The Financial Times Guide to Personal Tax 2007/2008

FINANCIAL TIMES

In an increasingly competitive world, we believe it's quality of thinking that will give you the edge – an idea that opens new doors, a technique that solves a problem, or an insight that simply makes sense of it all. The more you know, the smarter and faster you can go.

That's why we work with the best minds in business and finance to bring cutting-edge thinking and best learning practice to a global market.

Under a range of leading imprints, including *Financial Times Prentice Hall*, we create world-class print publications and electronic products bringing our readers knowledge, skills and understanding, which can be applied whether studying or at work.

To find out more about Pearson Education publications, or tell us about the books you'd like to find, you can visit us at **www.pearsoned.co.uk**

The Financial Times Guide to Personal Tax 2007/2008

Sara Williams and Jonquil Lowe

FT Prentice Hall
FINANCIAL TIMES

An imprint of **Pearson Education**
Harlow, England • London • New York • Boston • San Francisco • Toronto • Sydney • Singapore • Hong Kong
Tokyo • Seoul • Taipei • New Delhi • Cape Town • Madrid • Mexico City • Amsterdam • Munich • Paris • Milan

PEARSON EDUCATION LIMITED

Edinburgh Gate
Harlow CM20 2JE
Tel: +44 (0)1279 623623
Fax: +44 (0)1279 431059
Website: www.pearsoned.co.uk

The Financial Times Guide to Personal Tax was previously published as the *Tax Guide*

First published 2006
Second edition published by Pearson Education in Great Britain 2007

ISBN: 978-0-273-71415-6

British Library Cataloguing in Publication Data
A catalogue record for this book can be obtained from the British Library

10 9 8 7 6 5 4 3 2 1
11 10 09 08 07

Typeset in 9pt Stone Serif by 3
Printed and bound in Great Britain by Ashford Colour Press Ltd., Gosport

The Publisher's policy is to use paper manufactured from sustainable forests.

The authors

Sara Williams is a former investment analyst and financial journalist. She has contributed many articles on tax and finance for national newspapers and for a number of years wrote for *Which?*, including the *Which? Tax-Saving Guide* and the *Which? Book of Tax*. She is also the author of the *Financial Times Guide to Business Start Up*. She is now the CEO of AIM-listed Vitesse Media, an online, events and print media business. Its titles include *What Investment, Business XL, Growth Company Investor, M&A, The AIM Guide*, SmallBusiness.co.uk and GrowthBusiness.co.uk. She is a qualified investment manager and adviser.

Jonquil Lowe started out as an economist and worked for several years in the City as an investment analyst. She is a former head of the Money Group at Consumers' Association (now renamed Which?), a past editor of the *Which? Tax-Saving Guide* and was for many years a regular contributor to *Which? Way to Save Tax*. Jonquil now works as a freelance researcher and journalist. She writes extensively on all areas of personal finance for a diverse range of clients, including Which?, the Financial Services Authority and LexisNexis Butterworths. Jonquil holds the Diploma in Financial Planning (formerly called the Advanced Financial Planning Certificate) and is author of some 20 books, including *Be Your Own Financial Adviser, The Which? Guide to Giving and Inheriting, The Pension Handbook* (published by Which?), *The Which? Guide to Money in Retirement, The Which? Guide to Shares* and the *Personal Finance Handbook* published by the Child Poverty Action Group.

Contents

PART II FILLING IN YOUR TAX RETURN / 167

APPENDICES / 365

Acknowledgements

A tax guide of this type cannot appear without the help and hard work of a multitude of people too numerous to mention. However, we would like to give special thanks to Keith Gordon MA (Oxon), FCA, CTA, Barrister, who has helped us on the technical side.

Thank you

Sara Williams and Jonquil Lowe

Note

Both of us – along with everyone at Vitesse Media plc – have made strenuous efforts to check the accuracy of the information. If by chance a mistake or omission has occurred, we are sorry that neither we nor the Publisher can take responsibility if you suffer any loss or problem as a result of it. But please write to Sara Williams and Jonquil Lowe, *FT Guide to Personal Tax*, Octavia House, 50 Banner Street, London, EC1Y 8ST if you have any suggestions about how we can improve the content of the guide.

Dear Reader!

The *FT Guide to Personal Tax* went to press shortly after the 2007 Budget on 21 March and much may change before the Chancellor's proposals become law. If you want to keep abreast of developments, you can contact us in either of two ways:

- send for our free update, which will be issued in the autumn – see below for instructions on what to do

- log on to the Tax Guide website – at www.taxguide.co.uk

To get the paper version send an A4-sized self-addressed envelope with a 48p stamp on it to: Sara Williams and Jonquil Lowe, *FT Guide to Personal Tax*, Octavia House, 50 Banner Street, London EC1Y 8ST.

Yours sincerely

Sara Williams
Jonquil Lowe

Introduction

Half the UK population are taxpayers compared with just two-fifths some 30 years ago. We can expect to pay over £200 billion in taxes on income and wealth in the 2007–8 tax year. As the government digs more deeply, it makes sense to take all legal steps you can to minimise the tax you pay.

While paying the tax may hurt, the collection process is often fairly painless with tax automatically deducted through the Pay As You Earn (PAYE) system. But nearly 9 million people have to complete either a short or full tax return each year under the self-assessment system.

However your tax is collected, you are ultimately responsible for ensuring that all your income and any other taxable sums are declared and the correct tax paid. This means, for example, if you pay tax through PAYE, you should still check your tax bill and may have to complete a Tax Review Form (P810) from time to time. If you are one of the 1.5 million people invited to fill in a short tax return, it's still down to you to order the full return instead if the short one is not appropriate for you.

Everyone who is required to fill in a tax return – short or full – must stick to strict deadlines.

If you don't, fines and interest are added to your bill. Despite this, over a million taxpayers every year end pay their tax late and nearly as many deliver their tax return late. Remember there are:

- dates by which you have to send in your tax return (p. 28)
- rules about records that you must keep (p. 26)
- dates to pay your tax bill (p. 31)
- rules about which income you will pay tax on (p. 15)
- dates for reporting income (p. 26)
- penalties you have to pay if you don't stick to all the rules (p. 46)
- obligations that taxpayers must stick to (p. 26).

The taxes you might pay

There are a number of different ways in which the government raises money from taxpayers. Some of the taxes are as follows:

- income tax – some of your income is taxed at varying rates
- capital gains tax – some of the gains you make on investments or possessions may be taxed at varying rates
- inheritance tax – when you die, some of the money you leave to others could be taxed
- pre-owned assets tax – an income tax on the benefit you are deemed to get if you still use or enjoy something you have given away
- national insurance – this is compulsory only for people who are earning: employees and their employers, the self-employed or business partners.

Other taxes include council tax, corporation tax, business rates, value added tax, stamp duty land tax and excise duties.

The tax returns for the tax year ending 5 April 2007 should have landed on your doorstep during April 2007. These will cover your income and gains, reliefs and allowances. The information you provide will be used by you or your tax inspector to work out your income tax and capital gains tax bills and any pre-owned assets tax due.

How tax rules are changed

Strangely enough, income tax is a temporary tax and a new Act of Parliament is required each year to allow the government to go on collecting it. This provides the ideal opportunity for the government to ask Parliament to approve changes to the tax rules, so there is an annual cycle:

November/December before the start of the next tax year: Pre-Budget Report

The government announces complicated or tentative proposals to change the rules, often inviting experts and the public to comment.

March (usually): Budget

The government announces changes. Many apply from the start of the tax year. Other changes may take effect from different dates.

6 April: start of the new tax year

March/April: Finance Bill published

This is the draft legislation to implement the changes from the Pre-Budget Report and the Budget. Sometimes other last-minute government changes are slipped in too. Now Parliament sets about debating and amending the draft rules.

July (usually): Finance Act passed

The measures in the act become law – many are backdated to the start of the tax year, Budget Day or even earlier.

What is in this guide?

This tax guide explains the rules for income tax, capital gains tax, inheritance tax, pre-owned assets tax and national insurance. It covers most of the rules that the majority of taxpayers need to know, but it may not cover very specialised cases.

In Part I, the guide gives a broad outline of the rules and helps you to plan your affairs to minimise your tax bills. It covers what you need to know for the current tax year ending 5 April 2008 (the 2007–8 tax year). It includes the changes proposed in the March 2007 Budget. By following its advice you should be able to save tax in the current and future tax years.

The guide went to the printers in Spring 2007 and its advice is based on what was proposed in the Budget. Proposals are sometimes changed by debate in Parliament. You can receive notice of later changes by either visiting our website, www.taxguide.co.uk or sending an A4 stamped (48p), self-addressed envelope to Sara Williams and Jonquil Lowe, *FT Guide to Personal Tax*, Octavia House, 50 Banner Street, London EC1Y 8ST.

In Part II, the guide helps you to fill in your tax return and has the information and figures for the tax year ending 5 April 2007 (the 2006–7 tax year). It includes lots of tax-saving tips that help you to cut your tax bill for the last tax year.

How to pay less tax

1

Tax changes for 2007–8

The main headline in Budget 2007 was a 2p cut in the basic rate of income tax from April 2008, but compensating changes mean that many taxpayers will see no saving on their tax bill.

Income tax and allowances

In 2007–8, tax rates are unchanged from the previous year. Thresholds increase with inflation. The starting rate band is £2,230 (was £2,150) and higher rate tax starts at £34,600 (was £33,300).

For 2007–8, the personal allowances increase with inflation to £5,225 (was £5,035) for people under 65, £7,550 (was £7,280) if you are aged 65 to 74 and £7,690 (was £7,420) if you are 75 or over.

In 2008–9, the basic rate of tax is being cut to 20 per cent (from 22 per cent). The 10 per cent starting rate band will be abolished for earned income (such as salaries, profits, rents and pensions) though will be retained for savings income and capital gains. To compensate low income households and pensioners, tax credits (see below) and personal allowances for the over-65s will be increased.

In 2009–10, higher rate tax will start at incomes above £43,000 (compared with £39,825 in 2007–8) but income tax savings will be offset by higher national insurance (see p. 12).

Reliefs

The cut in basic rate tax from 2008–9 reduces the basic rate relief on pension contributions and Gift Aid donations. For example, tax relief on a £100 net payment will be just £25 instead of £28.21 as now. Higher rate tax-payers will continue to get relief at 40 per cent.

From 2007–8, benefits you can receive from a charity without losing Gift Aid relief are increased for donations above £1,000 to a maximum of 5 per cent (was 2.5 per cent) of the donation subject to an overall limit of £500 (was £250).

Tax credits

In 2007–8, the child element of child tax credit (CTC) is increased in line with earnings to £1,845. The family element is unchanged at £545. Working tax credit (WTC) elements increase in line with prices and the childcare element is unchanged.

In 2008–9, the child element of CTC is due to increase to £2,080 and the level of income at which you start to lose WTC is to increase to £6,420 (currently £5,220). However, the rate at which you lose tax credits will increase to 39p (currently 37p) for every £1 by which your income exceeds £6,420.

Paying and reclaiming tax

From the 2008 tax return onwards, the date by which you must send in paper returns is brought forward to 31 October (previously 31 January). This is also the new deadline if you want the Revenue to work out your tax bill for you (currently 30 September). The date for filing by internet is unchanged at 31 January following the end of the tax year. The Revenue will be able to open an enquiry into your return within one year from the date you file it.

From April 2008 onwards, there will be a new system of penalties for mistakes in tax returns. Penalties will depend on the amount of tax understated and your behaviour both in making the mistake and cooperating with the Revenue to put it right.

Homes and tax

The government is still considering a new planning gain supplement to tax the increase in land values following the grant of planning permission. The earliest it would be introduced is 2009.

If you have a holiday home abroad, you might own it through a company of which you are a director. Strictly, this means your use of the home is a taxable fringe benefit provided by the company. The government has said tax will not apply and, if you have paid such tax in the past, you can now claim it back.

Savings and investments

ISAs (individual savings accounts) will now be available indefinitely. From 2008–9, the yearly investment limit is being raised to £7,200 overall, of which up to £3,600 can be invested in a cash ISA. Also, from 2008–9, the distinction between mini and maxi ISAs is being abolished and you will be able to transfer your savings from cash ISAs to stocks and shares ISAs (but not vice versa).

From 2008–9, most foreign dividends will be taxed in the same way as UK dividends, with a 10 per cent tax credit, reducing the tax you pay. You will be eligible for the credit provided you hold less than 10 per cent of the company's shares and all your foreign dividends come to no more than £5,000 a year.

Changes to the enterprise investment scheme (EIS) and venture capital trust (VCT) rules will restrict the schemes to smaller companies, which will tend to increase the riskiness of these investments.

Sharia-compliant bonds (sukuk) are now taxed in the same way as comparable conventional interest-bearing bonds.

From 31 March 2007, commission rebate received when you invest in an investment-type life insurance policy ceases to be tax-free where the total you invest comes to £100,000 a year or more and the policy runs for less than three years.

The government is consulting on rules to tax UK-based unit trusts and open-ended investment companies that invest in property in the same way as real estate investment trusts. This means you would pay tax on distributions and gains in broadly the same way as if you were investing directly in property.

Pensions

If you opt for an alternatively secured pension (ASP) at age 75, death benefits from your scheme paid other than to your dependants or charity will be subject to both inheritance tax (up to 40 per cent) and up to 70 per cent tax as an unauthorised payment from the scheme. This makes using pension schemes for inheritance planning uneconomic.

From 6 April 2007, if you opt for an ASP, you must draw a pension equal to at least 55 per cent of the equivalent annuity (not 60 per cent as previously proposed).

Tax relief is no longer available for pension scheme contributions you pay to buy term insurance, unless you applied for the policy before 14 December 2006 (personal pension) or 29 March 2007 (occupational scheme). Existing policies and life cover paid for by employers are not affected.

Capital gains tax

The amount of net capital gains an individual can make without paying capital gains tax (CGT) rises to £9,200 (was £8,800) and £4,600 for most trusts.

With effect for disposals on or after 6 December 2006, you cannot claim tax relief on a loss made through a scheme contrived mainly to save tax.

HM Revenue & Customs is being given powers to alter which shares count as 'listed'. Any changes would affect the scope of, for example, CGT business asset taper relief and EIS and VCT reliefs.

Inheritance tax (IHT) and pre-owned asset tax (POAT)

As already announced, the threshold at which tax starts increases to £300,000 for 2007–8 (was £285,000). The threshold increases in the following years to £312,000, £325,000 and £350,000 by 2010–11.

You can escape POAT if you elect for assets to be taxed within the IHT regime. The normal date for this election is 31 January following the tax year in which you first become liable for POAT. But the Revenue now has powers to accept late elections.

Employees

The scales for taxing company cars in 2007–8 and 2008–9 have already been published. From 2008–9, you can claim a 2 per cent discount if you drive a car capable of being run on E85 fuel. The figure used to calculate the taxable value of fuel for private use is unchanged in 2007–8 at £14,400.

Certain non-cash benefits provided for retired former employees are tax-free, backdated to 6 April 2006. This can cover, for example, continuing to provide accommodation, recreational benefits and annual parties.

Businesses

First-year capital allowances for small businesses buying plant and machinery stay at 50 per cent until 5 April 2008. From 2008–9, first-year allowances are being abolished and replaced with a new annual investment allowance (AIA). The AIA will give 100 per cent relief for up to £50,000 a year of expenditure on plant and machinery.

From 2008–9, the maximum writing-down allowance for plant and machinery will be reduced to 20 per cent (currently 25 per cent). Writing-down allowances for other types of spending are also changing. There will be a new payable tax credit to give relief for losses made on investment in certain green technologies.

The government is continuing to consult on changing the capital allowance rules for cars.

The business premises renovation scheme goes ahead from 11 April 2007. It gives 100 per cent first-year capital allowances for the cost of converting or renovating premises in deprived areas to bring them back into commercial use. Properties refurbished by or used by companies in certain industries, such as fishing, coal and steel, are excluded.

The VAT registration limit increases to £64,000 from 1 April 2006 (was £61,000).

To remove incentives for businesses to choose their legal form for tax rather than commercial reasons, the small companies corporation tax rate (currently 19 per cent) is being increased in stages to 22 per cent by 2009–10.

Individuals providing their services to clients through a managed service company (MSC) face higher tax bills. Payments from 6 April 2007 onwards will be subject to income tax and Class 1 national insurance. If the MSC cannot pay the tax, the Revenue can seek payment from the director of the company (normally the individual providing the services) or whoever set up the MSC.

National insurance

The level of earnings (primary threshold) up to which no Class 1 contributions are paid increases to £5,225 (£100 a week) for 2007–8 (was £5,035). The upper earnings limit (UEL) increases to £34,840, equivalent to £670 a week (was £33,540). Rates are unchanged at 11 per cent on earnings between the primary threshold and UEL and 1 per cent on anything above the UEL.

In 2008–9, the UEL increases by £3,900 more than inflation and in 2009–10 will be aligned with the income level at which the higher rate of income tax starts to be paid (see above), expected to be £43,000. This means that more of your income will be taxed at the higher 11 per cent rate.

In 2007–8, Class 2 contributions paid by the self-employed increase to £2.20 a week and the threshold below which payment is optional rises to £4,635 a week (was £4,465). The lower and upper profit limits for Class 4 contributions increase to £5,225 and £34,840, respectively (were £5,035 and £33,540). Rates are unchanged at 8 per cent on profits between the two limits and 1 per cent on anything more.

In 2008–9 and 2009–10, the upper profits limit increases in line with changes in the UEL, meaning that more of your profits will be taxed at the higher 8 per cent rate.

Land and property

For spending on residential property from 6 April 2007, the landlords' energy-saving allowance (LESA) is extended to floor insulation and the allowance will apply per property (rather than per building as previously). The allowance will be available until 2015.

Trusts

Where, as a landlord, you hold service charges or a sinking fund in trust, income from the money will, from 6 April 2007, be taxable at 20 per cent (rather than the 40 per cent rate applicable to trusts) regardless of whether it falls within the £1,000 basic rate allowance.

Other

Members of the armed forces serving in some areas, including Iraq and Afghanistan, receive an armed forces operational allowance. From 1 April 2006 onwards this allowance is tax-free.

From 6 April 2007, provided they are not carrying on a trade, there is no tax on any income households make from putting into the national grid surplus power they have generated through solar panels, wind turbines and other microgeneration methods.

2

An overview of income tax

Broadly speaking, income tax is a tax on the regular sums that you receive
– for example, earnings from a job, profits from your business, pensions,
interest from savings and so on.

Quick guide

There are many complexities and exceptions in the way that income is
taxed. What follows is a broad brush outline. It gives some important
relationships:

Total income = (Income – Reliefs)
Taxable income = (Income – Reliefs – Allowances)
Income tax = Taxable income × the rate(s) of tax

Example

Jessica Jones has income from employment of £28,000. She pays £1,000 into an
occupational pension scheme and she can claim a personal allowance for 2007–8 of
£5,225. Her taxable income is:

	£
Income	28,000.00
Less reliefs: pension contributions	1,000.00
	27,000.00
Less personal allowance	£5,225.00
Taxable income	£21,775.00
Tax at 10% on first £2,230	£223.00
Tax at 22% on next £19,545	£4,299.90
Total tax bill	£4,522.90

Income is made up of what you earn from your job or self-employment and what you receive as income from other sources, such as pensions and investments. But not all the money you receive is income and some income you receive is tax-free (see p. 365). Some income you receive has had tax deducted (called *net* – see pp. 20 and 73) and some income is paid without tax deducted (called *gross* – see pp. 20 and 75).

Reliefs are amounts which you pay out and on which you get tax relief, such as pension contributions and donations to charity. Relief may be given in different ways (see p. 21).

Allowances are amounts to which you are entitled because of your personal circumstances. Personal allowance and blind person's allowance reduce your income before your tax bill is worked out, giving you relief at your highest rate of tax. But with married couple's allowance (available only to older people), relief is restricted and given as a deduction in your tax bill.

Taxable income is the figure on which your tax bill is based. The amount of income tax depends on how much taxable income you have and what rate of tax is paid on it (see below). From this initial tax bill you then deduct any reliefs and allowances that are given as a reduction in the bill. The maximum reduction is the amount needed to reduce your tax bill to zero.

Total income is a figure that is not important for most taxpayers, but it is for older people in receipt of age-related allowances. The amount of total income determines whether you get these allowances in full or only a reduced amount (see pp. 24, 54 and 226). Total income is the amount you have after you have deducted some reliefs from income, but before deducting allowances. The reliefs you deduct to arrive at total income include pension contributions, charitable donations under Gift Aid and gifts of shares or certain other investments to charity.

The rates of tax

There are different rates of tax:

- starting rate tax (10 per cent for the 2006–7 and 2007–8 tax years)
- basic rate tax (22 per cent for 2006–7 and 2007–8)
- higher rate tax (40 per cent for 2006–7 and 2007–8)

The levels at which these rates apply can vary from year to year. Here are the levels of income for each of these rates for 2006–7 and 2007–8:

2006–7 tax year

Income band £	Size of band £	Tax rate %	Tax on band £
0–2,150	2,150	10	215.00
2,151–33,300	31,150	22	6,853.00
Over 33,300		40	

2007–8 tax year

Income band £	Size of band £	Tax rate %	Tax on band £
0–2,230	2,230	10	223.00
2,231–34,600	32,370	22	7,121.40
Over 34,600		40	

Different tax rates apply to income from most savings and investments. The tax rates for savings income (for example, from building society accounts, gilts and corporate bonds) falling into each of the bands above are 10 per cent, 20 per cent (called the savings rate) and 40 per cent. Dividends from shares, distributions from share-based unit trusts and similar investments are paid with tax at 10 per cent already deducted. Non-taxpayers cannot reclaim this tax. There is no further tax to pay unless you are a higher rate taxpayer, in which case you pay a further 22.5 per cent.

From 2008–9, the 10 per cent starting rate is being abolished for earned income (meaning income from, for example, wages and salaries, profits from your business, rents if you let out property and pensions). It will still apply to savings income (and capital gains). At the same time, the basic rate is being reduced to 20 per cent (was 22 per cent).

Tax-saving idea 1

From 2008–9, despite the reduction in the basic rate of tax, the abolition of the starting rate band will increase the amount of tax you pay if you earn less than around £18,000 a year. There will be a compensating increase in tax credits. Therefore to protect yourself from a tax rise, make sure you claim tax credits if you are eligible (see page 60).

Tax credits

Since 6 April 2003, two state benefits – the working tax credit and child tax credit – are integrated into the tax system, with the amount you get based broadly on your 'total income' (see opposite). For details see p. 60.

Income

Your income will be made up of money or goods you receive or anything you get in return for a service – but not all payments you receive count as income (see below). The following *will* all normally be considered as income:

- what you earn from your work, including a job (see p. 231), a partnership (see p. 307) or self-employment (see p. 275), including salary, tips, fringe benefits and business profits
- rent from letting out property (see p. 311)
- income from investments, such as interest, dividends and distributions (see pp. 182 and 191)
- pensions (from the state, your previous employer or your own plan)
- social security payments, such as jobseeker's allowance
- casual, occasional or miscellaneous income, such as freelance earnings, income received after you close a business, income from guaranteeing loans, dealing in futures, income from underwriting, certain capital payments from selling UK patent rights, gains on many discounted securities, accrued income in bond and gilt strip prices
- income from a trust.

Payments that are not income

Some payments you receive are not income. For example:

- loans
- presents and gifts (but occasionally inheritance tax may be due later)
- lottery prizes
- gambling winnings (if you are a gambler rather than a bookmaker)
- proceeds from selling assets unless this is how you make a living (but capital gains tax may be due)
- maintenance from an ex-spouse or former partner
- money you inherit (though inheritance tax may have been deducted).

Tax-free income

Some other payments you receive are income but are specifically tax-free, including premium bond prizes, interest on National Savings Certificates and income from savings held in a cash individual savings account (ISA).

There is no capital gains tax either on items that are income. A comprehensive list is given on p. 365.

Main types of income for 2007–8 tax year

Type of income	Tax deducted?	At what rate?	More tax to pay?
Earnings from a job	yes	StR, BR, HR	no[1]
Taxable fringe benefits	yes, from earnings	StR, BR, HR	no[1]
Occupational or personal pension, retirement annuity contract	yes	StR, BR, HR	no[1]
Bank, building society interest from UK account	yes[2]	SR	yes – HR
Bank interest from offshore account	often, no		yes
Gilts and most other bonds	no[3]		yes
Income from annuity (other than pension annuities)	yes[2] [4]	SR	yes – HR
Dividends from shares	yes[5]	10%[5]	yes[6]
Distributions from share-based unit trusts and oeics	yes[5]	10%[5]	yes[6]
Distributions from Real Estate Investment Trusts	no		yes
Income from an executor before a will is sorted out	yes	10%[5], SR and BR	yes – HR
Income from a trust	yes	10%[5], SR and BR/32.5 per cent and HR[7]	yes – HR/no[7]
Income from self-employment or a partnership	no		yes
Social security benefits	no[8]		yes
Rent from property	no		yes
Pre-owned assets	no		yes

Key: StR = starting rate; BR = basic rate; HR = higher rate; SR = savings rate
(1) There could, of course, be more tax to pay if insufficient has been deducted.
(2) Non-taxpayers can have this income paid without tax deducted – see p. 75.
(3) But you can choose to have interest paid with tax deducted at the savings rate of 20 per cent.
(4) Tax is deducted from the part of the annuity which counts as income, not the part which counts as a return of the capital.
(5) Non-taxpayers cannot claim back the tax deducted.
(6) Higher rate taxpayers pay at a rate of 32.5 per cent.
(7) Depending on the type of trust – see p. 337.
(8) But if you return to work, tax, if due, will be deducted from your earnings.

How income is paid to you

Income which is taxable can be paid to you without any tax deducted (*gross*) or with tax deducted (*net*). The tax can be deducted at the savings rate, the basic rate and/or some other rate. The table on p. 19 lists types of income, whether or not they are paid with tax deducted and if any further tax will be due. There are more details of income in Chapter 12.

If you need to give a figure for gross income when you have received net income, there are ready reckoners which help you to gross it up in Appendix B on p. 369.

Tax-saving idea 2

Look for opportunities to arrange your income to be tax-free (see p. 365 for a comprehensive list). In the case of a couple, seek to distribute income between the two of you to the greatest advantage (see Chapter 5).

Tax-saving idea 3

From 6 April 2007, income from retirement annuity contracts will be paid to you through the Pay As You Earn (PAYE) system (see p. 35) with the right amount of tax deducted. Previously, this income was normally paid with basic rate tax deducted. HM Revenue & Customs estimates that 200,000 people receiving this type of net income were not liable for tax but failed either to claim the tax back or arrange to receive the income gross. If this applies to you, claim back the overpaid tax now. You can go back as far as the 2001–2 tax year, provided you put in your claim by 31 January 2008.

Reliefs

You make certain choices in life but sometimes the government gives a helping hand to encourage particular courses of action, such as saving for retirement or giving to charity. It does this by letting you have tax relief on what you pay. The items which qualify for this tax relief are known as reliefs, outgoings or deductions.

You can get a double boost from making some payments if they also reduce your 'total income'. This may save extra tax if you qualify for age allowance (see pp. 24, 54 and 226) or entitle you to extra tax credits (see p. 60).

How you get tax relief

Tax relief may be given in one of three ways, depending on the type of spending involved:

■ by deducting basic rate tax relief from the payment before handing it over. Any higher rate relief is given by raising the threshold at which you personally start to pay tax at the higher rate. Examples include contributions to personal pensions (including stakeholder schemes) and Gift Aid donations. For example, if you want a charity to receive £100 under Gift Aid, you hand over just £78. (When the basic rate falls to 20 per cent in 2008–9, you will need to donate £80 if you want the charity to receive £100.)

Tax-saving idea 4

Unless you are a higher rate taxpayer, the amount of tax relief you get on contributions to a pension scheme will fall from 2008–9 when the basic rate falls to 20 per cent (from 22 per cent now). Try to pay as much as you can into your pension scheme before 6 April 2008, so that you benefit from the higher 22 per cent relief. (You will get relief at the basic rate even if you are a non-taxpayer or pay tax at the starting rate provided you invest in a personal pension or stakeholder scheme.)

■ a reduction in your income before tax is worked out. This gives relief up to your highest rate of tax. Examples include contributions to an occupational pension scheme and payroll giving to charity

■ as a reduction in your tax bill. This applies, for example, to maintenance payments (available only to older people) and enterprise investment scheme investments. Relief is restricted to a percentage of the eligible payment.

Any relief not automatically given by deducting it from the payment, is given either through the PAYE system (so less tax is deducted from your salary) or by a claim through your tax return (in which case the appropriate deduction is made when working out your tax bill).

Main types of relief for 2007–8 tax year

Type of relief	Amount of relief	How do you get tax relief?
Business losses not already set against profits	StR, BR or HR	through your PAYE code or tax bill
Charity[1]: Gift Aid[2], gifts of shares, land or buildings	StR, BR or HR	BR: make lower payments HR: either PAYE code or tax bill
EIS (up to limits)	20%	through your PAYE code or tax bill
VCT (up to limits)	30%	through your PAYE code or tax bill
Community investment tax relief	5%	through your PAYE code or tax bill
Home income plan[3]	23%	lower payments through MIRAS
Interest on some loans to invest in business	StR, BR or HR	through your PAYE code or tax bill
Job expenses	StR, BR or HR	through your PAYE code or tax bill
Maintenance payments[4]	10% of £2,350	through your PAYE code or tax bill
Mortgage interest on a property you let	StR, BR or HR	lower tax bill on rental income
Landlord's energy-saving allowance (up to £1,500)	StR, BR or HR	lower tax bill on rental income
Pension contributions to employers' schemes	StR, BR or HR	through PAYE system
Personal pension payments (including stakeholder pensions)	BR or HR	BR: make lower payments HR: through PAYE code or tax bill
Retirement annuity contract payments	StR, BR or HR[5]	through your PAYE code or tax bill (or as for personal pensions)

Key: StR = starting rate; BR = basic rate; HR = higher rate
(1) And community amateur sports clubs that meet certain conditions.
(2) You make lower payments by deducting relief at the basic rate. If your tax bill is less than the relief deducted, the Revenue may claw back some of the relief.
(3) Relief not available for loans made on or after 9 March 1999.
(4) Since 6 April 2000, available only where one or both parties was born before 6 April 1935.
(5) Providers can choose to treat payments in the same way as those to personal pensions. The provider will tell you if this applies to your contract.

Example

Peter Atwell wants to put £2,400 into a stakeholder pension scheme. He makes the payment net – in other words, after deducting tax relief at the basic rate which comes to 22 per cent × £2,400 = £528. Peter is a higher rate taxpayer, so can claim extra relief of (40 per cent × £2,400) – £528 = £432. His pension contribution of £2,400 has cost him only £2,400 – £528 – £432 = £1,440.

Tax-saving idea 5

You have until 31 January five years after the end of a tax year to correct your tax bill if, say, you've forgotten to claim a relief or allowance. This means by 31 January 2008 you can go back as far as the 2001–2 tax year to claim tax relief for a deduction or allowance which occurred in that year. You get the tax relief at the rates which applied in the tax year for which you are claiming not the current one. (But relief for business losses must be claimed sooner – see p. 302.) For details of other tax deadlines, see Appendix D.

The table opposite lists the main types of reliefs and how you get them. There are more details about reliefs in Chapter 13.

Allowances

Everyone is entitled to an allowance to deduct from their income to ensure that some income is tax-free. This is called the personal allowance. But the amount of the allowance varies with age. There are a few other allowances that you might be able to claim – but these depend on your personal circumstances. There are details of allowances in the table overleaf and in Chapter 14.

Example

Lily Crabtree, 71, has a total income of £23,000. This is higher than the £20,900 limit. Her personal allowance is reduced to £7,550 – ½ × (£23,000 – £20,900) = £6,500

Details of allowances

Allowance	Age[1]	Tax year	Amount
Personal	up to 65	2006–7	£5,035
		2007–8	£5,225
	65–74	2006–7	£7,280[2]
		2007–8	£7,550[2]
	75 plus	2006–7	£7,420[2]
		2007–8	£7,690[2]
Married couple's[3]	72–74	2006–7	10% of £6,065[2]
	73–74	2007–8	10% of £6,285[2]
	75 plus	2006–7	10% of £6,135[2]
		2007–8	10% of £6,365[2]
Blind person's	any	2006–7	£1,660
		2007–8	£1,730

(1) On birthday falling within the tax year.
(2) The amount of these allowances is reduced if total income is above a certain amount. In 2006–7 the allowances were reduced if total income was over £20,100 and in 2007–8 the income limit is £20,900. For more details see below and pp. 54 and 226.
(3) From April 2000, this allowance was abolished for people born on or after 6 April 1935. Where the allowance received by an older person is restricted because of income – see note 2 above – it will not be reduced below £2,350 in 2006–7 and £2,440 in 2007–8.

Tax-saving ideas 6, 7 and 8

In 2007–8 you will be losing age allowance if your income is in the range £20,900 to £25,550 if you are aged 65 to 74 and £20,900 to £25,830 if you are aged 75 or more. (The upper limits will be higher if you also qualify for married couple's allowance – see p. 55.) Income for this purpose does not include any tax-free amounts (such as, your winter fuel payment or extra payment to help with council tax bills). If you are losing age allowance, you can cut your total income and so increase the allowance by switching from taxable to tax-free investments – for example, from an ordinary savings account to a cash ISA.

Making pension contributions and Gift Aid donations will be especially tax efficient because they also cut your total income and so increase your personal allowance.

If you are 65 (men) or 60 (women) or older, consider deferring your state pension to earn a state pension lump sum (see p. 197). The lump sum does not count as part of your total income and so does not reduce your age allowance.

The higher personal allowance for people aged 65 and over is reduced by £1 for each £2 by which your total income exceeds a certain amount (£20,900 in 2007–8). But it is never reduced below the basic personal allowance that everyone gets (£5,225 in 2007–8).

3

Paying and reclaiming tax

Self assessment started in 1996. It puts the onus on you to report any sources of income and gains, provide a figure for the tax due (though in practice you can ask the Revenue to crunch the numbers for you) and ensure that you make timely payments of the tax due. To discourage cheating, there are penalties for providing information late, failing to pay tax on time and failing to keep records. In addition, the Revenue can investigate your tax affairs to check that you are operating the system correctly (see Chapter 4).

Not everyone has to operate self assessment. Over two-thirds of taxpayers have their tax calculated and collected through PAYE (see page 35). But even they need to be aware that a change in their circumstances or a change in the tax system (such as the introduction of the pre-owned assets tax – see Chapter 10) can trigger an obligation under self assessment with the onus on the taxpayer to realise when this occurs.

Name change

The government department dealing with tax is HM Revenue & Customs (the 'Revenue' or HMRC). It was formed in 2005 by the merger of two former departments, the Inland Revenue and HM Customs & Excise.

In addition to acting as policeman of the system, the Revenue also tries to help its customers (taxpayers) to understand the system and operate it correctly. In this role the Revenue tries to put on a friendly public face. Normally a single tax office deals with your affairs, sending you returns, issuing your tax code, and so on. But, if you have a query or problem, increasingly you will deal with a website or remote call centre (see Appendix E).

Your obligations

New source of income or capital

If you don't receive a tax return, you must notify your tax inspector of any income or capital gains, which have not been previously declared, within six months from the end of the tax year in which you make the income or gain (i.e. by 5 October). This applies even if you don't yet know the amount of the income or gain and even if previously you have received a letter from the Revenue saying you do not need to complete a tax return.

There are certain circumstances in which you don't have to notify your tax office. This applies, for example, if all the income comes under the PAYE system or if the income is paid with tax already deducted and you pay tax at no more than the basic rate.

Note that, quite apart from the rules above, if you become newly self-employed, you must normally register with the Revenue within three months of the end of the month you start up or face a £100 fine (see p. 278).

Records

You are required to keep records, such as original copies of dividend vouchers, bank statements, certificates of interest received and any certificates showing foreign tax deductions, which you need to complete your tax return. If you don't have the original certificates, you can complete your tax return using information that can be verified by an external source. You don't have to send in your vouchers and other documents in order to get a tax refund. You must keep the originals in case of a Revenue enquiry (see Chapter 4), but if they are lost you will not be penalised providing you can produce other evidence for the information. You also need to keep a copy of the working papers that you used to work out your calculations.

If you don't run your own business or have letting income, the period to keep records is one year from the date by which you must send back the tax return (usually 31 January). If you run your own business or receive any income from letting, you need to keep records for five years from the date by which you should send in your tax return (31 January).

This period is extended if there is an enquiry into your affairs. Records must be kept until the enquiry is complete. The period to keep records is also extended if you send in your return late or need to correct it after you have sent it in. The documents need to be kept until one year after the end of the quarter in which you amended the return or sent it in late. Quarters end on 31 January, 30 April, 31 July and 31 October.

The failure to keep records can result in a swingeing penalty (see Chapter 4).

Tax-saving idea 9

Make sure you keep all your records and your working papers. If you don't, you may end up paying more tax than you should because you can't provide the evidence to back up your tax return. And don't forget you can be fined for not keeping your records. If you are in business or letting, for the tax year 2006–7, you must normally keep your records until 31 January 2013. Other taxpayers must keep records for that year until 31 January 2009.

Example

Roger Rose (a basic-rate taxpayer) is an employee paying tax under the PAYE system. He buys some shares in a UK company in October 2006 and receives a dividend of £84 some two months later. He also decides to do some freelance consulting on the side, as well as his job. He doesn't know how much income that will bring in, since part of his payment will be in the form of commission.

As a basic-rate taxpayer, Roger has no further tax to pay on the dividend. So, if this had been his only extra income in 2006–7, he would not have needed to take any action. But he also has the freelance income on which tax will be due. Even though he does not yet know how much the income will be, he must tell his tax office about it by 5 October 2007 (that is within six months of the end of the tax year). His tax office will then send him a tax return which he has three months to complete.

The tax return

Your tax return asks for details of your income, deductions and allowances for the 2006–7 tax year just ended, that is the year ending on 5 April 2007. Roughly 1.5 million people with straightforward tax affairs are sent a short four-page tax return – see Appendix C. If your affairs are more complex, you will receive the full return comprising a 12-page basic return, an additional form about pension schemes and up to nine supplements (see Chapter 11). It is your responsibility to check that you have received the correct tax return and supplements and to obtain any further supplements you need.

Example

For years, Helen Hickie has lived on her pensions and modest income from invest-ments. On this basis, the Revenue sends her a short tax return for the 2006–7 tax year. But during that year, Helen's sister who lived abroad died leaving Helen some foreign shares which now provide Helen with extra income. The short return is not suitable and Helen needs to contact the Revenue Orderline (see p. 170) to request a full return including the foreign supplement.

You must provide precise figures throughout your return. This means getting hold of the documents you need. If you are an employee, these include forms P60 (summary of income from a job and tax already paid), P45 (summary of income and tax paid where you have left a job), P11D or P9D (taxable fringe benefits and expenses). Your employer is responsible for supplying you with these forms by certain dates (see Appendix D). Where precise figures are not available (for example, where you are self-employed and the relevant accounting period has yet to end), give a provisional esti-mate and say when the final figure will be available. With subjective figures (for example, the value of an asset you have given away or received from your employer), get an independent valuation and give details in the additional information sections of the return.

If figures on returns from taxpayers like you are commonly subject to errors, or based on previous years your figures seem out of step with those for similar taxpayers, you may receive a letter from the Revenue suggesting you take particular care in completing that section of your return. Where applicable, give extra details (for example, the basis on which you are claiming a proportion of a part-private/part-business expense) in the additional information sections.

In general, you do not need to send supporting documents with your tax return. If you wish to draw the Revenue's attention to an item or explain the basis of your figures, it is normally best to make a note in the additional information boxes provided on the main return and its supplements. If you do send supporting documents, it is unlikely that they will be read unless your tax office decides to open an enquiry into your return (see Chapter 4).

Deadlines for your tax return

The key date for your 2006–7 tax return is 31 January 2008. Your tax return must normally reach your tax office by this date, otherwise you risk an automatic fine (see Chapter 4). From the 2007–8 tax return, this key date is changing (see the box opposite).

However, if you want to ask the Revenue to calculate your tax bill for you – and we recommend that you do this unless you are using a tax adviser – you should send in your return by 30 September 2007. There are no penalties for missing this deadline and the Revenue will still work out your tax for you if you send in the return later but it will not guarantee to be able to tell you how much you owe in time for the payment deadline on 31 January (see p. 31).

Tax-saving idea 10

> If you are paying tax under the PAYE system and have some other income, for example from investments, on which you will need to pay tax, send in your 2006–7 tax return by 30 September 2007 or 30 December 2007 if you file by internet. If you do this, and the amount of tax due is less than £2,000, you will not have to pay tax on this extra income by 31 January 2008. Instead, it will be included in your PAYE code for the 2008–9 tax year, thus spreading out and delaying the payment.

Alternatively, you can file your return by internet at any time and the software will immediately tell you the amount of tax to pay. Although you can't file the short return online, there is nothing to stop you using the online service (which is based on the full return) instead if you want to.

You should also file by 30 September if you owe less than £2,000 tax and want it collected through PAYE over the coming tax year instead of paying the whole lot as a single lump sum in January. But, if you file by internet, you have an extra three months until 30 December.

Where a tax return has been issued after 31 October, you are given three months to complete it and send it back to your tax office. If the return is issued after 31 July and you want your tax inspector to calculate the tax due, it must be returned within two months.

Changes from the 2007–8 return onwards

> The Revenue is keen to encourage as many people as possible to manage their tax affairs online. To encourage this, from the 2007–8 tax return onwards, the filing deadlines are being changed. For 2007–8, they will be:
>
> ■ 31 October 2008 for paper tax returns – in other words, three months earlier than the current deadline. Provided you meet the deadline, the Revenue will calculate your tax bill for you
> ■ 31 January 2009 if you file by internet. The software will immediately calculate your tax bill.

▶

Penalties will apply for missing either of these deadlines. In 2008, the Revenue is also planning to replace the existing main return with a new paper tax return. Like the present short tax return (see Appendix C), this will be read by machine and so you will need to take care to fill it in correctly. You will no longer automatically be sent the Revenue's tax calculation guide (but can request a copy if you want). For the self-employed, there will be a choice of supplements with a simplified version for small businesses (expected to mean turnover less than £40,000 a year) with straightforward tax affairs.

Filing by internet

You can file the full tax return (but not the short return) by internet. This is free if you use the Revenue's software but unfortunately this is limited to the basic return; the supplements for employment, self-employment, partnership and land. If you use other supplements, you need to buy commercial software – see the Revenue website www.hmrc.gov.uk for a list of suppliers.

The main advantages of internet filing are that the software prompts you to correct common errors, immediately tells you the amount of tax you owe and immediately states whether your return has been received. Also, the additional information sections are part of the electronic return and so definitely passed to your tax office, whereas such details on a paper-based return are not transferred to the Revenue's computer system and sometimes get overlooked. You can attach supporting documents as pdfs (maximum file size 5Mb) but these are unlikely to be read unless the Revenue is opening an enquiry into your return. Therefore, if you especially want to draw the Revenue's attention to extra information, it is best to type it into the additional information sections.

To file by internet you must first register which can take up to seven days. Follow the instructions supplied with your return or on the Revenue website. You can also pay tax electronically – see the Revenue website for details.

If you don't send in your tax return

Failing to send back your completed tax return means you can be charged a penalty (see Chapter 4) and allows the Revenue to issue what's called a determination. This is an estimate of the tax you might owe and is often deliberately on the high side. The tax shown on this determination is payable; you cannot appeal against it or postpone it. The only way you can overturn this estimate is to complete your tax return and tax calculation.

You must do this within five years of the date by which you should have sent it in, or, if it is later, within a year of the determination by your tax inspector.

Your tax inspector cannot normally make a determination if five years have passed since the date you should have sent in your tax return. If there is reason to believe you have been fraudulent or negligent, the inspector can go back 20 years.

Tax calculation

After you have sent in your tax return, the Revenue checks it for obvious errors, such as arithmetical mistakes or failing to copy figures correctly from one part to another. You will be sent a tax calculation form (SA302) only if the Revenue has to make any corrections or you have asked the Revenue to work out your tax bill for you. The form sets out the tax the Revenue thinks you owe and the amount of any payments you have to make. Check this carefully as soon as it arrives. If there is anything you do not understand, or you disagree with the figures, write to or phone your tax office – otherwise you will be expected to pay the amounts shown on the form.

Tax-saving idea 11

Always check tax forms, such as a tax calculation or coding notice (see p. 36) to make sure your tax inspector has got the sums right.

Tax payments

Self assessment is used to collect income tax, capital gains tax and, if you are in business, Class 4 national insurance contributions (NICs). You, your adviser or your tax inspector works out the total amount due. The tax is usually paid in three instalments.

Interim and final payments

Self assessment requires two interim payments on account. The first is due on 31 January during the tax year; the second on 31 July following the tax year. Each payment is normally half the amount of your income tax and Class 4 NICs bill for the previous year less any tax paid through the PAYE system, dividend tax credits, and so on. There is no adjustment for changes in tax rates and allowances from one year to the next. However, if you expect your income to be lower this year than last, you can ask for a reduction in the payments on account (see overleaf) – but, if you turn out to be wrong, you'll have to pay interest on the tax paid late.

The final balancing income tax payment or repayment will be made on 31 January following the end of the tax year after completion of the tax return. Any capital gains tax due will also be paid with this third instalment.

Working on the basis of the tax due for the previous tax year, if the total tax payable, net of tax deducted at source (including PAYE), is less than £500 or if tax deducted at source (including PAYE) is more than 80 per cent of the total income tax plus Class 4 national insurance due, then interim payments won't be required.

Employees can put off paying a final tax bill of less than £2,000 by asking for it to be included in next year's PAYE code. To achieve this, you have to send in your 2006–7 tax return by 30 September 2007 (or 30 December 2007 if you file by internet).

An effect of the self assessment payment system is that, if your income increases from one tax year to the next, you may face a hefty tax bill in the following January. This is because the jump in income produces a final payment to scoop up tax underpaid in the last tax year plus an increased payment on account for the current tax year – see Example on p. 35. Make sure you set aside enough money to cover the tax bills.

Conversely, if your income falls from one year to the next, there may be a large drop in your January tax payment if you stand to get a refund of tax overpaid and a lower first payment on account.

Tax-saving idea 12

Payments on account are based on last year's tax bill. If you expect your income to be lower this year or your allowances and reliefs to be higher, you can make reduced payments – see opposite.

Self assessment statement

Shortly before a payment on account falls due, you will usually receive a self assessment statement (form SA300) showing the amount to pay and with a pay slip attached. If you are registered for the Revenue's internet service, you can view recent statements online.

These statements (previously called statements of account) used to be notoriously difficult to understand but, since August 2006, you will normally get a simpler, personalised statement along the lines of the example overleaf. You can request an old-style statement if you would prefer it. The key figure is the 'Amount due by . . .', which shows what you must pay and when. Paying late means paying interest, so it's vital to check your statements.

How to reduce your payments on account

If you think your tax bill this year, for the types of income covered by your self assessment statement, will be lower than in the previous year, you can claim to make lower payments on account than the Revenue is asking for. This might happen because your income has dropped – for example you are getting less in profits or rents. Or maybe you have become newly eligible for a tax allowance or extra relief, for example because you have increased your pension contributions.

If this is the case, carefully work out your expected tax bill for this year (including Class 4 national insurance if you are self-employed – see p. 304). Halve the total to find the amount for each payment on account. Then fill in form SA303 which you can get from your tax office or the Revenue website at www.hmrc.gov.uk. To reduce a forthcoming payment, return the form before the 'due by' date on the statement of account. If later you realise you will owe even less tax, you can make a further claim, again using form SA303.

Tax-saving idea 13

Always check your self assessment statement to see if you can claim a reduction in the interim payments on account. But, if in doubt, it is better to pay slightly more than to ask for a reduction. You will be charged interest if you pay too little, whereas tax you have overpaid earns interest. The interest charged on underpaid tax is over twice as much as that added to overpaid tax. You can also be fined if you knowingly reduce your payments on account by too much.

What your self assessment statement might look like

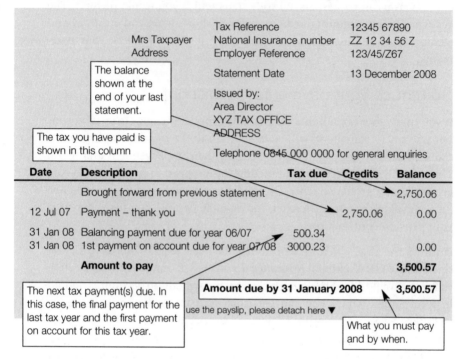

Interest and surcharges

Provided you pay the original payments on account demanded on time, no interest is normally charged even if your tax bill for the year turns out to be much higher. In other cases, interest is payable on tax paid late.

On the other hand, any tax you have overpaid also earns interest. Any interest charged or received will be shown on your self assessment statement.

Interest is automatically charged on any tax left unpaid after the 31 January or 31 July payment deadlines. If the tax due on 31 January 2008 is still not paid by 28 February 2008, there is a surcharge of 5 per cent of the unpaid tax. A further 5 per cent surcharge of the amount of tax still unpaid after 31 July 2008 is imposed. Interest will be added to any unpaid surcharge, starting 30 days after the notice of the surcharge.

Example

Shalini Edwards is self-employed. Her profits are usually around £32,000 but, for 2006–7, they jumped to £40,000. During 2007, her tax bills were £4,000 in January and £3,940 in July. Of these, 2 × £3,940 = £7,880 were payments on account for 2006–7. But due to the profit increase, the total bill for the year is £9,779. Shalini must make a final payment on 31 January 2008 of £9,779 − £7,880 = £1,899. The increased total bill feeds through to a higher first payment on account for 2007–8 (½ × £9,779 = £4,890), also due on 31 January 2008. Her total tax bill for January 2008 is £6,789. This is two-thirds more than the previous January's bill, even though her profits increased by only a quarter.

The PAYE system

Your employer is an unpaid tax collector for the Revenue using the PAYE system – Pay As You Earn. Every time employees are paid, income tax and national insurance contributions (NICs) are deducted from the earnings and sent in a batch to the collector of taxes. Your employer is also responsible for collecting student loan repayments on behalf of the government (see p. 256) through your pay packet.

Your employer needs various bits of information to operate the PAYE system, in particular a PAYE code for each employee. This is issued by the Revenue and tells the employer how much tax-free pay to give you each month or week. The Revenue also sends you a notice of your PAYE code, for example in January or February in time for the coming tax year or when your circumstances change. You will not necessarily get a notice every year. You can request a coding notice at any time.

Tax-saving idea 14

According to the National Audit Office (a body that keeps a watch on the government's money management), around three out of ten coding notices contain errors. If your PAYE code is wrong, you may pay too much tax and have to wait for a rebate. And, although paying too little tax might seem attractive, you will have to make up any underpayment in the following tax year – often in one go if it is £2,000 or more. So it makes sense to check your PAYE code carefully whenever you receive a notice of coding.

The coding notice

The coding notice (form P2) sets out the Revenue's calculations to arrive at your PAYE code. Your employer uses the code in conjunction with tax tables supplied by the Revenue to work out how much tax to deduct from your pay.

If you work for two employers, you should have two PAYE codes – one for each job – and two coding notices. If you are retired and receive an occupational and/or personal pension, you will also have tax deducted through PAYE. If you have just one main pension, you'll get one PAYE code. If you have two or more substantial pensions, you may get a code for each one.

Your PAYE code reflects the amount of allowances your tax inspector estimates you can set against your earnings in the current tax year. It may be adjusted to collect tax on fringe benefits and income, such as freelance earnings, odd pensions and savings interest. The amounts are based on information in your tax return (if you get one), from your employer or from other organisations that send details of payments to the Revenue. You may also be asked to complete a tax review form (P810). This is a one-page form, which asks for details of your income and payments that qualify for tax relief, so that the Revenue can update and correct the information it holds.

Your employer usually makes various other adjustments to your gross salary to arrive at your take-home pay. These can include deduction of national insurance, student loan repayments, pension contributions and donations to charity through payroll giving. None of these is reflected in your PAYE code.

Checking a coding notice

In 2005, the Revenue tested a new type of coding notice (see p. 38) which is now being used nationwide. Instead of a rather standardised form with an explanatory booklet, you now get a short, personalised form with the relevant notes on the form itself. The Revenue hopes that this will be easier to understand.

The main figures on the coding notice are in two columns. The column on the right is the main sum which starts with your allowances and reliefs and then subtracts the total of any adjustments. The column on the left details the adjustments. For example, if you will have taxable fringe benefits (such as a company car) in the current year, their value will be listed in this column. So will the amount you are expected to get from other sources of untaxed income, such as freelance earnings, taxable state pensions and benefits, and savings income that has not already been taxed.

Tax-saving idea 15

You do not have to agree to have untaxed income taxed through PAYE. You can opt for it to be taxed, instead, through the self assessment system described in the first part of this chapter. Self assessment means you pay the tax later (through payments on account and any final payment) but does involve more admin than PAYE.

Checking the entries on your coding notice is very straightforward. Start by making sure that you have all the allowances and deductions to which you are entitled in the right-hand column. Some allowances and deductions are not included if you have already been given the correct amount of tax relief at source – for example, where a basic rate taxpayer makes contributions to a personal pension or Gift Aid donations to charity. If you pay tax at the higher rate, there will be an entry on your coding notice to give you the extra relief due (see Example).

Example

> Gerry Walker puts £5,000 gross (before tax relief) into a stakeholder pension scheme in 2007–8. Since the basic rate of tax is 22 per cent, he gets relief at source of 22% × £5,000 = £1,100. So he actually hands over just £3,900. But Gerry is a higher-rate taxpayer so he is entitled to relief of 40% × £5,000 = £2,000. The extra £900 relief is given by increasing his tax allowances by £2,250 since 40% × £2,250 = £900.

Next check the amounts in the left-hand column that are to be taken away. Most are straightforward. The main complications are:

▪ **interest without tax taken off** collects tax on interest you are expected to get during the tax year which will be paid gross – for example, from NS&I income bonds (see Example overleaf). If you are a basic rate taxpayer, the amount entered here will be less than the actual interest you receive. This is because the interest needs to be taxed at 20 per cent (see p. 17) but PAYE will give you relief at 22 per cent. Deducting the smaller amount shown on the coding notice will ensure the correct tax is paid

▪ **allowance restriction** if you get married couple's allowance and/or qualify for tax relief on maintenance payments (both now available only for people born before 6 April 1935). These give tax relief only at a rate of 10 per cent. If your top rate of tax is expected to be just 10 per cent (the starting rate), then the full amount of the allowance will be added to your personal allowance. But, if your top rate of tax is higher than 10 per cent, an adjustment is needed to prevent PAYE giving you too much relief. The Example on p. 39 shows how this is done.

▪ **higher rate tax adjustment** collects extra tax due at the higher rate on interest, dividends and some other sorts of income which are paid after deduction of tax that covers any basic rate tax due. See Example on p. 39.

HM Revenue & Customs

PAYE Coding Notice

Tax code for tax year

2007 – 2008

Please keep all your coding notices. You may need to refer to them if you have to fill in a tax return. Please also quote your tax reference and National Insurance number if you contact us.

010000:00000080:001   491/1
MR B ANDREWS
MATHESON HOUSE
GRANGE CENTRAL
SOMERSET STREET
TELFORD
SHROPSHIRE   TF3 4HQ

H M INSPECTOR OF TAXES
NORTH WEST MU1
5 ABBEY FOREGATE
SHREWSBURY
SALOP
SY2 6AD

Inland Revenue office phone	Date of issue
01567 3456789	13 FEB 2008

Tax reference	National Insurance number
491/G7070/HD	CE 00 00 30 A

Dear MR B ANDREWS

Your tax code for the year 6th April 2007 to 5th April 2008 is 172T

You need a tax code so Giveus Abreak can work out how much tax to take off the payments they make to you from 6th April 2007. We have worked out your tax code but need you to check that our information about you is correct. The wrong tax code may mean you pay too much, or too little tax. Please keep your Coding Notices, you may need them if we send you a Tax Return.

Here is how we worked it out			
your personal allowance		£5,225	(see Note 1 below)
car benefit (new rules)	- £1,500		(see Note 2 below)
car fuel benefit	- £1,500		(see Note 3 below)
interest without tax taken off (gross interest)	- £501	- £3,501	(see Note 4 below)
a tax free amount of		£1,724	(see Note 5 below)

If we have got it wrong, or if your circumstances have changed and you think it could affect the tax you pay, please tell us. Our telephone number and address are above. We turn £1,724 into tax code 172T to send to Giveus Abreak. They should use this code with the tables they receive from HM Revenue & Customs to take off the right amount of tax each time they pay you from 6th April 2007. Giveus Abreak do not know the details of 172T or how it is worked out - that is confidential between us.

Notes

1   The law allows everyone who lives in the UK to receive some income before tax has to be paid - a "tax free amount" of income. That tax free amount starts from a "personal allowance" that depends on your circumstances. Our records tell us you are entitled to £5,225 for this tax year, the standard personal allowances for people who will be under 65 at 5th April 2008.

2   We have to see if anything should reduce your tax free amount. We understand you have a company car from Giveus Abreak. You have to pay tax on the benefit of using that car for your private motoring. By taking into account the

   – car's cost,

■ **tax underpaid** is an adjustment to collect any tax of less than £2,000 outstanding from a previous tax year. For example, if you owe £500 and pay tax at the basic rate of 22 per cent, £2,273 will be deducted from your allowances so that 22% × £2,273 = £500 tax is collected.

Example

Burt Andrews gets £551 interest from an NS&I investment account in 2007–8. He should pay tax of 20% × £551 = £110. But he is a basic rate taxpayer, so simply deducting £551 from his allowances would collect too much tax (22% × £551 = £121). Instead the tax inspector deducts £501. This will collect the right amount of tax because 22% × £501 = £110.

Example

Bill Svensen is married and was born before 6 April 1935. He gets £6,365 married couple's allowance in 2007–8. This amount is shown in the right-hand column on his coding notice. But he is a basic rate taxpayer and if £6,365 of his income were tax-free, this would give him 22% × £6,365 = £1,400.30 in tax relief. This is £763.80 too much because the married couple's allowance gives relief only at 10 per cent (10% × £6,365 = £636.50). Therefore an allowance restriction of £3,471 is deducted in the left-hand column. Since 22% × £3,471 = £763.62, this claws back virtually all of the excess relief.

Example

Betty Pinder pays tax at the higher rate and receives £800 of interest from which tax at 20 per cent (£200) has already been deducted. But Betty should have paid tax at 40 per cent on the gross amount, which means she owes a further £200 tax. To collect this, a higher rate adjustment of £500 is deducted from her allowances, since 40% × £500 = £200.

Calculating your PAYE code

All the adjustments are subtracted from the allowances and reliefs to find the net amount of tax-free pay for the year. This is converted into a PAYE code, normally by knocking off the last figure and adding one of the following letters, depending on your allowances and tax rate:

■ L – personal allowance at the rate for those aged under 65 only

■ P – personal allowance for those aged 65–74 only

■ Y – personal allowance for the over-75s only

■ V – personal allowance for those aged 65–74 and married couple's allowance for those born before 6 April 1935 and under age 75, paying tax at the basic rate.

So, if your only tax allowance is the single person's allowance for people under 65 of £5,225 and you have £3,501 deductions to collect extra tax, your total tax-free amount for the year will be £5,225 − £3,501 = £1,724. Your code is found by knocking off the last figure to give you 172 and adding L. Your PAYE code will be 172L.

When it comes to deducting tax from your pay, the employer's tax tables say that an employee with a code 172L is entitled to £1,729 of tax-free pay and this is spread equally over all the pay periods in the year.

The letters after the number enable your tax bill to be automatically adjusted when tax allowances change without a new code being issued.

T and K codes

If your code ends in the letter T, your tax position is more complicated – you may be getting other allowances (such as blind person's allowance), have fringe benefits (such as a company car) or you have asked for the T code because you do not want your employer to know what allowances you are entitled to. Your tax bill can't be automatically adjusted if you have this sort of code and you will have to wait for your tax office to tell your employer what adjustment to make.

If, in working out your code, the deductions come to more than your allowances, you will have a PAYE code starting with the letter K. This tells your employer to add an extra amount to your pay before working out tax – see Example below. K codes have to be recalculated every time the tax allowances change or there is some other alteration in your circumstances.

Example

Rasheed Patel is a single man and his only tax allowance is the personal allowance of £5,225. However, he has a company car with a taxable value of £6,000, so his tax-free amount for the year is £5,225 − £6,000 = −£775. His PAYE code is found by dropping the last digit to get 77. Then he subtracts 1 to get 76, giving a code of K76. This means, Rasheed will have £769 added to his pay for the year before tax is worked out (instead of having some allowances deducted).

More than one source of income

There are special PAYE codes that don't have numbers or have numbers that don't stand for tax allowances. These are mainly used for deducting tax from second or third sources of income:

■ BR – this income is all taxed at the basic rate. This is where other sources of income have used up all your allowances and your starting rate tax band

■ DO – this income is all taxed at the higher rate because other sources of income have used up your allowances and both your starting and basic rate tax bands

■ OT – you are not entitled to any tax-free pay but this income is to be taxed at the starting rate, then the basic rate and, if necessary, the higher rate

■ NT – this income is to be paid without any tax deducted, perhaps because it is less than your tax-free allowances.

Claiming a tax refund

If you have paid too much tax through PAYE because you have stopped doing a job part way through the tax year, a refund will automatically be arranged by your new employer or the Jobcentre Plus office handling your benefit claim. But, if you are neither going to a new job nor getting benefit, claim a tax rebate using form P50.

In other cases where you have paid too much tax – for example, because tax has been deducted from your savings income but you are a non-taxpayer – claim a refund using form R40. Do not send any documents, such as certificates of tax deducted, with the form but keep them safe in case your tax inspector asks to see them. The Revenue aims normally to process your claim within 28 days. Refunds are based on the information you provide, but the Revenue can open an enquiry either before or after paying the refund. You do not have to wait until the end of the tax year to make a claim but repayments of less than £50 are not usually made mid-year.

Either ask your tax office for the relevant claim form or download it from www.hmrc.gov.uk. You can't submit these forms by internet.

4

Dealing with tax problems

Given the complexity of the UK tax system, it is hardly surprising if your tax affairs do not always run smoothly. Here are some ideas on how to cope with the most common problems you are likely to face.

Changes to your tax return

Estimates, mistakes and corrections

If you have put a provisional figure in your return (see p. 28), you must supply the final figure as soon as it is known. If extra tax is due and the normal payment date has passed, you will be charged interest but no penalties or surcharges unless you have been negligent or fraudulent. You will receive interest if a refund is due.

You might make a mistake when you complete the return. You have 12 months from the filing date within which you can amend your return with a minimum of fuss. Simply phone or write to your usual tax office explaining the amendment required. If, within nine months of the date you sent in the return, the Revenue picks up any obvious errors, it too can amend the return.

You also have five years from the date the tax return had to be in by – for example 31 January 2013 in the case of the tax return for the year 2006–7 – to correct any mistakes and claim back any tax overpaid as a result. You should notify your tax office in writing. However, you can't use this route to make a back claim for a tax relief where the time limit for making the claim has already expired. (This applies, for example, to some types of loss relief if you run a business.)

Any tax due as a result of a revised self-assessment should be paid either by the normal payment date or 30 days after the making of the self-assessment (but this does not put off the date from which interest is charged).

Interventions

Since July 2006, the Revenue has been piloting a range of informal methods to help taxpayers get their tax right where the Revenue suspects there may be problems. These 'interventions' can take the form of letters, phone calls or visits. The Revenue may ask you to review the way you keep your business records, fill in a questionnaire to review the tax-compliance risks you face, or reconsider particular entries on your tax return. Where it has third-party information, the Revenue might correct your tax return and ask you to explain the perceived error and to take steps to avoid it happening again. So far, it is up to you to choose whether to take part in these interventions.

Enquiries

Your tax inspector has the right to open a formal enquiry into your tax return. A small proportion of all returns is selected at random for enquiry. But most are chosen because the inspector thinks there may be something wrong. Your tax inspector must tell you if the enquiry is into your whole return or just some aspect of it (such as a particular expense you have claimed).

Your tax inspector must give you written notice of an enquiry. For your 2006–7 return, the enquiry must normally start by 31 January 2009, assuming you sent your return in by the 31 January 2008 deadline. If your return was late or you amended it, the enquiry deadline is extended to one year from the end of the calendar quarter in which you sent in your late or amended return. From the 2007–8 tax return onwards, the enquiry window will be one year from the date the Revenue receives your tax return.

In effect the enquiry window can be extended to five years if your return includes a valuation, some other value judgment or you have interpreted tax law in a different way from the Revenue and you are deemed to have given insufficient information about this on your return. In this situation the Revenue is allowed to make a discovery assessment (see opposite) following the ruling in a case called *Langham* v *Veltema*. You can find guidelines on the Revenue website (www.hmrc.gov.uk) on the information you should supply to avoid a discovery assessment.

Your tax inspector has the right to demand that you produce certain documents. When you receive a notice of an enquiry, you may also receive a notice to produce these within 30 days. You can provide copies, but your tax inspector may insist on seeing the originals. You can appeal within 30 days against this notice to produce documents.

You can also appeal to the general commissioners (see p. 48) if you consider that an enquiry should not have been undertaken or is being continued unnecessarily. If they agree, the general commissioners can issue a notice to the Revenue requiring it to close the enquiry.

When the subject of an enquiry is complete, your tax inspector will issue you with a formal notice telling you so, how much tax you are considered to owe (if any) and requiring you to amend your self assessment. You can appeal against it, if you don't agree. The result of a tax enquiry may also lead to a revision of any tax credits you claim (see p. 60). Once the enquiry is closed, no further enquiry can be made into the same return but a discovery assessment (see below) is possible. For more information about enquiry procedures and your rights, see Revenue booklet IR160 *Enquiries under self assessment* or www.hmrc.gov.uk/compliance.

Discovery assessments

The law allows a discovery assessment if you are deemed to have been acting fraudulently or negligently and in some other limited circumstances.

A discovery means that your tax inspector has discovered that some income or gain on which you should have paid tax has not been included in your self assessment, or the assessment is too low, or the amount of relief given is too much. A discovery assessment would be to collect the extra tax due. You can appeal against a discovery assessment (see p. 48).

A discovery assessment cannot be made if full and correct information was sent with your tax return to the Revenue and it should have been possible to work out the correct tax. If the tax lost results from an error in the taxpayer's return but the return was made in accordance with prevailing practice at the time, no discovery assessment can be made.

Penalties, appeals and complaints

Penalties

The self assessment system is underpinned by a range of penalties, the most important of which are summarised in the table opposite. In addition, interest is added to overdue tax and also to penalties that remain unpaid. The tax inspector has discretion to reduce some penalties based, for example, on the gravity of your case and the extent of your cooperation.

At the time of writing, the penalty arrangements for incorrect tax returns were under review and a new system is expected to start for tax returns filed from April 2009 onwards. Under the new system, there will be four levels of penalty:

- nil, if you made a genuine mistake

- moderate, if you had not taken reasonable care

- higher, if you deliberately understated your tax

- even higher, if you deliberately underpaid and tried to conceal this.

The penalties may be reduced according to whether you voluntarily own up, admit the error when confronted and you cooperate with the Revenue. The Revenue might also suspend penalties for careless mistakes if it thinks that this will help you comply in future.

Tax-saving idea 16

Don't be late sending in your tax return. The 2007 return must be sent back by 31 January 2008 to avoid an automatic £100 penalty.

Action/omission triggering penalty	Penalty	Deadline for 2006–7 tax year
Failure to tell your tax office (if you have had no tax return) within six months of the end of the tax year about income or gains on which tax is due	Equal to the amount of tax due and unpaid by 31 January following end of tax year	5 October 2007
Failure to send in tax return by the due date	£100 or, if less, penalty equal to amount of tax due	31 January 2008
Tax return still not sent in six months after due date	Further £100 or, if less, penalty equal to amount of tax due	31 July 2008
Tax return still not sent in one year after due date	Equal to amount of tax due	31 January 2009
Continued failure to submit return	Up to £60 a day	
Fraudulently or negligently sending incorrect return	Equal to amount of tax due on income or gains undeclared	
Failure to keep records for a tax or accounting year and to preserve them for required period	£3,000	
Failure to produce documents on request	£50	
Continuing failure to produce documents	Up to £30 a day or, with permission of commissioners, up to £150 a day	
Final payment of tax unpaid more than 28 days after the due date	Equal to 5% of the unpaid tax	28 February 2008
Final payment of tax unpaid more than six months after due date	Further 5% of unpaid tax	31 July 2008

In 2001, a criminal offence was introduced of being 'knowingly concerned in the fraudulent evasion of income tax'. This is aimed at catching people who deliberately dodge tax, for example, employers and employees colluding to pay less through PAYE, or householders and tradesmen deliberately negotiating a cash price so they benefit from tax saved. The maximum penalty for serious cases is an unlimited fine and/or seven years in prison.

Appeals and complaints

You can appeal against the following: an assessment which is not a self assessment, an amendment to your self assessment by the Revenue after an enquiry, an amendment of a partnership statement where a loss of tax is discovered, a disallowance in whole or in part of a claim or election included in a tax return, penalty determinations, or a formal notice requesting documents.

Tax-saving idea 17

> You can appeal against the £100 penalty for missing the deadline for sending in your tax return. You would need a reasonable excuse, for example, an unexpected postal strike, serious illness, the death of a close relative, or loss of records due to fire, flood or theft. Pressure of work, a failure by your tax adviser or lack of information would not be regarded as a reasonable excuse.

You have to give written notice of appeal within 30 days after the issue of the notice of assessment, amendment or disallowance. But you may not appeal against an amendment as a result of an enquiry until you've had notice that the enquiry is complete, although certain questions may be referred for decision to the special commissioners or the courts while an enquiry is in process.

If you disagree about the amount of the tax bill, you should first of all exhaust the avenues within the Revenue. Appeal to your tax officer – they may not have made the original decision. However, if it becomes clear that the two of you are not going to agree, there remains the option of appealing to the commissioners – and if that doesn't work you could appeal to the High Court, then to the Court of Appeal (or equivalents for Scotland and Northern Ireland) and ultimately to the House of Lords, but this would be costly.

There are two types of commissioners. The general commissioners are not tax experts, but often local people acting in the same way as magistrates. There will be a clerk with expert knowledge on hand to advise them. The second group are known as special commissioners. They are tax experts in their own right.

If you are dissatisfied with the way the Revenue handles your tax affairs, you should first complain to your tax officer. If you get no satisfaction, you should direct your complaints to the regional controller responsible for your tax office (ask the tax office for the name and address). If this doesn't work, you should channel your next communication to the independent

Adjudicator's Office. The Adjudicator's remit covers matters such as excessive delay, errors, discourtesy or the way your tax inspector has exercised his or her discretion.

New appeals system

The present system of general and special tax commissioners is due shortly to be replaced. New legislation is creating an integrated two-tier tribunal system that will cover most types of dispute including tax cases. The First-Tier Tribunal will handle most tax disputes in the first instance, with a right of appeal to the Upper Tribunal, but complex cases might go straight to the Upper Tribunal. Access to the system will be via the Tribunals Service (www.tribunals.gov.uk).

Getting help

Although you can handle disputes with the Revenue yourself, this can be difficult and daunting, especially if you are faced with a Revenue enquiry or need to take a case to the commissioners or the new tribunals. You may need the help of a tax adviser – contact the Chartered Institute of Taxation (www.tax.org.uk) for a list of its members.

If your income is low and you cannot afford to pay a tax adviser, you may be eligible for free professional tax advice through TaxAid (www.taxaid.org.uk). Older people on low incomes can get free tax advice through TaxHelp for Older People (TOP). Both organisations target their help at households with an income of £15,000 or less. See Appendix E for contact details.

5

Tax and your household

In general, the tax system treats you as an independent person. But there are special rules designed to help (or sometimes to prevent tax avoidance) where particular circumstances relate to you or your household. This applies, for example, if you are married, in a civil partnership, have children or you are on a low income.

Marriage and civil partnerships

Married couples and civil partners are treated as two independent entities for the purpose of paying tax (though not when it comes to claiming tax credits – see p. 60). Each person is taxed on their own income and gains and has their own allowances. Each is responsible for filling in their own tax return and paying their own tax bills. There is no longer a tax allowance for married couples unless either or both husband and wife were born before 6 April 1935 – this allowance is now also available to older civil partners.

However, there are some aspects of the tax system which recognise that husband and wife, or civil partners, are more than just two individuals living together. One is that they can transfer some allowances between them in certain circumstances. Gifts between them don't normally trigger a capital gains tax or inheritance tax bill. And by sharing their wealth, a couple can each use their tax-free allowances to reduce the amounts paid in tax.

Tax-saving idea 18

If one of you pays tax at a higher rate than the other, you should consider giving investments which produce a taxable income to the spouse or civil partner who would pay least tax on the income. (But see opposite if you have shares in a close company.)

Gifts between married couples or civil partner must be genuine with no strings attached. If you are reluctant to give away the investments completely, consider putting them into joint names so the income is shared equally (see below).

Example

Janet Lardon is on a salary of £60,000 a year and has interest from savings accounts of £5,000 a year before tax. She pays tax at the higher rate of 40 per cent on her earnings – and that will be the rate for any savings interest.

She decides to share the savings accounts with her husband Ted, who pays tax at the basic rate only. She puts them in their joint names, so £2,500 of the interest is taxed as his. He has to pay tax on interest at 20 per cent (see p. 17), so they save higher rate tax of 20 per cent of £2,500, that is £500 a year.

This section explains the opportunities to save tax in marriage or civil partnership. For how marriage or civil partnership affects home ownership, see p. 68; information about capital gains tax is on p. 145, and on inheritance tax on p. 151.

Civil partnership

Since 5 December 2005, same-sex couples who register their relationship as a civil partnership are treated for tax in the same way as married couples.

Jointly owned assets

If you have investments which are jointly owned, your tax officer will assume the income from them is split equally between you. If the investments are not owned in equal proportions, you can have the income divided between you to reflect your actual shares of it. You do this by both signing a declaration of beneficial interests on form 17 (available from tax offices) and sending it to your tax officer.

The new split of joint income applies from when the declaration is signed – it can't be backdated. If you acquire new assets on which the 50:50 split is not to apply, you must make a further declaration. Note the split for income will also be used to allocate any gain on selling an asset between you when you dispose of it (see p. 122).

The exception to the above rules is where you jointly own shares in a close company. (A close company is basically one controlled by five or fewer people. Typically this could be a company that you or your spouse or civil partner owns and manages.) Since 6 April 2004, you will automatically be taxed on dividends from these shares according to the actual proportion in which you own them or have rights to income from them.

Personal allowances

A husband, wife and civil partner are each entitled to a personal tax allowance in the same way as single people – usually £5,225 in 2007–8 but more if aged 65 or over (see p. 24).

Married couple's allowance

Since 6 April 2000 married couple's allowance is given only where one (or both) of a couple was born before 6 April 1935.

The allowance gives tax relief at 10 per cent as a reduction in the tax bill.

The table overleaf shows the amounts of married couple's allowance in 2006–7 and 2007–8. The allowance is made up of two parts: a basic element and an age-related addition.

For couples who were married before 5 December 2005, the whole allowance is initially awarded to the husband, but half or all of the basic amount may be transferred to the wife. But the age-related addition stays with the husband (unless his income is too low to use it – see p. 55).

For couples who marry, and for same-sex couples who form a civil partnership on or after 5 December 2005, the whole allowance is initially awarded to whichever of the couple has the highest income. Once again, half or all of the basic amount (but not normally any of the age-related addition) can be transferred to the other spouse or partner.

You must normally make an election to transfer half or all of the basic amount before the start of the tax year – for example, an election for 2007–8 must have been made before 6 April 2007.

Married couple's allowance

Age of older partner during tax year	2006–7 tax year		2007–8 tax year	
	Maximum allowance (1)	Which would save this much tax:	Maximum allowance (1)	Which would save this much tax:
72–74	£6,065	£606.50		
73–74			£6,285	£628.50
75 and over	£6,135	£613.50	£6,365	£636.50
Of which: basic amount	£2,350	£235.00	£2,440	£244.00

(1) Total income limit at which allowance reduced: £20,100 in 2006–7 and £20,900 in 2007–8.

The married couple's allowance is reduced if the 'total income' of the person who gets the age-related addition is above a certain level. But the allowance is never reduced below the basic amount (£2,440 in 2007–8). The allowance is reduced by £1 for each £2 of income over £20,900 in 2007–8 (£20,100 in 2006–7). But any age-related personal allowance (see p. 24) is reduced first.

For example, suppose a husband aged 73 (married before 5 December 2005) has an income of £25,800. This is £4,900 above the income limit for 2007–8 of £20,900 which means he stands to lose ½ × £4,900 = £2,450 of age-related allowances. He initially has a personal allowance of £7,550 but this is reduced by £2,325 to the standard £5,225 because of his excess income. That leaves a further reduction of £125 which is set against his married couple's allowance of £6,285 reducing it to £6,160.

The table opposite shows the income level in 2007–8 at which all the age-related married couple's allowance would be lost (and so only the basic amount would be given).

Income level at which all age-related married couple's allowance lost in 2007–8

Age recipient of the age-related addition reches during tax year	Age partner reaches during tax year	Income level at which allowance reduced to basic amount (£2,440)
Under 65	73–74	£28,590
Under 65	75 and over	£28,750
65–72	73–74	£33,240
65–72	75 and over	£33,400
73–74	Any age under 75	£33,240
73–74	75 and over	£33,400
75 and over	Any age	£33,680

Tax-saving idea 19

Is one of you 73 or over in 2007–8? And does whichever of you gets the age-related part of the married couple's allowance have 'total income' high enough to be losing part of the allowance? You may be able to save tax by transferring investments that produce income to the other spouse or partner.

Transfer of allowances because of low income

If either spouse or civil partner has a tax bill which is too low to use up all their married couple's allowance, they can ask to have the unused part deducted from the tax bill of their spouse or partner. Even the age-related addition can be transferred in these circumstances. You can do this after the end of the tax year in which you got the allowance – see p. 229 for how to claim this. You have up to five years and ten months after the end of the tax year to transfer the unused allowances.

Example

Jasper Duffy, 73, has a total income of £26,800 – of which £11,800 a year is from savings and investments. Because his total income is well over the £20,900 limit, it reduces the amount of personal allowance he gets to the amount for under-65s. But it is also high enough to reduce the married couple's allowance the Duffys get from £6,285 to £5,660.

He decides to share his savings and investments equally with his wife Ellen, whose total income is well below the £20,900 limit. He puts them all into their joint names, which means only half the income they produce is his. This reduces his total income by half of £11,800 = £5,900 to £20,900.

▶

> The Duffys will thus get the full amount of married couple's allowance for people aged 73 to 74. And Jasper will get the full higher personal allowance for those aged 65 to 74.

Tax-saving ideas 20 and 21

> If your income is too low to use all the married couple's allowance, even the age-related part can be transferred to your spouse or civil partner.
>
> Married couples and civil partners of any age can transfer blind person's allowance between them if the recipient has too little income to be able to use the allowance fully. The unused part can be transferred to the spouse or partner even if they themselves are not blind.

Just married or registered?

If you newly marry or register a civil partnership and either of you was born before 6 April 1935, you qualify for the married couple's allowance.

In the tax year of your marriage or registration, you get one-twelfth of the allowance for each month or part-month of the union. In the 2007–8 tax year, you could get an allowance of up to £524 a month if either of you is aged 73 to 74 and £531 if 75 or over. A month runs from the sixth day to the fifth day of the next calendar month.

As described on p. 53, you can elect to transfer half or all of the basic amount of the allowance to your spouse or partner. In the year of marriage or registration only, you have until the end of the year to make this election – in other words until 5 April 2008 for the 2007–8 tax year.

Separation and divorce/dissolving a partnership

Separation, divorce or dissolving a civil partnership may affect:

- tax relief on maintenance you pay, but only if you or your spouse or partner were born before 6 April 1935
- national insurance contributions you pay if you are a married woman who has been paying contributions at the married women's reduced rate
- your entitlement to tax credits (see p. 60)

■ the tax allowances you get in the year it happens, but only if you or your spouse or partner were born before 6 April 1935.

If any of the above apply to you, you should tell your tax officer when you separate (and within three months for tax credits), even if you have not yet made a formal deed of separation or sought a court order. The Revenue will then treat you as no longer living with your spouse or partner, provided your circumstances suggest that the separation will be permanent.

Maintenance payments

Maintenance can take several forms, including direct payments of cash or the provision of support such as a home to live in. The person receiving maintenance does not pay any tax on the amount they get.

Where the maintenance is provided voluntarily – that is, the payment cannot be enforced – the person paying it gets no tax relief. This is also true for enforceable maintenance payments, except where you or your spouse or partner were born before 6 April 1935.

Provided you or your former (or separated) spouse or partner were born before 6 April 1935, you can claim relief for payments made under a legally binding agreement, such as a court order, a Child Support Agency assessment or a written agreement. Only payments up to a set limit qualify for relief. The limit is £2,440 in 2007–8. Relief is given at a fixed rate of 10 per cent through your PAYE code (see Chapter 3) or through an adjustment to your tax bill.

National insurance contributions

Paying certain types of national insurance contributions entitles you to some state benefits, such as state retirement pension. If you are a woman and you married before May 1977, you may have opted to pay contributions at the 'married women's reduced rate'. In return for paying less national insurance, you gave up the right to those state benefits and instead relied on your husband. Although, from May 1977 onwards, wives could not newly opt to pay the reduced rate, anyone who had already made the option could continue.

Your right to pay national insurance at the reduced rate ends at the time your marriage ends – generally, on the date of the decree absolute. If you are an employee, tell your employer so that he can arrange for you to pay full rate contributions. If you are self-employed, notify your tax office. For more information, see the Revenue website at www.hmrc.gov.uk/faqs/women_reduced_rate.htm

Capital gains tax and inheritance tax on separation

You can carry on making gifts to your ex-spouse or ex-partner in the year of separation without falling into the net for capital gains tax. After this, gifts may lead to a capital gains tax bill in the same way as for any other gifts (see p. 146).

However, if one of you moves out of the family home and gives or sells it to the other within three years of the separation, there will be no capital gains tax to pay. Even after that, there may be no capital gains tax if your ex-spouse or ex-partner is still living there and you have not claimed any other property as your only or main home.

Gifts between separated spouses or separated civil partners are free of inheritance tax (see p. 153). Once you are divorced or the relationship is dissolved, gifts may fall into the inheritance tax net unless they are for the maintenance of the ex-spouse, ex-partner or any children.

Married couple's allowance

Each of you retains your personal allowances. And each of you will retain any married couple's allowance you were getting before the separation – but only for the rest of the tax year.

Bereavement

If your husband, wife or civil partner dies, you carry on getting your own personal allowance as usual. If you have been claiming tax credits, within three months of becoming bereaved you need to make a new claim as a single person (see p. 62).

If you or your spouse or partner were born before 6 April 1935, you keep any married couple's allowance you were getting for the rest of the tax year in which death occurs. Any married couple's allowance unused in the year of death by the person who has died can be transferred to the surviving spouse or partner. Married couple's allowance ceases from the following year.

Living together

If you live with someone without being married or registered as a civil partnership, you are treated for tax purposes as single people. However, the same is not true for tax credits (see p. 60). The amount of any tax credits you can claim depends on your household income and couples are treated as being part of the same household whether or not they are married.

Children and young people

In general, the tax system does not treat people differently on the grounds of age. Therefore a child, just like an adult, has their own income tax allowance, tax bands and capital gains tax allowance. However, there are some rules specific to children and young people, in particular:

- to counter tax avoidance, where a parent gives money or investments to a child and these produce an income, that income is taxed as the income of the parent not the child unless it comes to no more than £100 a year. The £100 limit applies per parent per child

- individual savings accounts (ISAs) – see Chapter 7 – are generally not available to people under age 18 except that young people may hold cash ISAs from age 16 onwards

- child trust funds – see Chapter 7 – are tax-efficient investments available only to children born on or after 1 September 2002 up to their 18th birthday

- some payments commonly received by young people and students are tax-free. These include: educational maintenance allowance; student loans, grants and bursaries; and most youth training scheme allowances

- although children can be taxpayers, until they reach age 16 they have no liability for national insurance on any earnings or profits

- if you are a student working only during your holidays and earning too little to pay tax, you can arrange to receive your wages without any tax deducted by giving your employer a completed form P38S available from tax offices and the Revenue website

- since 6 April 2006, if a parent puts assets into a trust which can benefit their child, the trust counts as 'settlor-interested'. Both income and gains made by the trust are taxed as those of the parent

- transfers to most types of trust on or after 22 March 2006 count as taxable gifts for inheritance tax and the trust may periodically have to pay inheritance tax (see Chapter 10). These rules do not apply where a trust is set up in a parent's will to benefit their dependent child (called a 'bereaved minor's trust')

■ accumulation and maintenance (A&M) trusts have in the past been a popular way to make gifts to children and grandchildren because of favourable inheritance tax treatment. This treatment no longer applies for A&M trusts set up on or after 22 March 2006. Existing A&M trusts have until 5 April 2008 to change their terms or become subject to the harsher treatment (see Chapter 10 and Tax-saving ideas below).

Tax-saving ideas 22, 23 and 24

If you give capital to your children and it produces over £100 income a year, that income will normally be taxed as yours. Choose investments that produce a tax-free income instead (see Chapter 7).

If you are a student with an income of no more than £5,225 in 2007–8, you should not be paying tax. Claim back any tax deducted from earnings through your employer by using form P50 and claim back any tax deducted from savings using form R40 (see p. 41). Arrange to have savings interest paid without tax deducted by giving the bank or building society form R85 (see p. 75). If you work only in the holidays, arrange to get your wages paid gross by filling in form P38S. All forms are available from tax offices and the Revenue website, www.hmrc.gov.uk.

You can protect an A&M trust set up before 22 March 2006 from inheritance tax charges from 6 April 2008 onwards, if you change the trust rules so the beneficiaries become entitled outright to the trust assets by age 18. Alternatively defer entitlement to as late as age 25. The trust may then have to pay inheritance tax for the years from age 18 to 25 but only at a maximum 4.2 per cent of the value of the trust assets.

Households with children or on a low income

If you are working and have a low income or if you have children (in which case you do not need to be working and can have a fairly substantial income), you may be eligible for tax credits.

Tax-saving ideas 25 and 26

Households with children and an income up to £58,175 (£66,350 for the year a new child is born) are eligible for child tax credit. This is not given automatically – make sure you claim (see p. 64).

Even with an income up to nearly £50,000, you might qualify for working tax credit if you pay for childcare. In 2007–8, the maximum childcare element is worth up to £12,480. However, you might instead be able to get help with childcare costs from your employer (see p. 104).

Working tax credit (WTC) and child tax credit (CTC) are – despite their names – state benefits, not tax allowances. However, the amount you can get depends broadly on your income for tax purposes (or joint income if you are married, in a civil partnership or living with someone). This means that measures which save you tax might increase your tax credits too. And don't assume these are benefits just for the poor. If you have children, you might qualify even with an income well over £60,000 a year.

Tax credits if you have no children

You may be able to claim WTC if you or your partner are in work but on a low income. You must either be: aged 25 or more and working at least 30 hours a week; 16 or more, working at least 16 hours and disabled; or aged 50 or more and have recently started work after a period claiming certain state benefits. You are unlikely to be eligible in 2007–8 if your income comes to much more than about £11,800 a year (single) or £16,400 (couple) – unless you are entitled to the extra credits available to people with a disability or some over-50s.

Tax credits if you have children

You may be eligible for both the credits or just the CTC. For 2007–8, you can get at least some CTC provided your household income does not exceed £58,175 (or £66,350 if you have a child under one).

How the credits work

WTC is made up of eight elements – see the table overleaf. Your claim is based on as many of these elements as apply to you and you add on the relevant individual element of CTC for each child you look after. However, for every £1 by which your income (see overleaf) exceeds the first threshold (£5,220 in 2007–8), the credits are reduced by 37p. WTC is reduced first with the childcare element being the last to go, then the CTC.

If you qualify only for CTC and no WTC, the first threshold at which you start to lose the individual elements of CTC is higher (£14,495 in 2007–8).

Every household with children also qualifies for the family element of CTC. This is not reduced at all until the household income reaches the second threshold (£50,000 in 2007–8). You then lose £1 of credit for every £15 of income over the threshold.

Rate of tax credits in 2007–8

Element Working Tax Credit (WTC)	Who qualifies[1]	Amount
Basic	Everyone eligible for WTC	£1,730
Lone parent	Single, caring for a child	£1,700
Second adult	Most couples	£1,700
30-hour	Working at least 30 hours a week	£705
Disabled worker	Satisfy range of disability conditions	£2,310
Severe disability	Eligible for highest rate of disability benefit	£980
50-plus	Aged 50 or more and returning to work. Higher rate applies if work at least 30 hours a week	£1,185 or £1,770
Childcare	Incurring eligible childcare costs	80% of eligible costs[2]
Child Tax Credit (CTC)		
Individual element	For each child in your care	£1,845[3]
Family element	First year following new birth	£1,090
Family element	Families without a newborn child	£545

(1) The rules are complicated and just a brief indication is given here.
(2) Eligible costs are up to £175 a week for one child and £300 a week for two or more.
(3) Increased to £4,285 or £5,265 for a disabled child depending on severity of disability.

Income on which your tax credits are based

The amount of tax credits you get for any year is based on your income for that same year. However, because there is a delay before you know your income for the year, your claim is initially based on your income for the previous tax year. So, for the 2007–8 tax year, your credits are based initially on your income for 2006–7 and then revised after 5 April 2008 when your actual income for 2007–8 is known.

If it turns out that your income was lower than initially estimated, you will have received too little in tax credits and should receive an extra sum after the end of the year. Conversely, if it turns out that your actual income was higher than the estimate, you will have received too much in tax credits and the excess may be clawed back. But increases in income up to £25,000 are disregarded. You are required to report some changes in your circumstances during the year instead of waiting for the end-of-year review.

Example

Julie Brown is a single parent, working full-time and earning £13,000 a year. She has two children both at primary school and spends £225 a week (£11,700 a year) on childcare. She qualifies for both WTC and CTC in 2007–8 as follows:

Income in excess of first threshold	
(£13,000 − £5,220)	£7,780
Taper (37p for each £1 of excess)	£2,878
WTC	
Basic element	£1,730
Lone parent element	£1,700
30-hour element	£705
Childcare element (80% × £11,700)	£9,360
WTC before taper	£13,495
WTC after deducting taper (£2,878)	£10,617
CTC	
Individual elements (2 x £1,845)	£3,690
Family element	£545
Total CTC	£4,235
Total credits after taper	£14,852

Julie receives £14,852 in tax credits taking her income (before tax and national insurance) to £27,852 a year.

Tax-saving ideas 27 and 28

If your income for 2006–7 was over the limit for tax credits but you do not know what your income for 2007–8 will be and so do not know whether you will be eligible for credits this year, you should nevertheless put in a claim by 5 July 2007. Otherwise, if you do turn out to be eligible, it will be too late to backdate your claim to the start of the tax year. This might apply if, for example, you are self-employed with income that varies from year to year, or an employee fearing redundancy.

Any payment that qualifies for tax relief can be super tax-efficient if it also reduces your income and so increases the amount of CTC or WTC you can claim. This applies to, for example, pension contributions, Gift Aid donations, purchases through your business if you are self-employed, and claims against income for loss relief. See Example below.

Example

Douglas and Angela Adams have two children and a household income of £55,000. They qualify for the family element of CTC. The basic amount is £545 in 2007–8, but the couple lose £1 of credit for every £15 by which their income exceeds £50,000. The credit is reduced by (£55,000 − £50,000) ÷ 15 = £333 to £212.

▶

However, Douglas pays £5,000 into his personal pension. He is a higher-rate tax-payer, so in total he gets 40% × £5,000 = £2,000 tax relief on the payment. The pension contribution is also deducted from the household income for the purpose of CTC. This reduces Douglas' and Angela's income to £50,000 and increases their CTC to £545. Effectively, Douglas has had tax relief of (£2,000 + £333) ÷ £5000 = 46.7 per cent on the contribution.

Between April and July 2007, you will receive an annual review form (TC603R) to finalise your award for 2006–7. You are asked either to confirm the details on the form or to notify any changes by 31 August 2007. If you still do not know your income for last year, give a provisional figure and then supply the exact figure once known but no later than 31 January 2008.

Broadly, credits are based on your income for tax purposes, but there are differences. For example, some fringe benefits, such as cheap loans, are ignored, as is the first £300 of income from savings and pensions. Deduct any amounts paid to a pension arrangement or under Gift Aid but ignore the Gift Aid carry back rules (see p. 222) and deduct only what you actually paid during the year. Business losses are taken into account in the year in which they arise and, unlike the tax rules, are set against the income of the couple in a joint tax credit claim. Losses not used in this way may be carried forward for tax credit purposes, regardless of the way they have been claimed for tax.

How to claim

Tax credits are not paid automatically – you must claim them. You make a single claim for both credits by phoning the Tax Credits Helpline (0845 300 3900). Claims can be backdated no more than three months, so you need to send in a new claim by 5 July to get credits for the full tax year.

6

Tax and your home

Buying a home is probably the biggest purchase you will make. This chapter explains the limited situations in which you can still get tax relief on mortgage interest and how to make sure you don't pay a hefty capital gains tax bill if you sell your home for a lot more than you paid for it.

Mortgage interest tax relief

Home income schemes

People aged 65 or over can still get tax relief on the interest paid on a mortgage loan taken out as part of a home income scheme before 9 March 1999. Provided 90 per cent or more of the loan was used to buy an annuity, tax relief is given on the interest payments on up to £30,000 of the loan at a rate of 23 per cent. You go on getting tax relief even if you move house or switch mortgage. Usually relief is automatically deducted from the interest.

Running a business or letting your home

If you use your home for business purposes, you may be able to set off some of the interest against business income (see p. 295).

If you take out or extend a mortgage against your home and use the money raised in your business or to finance property you rent out, you can claim part of the interest as an allowable expense (see pp. 299 and 316).

If you let part or all of your home, you may be able to deduct mortgage interest when working out your profit or loss (see Chapter 19).

Capital gains tax on homes

If you sell most types of investments (including property) for more than you paid for them, there may be capital gains tax to pay (see Chapter 9). But if you sell your only or main home, there is normally no capital gains tax. This exemption is known as private residence relief.

If you own more than one home, only one of them qualifies for private residence relief. And you might lose the relief if you use the home for business, leave it for prolonged periods or let it out. If you do have to pay capital gains tax on selling a home, it can mean a hefty tax bill – the gain, adjusted for various reliefs, can be taxed at up to 40 per cent.

Which homes?

Private residence relief is given for your only or main home, whether it is a house or flat, freehold or leasehold, and wherever in the world it is.

You must occupy the home exclusively as your residence if it is to be free of capital gains tax. If part of the home is used exclusively for business, you may have to pay tax on part of the gain (see p. 69). And letting out some or all of your home can also mean a capital gains tax bill (see p. 71).

If you live in a caravan or houseboat, there's normally no capital gains tax to pay on it, even if it is not your only or main home. Caravans and boats count as wasting assets with a useful life of 50 years or less – and are thus outside the net for capital gains tax (see p. 120). But if you own the land on which a caravan stands, you might have to pay capital gains tax if you sell it, unless the caravan was your only or main home.

Gains on a former home that continues to be occupied by your ex-spouse are tax-free if you sell within three years of your leaving. A longer exemption period applies if this is your ex-spouse's only or main home and you have not nominated any other property as your own only or main home.

A home which a dependent relative lives in rent-free is also free of capital gains tax provided it fell into this category on or before 5 April 1988. This exemption lasts only as long as the relative continues to live in the home. Dependent relatives are: your mother or the mother of your spouse or civil partner if she is widowed, separated or divorced; any relative of yours or your spouse or civil partner who is unable to look after themselves because of permanent illness, disablement or old age (usually 65 or over).

Gardens

Private residence relief extends to the garden that goes with your home provided either the area of your home and garden come to no more than half a hectare (about 1¼ acres) or, if larger, a garden of that size is required for the reasonable enjoyment of the home. Gains related to any extra land will usually be taxable.

If your plot is no more than half a hectare, you can sell part of it without having to pay any capital gains tax even if you have obtained planning permission to build on the land. But the relief is lost if you fence off or start to develop the land and then sell it.

Tax-saving idea 29

The government is considering a possible new tax (the planning gain supplement) but will not introduce it before 2009. It aims to tax the increase in the value of land due to the grant of planning permission. Minor home improvements, such as adding a conservatory, are expected to be exempt. But, say, building new homes on part of your garden would be caught. It is likely the developer of the land would have to pay the tax but this would be reflected in the price you could get for your land. It seems the tax will be charged on the development value of the land less its 'current use value'. The current use value would take into account the value of any planning permission already granted before the new tax starts. Therefore, if you have any projects like this is mind, it might be better to get planning permission sooner rather than later.

If your plot exceeds half a hectare and you sell part of it, the Revenue will usually argue this is strong evidence that the garden was larger than required for reasonable enjoyment, so a gain will be taxable. Exceptions may be where you sell to a family member or where the sale was forced on you by financial necessity.

Private residence relief does not apply to a garden if you have already sold (or given away) the home that went with it.

If you have more than one home

If you have more than one home, you can choose which is your main one and so free of capital gains tax. It doesn't have to be the home where you spend most time.

Tax-saving ideas 30 and 31

If you have more than one home, you can nominate which one is to be treated as your main home for tax purposes. Normally, choose the one on which you expect to make the largest gain.

Married couples and registered civil partners must nominate just one home between them as their main home. But unmarried and unregistered partners can each elect a different residence as their main home even if, say, one is used only for weekends.

Tax-saving ideas 32 and 33

Every time the number of homes you have – whether or not you own them – changes you have a new opportunity to elect your main home. You could create a new opportunity by, for example, renting a flat for a few weeks. This could be worth doing if you previously missed the two-year time limit for electing which of two homes should count as your main home.

Electing a second home as your main home even for just a week can save you capital gains tax if it means you can claim other reliefs such as the last three years of ownership (see p. 70) or lettings relief (see p. 71).

Example

Mahmoud Sherani has a flat in London and a house in Dorset. Years ago he elected the London flat as his main home. He now plans to sell the house in Dorset on which he will make a large gain. On 1 May 2007 he changes his election so that the Dorset house is treated as his main home. A week later, he changes the election back to the London flat. Because the Dorset house has now been his main home albeit for a very short time, gains relating to the last three years of ownership are tax free. When he sells the London flat, gains attributable to one week will be taxable but should fall comfortably within his capital gains tax-free allowance (see Chapter 9).

You must make the election in writing and within two years of acquiring a second or further home. Once made, you can vary the election whenever you like and as often as you like and any variation can be backdated up to two years.

The Revenue takes the view that, if you miss the two-year deadline, you have lost the opportunity to make any election at all. Your main home will then be determined by the facts, such as your postal address and where you are registered to vote and you can be required to provide evidence to support this.

Married couples and civil partners can have only one main home even if in reality they spend a lot of time living in separate homes (for example, because one works away during the week). Unmarried and unregistered couples can each have a different main home.

Tax-saving idea 34

If you live most of the time in rented accommodation but also own a home and did not realise you needed to nominate the one you own as your main home in order to ensure there is no tax when you sell it, the Revenue will, by concession, waive the two-year limit. You must make the nomination within a reasonable time of becoming aware of your need to do so and it can be backdated to the time when you first started to have two homes.

Working from home

If any part of your home is used exclusively for business, there may be a capital gains tax bill (see Chapter 9) when you sell the home. This will not usually apply if you are an employee working from home, but could do if a substantial part of your home is set aside exclusively for the work.

If you use one or more rooms entirely for business (as an office or workshop, for example), there will be tax on part of the gain when you sell the home. You will have to agree the proportion with the tax officer, who may base it on the number of rooms you use or market value if the business part could be sold separately. If you claim part of the mortgage interest as a business expense (see p. 295), the same proportion of the gain is likely to be taxable.

Away from home

If you don't live in your home for all the time you own it, you might lose some of the private residence relief – even though it is the only home you own or you have nominated it as your main home. Normally you will have to pay capital gains tax on the following proportion of the taxable gain:

$$\frac{\text{Number of complete months of absence}}{\text{Number of complete months of ownership}}$$

Only months of ownership or absence since 31 March 1982 count in working out the proportion – earlier gains are outside the scope of the tax (see p. 129).

In practice, you can be away from the home for considerable spells of absence without losing any private residence relief. You can retain it during absence for the following periods:

- the first year of ownership while you are building, rebuilding or modernising the home. This can be extended for another year if you can convince the tax inspector it is necessary. To retain the exemption, you must move in within the one-year (or two-year) period
- the last three years of ownership – even if you have already moved out
- any other absences totalling up to three years, provided you live in the home both before the first absence and after the last.

You may also be able to retain private residence relief if work takes you or your spouse away from home. If your employer requires you to live away from home in the UK, you can go on getting private residence relief for up to four years of absence. If your employer requires you to work abroad, you can get relief indefinitely. But you must live in the home before the first absence and normally also after the final absence.

Provided you intend to live in your home in the future, private residence relief continues if you or your spouse are required to live in job-related accommodation (see p. 104). Self-employed people who have to live in work-related accommodation (for example, over the shop or at the club) can go on getting relief on their own homes as long as they intend to live there eventually.

Tax-saving idea 35

> If you are away from home for quite long periods, keep an eye on the capital gains tax position so that you don't lose private residence relief.

Example

> Linda March bought a house on 24 June 1996. On 6 July 1999 her employer sent her on an overseas posting lasting until 10 November 2001. On Linda's return to the UK, her employer sent her to work away from home until 15 August 2005. She lived in the home until 22 October 2005, when she bought a new home, eventually selling her old home on 27 February 2007.
>
> During the ten years and eight months Linda owned the home, she was absent for three periods totalling seven years and three months. But she will get private residence relief for the entire time she owned the house.

The two years and four months from July 1999 to November 2001 count for private residence relief because they are a period of employment spent entirely abroad.

The three years and nine months from November 2001 to August 2005 are less than the four years of employment elsewhere in the UK possible without losing private residence relief.

The year and four months from October 2005 to February 2007 are part of the last three years of ownership.

Capital gains tax on lettings

There is no capital gains tax to pay if you take in one lodger who is treated as a member of the family – sharing your living rooms and eating with you. But in other circumstances, there may be capital gains tax to pay when you sell a home that has been let out wholly or in part.

If you let out the whole house for a period, the gain attributable to that period is taxable.

If you let part of your home, you may have to pay capital gains tax on the part that is not occupied by you. If you let two of your six rooms, for example, one-third of the gain on selling the home is taxable (less if you haven't let the two rooms for all the time that you've owned the home).

However, there may still be no capital gains tax to pay if you can claim lettings relief for homes which have been wholly or partly eligible for private residence relief. Lettings relief reduces the taxable gain by £40,000, or the amount of private residence relief if this is lower – see the example below.

Tax-saving idea 36

You can claim letting relief only in respect of a residence that has been your main home at some time. So, if you buy a property mainly to let out, it could be worth moving in and making it your home for a while. There is no minimum time period but you must be able to prove that it was genuinely your permanent home while you were there.

Example

Jane Mortimer lived in her home for four years and then let it out for six. She sold it making a taxable gain of £50,000.

▶

Jane qualifies for private residence relief for the four years she lived in it, plus the last three years of ownership – seven years in all. The gain attributable to the remaining three years is 3/10 of the £50,000. This £15,000 is taxable.

Jane next works out how much lettings relief she is entitled to. The amount is the lower of £40,000 or the value of private residence relief on the house, which is £50,000 – £15,000 = £35,000. She can reduce the gain by £35,000; that means no taxable gain on the letting.

Property dealings

If you regularly buy and sell houses for profit, there might be a capital gains tax bill when you sell one – even if you have been living in it as your only or main home. This is meant to catch people who are making a business out of doing up unmodernised homes for sale. If your property dealings are substantial, you could be classified as a dealer in land. You would then have to pay income tax on the profits as a self-employed person (see Chapter 17).

Inheritance

If you inherit a property – for example, a family home on the death of your parents – you are deemed to have acquired it at its market value on the date of death. If you do not take up residence, there could be capital gains tax to pay if you sell the property and its value has risen since the date of death.

7

Savings, investments and pensions

To encourage savings, the government offers various tax incentives to investors, including a lower tax rate on savings income for basic-rate tax-payers and tax relief on pension contributions. There are also special tax rules to persuade you to build up some savings for yourself (individual savings accounts – ISAs) or your children (child trust fund), take out long-term life insurance policies, and invest in new businesses (for example venture capital trusts).

This chapter guides you through the various types of savings and investments and how they are taxed. It explains the rules and tells you how to cash in on the tax breaks offered by the government.

Income tax on investments

Income from some investments is tax-free (that is, there is no income tax to pay). For a list of these, see p. 367.

All other investment income is taxable. With more and more investments, tax is deducted from the income before it is paid to you. There is no further tax to pay on such income unless you pay tax at the higher rate. If you should have paid less tax than was deducted, you may be able to get a refund.

Interest paid after deduction of tax

Interest on most kinds of savings is now normally paid after tax has been deducted from it. This applies to building society accounts, bank accounts, annuities (other than pension annuities) local authority loans and bonds and National Savings & Investments (NS&I) fixed rate savings bonds.

On these types of interest, tax is deducted at 20 per cent from the gross income before handing it over to you. There is no further tax bill if you pay tax at the basic rate on your income – which is the case for the vast majority of taxpayers. If you pay tax at the higher rate, there will be extra tax to pay on this income (see below). If your income is too low to pay tax or you pay tax on the rest of your income at the starting rate of 10 per cent only, you can reclaim all or some of the tax which has been deducted.

The savings income is treated as an upper slice of your income. This means it does not reduce the amount of earnings or other income that can be taxed at the starting rate – the £2,230 taxable at 10 per cent in 2007–8.

Example

> Sonny Dasgupta pays tax at 40 per cent on his income. NS&I certificates offer him an average return of 3.65 per cent a year tax-free over two years. He could get 5.0 per cent a year over the same period in a bank term account.
>
> Sonny invests in the NS&I certificates, since that will give him 3.65 per cent a year whatever his tax rate. The interest rate he would get on the bank account after paying tax at 40 per cent would be lower: 60 per cent of 5.0 per cent, that is 3.0 per cent a year.

Higher rate tax on income paid after deduction of tax

If you get interest after tax has been deducted and pay tax at the higher rate of 40 per cent, there will be a further tax bill to pay – as the first example on p. 76 shows. The higher rate tax will be collected by the Revenue in one of two ways:

- by increasing the amount of tax you pay on your earnings through PAYE (see Chapter 3)
- through the payments you have to make in January and July under the self assessment system (see Chapter 3).

Grossing-up

> If you receive investment income after some tax has been deducted from it, what you receive is known as the net income. But you may need to work out how much the income was before tax was deducted from it (the gross income).
>
> You can find the gross income by grossing-up the net income using the ready reckoners in Appendix B (p. 369), or by using the following formula:
>
> $$\text{Amount paid to you} \times \left(\frac{100}{100 - \text{rate of tax}} \right)$$

For example, if you receive £50 of income after tax has been deducted at 20 per cent, the grossed-up amount of the income is: £50 × 100/(100 − 20) = £50 × 100/80 = £62.50.

Too much tax deducted?

If too much tax has been deducted from your interest, the excess can be claimed back. This would happen if the rest of your income is below the level at which you pay tax or you pay tax at the lower rate of 10 per cent only on the rest of your income – as the second example overleaf shows. For how to claim back tax, see p. 41.

Tax-saving ideas 37 and 38

If you pay tax at the top rate of 40 per cent, tax-free investments can be very attractive. Even if you could get a higher advertised rate of return on a taxable investment, the after-tax return could be considerably lower.

If you have been over-taxed on your savings, claim a refund using form R40 (see p. 41). You can go back nearly six years to claim tax back – for example, if you claim by 31 January 2008, you can claim back tax paid as long ago as the 2001–2 tax year. Non-taxpayers can arrange to receive gross interest in future by completing form R85.

Not a taxpayer?

If your income is too low to pay tax, you can arrange with the bank or building society to be paid interest without deduction of tax. Fill in form R85 which is available from banks, building societies and post offices, as well as from tax offices and www.hmrc.gov.uk. Also see Revenue leaflet IR111 *Bank and Building Society Interest – Are You Paying Tax When You Don't Need To?* or www.hmrc.gov.uk/taxback. Once made, the declaration runs indefinitely, so remember to review it if your circumstances change (for example, on the death of a spouse). There are hefty penalties for making a false declaration.

Arranging for interest to be paid without deduction of tax not only saves you claiming back the tax which has been deducted, you also get the money much earlier. But not all banks and building societies can manage to pay half the interest without tax deducted where only one joint holder is a non-taxpayer.

Example

Niamh Fagan gets £80 interest on her building society account in 2007–8. Tax has already been deducted from the interest at 20 per cent before it is credited to her account, so this £80 is the net (that is, after deduction of tax) amount.

To work out the gross (before deduction of tax) amount of interest, Niamh must add the tax back to the net amount. The grossed-up amount of interest is: £80 × 100/(100 − 20) = £80 × 100/80 = £100

In other words, Niamh has paid £100 − £80 = £20 in tax and this covers her basic rate tax on the interest.

If Niamh should pay tax at 40 per cent on this interest, her overall tax liability is 40 per cent of £100 = £40. Since she has already paid £20 in tax, she has to pay only £40 − £20 = £20 in higher rate tax. This leaves her with £80 − £20 = £60 of interest after higher rate tax has been paid.

Example

Niall O'Halloran has earnings of £5,300 in 2007–8 and received interest from his savings of £400. The correct tax has already been paid on his earnings. Tax has been deducted from this interest at 20 per cent but Niall reckons he should be paying tax on it at the lower rate of 10 per cent only. He checks to see if he is due a rebate.

First he works out the gross amount of interest he received – the amount before deduction of tax at 20 per cent: £400 × 100/(100 − 20) = £400 × 100/80 = £500.

This means he has been paid a gross amount of £500 from which £100 of tax has been deducted.

He adds the £500 to the £5,300 of earnings to find his total income of £5,800. Like all taxpayers, he is entitled to a personal allowance of £5,225 for the tax year, so his taxable income is £5,800 − £5,225 = £575.

Starting rate tax of 10 per cent is due on the first £2,230 of taxable income, so that is the rate he should have paid on the £500 of gross interest. 10 per cent of £500 is £50, so he is due a rebate of £100 − £50 = £50 on the interest.

Offshore bank accounts

Interest from UK banks and building societies is usually paid with tax deducted. But, if you have an account based in, say, the Channel Islands, Isle of Man or elsewhere offshore, the interest is generally paid gross. If you are a UK resident, you must nevertheless declare this interest and pay any tax due.

Tax-saving idea 39

The Revenue is pursuing a campaign to track down taxpayers who have failed to declare interest from offshore accounts. After several rulings by the special commissioners, the Revenue has the power to force banks and other institutions to disclose details of customers with offshore accounts or credit card transactions linked to such accounts. Taxpayers who voluntarily tell their tax office about such accounts are likely to be charged a reduced penalty and less likely to face prosecution.

Shariah-compliant products

Alternative financial products, where the return is in the form of a share of profits or a mark-up paid at a future date, have been developed to comply with Shariah law. The return on these is treated in the same way for tax as interest.

Gilt-edged stock

Since 6 April 1998, interest on all British government stocks (gilts) is usually paid gross – i.e. without any tax already deducted. But, if interest you started to receive before 6 April 1998 was originally paid net, it will continue to be paid with tax at 20 per cent already deducted unless you ask to be paid gross instead. Similarly, if you are receiving interest gross, you can ask to receive interest net of tax. To change the way your interest is taxed complete the appropriate form from Computershare (Tel: 0870 703 0143 www.computershare.com).

Corporate bonds

Interest from bonds listed on a stock exchange is paid gross (without any tax deducted).

Bond-based unit trusts

Unit trusts and open-ended investment companies (oeics) that invest wholly or mainly in gilts and/or corporate bonds pay 'income distributions'. They are taxed like other savings income and paid with 20 per cent tax deducted. Distributions from share-based unit trusts are taxed differently (see below).

Shares and unit trusts

Dividends from UK companies and distributions from share-based unit trusts are paid with a tax credit – the amount is given on the tax voucher which comes with the dividend or distribution. The tax credit is 10 per cent of the gross amount. So if you receive a dividend of £80, the grossed-up amount of this dividend is:

$$£80 \times \left(\frac{100}{100 - 10}\right)$$

$$= £80 \times \frac{100}{90}$$

$$= £88.89$$

The tax credit is £88.89 − £80 = £8.89.

The tax on the grossed-up amount of dividends and distributions is 10 per cent for starting rate and basic rate taxpayers. Since this is the same amount as the tax credit, they need pay nothing extra. Note that the 10 per cent tax credit does not eat up any of your starting rate band: you can still have up to £2,230 of other income taxed at the 10 per cent starting rate in 2007–8.

If you pay tax at the higher rate, there is extra tax to pay. Higher rate taxpayers pay tax on the grossed-up amount of dividends and distributions at 32.5 per cent. So on a net dividend of £80, your total tax bill is 32.5 per cent of the grossed-up amount of £88.89 = £28.89. Since you have a tax credit of £8.89, the higher rate tax due is £28.89 − £8.89 = £20. That leaves you with £80 − £20 = £60 after paying the higher rate tax.

The tax credit cannot be claimed back if the income is not taxable in your hands. So if your income is too low to pay tax you cannot claim it back. This means that if most or all of your income is dividends and distributions, you might not get the full value of your tax allowance.

From 2008–9, dividends you receive from foreign companies will be taxed in the same way as UK dividends provided you own less than 10 per cent of the company concerned and your total foreign dividends do not come to more than £5,000 a year.

Real estate investment trusts

Investment trusts are companies, quoted on a stock exchange, whose business is running an investment fund. You invest by buying shares in the fund and, in general, your investment is taxed in the same way as any other shares would be.

However, from 1 January 2007, a new type of investment trust called a real estate investment trust (REIT) has become available. A REIT is a company that invests mainly in a portfolio of rented commercial and/or residential properties. Provided various rules are met, including that at least 90 per cent of all the profits received by the REIT are distributed to shareholders, the REIT pays no tax on the profits.

As an investor, you pay tax on your REIT income at the same rate that you would if you invested direct in rental property. The REIT pays out dividends – called property income distributions – with tax at the basic rate (22 per cent in 2007–8) deducted. If you are a non-taxpayer, you can claim this back. If you are a starting-rate taxpayer you can claim back part of the tax. Higher-rate taxpayers have extra tax to pay.

Tax-saving idea 40

> You can hold REITs through an individual savings account (see p. 90), self-invested personal pension plan (see p. 89) or a child trust fund (see p. 93), in which case distributions, as well as any gains from selling the shares, will be tax-free.

Investing for capital gains

One way of reducing your income tax bill is to invest for capital gains rather than income. Capital gains tax is paid on increases in the value of investments – for example if the value of shares rises and then the shares are sold. The chargeable gain is added to your income and taxed at the same rate as savings (interest) income.

Example

> Maggie East, 70, has income of £14,000 in 2007–8 made up of £9,000 in pensions, £1,500 building society interest (grossed up to include the 20 per cent tax) and £3,500 in dividends (grossed up to include the 10 per cent tax credit). She has a personal allowance of £7,550 and wonders how the tax bill is allocated between these different types of income.
>
> Her allowances and tax bands are set against her income in the following order: income other than from savings and investments, savings income, dividend income (but bearing in mind that allowances cannot be used to reclaim dividend tax credits). So her tax position is as follows:
>
> ▶

	'Other' income	Savings income	Dividend income
Income	£9,000	£1,500	£3,500
Less personal allowance	£7,550	£0	£0
Taxable income	£1,450	£1,500	£3,500
Starting rate band	£1,450	£780	£0
Basic rate band	£0	£720	£3,500
Tax at 10%	£145.00	£78.00	£350.00
Tax at 20%	n/a	£144.00	n/a
Tax at 22%	£0	n/a	n/a
Less tax already paid	£145.00	£300.00	£350.00
Tax refund/extra to pay	£0	£78 refund	£0

The allowance reduces Maggie's taxable income other than savings and investments (her 'other' income) to £1,450 and this is all taxed via PAYE at the starting rate. Her 'other' income is too low to use up all the starting rate band, so the unused part is next set against her savings income. This means £780 of her savings income should have been taxed at 10 per cent rather than the 20 per cent already deducted. Therefore Maggie can claim a tax refund of £78. Tax due on the dividend income matches the tax credit so there is nothing further to pay.

But there's no tax to pay if your total net capital gains in 2007–8 are below £9,200. A husband and wife and civil partners can each make total net capital gains of this amount before paying capital gains tax. And you can often make gains of more than the £9,200 limit, because of the deductions you can make in calculating your net capital gains. These include taper relief which reduces the tax bill according to how long you have owned the investment since 6 April 1998. A few investments – shares in unquoted trading companies including those listed on the Alternative Investment Market (AIM) and employee shares – count as business assets and so benefit from higher relief (see p. 134).

Tax-saving idea 41

Many people are careful to make the most of their income tax-free allowances each year, but overlook the tax-free capital gains limit. To make regular use of the limit, you could consider selling assets each year and buying them back later or immediately buying similar assets (see p. 137).

For more about capital gains tax and how to minimise it, see Chapter 9.

Life insurance policies

Many types of life insurance build up a cash-in value which makes it possible to use them as a form of investment. With most, the insurance company has paid tax on the investment income and gains before paying out the return to you. This is deemed to be equivalent to tax at the savings rate but you cannot reclaim any of it even if you pay tax at less than this rate. However, provided certain rules are met, higher-rate taxpayers do not have any further tax to pay on the return. There may be higher tax to pay if you cash in a savings-type life insurance policy after less than ten years or three-quarters of the term, if this is shorter (see p. 201).

Tax-saving idea 42

Although there is often no tax for you to pay when you cash in a life insurance policy, the insurance company has already paid tax which you can't reclaim. Unless you are a higher rate taxpayer, other investments will usually be more tax-efficient. For example, consider unit trusts, investment trusts or open-ended investment companies as alternatives to unit-linked life insurance policies.

Tax-saving idea 43

Everyone should try to make sure that they are saving for retirement through a pension – and the earlier you start, the better the pension you should get at the end. Don't delay. You can get tax relief at your highest rate of tax. This means a contribution of £1,000 costs you just £600 if you are a higher rate taxpayer, and just £780 if you are a basic rate taxpayer in 2007–8. If your income level means you are losing tax credits, a £1,000 pension contribution could increase your credits by up to £370, or £67 if you just get the child tax credit family element. The effective cost of a £1,000 contribution after tax relief and credits could be reduced to £230 for a higher rate taxpayer and £410 for a basic rate taxpayer.

Pensions

The government offers tax incentives to encourage you to provide for your retirement by saving with an employer's occupational pension scheme or through your own personal pension or stakeholder scheme. These mean that saving for the future through a pension often provides a better return than any other type of investment:

- there is tax relief on your contributions to the scheme (within limits)
- any employer's contributions made for you are not taxable as your income or as a fringe benefit
- the fund the money goes into pays no capital gains tax and some of the income builds up tax-free
- you can trade in some pension to get a tax-free lump sum when you retire.

New rules since April 2006

A single, unified regime for all types of pension scheme was introduced from 6 April 2006, replacing the previous patchwork of eight different sets of rules. The new regime gives most people much greater flexibility over the pension schemes they use and the ability to save more. However, original proposals that increased choice about how you invest your pension savings and how you draw your pension in retirement have been severely cut back.

How much you can save

There is now no limit at all on the amount that you can pay into registered pension schemes (which means virtually all occupational and personal schemes). But you can get tax relief only on contributions you pay under age 75 and up to the greater of:

- £3,600 a year, or
- 100 per cent of your relevant UK earnings for the year. Relevant earnings means earnings chargeable to tax, including, for example, salary, bonuses, taxable fringe benefits and profits if you are self-employed.

This annual limit for relief applies to contributions paid by you and by most people on your behalf, but excludes, for example, contributions paid by your employer and amounts paid in by the government because you are 'contracted out' of part of the state pension scheme. It applies to the total of your contributions to all your pension schemes.

If you are a high earner, the amount you pay in might also be restricted because of the annual allowance (see p. 84).

Tax-saving ideas 44, 45 and 46

Everyone – even a child – can put at least £3,600 a year into a pension scheme. You can make contributions on behalf of someone else – for example, your child or a non-working partner.

In any one year, you can get tax relief on payments into pension schemes up to 100 per cent of your UK earnings for the year. This may give you scope, for example, if you inherit a lump sum to invest the whole amount tax efficiently for retirement.

Usually your contributions have to be in money but if you get shares from an employee savings-related share option scheme or share incentive plan (see Chapter 16) you can transfer these to a pension scheme within 90 days of acquiring them. Future capital growth will then be tax-free and higher rate taxpayers will also pay less tax on any dividends they produce.

How you get tax relief: occupational schemes

If you pay into an occupational scheme, the contributions are deducted from your pay before income tax is worked out ensuring that you get tax relief on the contributions up to your top rate of tax.

How you get tax relief: other schemes

You get relief on contributions to a personal pension by making payments from which you have deducted tax relief at the basic rate (22 per cent in 2007–8). For example, if you want to pay in £3,600, you first deduct 22% × £3,600 = £792 and hand over just the remaining £2,808. The pension provider then claims the £792 from the Revenue and adds it to your scheme. In this way, £3,600 is paid in at a cost to you of £2,808. This system applies to everyone, even if they pay tax at less than the basic rate.

If you are a higher rate taxpayer, you can get extra relief through PAYE or self-assessment. Either claim through your tax return or tax review form P810. Extra relief is given by raising the threshold at which higher rate tax starts. In the example above, up to £3,600 would be taxed at the basic instead of higher rate giving maximum extra relief of (40 − 22)% × £3,600 = £648.

Tax relief on contributions to retirement annuity contracts can be given as described above. But normally you pay gross contributions and need to claim all the tax relief due through your tax return or form P810.

Tax-saving ideas 47 and 48

From 2008–9, unless you are a higher rate taxpayer, the amount of tax relief you can claim on contributions to a personal pension (including stakeholder schemes) will fall from 22 per cent to 20 per cent. If possible, make contributions before 6 April 2008 so that you get the higher relief.

If you are in work and currently pay tax at the starting rate, from 2008–9 your earnings will be taxed more heavily because the 10 per cent starting rate band is being abolished and replaced with an extended 20 per cent basic rate band. But it does make contributions to an occupational pension scheme an even more attractive way to save because you will get tax relief on them at 20 per cent.

Tax-saving idea 49

If you are a starting rate taxpayer or non-taxpayer, you still hand over contributions to a personal pension after deducting tax relief at the basic rate. The relief is claimed by the provider from the Revenue and added to your scheme. In this way, you are getting a bonus added to your pension savings. As a non-taxpayer, for every £10 you contribute, the bonus increases your savings by £2.82 in 2007–8.

Examples

Marion Mould is an employee. Her monthly contributions of £50 to her employer's occupational pension scheme are deducted from her salary before tax is worked out under PAYE.

Margaret May is an employee. She saves for retirement through a stakeholder scheme. She saves £50 a month but hands over only £39 to the pension provider because she has deducted £11 basic rate relief (at 22 per cent in 2007–8). The provider claims £11 from the Revenue and adds it to her scheme.

Marcia Mumps is self-employed, saving £50 a month through a retirement annuity contract. She hands over £50 to the provider each month and claims tax relief through her tax return.

Example

In 2007–8, Arif Gupta has earnings of £60,000 on which he pays tax of £15,414. He inherits £46,800 and decides to pay the whole lot into a personal pension. The £46,800 is treated as a net contribution from which tax relief at 22 per cent has already been deducted. The relief comes to £13,200 which is 22% × (£46,800 + £13,200). He also gets some higher-rate tax relief given by raising the threshold at which he starts to pay higher rate tax by the amount of the gross pension contribution (£60,000). This reduces his tax bill to £11,783, giving higher-rate relief of £15,414 − £11,783 = £3,631. In total, the tax relief on the contribution comes to £13,200 + £3,631 = £16,831. This exceeds the tax he would actually have paid due to the way relief is given on personal pensions.

Annual allowance

Each year you have an allowance to cover the increase in your pension savings and/or the value of your pension rights. If your savings/rights increase by more than the annual allowance, you have to pay tax on the excess at a rate of 40 per cent. The annual allowance for 2007–8 is £225,000 – see the table on p. 85 for the level in future years. How the increase in your savings/rights from each scheme is measured depends on the type of scheme – your scheme can advise.

The annual allowance does not apply in the year that you start to draw benefits. This clears the way, for example, for your employer to pay a large contribution to your scheme if you are retiring early because of ill health or as part of a redundancy deal.

Annual and lifetime allowances

Tax year	Annual allowance	Lifetime allowance
2006–7	£215,000	£1.5 million
2007–8	£225,000	£1.6 million
2008–9	£235,000	£1.65 million
2009–10	£245,000	£1.75 million
2010–11	£255,000	£1.8 million

Tax-saving idea 50

Your employer can pay up to £225,000 into a pension scheme for you in the 2007–8 tax year. This can be particularly useful if you run your own company and so can control how much the employer (the company) pays in. The company gets tax relief on the contributions provided they are 'wholly and exclusively' for the purpose of the business. In practice, this means the contributions must be proportionate to the value of your work.

Topping up your pension

The tax rules no longer put any restriction on the combination of pension schemes you have. For example, there is now nothing to stop a member of an occupational scheme also paying into a personal pension, regardless of how much they earn. However, individual schemes may impose restrictions on who can join, so check the rules.

Options at retirement

Under the tax rules, you can now start to draw your pension at any age from 50 (being increased to 55 by 2010), though individual schemes may set their own age limits.

You do not have to stop work in order to start your pension. So, provided your employer and the pension scheme rules allow it, you could, perhaps, switch to part-time work while drawing part of your pension to top up your earnings.

Depending on the scheme, you may have various pension options:

- **scheme pension**. This is a pension determined by your occupational scheme
- **lifetime annuity**. All money purchase schemes (occupational or

personal) must let you shop around with your pension fund to buy a lifetime annuity. This is an investment where you swap your fund for an income payable for the rest of your life

- **short-term annuity**. You use part of your fund to buy an annuity which pays an income for up to five years. You can then buy another short-term annuity or take up another or the options. But any short-term annuity must end before you reach age 75

- **income withdrawal**. You leave your pension fund invested and draw a pension direct from the fund. If you are under age 75, this is called an 'unsecured pension' and must be broadly between nil and 120 per cent of the lifetime annuity you could otherwise have had. From age 75 onwards it is called an 'alternatively secured pension'. Originally, the pension had to be between nil and 70 per cent of the annuity you could otherwise have had but, from 6 April 2007, a pension must be drawn and must be between 55 and 90 per cent of the comparable annuity.

When you become entitled to start a pension, the tax rules let you take part of your benefits as a tax-free lump sum. The maximum tax-free lump sum is normally 25 per cent of the pension fund or, in the case of a defined benefit scheme, 25 per cent of the capital value of the pension plus the lump sum. The capital value of the pension is usually the yearly pension multiplied by 20.

Tax-saving ideas 51, 52 and 53

Provided the individual scheme rules allow it, you can now take a tax-free lump sum from any type of pension scheme – this includes additional voluntary contribution schemes and all contracted-out schemes.

If you opt for income withdrawal before age 75, you do not have to draw any pension at all. You could just take a quarter of your fund as tax-free cash and leave the rest of the fund invested for later. But income withdrawal involves extra costs and investment risks so is not suitable for everyone.

If you are at least age 50 and want to make a sizeable contribution to your pension fund, consider borrowing part of the outlay, immediately opting for income withdrawal and using the tax-free lump sum in order to repay the loan – see Example.

Example

Mark Fisher, aged 60, has relevant earnings of around £80,000 in 2007–8 and has £21,000 to pay into his personal pension. First he borrows £25,800 boosting the amount he can pay in to £46,800. This is treated as a contribution net of basic rate tax relief making a gross contribution of £60,000. He immediately starts income draw-down, opting for a nil pension but drawing 25% × £60,000 = £15,000 cash. As a higher-rate taxpayer, Mark also gets £10,800 higher-rate tax relief. He uses the lump sum and extra tax relief, £15,000 + £10,800 = £25,800 to repay the loan. Borrowing has enabled Mark's £21,000 investment to produce a pension fund of £45,000 (but less after charges). Note that anti-avoidance rules generally prevent this and other methods of 'recycling' the tax-free lump sum, but the anti-avoidance rules do not apply where the lump sum involved is no more than 1 per cent of the standard lifetime allowance – in other words, £16,000 in 2007–8.

Lifetime allowance

Unlike the pre-April 2006 rules, there is now no limit on the value of pension and other benefits that your pension schemes can provide. Instead, you have a lifetime allowance and anything above that is taxed at a rate of 25 per cent of the excess if drawn as (taxable) pension and 55 per cent if it is drawn as a lump sum. The lifetime allowance for 2007–8 is £1.6 million – the allowance for following years is shown in the table on p. 85.

The total of any lump sums you take must not come to more than 25 per cent of your available lifetime allowance.

You have to compare the benefits you are drawing against the allowance each time there is a 'benefit crystallisation event'. These events are: becoming entitled to a scheme pension or lifetime annuity, starting income withdrawal, reaching age 75 without having already started a scheme pension or lifetime annuity, becoming entitled to a lump sum, a lump sum being paid out on your death (see below), a large increase in your pension after it starts, and transferring to an overseas pension scheme. Each benefit crystallisation event uses up part of the lifetime allowance leaving less to be set against the next event.

Example

In 2007–8, Bina Zengeza retires at 65. She qualifies for a pension of £40,000 from her final salary scheme plus a lump sum of £120,000. She also has £20,000 in an additional voluntary contribution scheme. Her schemes advise that the value of her pension savings and rights is £940,000. This is within the lifetime allowance of £1.6 million so there is no lifetime tax charge.

Using pension schemes to provide life cover

On death at any age, a pension scheme can pay out pension(s) to your dependants. A dependant is your spouse or civil partner, children under age 23 and anyone else who was fully or partly financially dependent on you (which could include, for example, an unmarried partner with whom you shared household expenses).

If you die before age 75 and without having started to draw any benefits, a scheme can pay out a tax-free lump sum to your heirs (who do not have to be dependants). The lump sum may be provided by life cover and/or through paying out any pension fund.

If you die before age 75, having already started your pension or income withdrawal, a lump sum can still be passed to your heirs but only after deduction of income tax at 35 per cent. The lump sum might be provided by, say, an option available with an annuity or the remainder of your pension fund. Normally there will be no inheritance tax on this lump sum. The exception is where you had made choices in order to deliberately leave a bigger inheritance to heirs other than genuine dependants at a time when you knew you did not have long to live.

On death from age 75 onwards, a lump sum can be paid out only if it goes to a charity you have nominated. Otherwise any remaining pension fund must be used to provide dependants' pensions.

Originally, it was also possible to transfer any remaining pension fund to other pension funds of members of the same scheme but, from 6 April 2007 onwards, this would trigger such punitive tax charges that it is no longer worth considering.

It has long been possible to use pension contributions to buy life cover, which means that you get tax relief on the premiums you pay. The new April 2006 regime initially removed restrictions on the amount you could pay towards such cover. However, in a government U-turn, it is no longer possible to buy life cover through a personal pension. If you applied for your policy before 14 December 2006, the policy can carry on and you continue to get tax relief on the premiums. For policies taken out since then, tax relief ceased from 6 April 2007 onwards. Employers can still provide life cover through occupational schemes.

Tax-saving idea 54

> If you are getting tax relief on premiums for life cover applied for before 14 December 2006 through a personal pension, be wary of switching to another policy or provider. Premiums for your new policy will not qualify for tax relief and so are likely to cost more overall.

Pension scheme investments

If you save through a self-invested personal pension (SIPP), you can choose how your pension fund is invested. However, the government puts some restrictions on your choice (by imposing hefty tax penalties). In particular, you may not invest either directly or indirectly in:

- ■ tangible moveable property – for example, art, wine, cars, boats, jewellery, stamps, books, and so on

- ■ residential property (including beach huts). But you may invest in hotels (provided you do not have any rights to stay there), prisons, care homes, student halls of residence and similar. You may also invest indirectly through a real estate investment trust (see p. 78) or through an investment vehicle which meets certain conditions. The conditions include: the vehicle holds at least £1 million of property or at least three separate properties and no single property accounts for more than 40 per cent of the total; and there are a number of unconnected investors none of whom holds more than 10 per cent of the vehicle.

Protecting pre-April 2006 pension rights

If by 6 April 2006, your pension savings/rights already exceeded the standard lifetime allowance, you can register for 'primary protection' by 5 April 2009. This gives you a personalised lifetime limit equal to the value of your savings/rights on 5 April 2006. This limit will be increased each year in line with increases in the standard limit. Any increase in your savings/rights above that – for example, because of exceptional investment growth – will be taxable. You can continue to build up further pension savings and rights if you want to, but they will be in excess of your lifetime limit and so taxed when you start to draw benefits from them.

Whether or not your pension savings/rights exceeded the lifetime limit by 6 April 2006, you can ask for 'enhanced protection' by 5 April 2009. This ensures that all the savings/rights you had built up by 5 April 2006 will not be taxed however much they increase up to the time you start to draw benefits. But, in this case, you may not build up any further savings or rights – if you do, the enhanced protection is lost, though if applicable you can revert to primary protection instead.

Under the pre-April 2006 rules, it was possible to build up tax-free lump sums equal to more than 25 per cent of your pension fund. Provided the scheme has a record of your entitlement, you keep your right to draw this extra-large tax-free sum later on. But you normally lose this right if you transfer to another scheme. There is no need to register with the Revenue for this protection.

Tax-saving idea 55

There is no need to register to protect the right to a tax-free lump sum that by 6 April 2006 exceeded 25 per cent rule. But, to escape an eventual tax charge, the scheme must have records of your entitlement. Write to the scheme asking it to confirm your entitlement and store its response in a safe place.

Individual savings accounts

Individual savings accounts (ISAs) let you invest tax-efficiently in two ways:

- **cash ISAs.** These are savings accounts with banks, building societies or National Savings & Investments

- **stocks and shares ISAs**. These invest in stockmarket investments, such as shares, gilts and corporate bonds or funds investing in these investments (for example, via unit trusts and insurance policies).

Originally, the government had promised that ISAs would be available only until 2010. But now it has said that they will continue to be available indefinitely.

Each tax year, you can take out up to two mini-ISAs, comprising one cash ISA and one stocks and shares ISA. Alternatively, you can take out one maxi ISA which automatically has a stocks and shares component and can also have a cash component. The table shows the amount you can invest in each.

From April 2008, the distinction between mini- and maxi-ISAs is being abolished and the limits on the overall amount you can invest in ISAs and the maximum you can invest in a cash ISA are increased slightly (see table opposite).

Under the present rules, you cannot take out both mini-ISAs and a maxi-ISA in the same tax year. If you realise by mistake you have taken out too many ISAs, tell the manager of the last one you bought. The tax due on any income or gains will have to be paid by the manager and you will be sent details to enter on your tax return.

How much you can invest in ISAs each tax year

Type of ISA	Each tax year you can invest up to 2007–8	2008–9
Stocks and shares ISA	£7,000 less any amount invested in a cash ISA	£7,200 less any amount invested in a cash ISA
Cash ISA	£3,000	£3,600

The age limit for investing in a cash ISA is 16. The age limit for other ISAs is 18.

The accounts are provided by ISA managers – banks, building societies, insurance companies, investment managers and other financial institutions.

You can take your money out of an ISA at any time and there will be no capital gains tax to pay when you cash in part or all of an ISA. Interest and interest distributions from accounts and investments in an ISA are tax-free. Dividends and similar income are taxed at 10 per cent (because ISA managers cannot reclaim the tax credit – see p. 77). However, income from real estate investment trusts (see p. 78) held in an ISA is tax-free.

Tax-saving ideas 56, 57 and 58

Saving through a cash ISA means no tax to pay on your interest. If you would, in any case, save with a bank or building society make sure you use your ISA allowance each year.

Higher-rate taxpayers pay less tax on dividends and similar income earned by investments held in a stocks and shares ISA. This does not apply to other taxpayers – their income is taxed the same whether these investments are held in or outside the ISA. But stocks and shares ISAs investing in gilts and/or corporate bonds produce tax-free income for everyone.

Stocks and shares ISAs can still be a tax-efficient growth investment if you normally use up your capital gains tax allowance each year or if you use them to invest in real estate investment trusts (REITs), since these provide tax-free income when held within an ISA.

You declare neither income nor gains from ISAs on your tax return. This can give a big administration saving over holding investments outside an ISA.

Note that you have to be resident in the UK (unless you are a Crown servant working abroad, or their spouse or civil partner) to put money into an ISA, but if you go abroad after starting one, you don't have to cash it in – it still goes on getting tax relief.

Investing in ISAs

Normally you must pay cash into an ISA, so if you want to transfer in shares or other investments that you already own, you must sell them first and buy them back within the ISA.

However, if you receive shares from a savings-related share option scheme or share incentive plan (see Chapter 16) you can transfer these directly into an ISA up to the maximum you are allowed to invest. So in 2007–8, you can transfer £7,000 of such shares into an ISA provided you made no other ISA investments in the tax year. There will be no capital gains tax to pay on the transfer and no capital gains tax on any profits on selling the shares later. You must make the transfer within 90 days of the shares being issued.

If in any tax year you decide to go for two mini-ISAs, you can have a different manager for each one. Whether you have mini-ISAs or a maxi-ISA, next year you do not have to stick with the same ISA manager(s) you chose this year.

You can transfer your existing ISAs from one manager to another. In the year the ISA was taken out, however, you can do this only by closing the old ISA and switching everything in it to a new one. Once the tax year in which you took out the ISA has ended, you can switch just part without closing the old one. Ask the ISA managers to organise the switch – you may lose tax relief if you withdraw cash yourself from one ISA to pay into another. Note that there may be charges for switching.

At present, you cannot switch from a cash ISA to a stocks-and-shares ISA or vice versa. However, from April 2008, you will be able to transfer your savings from cash ISAs to stocks-and-shares ISAs. The government hopes this will encourage people to diversify their assets and widen share ownership.

Tax-saving idea 59

Keep your old PEPs going if you can afford to – together with saving through ISAs, you can build up a sizeable chunk of tax-efficient savings. From 2008, the distinction between PEPs and ISAs will be abolished, so all your old PEPs will automatically become ISAs.

Personal equity plans (PEPs)

A personal equity plan (PEP) is a way of investing in various stockmarket investments such as shares and unit trusts without paying capital gains tax on the proceeds. Dividends and similar income earned by investments in PEPs are taxed at 10 per cent (because the PEP manager cannot reclaim the tax credit) but other types of income are tax-free. PEPs came to an end on 5 April 1999, so you can no longer invest new money in them. But you can continue to own PEPs taken out on or before that date and get the tax benefits. The government has said that, from April 2008, PEPs will become ISAs in order to simplify savings and reduce administration costs.

Under the present rules, PEPs can hold the same range of investments as stocks and shares ISAs. In the past different types of PEP were issued (for example, some investing in just a single company) but you can now merge different types of PEP. You can transfer the whole or part of any PEP from one PEP manager to another.

Tax might be due on PEP proceeds if some of your money is held as cash on deposit and earns interest which is paid out to you. If more than £180 of interest is paid out to you in a year, the plan manager must deduct tax at 20 per cent and hand this over to the Revenue. The net interest is treated in the same way as any other interest you receive after deduction of tax – higher-rate taxpayers face an additional tax bill (see p. 74). From April 2008, this rule is expected to cease and, in line with the current rules for stocks-and-shares ISAs, all cash held within the former PEPs will be taxed at 20 per cent.

Child trust fund

To encourage the savings habit and help young adults take advantage of opportunities that require some capital, the government has introduced the child trust fund (CTF). The scheme covers every child born on or after 1 September 2002.

A CTF is awarded automatically to your child if you are receiving child benefit and the child lives in the UK. You receive a voucher from the government for £250 with which to open the account. If your household income is low, the government adds a further £250 to the fund. If you haven't opened the CTF within a year, the Revenue will open it instead opting for a stakeholder account (see below). The government will pay a further amount (£250 or £500 depending on household income) into the account when the child reaches age seven and is consulting on a further top up at secondary school age.

You, other family members and friends can also pay into your child's CTF. The maximum you can contribute between you is £1,200 a year.

Your child can't take money out of the CTF until he or she reaches age 18 but then there are no restrictions on the amount withdrawn or what it can be used for. The government has proposed that, on maturity, a CTF should be able to roll over automatically into an ISA to encourage the young person to carry on saving.

Money in the CTF may be invested in a choice of ways – for example, cash, unit trusts or investment-type life insurance. Every provider must offer a stakeholder account which is invested at least partly in shares and is 'lifestyled' so that it automatically shifts towards safer investments as your child approaches age 18.

CTF managers will not be able to reclaim the tax credit on dividends and similar income from share-based investments in the CTF, so such income will effectively be taxed at 10 per cent. But other income and gains from investments in the CTF will be tax-free. CTFs can invest in real estate investment trusts (REITs) – see p. 78 – and the income, as well as gains, from these is tax-free within a CTF.

Tax-saving idea 60

If you give capital to your child and it produces over £100 income a year, that income will normally be taxed as yours. You can avoid this trap by investing in a child trust fund, friendly society tax-efficient plan ('baby bond'), NS&I children's bonus bonds or a stakeholder pension scheme.

Savings gateway

This is a government scheme to encourage low income households to save. Several pilot schemes are being tested.

Savers open an account which does not earn any interest. Instead the government adds a bonus for each £1 the saver has paid in. For example, the bonus might be £1 for each £1 saved, but the government is experimenting with different levels of matching. The government bonus is added when the account matures at the end of 18 months. Savers can withdraw their own money at any time provided they leave at least £1 in the account.

The bonus counts as a gain not income and could be subject to capital gains tax. In practice, savers are likely to have enough unused capital gains tax-free allowance to cover the bonus. Exceptionally where this is not the case the government increases the bonus by enough to meet the tax bill.

Investing in growing businesses

The government offers a variety of incentives to encourage you to invest in small and growing companies or to support social regeneration. The tax breaks are welcome, but bear in mind these are, by their nature, high-risk investments, so losses could outweigh any up-front tax relief and returns might not materialise to become tax-free. However, if a company does take off, your handsome profits will be sheltered from tax and at least losses can be set off against other capital or income. The main incentives are:

■ loss relief

■ enterprise investment scheme

■ venture capital trusts

■ community investment tax relief (unlikely to produce a gain – see p. 100).

The table overleaf broadly summarises the tax incentives you can get.

Tax reliefs for investment in unquoted trading companies

Type of investment	Income tax relief on amount you invest	Capital gains deferral relief	Tax-free income	Tax-free gains	Can set losses against taxable gains on other assets	Income tax relief on losses
Investing direct in unquoted trading company shares	No	No	No	No[1]	Yes	Yes
Enterprise investment scheme	Yes at 20%	Yes	No	Yes	Yes	Yes
Venture capital trusts	Yes at 30%[2]	No[3]	Yes	Yes	No	No

(1) But gains qualify for business asset taper relief (see pp. 133–6).
(2) 40 per cent applied to period 6 April 2004 to 5 April 2006.
(3) Ceased to be available from 6 April 2004 onwards.

Income tax loss relief

If you buy newly issued shares in an unquoted trading company and sub-sequently sell them at a loss, you can under the normal capital gains tax rules set the loss against capital gains you make on other assets (see p. 131). Alternatively, you can deduct the loss from:

■ your income for the tax year in which you make the loss, and/or

■ your income for the tax year before the one in which you make the loss.

To be eligible for this relief, the shares must match the definition of shares that can qualify for the EIS (see below) and meet certain other conditions, but you do not have to have invested in the shares through an EIS.

You must claim loss relief in writing within one year of 31 January following the year in which you make the loss. For example, if you make a loss in 2007–8, you must make your claim by 31 January 2010.

See p. 309 for information about loss relief if you provide financial backing by being a non-active partner in a venture.

Enterprise investment scheme (EIS)

If you invest £500 or more in new shares issued by certain unquoted trading companies, you can get tax relief on the investment – provided you hold the shares for a minimum period of three years from the issue of the shares (or when the company starts trading if this is later). The period is not broken if the company floats on a stock exchange, provided the flotation had not been arranged at the time you invested in the shares.

Investments in EIS-approved investment funds which invest in such companies also qualify – even if less than £500.

If you dispose of the investments after the minimum period, there will be no capital gains tax to pay when you sell your investment. To further encourage you to invest in growing companies, a series of investments in EIS shares will be treated as a single investment when working out taper relief for capital gains tax – see p. 134. This means that 'serial investors' can still reduce the capital gains tax bill on EIS shares held for less than the minimum period.

You get income tax relief at 20 per cent on up to £400,000 from 6 April 2006 (previously £200,000) of EIS investments in any tax year. But if you make the investment between 6 April and 5 October inclusive, half the investment up to a maximum of £50,000 (previously £25,000) can be set off against your income for the previous tax year. With a married couple or civil partnership, each of you can invest up to these limits.

Making EIS investments can also allow you to put off paying capital gains tax made on other assets if you are able to claim capital gains deferral relief (see p. 148). To get the relief, you must reinvest at least part of the proceeds within a period starting one year before and ending three years after receiving them.

The companies you can invest in must be unquoted; this includes those with shares traded on the Alternative Investment Market (AIM). They have to be trading companies, which excludes those engaged in banking, insurance, share-dealing, dealing in land or property, farming, market gardening, forestry, managing hotels, leasing and legal or accountancy services. The company must be trading in the UK, but it does not have to be registered or resident in the UK. Investments in schemes where a substantial part of the return is guaranteed or backed by property are also excluded.

Warning

There have been several changes to the EIS rules that limit your investment to smaller and possibly riskier companies:

■ from 6 April 2006, to be eligible for EIS, a company can have assets only up to £8 million (previously £16 million) including money raised from investors through the scheme
■ from 6 April 2007 onwards, a company must have fewer than 50 employees and the total venture capital the company can raise through EIS, VCT and similar schemes is restricted to £2 million over the previous 12 months.

You won't get tax relief on investments if you are connected with the companies – broadly this means being an employee or director or owning over 30 per cent of the shares. In deciding how much of a company you own, you must include the holdings of connected persons – your spouse, civil partner and your or their children, parents and grandparents (but not brothers or sisters) – and associates such as business partners. Once you have made your EIS investment, however, you can take part in the active management of the company as a paid director (or 'business angel') provided you had not been connected with the company before you made the EIS investment.

You can't claim the tax relief until the company has carried out its qualifying trade for at least four months, and you lose it if it ceases to do so within three years. If you sell the shares within the minimum period, you lose tax relief on the amount you sell them for (that is, if you sell them for more than they cost you, you have to pay back all the relief). If you sell the shares after the minimum period and the company still qualifies under the scheme there will be no capital gains tax to pay on any gain you make. If you make a loss, this can be set off against other income or capital gains (see loss relief on p. 96) – reducing your overall tax bill for the year.

Tax-saving idea 61

If you want to put off a large capital gains tax bill (say, to a future year when you may have more allowances and reliefs available), consider reinvesting your money in an EIS and claiming capital gain tax deferral relief – but only if you are comfortable with this type of high-risk investment.

Venture capital trusts (VCTs)

VCTs are a type of investment trust listed on the stock exchange whose business is investing in the shares of unquoted trading companies. By buying VCT shares, you are investing in a spread of different small, growing companies. This should help to spread your risks, and the fact that the VCT is itself quoted might make it easier to find buyers if you want to sell your investment later on.

Warning

There have been several changes to the VCT rules that mean your money is likely to be invested in smaller and possibly riskier companies than in the past:

- ■ from 6 April 2006, a VCT can have assets only up to £8 million (previously £16 million) including money raised from investors through the scheme
- ■ from 6 April 2007 onwards, a VCT can invest only in companies that have fewer than 50 employees and have raised no more than £2 million over the previous 12 months through EIS, VCT and similar schemes.

You must be aged at least 18 to invest in a VCT and you must buy the VCT shares when they are newly issued. The shares must give you no preferential rights to dividends or a share of the assets if the VCT is wound up, and there must be no promise or guarantee that you'll get your money back.

The unquoted trading shares in which the VCT invests must meet basically the same definition as shares eligible for EIS (see p. 97).

Provided you hold the shares for at least five years for investments before 6 April 2006 (previously three years), you get income tax relief on up to £200,000 invested in VCT shares each tax year. For shares issued during the two-year period 6 April 2004 to 5 April 2006, tax relief was increased to a rate of 40 per cent but is now reduced to 30 per cent.

You get tax relief on any dividends paid by the VCT provided certain conditions are met.

Provided you've held the shares for five (previously three) years, there is no tax on any gain you make when you sell VCT shares. But any loss you make is also ignored – so it can't be used to reduce capital gains tax on other assets or set off against your income.

Until 5 April 2004, making VCT investments allowed you to put off paying a capital gains tax bill on the disposal of other assets if you claimed capital gains deferral relief (see p. 148). To get the relief, you had to reinvest the proceeds in VCT shares within one year before or one year after making the gain (and you must have received some income tax relief on the VCT investment). Deferral relief is not available where you buy VCT shares issued on or after 6 April 2004.

Community investment tax relief

This scheme offers tax relief on money you invest or lend that is used to set up small businesses or community projects in socially deprived areas. (The scheme may also be extended to loans to individuals.) You cannot invest directly in these ventures – only via an accredited community development finance institution.

In general, the scheme is most likely to appeal to companies who want to 'put something back' into their local communities. But a useful way for individuals to invest is via a community investment tax relief account (CITRA) with Charity Bank (www.charitybank.org). The minimum investment is £1,000 for five years. Your return is made up partly of the tax relief you can claim (see p. 216) and partly of interest which you can opt to donate to charity. Charity Bank is a fully authorised bank and investors are protected by the same compensation scheme that applies to the big high street banks.

8

Making the most of fringe benefits

Many employers give their employees non-cash fringe benefits as part of their pay package. Typical examples are employer's contributions to a pension scheme, company cars, luncheon vouchers or interest-free loans to buy your season ticket for the railway.

Tax-free for all

There are many fringe benefits which are tax-free for all employees regardless of what you are paid – see the list below. There are also a number of other benefits which are tax-free for some employees, but not all. There are more details of these on p. 110.

Your employer's goods and services

Where these are provided to you free or at a lower price than the public would pay, they are tax-free as long as they cost your employer nothing to provide. The courts have decided the cost to your employer is nothing if the extra (marginal) cost is nil regardless of the average cost. Tax-free items could include, for example, goods sold to you at the wholesale price, cheap conveyancing for solicitors where the firm does not have to take on extra staff, and free bus travel for bus company employees which does not displace fare-paying customers.

Tax-free mileage allowances

■ If you use your own car for work, mileage allowance up the Revenue's authorised scale is tax-free. The scale is 40p per mile for the first

10,000 business miles and 25p for each additional business mile. See p. 109 for mileage allowance in excess of the authorised scale.

- Up to 20p per mile if you use your own bicycle for business.
- Up to 24p per mile if you use your own motorbike on business.
- Up to 5p per passenger per mile if colleagues travel on business in your car.

Tax-saving ideas 62 and 63

Many fringe benefits are tax-free, and even those which are not can remain good value for employees because the taxable value put on them may be less than it would cost you to pay for the benefit yourself. Try to take advantage of fringe benefits in negotiations with your boss. You do not normally pay national insurance contributions on fringe benefits unless they can be readily converted to cash.

With some fringe benefits, such as pension contributions and childcare vouchers, your employer saves national insurance too and so might be particularly willing to consider a salary sacrifice arrangement. Your contract is amended so you receive less salary but get extra benefits instead. This can be worth doing if you will be better off overall, taking into account the value of the benefits, the tax and national insurance you save and any savings your employer is willing to share with you. But check whether you'll lose out on other pay-related items, such as sick pay.

Tax-saving ideas 64 and 65

If your employer pays mileage allowance at less than the tax-free authorised rates or doesn't pay any allowance at all, you can claim the shortfall up to the amount of your actual costs or the authorised rate, whichever is lower as an allowable expense (see p. 251).

The tax-free authorised mileage rates will not cover all your costs if you drive a gas-guzzler car. You can save most tax by using a small, fuel-efficient car.

Other tax-free travel benefits

- Travel to and from work in a company van you have to take home (including cost of the fuel used) provided your employer prohibits any other substantial private use of the van.
- For members of the police, fire and ambulance services, having an emergency vehicle available for private use if you have to take it home because you are on call.
- A car parking or bicycle space at or near work.

- The loan of bicycles and safety equipment for employees for cycling between home and work.
- Work buses which can transport nine or more employees; discounted or free travel on public bus services subsidised by your employer.
- The cost of transport home if you are occasionally required to work after public transport has shut down or cannot reasonably be used.
- Reasonable extra travel or overnight subsistence expenses paid to you because of disruption to public transport by industrial action.
- Financial help with the cost of travelling to and from work if you are severely and permanently disabled and cannot use public transport. This could be the loan of a car provided it is adapted for your use and you are not allowed to make private journeys other than travel between home and work.
- Travel expenses paid for your spouse if they accompany you when you go to work abroad subject to certain conditions.
- Incidental overnight expenses (for example, newspapers and phone calls home) paid or reimbursed by your employer if you are away overnight on business. The maximum is £5 per night (£10 outside the UK). If more is paid, the whole amount not just the excess is taxable.

Tax-free financial benefits

- Your employer's contributions to a pension, life insurance or sick pay insurance policy for you. (But premiums to a private medial insurance policy are a taxable benefit unless related to overseas business travel.)
- Loans on preferential terms (including Shariah-compliant loans) where the total loan(s) outstanding does not exceed £5,000.
- Pensions advice arranged by your employer up to a cost of £150 per employee per year. (If it costs more, the whole amount is taxable not just the excess.)

Tax-free meals, subsistence and entertainment benefits

- Free or subsidised meals at work provided they are available to all employees and not in a public restaurant.
- Luncheon vouchers (or equivalent) up to a maximum 15p per day.
- Free meal on arrival if you participate in cycle-to-work days.
- Annual parties or similar functions, such as a Christmas dinner, which

are open to staff generally and together cost your employer no more than £150 per head per year.

■ Entertainment for you and your family provided by someone other than your employer purely as a gesture of goodwill – but not if there are strings attached or if the gift counts as payment for your services.

■ Sports facilities generally available to all staff and their families (and not available to the general public).

Tax-free accommodation benefits

■ Living accommodation provided it is either necessary for you to do your job, or beneficial and customary for someone in your line of work (for example, a caretaker). Not tax-free if you are a director unless you have no material interest in the company and you are either a full-time working director or director of a not-for-profit company or charity.

■ Living accommodation (and other security precautions) provided as part of special security arrangements if there is a security threat to you because of your job.

■ Council tax paid by your employer if either of the two living accommodation benefits above applies to you.

■ Relocation expenses if you move home for your job, such as the costs of buying and selling property, some travel and subsistence costs, and bridging loan expenses. The maximum is £8,000 per move. Any excess is taxable.

Other tax-free benefits

■ Up to £55 (£50 before 6 April 2006) a week of employer-contracted approved childcare or vouchers to pay for such care. Approved childcare can include, say, a nursery, childminders or after-school club. The £55 limit applies per employee regardless of number of children.

■ Childcare (up to any value) in a nursery or play scheme run by your employer or at least partly financed and managed by your employer (often referred to as a 'workplace nursery').

■ Up to £2 a week towards extra household expenses if you work from home under an arrangement agreed with your employer. (More if your employer has evidence to show you incur higher extra costs.)

■ Private use of a mobile phone provided by your employer. This includes more sophisticated handheld devices that include a mobile. For phones provided from 6 April 2006 limited to one per employee.

■ The ongoing loan of computer equipment worth up to £2,500 even if for private use where the loan started before 6 April 2006. For loans after that date, the normal rules for use of an asset apply – see p. 118.

■ Changing room or shower facilities at work, provided they are available to all employees.

■ Routine medical check-ups or medical screening for you or your family.

■ Cost of medical treatment while working abroad (or insurance for it).

■ Equipment, for example, a hearing aid or wheelchair, provided if you are disabled and which is primarily to enable you to do your job even if you also use it privately.

■ Retraining and counselling costs paid by your employer when you leave a job, provided you have worked for your employer for at least two years.

■ The cost of fees and books for further education or training courses paid for by your employer if the course is either necessary or directly beneficial for your work, or if you are under 21 when starting a general education course. If you have to be away from your normal workplace for no more than 12 months and will return after training, some travel and subsistence too.

■ Payments from your employer up to £15,000 a year (£7,000 before September 2005) to cover lodging, subsistence and travelling if you are released to attend a full-time course lasting at least a year at a university or a technical college.

■ Truly personal gifts from your employer of an appropriate size and nature (not cash), including gifts on marriage, and long-service awards of things or shares in the company. However, long-service awards are tax-free only if they are to mark service of 20 years or more, they do not cost more than £50 for each year of service and you have received no similar award in the previous ten years.

■ Small non-cash gifts from someone other than your employer. To qualify, the total cost of all gifts you received from the same donor must be no more than £250 in any tax year and they must not be provided on any sort of conditions, for example, that you will provide a particular service.

■ Suggestion scheme (incentive) awards (see p. 239).

Tax-saving ideas 66 and 67

You can receive up to £104 a year tax-free from your employer towards additional household expenses without having to keep records if you have to work from home. Higher amounts can be tax-free but you'll then need records to back up the claim. Additional expenses might include, say, heating, lighting, metered water and business phone calls.

If you can arrange your work so that you count as self-employed rather than an employee, you will be able to claim a much wider range of expenses (see Chapter 17). But remember there may be disadvantages in not having the protection of employment law. For more about the distinction between employees and the self-employed, see p. 275.

Taxable for all

There are four types of benefits which are always taxable. These are:

■ assets transferred to you or payments made for you

■ vouchers (with a few exceptions – see p. 108) and any goods or services paid for by credit card

■ living accommodation provided by your employer (apart from the few exceptions listed on p. 104)

■ mileage allowances in excess of the authorised rate if you use your own transport for work.

Tax-saving ideas 68 and 69

Check carefully whether employer-provided childcare is a good idea for you. Anything your employer pays is balanced by a reduction in any working tax credit childcare element for which you qualify (see p. 60). Bear in mind that if accepting childcare benefits ultimately means you are paid less, any pay-related benefits such as pension savings and life cover would be reduced.

Childcare vouchers from your employer can be used only to pay for approved childcare. This could include, say, a grandparent who gets approval, provided they also look after at least one other unrelated child and the care is not in your own home.

Assets transferred to you or payments made for you

Your employer may give you as a present, or allow you to buy cheaply, an item such as a television set, furniture, groceries or your employer's own product. These payments in kind may be taxed in a number of ways depending on how much you earn and whether you have the alternative of cash instead.

If you earn less than £8,500 (see p. 110)

The taxable value is the second-hand value of the payment in kind (whether or not you actually sell it). Since many assets have a much lower second-hand value than the cost of buying them new this can be advantageous to you.

If you earn at the rate of £8,500 or more (see p. 110)

The tax rules are tougher for those who earn at a rate of £8,500 or more, or directors. They pay tax on the larger of:

■ the second-hand value, or

■ the cost to the employer of providing the asset, including ancillary costs such as installation or servicing. Remember, though, that if it is the employer's own product, you pay only the extra cost to the employer. So if it does not cost the employer anything (after taking into account anything you have paid for it) it should be tax-free.

If you are being given something you have already had the use of (apart from a car), the taxable value is the larger of the following, less any amount you have paid:

■ the market value when you are given it (since 6 April 2005, this basis always applies to a bicycle or up to £2,500-worth of computer equipment provided as a tax-free benefit), or

■ the market value of the asset when it was first loaned out (either to you or to anyone else), less the total amount on which tax has already been charged. This is because assets which have been on loan will already have had some tax paid on them.

If you are given a car, for example on leaving a job, you are taxed on its second-hand value when you are given it, less anything you pay for it. If you buy your company car for a low price, you may have to pay tax on the difference between the price you paid and what your tax office reckons it would fetch on the open market.

Cash or perks?

You may be given the alternative of either a particular payment in kind, such as free board and lodging, or cash. If you have a perk you can convert into money either immediately or at short notice, you have to pay tax on the value of the cash alternative, even if you opt for the perk. However, note that there is a concession for some workers, including farm workers, and for cash alternatives to cars. And you usually will not be taxed on a reduction in salary in exchange for your employer paying for work-related training or lending you up to £2,500-worth of computer equipment under a pre-6 April 2006 arrangement.

Payments made for you

However much you earn, you pay tax on the full amount of any bill paid directly by your employer on your behalf, such as:

- your phone bill
- your personal credit card bill
- your council tax (unless it is tax-free because you live in tax-free accommodation, see p. 104)
- rent paid direct to your landlord
- a tax bill.

Note, though, that this normally applies only to payments settled directly by your employer, for example to the telephone company, the credit card company or your landlord. If you were given cash to settle the bill yourself, it should already have been added to your other pay on your payslip and taxed through PAYE.

Vouchers and credit cards

You may be given a voucher for a particular service (for example, a season ticket), a credit token or a company credit or charge card. If so, you are taxed on their cash equivalent unless they appear in the list of tax-free fringe benefits on pp. 101–6 (for example, childcare vouchers, gift vouchers which count as a small gift), or the voucher gives you access to benefits that are in the tax-free list, such as a pass for an employer-subsidised bus service. Cash vouchers worth a specified amount of cash will usually be taxed under PAYE.

For vouchers and cards which do count as a taxable fringe benefit, broadly speaking you pay tax on the expense incurred by the person who provided them, less any amount that you have paid yourself. You will not have to pay tax on any annual card fee or interest paid by your employer.

Company credit cards and charge cards are often provided as a convenient way of paying business expenses. But you will have to pay tax on anything which is not an allowable business expense.

Living accommodation

In some cases living accommodation may count as a tax-free fringe benefit – see the list on p. 104. But if it does not, it counts as a taxable perk however much you earn. It includes houses, flats, houseboats and holiday homes but not board and lodging or hotel-type accommodation where typically you get food and other services.

The taxable value of the accommodation is based on the higher of:

■ the rateable value of the property, or

■ if the property is let, the rent paid for it.

From the taxable value, you can deduct anything you pay for the accommodation, and also, if part of the property is used exclusively for your work, a proportion for that.

Rateable values are still used, although rates are no longer payable. However, for properties in Scotland, where rateable values were revalued more recently than elsewhere, only a percentage of the rateable value is used (found by multiplying the rateable value by 100 and dividing by 270). If there is no rateable value your employer will have to agree a value with your tax office.

If the tax is based on the rateable value, there may be an extra charge if the property cost more than £75,000, including the cost of any improvements made before the current tax year, but deducting anything you paid towards the cost. Broadly, you pay interest at the Revenue's official rate at the start of the tax year (6.25 per cent from 6 April 2007 (and 5 per cent throughout 2006–7)) on the excess over £75,000, reduced in line with the number of days you do not have the property if it is provided for only part of the year. You can deduct any rent you pay not already deducted when working out the basic taxable value, and an amount for business use.

Mileage allowances

If, when you use your own transport for work, your employer pays you a mileage allowance that is more than the Revenue authorised rates (see

p. 101), the excess is taxable. This is the case even if your actual costs are so high that you do not make any profit from your mileage allowance.

Taxable for some, tax-free for others

The following benefits are tax-free if, for the particular employment, you earn at a rate of less than £8,500 and are not a director:

- a company car or van
- private medical or dental insurance
- services without a second-hand value, such as hairdressing at work
- loans of things or money.

However, these benefits are taxable for employees who earn at the rate of £8,500 or more. You cannot get around this by asking to be paid under £8,500 and getting substantial perks instead. To work out whether you earn at a rate of £8,500 a year, you need to take into account two rules:

Rule 1

Your earnings for this purpose are any kind of pay you receive for the job – that is, including your expenses and the taxable value of any perks worked out as if you earned £8,500 or more. However, you can exclude any contributions you make to an employer's pension scheme, and payroll giving donations.

Rule 2

The earnings are worked out assuming you work full-time for a whole year. So if you leave a job half-way through the year, having earned £5,000, you will still count as earning more than £8,500 – because in the second part of the year you would have earned another £5,000, that is, £10,000 in total.

If you are a director you are automatically counted as earning £8,500 or more unless all of the following three conditions apply:

- you are either a full-time working director or a director of a charity or non-profit-making concern
- you do not own or control more than 5 per cent of the share capital
- you earn under £8,500.

Your employer should take account of your rate of earnings when filling in your taxable benefits and their cash equivalent: you can tell what category you fall into depending on whether you get a form P11D (which is the form for people who earn at a rate of £8,500 or more) or P9D (the alternative form if you earn under £8,500).

Company cars

Some employers provide a company car that is also available for your private use (including travel between home and work). Since 6 April 2002, the way of taxing this benefit aims to cut polluting emissions and you'll pay a lot of tax if you drive a gas-guzzler. Some employers offer employees cash instead of a car and require you to use your own car for business – but the structure of the mileage allowance (see p. 101) aims to stop you or your employer profiting from this move. If you only need a car for work occasionally, note that a 'pool car' is tax-free. To qualify it must not normally be kept overnight near your home, it must be used by more than one employee, and any private use must be a consequence of business use. But before you can work out which option is better for you, you need to be able to work out the taxable value of a company car and any free fuel you get.

Working out the tax on a company car

The taxable value of your company car is usually its price when new multiplied by a percentage based on the carbon dioxide (CO_2) emissions figure for your type of car. There are five steps to arrive at the taxable value:

- take the list price of your car when new
- find out the CO_2 emissions figure for your car
- use Revenue tables to find out the percentage corresponding to that CO_2 emissions figure
- increase or reduce the percentage by any supplement or discount (but only if the car was registered on or after 1 January 1998)
- multiply the list price by the percentage.

If you had the car for only part of the year, you can scale down the taxable value in proportion to the number of days in the tax year it was not available. And, you can deduct anything you pay yourself for use of the car.

The car's list price when new

This is the list price of the car at registration (not the dealer's price), including delivery charges, VAT and car tax. Any contribution you make towards the cost of the car is deducted from its price, up to a limit of

£5,000, and the maximum price for tax purposes is capped at £80,000. For cars without a list price, your employer will have to reach agreement with the Revenue, usually on the basis of published car price guides. The market value is used for classic cars worth at least £15,000 and aged 15 years or more at the end of the tax year.

Tax-saving idea 70

> The taxation of large and inefficient company cars is onerous. If you are about to get a new car, consider a smaller, more fuel-efficient model.

You cannot create an artificially low price by getting a basic model and adding accessories. The price includes any accessories fitted before the car was made available to you, and any accessories or set of accessories worth more than £100 which are fitted after that. Accessories needed because you are disabled are excluded.

The CO_2 emissions figure

Cars registered in the UK from 1 March 2001 onwards have an official CO_2 emissions figure which is shown on the vehicle registration document. You can also get the figure for your car from the Vehicle Certification Agency: VCA (FCB requests), 1 The Eastgate Office Centre, Eastgate Road, Bristol BS5 6XX, Tel: 0117 951 5151 www.vcacarfueldata.org.uk.

Cars registered between 1 January 1998 and 28 February 2001 also usually have an emissions figure but this is not shown on the registration document. You can get the figure either free from the Society for Motor Manufacturers and Traders website (www.smmt.co.uk/co2/co2intro.cfm) or from the car manufacturer or importer (there may be a small charge).

Cars registered before 1998 – and a few other more recent but unusual models – do not have a CO_2 emissions figure. Instead, the taxable value is the list price multiplied by a percentage based on the car's engine size (see table opposite).

The percentage charge

The CO_2 emissions figure is given in grams per kilometre. The minimum percentage of list price that you will be taxed on is normally 15 per cent (for cars emitting 140 g/km in 2006–7 and 2007–8). The percentage increases in steps of 1 per cent for every extra 5 g/km up to a normal maximum percentage of 35 per cent – see table opposite. If the emissions figure for your car does not end in '0' or '5' you round it down to the nearest amount that does.

CO₂-related car benefit percentage charges for 2006–7, 2007–8 and 2008–9

% of car's price to be taxed	CO₂ emission figure (g/km) 2006–7 and 2007–8	2008–9	% of car's price to be taxed	CO₂ emission figure (g/km) 2006–7 and 2007–8	2008–9
10	Not applicable	120	25	190	185
15	140	135	26	195	190
16	145	140	27	200	195
17	150	145	28	205	200
18	155	150	29	210	205
19	160	155	30	215	210
20	165	160	31	220	215
21	170	165	32	225	220
22	175	170	33	230	225
23	180	175	34	235	230
24	185	180	35	240 or more	235 or more

Car benefit percentage charges for cars without a CO₂ emissions figure

Engine size	Percentage of car's price to be taxed Cars registered before January 1998	Cars registered on or after 1 January 1998
Up to 1,400 cc	15	15
1,401–2,000 cc	22	25
Over 2,000 cc	32	35
Cars without a cylinder capacity	32	35

Supplements and discounts for cars registered on or after 1 January 1998

If your company car is a diesel, you must add an extra 3 per cent to the percentage charge, but the overall percentage is still capped at 35 per cent. The diesel supplement is waived for some cars meeting EU standards for cleaner diesels, but the waiver was cancelled from 6 April 2006 for cars registered from 1 January 2006 onwards.

The system encourages the use of cars powered by alternative fuels by giving discounts which from 2006–7 onwards are: 6 per cent for electric only; 3 per cent for hybrid electric; and 2 per cent for gas or bio-fuel with a CO_2 emissions figure for gas. These discounts will not apply where your car qualifies for the new 10 per cent rate from 2008–9.

Tax-saving idea 71

If you drive a company car or van in central London, the taxable value of your vehicle already includes any congestion charges (or related penalty charges) that are reimbursed by your employer. There is no need to declare these amounts separately and no further tax to pay on them.

Example

Sanjay O'Rourke chose a new company car in March 2007. He could have any make or model up to a cost of £20,000. He was thinking about an Alfa Romeo 159. He checked its CO_2 emissions figure which was 205 g/km. The table (see p. 113) told him that he would be taxed on 28 per cent of the car's list price: 28% × £20,000 = £5,600. As Sanjay is a higher rate taxpayer, the car would cost him 40% × £5,600 = £2,240 in tax in 2007–8. Instead Sanjay opted for a Toyota Prius hybrid fuel (petrol-electric) car. It cost the same, but with an emissions figure of just 104 g/km and the 3 per cent discount for hybrids, he is taxed on just 12 per cent of the list price, giving a taxable value of 12% × £20,000 = £2,400 and a tax bill of 40% × £2,400 = £960. Going green has saved Sanjay £1,280 tax this year. From 2008–9, the Toyota Prius will qualify for the new 10 per cent rate.

Fuel for company cars

If you get a company car, you may get free fuel for private use as well. The taxable value of fuel is a percentage of a set figure which is £14,400 in 2006–7 and unchanged for 2007–8. The percentage is the same as that used to find the taxable value of the company car (see p. 113). Therefore in 2007–8, the taxable value of fuel will normally lie between 15% × £14,400 = £2,160 and 35% × £14,400 = £5,040. But it will be lower if you drive a fuel-efficient car running on alternative fuel and higher if you drive a standard diesel. The fuel charge is proportionately reduced if you stop receiving free fuel for part of the tax year or your company car is not available for the full year. There is no fuel charge for an electrically powered company car.

You can avoid the fuel charge if you are required by your employer to reimburse the full cost of fuel used for private purposes and you actually do so. Bear in mind that commuting between home and work normally counts as private use. But fuel provided for travel between home and work for disabled employees is tax-free.

Vans

A van available for your private use was very lightly taxed in the past compared with a company car, but this has changed from 6 April 2007 onwards. In 2007–8, the taxable value is £3,000 a year. The taxable value is reduced if:

- the van is unavailable for part of the tax year in line with the number of days it is unavailable
- the van is shared with other employees. The taxable value is split between the employees concerned on a just and reasonable basis
- you have to pay your employer for your private use. The amount you pay is deducted from the taxable value.

From 2007–8, the taxable value of fuel provided by your employer for private use of the van is £500, reduced by any amount you have to pay.

However, since 6 April 2006, a van you take home each night is a tax-free benefit provided the only private use you (and your family and household) are allowed to make is commuting to and from work. In practice, incidental private use – such as an occasional trip to the rubbish dump or stopping to buy a newspaper en route to work – is overlooked. But using the van to, say, do your weekly shop would breach the rules and bring the van into the taxable benefit rules above.

In 2006–7 and earlier years, the taxable benefit of a van available for private use was £500 a year (£350 for vans four or more years old) with no charge for fuel.

Tax-saving idea 72

If your employer provides you with a van you take home at night, consider asking your employer to put in writing that you are not allowed to use the van privately. Then, provided any private use is only incidental, the van will be a tax-free benefit. Otherwise, the taxable value of the van and fuel will be £3,500 a year which would mean a yearly tax bill of 22% × £3,500 = £770 if you are a basic rate taxpayer.

Cheap or free loans

The basic rule is that if your employer provides a cheap or interest-free loan, you have to pay tax on the difference between the interest you pay and the interest worked out at an official rate – 6.25 per cent from 6 April 2007 (and 5 per cent throughout 2006–7). You do not need to worry about any of this, however, if:

■ your employer lends money as part of its normal business, comparable loans were available to members of the general public (a substantial proportion actually being sold to them), and the loan was made to you on the same terms as those comparable loans. Such loans are tax-free

■ the total loans you have outstanding are no more than £5,000 throughout the tax year. If you have several loans, one of which qualifies for tax relief, then the qualifying loan is ignored when deciding whether the other loans fall within the limit.

Example

Lene Mikkelsen has a £10,000 loan from her employer to help buy a flat, at a special low interest rate of 4 per cent (compared with the official interest rate of 6.25 per cent). She paid off £1,000 of the loan halfway through the year. The taxable value of the perk is £213 in 2007–8, worked out as follows:

Amount outstanding:	
At start of tax year	£10,000
At end of tax year	£9,000
Average:	£19,000 ÷ 2 = £9,500
Interest payable at official rate	£9,500 × 6.25% = £593
Actual interest payable	£380
Difference (taxable value)	£213

Lene is a basic rate taxpayer, so the loan costs her 22% × £213 = £46.86 in tax in 2007–8.

To work out the tax on a loan, you take the average amount owing during the year (the whole amount, not just the amount above £5,000), adjusted if the loan was only outstanding for part of the year. You then multiply the average loan by the average official rate of interest for the period in the year during which the loan was outstanding (your tax office should be able to tell you this). Lastly, you deduct the interest you were actually liable to pay during the tax year, to find the amount on which you will be taxed.

If you think that you will lose out under this averaging method, you can choose to calculate the figures using the daily amounts of the loan and official rates of interest. However, you have to use the same method for all your taxable loans, and the calculations can get quite complex. If you want to make this choice, you have to tell your tax office within roughly 21 months of the end of the tax year in question.

Note that under either method, if the loan qualifies for tax relief, you get tax relief on both the interest you actually paid and the difference between that and the official rate of interest. Effectively, the tax relief is worked out assuming you paid the official rate of interest.

Private medical or dental insurance

If your employer pays premiums for a private medical expenses policy for you (for example, through a group scheme for all employees), the amount is a taxable benefit. The same applies to dental insurance schemes. You pay tax on the cost to your employer, less any amount you pay for the benefit. However, private medical insurance is a tax-free benefit if related to overseas business travel.

Other benefits

There is a variety of other perks taxable only if you earn at the rate of £8,500 a year or more. These include:

■ relocation expenses which would normally be tax-free but which are above the £8,000 tax-free limit for each move

■ approved childcare paid for by your employer in excess of the £55 limit (see p. 104). This does not apply to 'workplace nurseries' which are not subject to the £55 limit

■ services supplied, such as free hairdressing, holidays, gardening or a free chauffeur – but remember that you pay tax only on the extra cost to your employer, so services that your employer provides as part of their normal business may be tax-free

- share schemes or share options which are not tax-free – see Chapter 16

- subscriptions and fees paid for by your employer for you to join professional bodies, societies, leisure or sports clubs, etc. Note that if you had paid a professional subscription yourself and could have claimed the cost against your tax because it was necessary for your work (see p. 253), there will be no tax charge

- any income tax paid for you by your employer, other than through PAYE. This may sometimes apply if PAYE was not deducted from your pay at the proper time, and the tax was later paid for you or if there was insufficient pay from which to deduct the tax under PAYE

- the value of anything provided for your use, except for cars, vans, mobile phones and living accommodation (for example, a television, furniture, a yacht or aircraft). The value is 20 per cent of the market value when it was first provided (to you or to anyone else), plus any expense of providing it met by your employer. If you are later given whatever it is, you will be taxed as explained on p. 107

- help with educating your children (unless this is nothing to do with your job, for example it is pure coincidence that your child gets one of the generally available scholarships your employer's firm provides).

9

Minimising capital gains tax

If you own items which increase in value, you may find yourself paying capital gains tax. For example, shares, unit trusts, land, property and antiques can increase in price, giving you a capital gain. If you sell them – or even give them away – you may be faced with a tax bill at up to 40 per cent of the chargeable gain.

The average taxpayer is unlikely to pay capital gains tax, however. There is a long list of assets on which gains are tax-free (see pp. 120–1). And there are various allowances and reliefs you can claim to reduce any potentially chargeable gains. If after all that there is still any chargeable gain left, part or all of it may be covered by your annual tax-free allowance (£8,800 in 2006–7 and £9,200 in 2007–8).

This chapter explains how capital gains tax works and the details of the various reliefs and allowances. It tells you how to keep your capital gains tax to a minimum. And it sets out the complicated rules for calculating the tax when you buy and sell shares. But it begins with a guide to when you might face this tax.

When do you have to pay capital gains tax?

You may have to pay this tax whenever you dispose of an asset. What is meant by dispose is not defined by law. But if you sell an asset, swap one asset for another or give something away, this will normally count as a disposal. So will the loss or destruction of an asset (although not if you replace or restore it by claiming on an insurance policy, or by using compensation received).

There are some occasions when there is no capital gains tax to pay, regardless of what is being disposed of or how much it is worth:

- assets passed on when someone dies
- gifts to a husband or wife or between civil partners, unless separated
- gifts to charity and community amateur sports clubs.

Although there are no taxable gains in these circumstances, there are also no losses if the asset is worth less than when you acquired it.

Tax-saving idea 73

If you are thinking of making a gift to charity of an asset which is showing a loss, think again. You won't be able to claim the loss to reduce other taxable gains (though with gifts of quoted shares or property, you may be able to claim income tax relief – see p. 222). Ideally, find something which is showing a taxable gain to give – there will be no tax to pay on the disposal. Alternatively, sell the asset which is showing a loss and give the proceeds to the charity. That would create an allowable loss which could reduce your tax bill on other disposals.

Example

Leonie Dale is trying to decide whether to give some shares worth £12,000 to a charity or whether to make a cash donation. If she sells the shares on the stock market, they would produce an allowable loss of £10,000. But she sold her share of a rental property earlier this tax year, making a chargeable gain of £10,000, so her best course of action would be to sell the shares and give the resulting proceeds to charity. She can then deduct the loss on the shares from the gain on the property sale, saving herself £4,000 capital gains tax.

Tax-free gains

There is no capital gains tax to pay on any gain you make on the following assets:

- your home (though not a second home in most cases – see Chapter 6)
- private cars
- wasting assets with a useful life of 50 years or less (for example, a boat or caravan), so long as you could not have claimed a capital allowance on it
- personal belongings – known as chattels – sold for less than £6,000 (see p. 130)

■ British money, including sovereigns dated after 1837

■ foreign currency for your personal spending abroad (including what you spend on maintaining a home abroad), but not foreign currency accounts

■ gains on insurance policies, unless you bought them and were not the original holder, or your wife did so and gave them to you (though you may have to pay part of the insurance company's capital gains tax bill – see p. 201)

■ betting, pools or lottery winnings

■ National Savings & Investments such as NS&I Certificates and Capital Bonds

■ Individual savings accounts (ISAs) – see p. 90

■ Personal equity plans (PEPs) – see p. 93

■ Enterprise Investment Scheme (EIS) shares, provided you have owned them for a minimum period and they carried on their qualifying activity for at least three years – see p. 96

■ shares in venture capital trusts (VCTs) – see p. 98

■ terminal bonuses on Save-As-You-Earn (SAYE) contracts

■ British government stock and any options to buy and sell such stock

■ certain corporate bonds such as company loan stock and debentures issued after 13 March 1984 and options to buy and sell such bonds

■ interests in trusts or settlements, unless you bought them

■ decorations for bravery, unless you bought them

■ gifts to certain bodies (such as museums) and gifts of certain heritage property in line with the inheritance tax exemptions (see p. 153)

■ gifts to charity and to community amateur sports clubs

■ damages or compensation for a personal injury or wrong to yourself or in your personal capacity (for example, libel)

■ compensation for being given bad investment advice that left you worse off after being persuaded to buy a personal pension between 29 April 1988 and 30 June 1994.

Tax-saving idea 74

If your spouse or partner is terminally ill, consider giving them any assets you own that are showing large taxable gains, assuming your spouse or partner plans to leave you their estate in their will. There is capital gains tax neither on the transfer to them nor on death. Moreover, you inherit the assets at their market value at the time of death, wiping out the previous gains. Bear in mind that the initial gift will not be accepted as genuine and will not save the intended tax, if leaving the assets back to you in the will is a condition of the gift.

Disposals of land to housing associations may also be free of capital gains tax.

If an asset is one where there is no capital gains tax to pay on disposal, any loss you make on it cannot normally be used to reduce your overall tax bill. Exceptions are enterprise investment scheme shares (see p. 96) and chattels worth £6,000 or less (see p. 130).

Who has to pay?

Capital gains tax applies to you as an individual in your private life or in your business whether self-employed or in partnership. Trustees may also have to pay capital gains tax on the assets that are held in trust (see below).

Executors of the estate of someone who has died may have to pay capital gains tax on any increase in value of estate assets between the death and distributing them to beneficiaries.

Any capital gains tax for 2006–7 will have to be paid by 31 January 2008, along with the final payment for any income tax still unpaid from the same tax year. Capital gains tax for 2007–8 will have to be paid by 31 January 2009.

Married couples and civil partners

A husband and wife are treated as two single people for capital gains tax purposes, and each is responsible for paying their own capital gains tax bills. With assets jointly owned by husband and wife – second homes, shares, valuables and so on – the gain or loss should be split 50:50 between you unless you own them in different shares.

You may have filled in form 17 (see p. 52) to allocate income from the asset in unequal shares. If so, the same shares are presumed to apply for capital gains tax. Otherwise, the gain or loss is split in whatever proportions the evidence supports. If you have no evidence, the split is assumed to be 50:50.

Since 5 December 2005, same sex couples who register their relationship as a civil partnership are treated for tax in the same way as married couples.

Trusts

Where assets are held in trust, the trustees are liable for capital gains tax on disposals of the assets in the trust, in much the same way as individuals. The rate of capital gains tax paid by trustees is 40 per cent in 2006–7 and 2007–8.

Trusts are entitled to a tax-free capital gains tax allowance in the same way as individual taxpayers. For most trusts, the allowance is half the figure that applies to individuals. So for 2006–7, the first £4,400 of net chargeable gains is free of tax for a trust; for 2007–8, the tax-free allowance for trusts is £4,600. Trusts for certain disabled people get the same tax-exemption as individuals: £8,800 for 2006–7; £9,200 for 2007–8.

Estates

There is no capital gains tax on assets you leave when you die. But any increase in their value between your death and their being distributed may be taxed at the same rate that applies to trusts: 40 per cent. The executors (or administrators if there is no will) are responsible for paying the tax.

In the tax year of death and the following two tax years, the executors are entitled to the same tax-free capital gains tax that individuals get (£8,800 in 2006–7 and £9,200 in 2007–8). After that, there is no tax-free allowance at all. Therefore, executors may wish to ensure that before the start of the third year assets, even if still unsold, are transferred to beneficiaries, who can then set their own tax-free allowances against any gains.

How to work out the gain or loss

The gain or loss on an asset disposed of in 2007–8 is worked out broadly as follows (and see the example on p. 125):

Step 1: Find the final value of the asset – what you get for selling it or its market value if given away.

Step 2: Find its initial value – normally what you paid for it or its market value (see p. 126). There are special rules for valuing assets owned on or before 31 March 1982 (p. 129) and for shares and unit trusts (p. 137).

Step 3: Deduct the initial value from the final value to find the gross capital gain or gross capital loss.

Step 4: If you incurred any allowable expenses in acquiring, owning or disposing of the asset (p. 127), these can be deducted to reduce the gross capital gain or increase a capital loss. This gives your net capital gain or net allowable loss.

Step 5: If you have made a net capital gain on an asset owned on or before 5 April 1998, you can reduce this by claiming indexation allowance which reflects the impact of inflation before that date on the figures (p. 128).

Step 6: You may be able to claim special reliefs to reduce a gain further or increase a net allowable loss – for example, when disposing of your only or main home (Chapter 6).

Step 7: Subtract your total allowable losses for the year from the total of your chargeable gains to find your net chargeable gain or your net allowable loss. If the losses exceed the gains, there is no capital gains tax to pay and your net allowable loss can be carried forward to set against gains in future years (p. 131).

Step 8: If you have made a net chargeable gain, you can deduct any losses carried over from previous years (p. 132). If the result is equal to or less than the tax-free capital gains tax allowance for the tax year (£9,200 for 2007–8), there is no capital gains tax to pay.

Step 9: If the result of deducting losses from previous years from your net chargeable gain is more than the tax-free allowance, you must next work out if you are entitled to taper relief on any of the gains you have made in this tax year. If you have owned an asset since 5 April 1998, taper relief reduces the net capital gain on it according to the number of whole years it was owned after that date (p. 133). Personal (but not business) assets owned before 17 March 1998 and sold on or after 6 April 1998 qualify for one bonus year of taper relief (see p. 134).

Step 10: Now deduct your losses for the tax year and previous tax years from the net capital gains made on each asset, starting with those that do not qualify for taper relief, going on to those with the lowest rate of taper relief, then to those with the next lowest rate and so on.

Step 11: When all the losses are used up, you can reduce each of the remaining chargeable gains by the appropriate rate of taper relief.

Example

Ben Barber bought a small paddock for £7,000 in April 1987 paying a valuation fee of £100. In the same week, he spent £500 laying a water supply to the field. The paddock was sold in May 2007 for £35,000 with an estate agent's fee of £250. Ben calculates the tax due as follows:

Step 1: The final value of the paddock is what he sold it for – £35,000.

Step 2: The initial value is what he paid for it – £7,000.

Step 3: He deducts the initial value from the final value to find the gross capital gain of £28,000.

Step 4: He incurred allowable expenses of £850: the £100 fee paid for valuing the paddock, the £500 spent on the water supply and the £250 fee paid when selling it. He deducts this from the £28,000 gross capital gain to get the net capital gain of £27,150.

Step 5: He can claim indexation allowance for the £7,000 cost of buying the paddock, the £100 valuation fee and the £500 cost of installing the water supply. The allowance is £4,538 (for how he calculated this, see p. 129). Ben subtracts this indexation allowance from the net capital gain of £27,150 to get a chargeable gain of £22,612.

Step 6: Ben can claim none of the special reliefs against capital gains tax.

Step 7: This is his only chargeable gain for the tax year and he has no allowable losses from the same tax year to deduct from it.

Step 8: Ben has £3,500 of allowable losses from previous tax years to set off against this chargeable gain. Deducting this from his £22,612 net chargeable gain gives £19,112 – well above the £9,200 capital gains tax-free allowance for the tax year, so he will pay capital gains tax.

Step 9: He will be entitled to taper relief on the chargeable gain made on the paddock. He has owned it for nine full years after 5 April 1998 and he gets a bonus year for having owned it before 17 March 1998. This is a personal asset rather than a business asset, so ten years entitles Ben to 40 per cent taper relief (see p. 134).

Step 10: Ben deducts the £3,500 loss from previous tax years from his net chargeable gains of £22,612 to get £19,112.

Step 11: Ben now deducts taper relief to arrive at a tapered gain of 60% × £19,112 = £11,467.

Step 12: The tax-free allowance for 2007–8 is £9,200. He subtracts this from the total chargeable gain to get £2,267.

Step 13: The £2,267 is added to Ben's taxable income for 2007–8 and tax is charged on it. His income is already high enough for him to be paying tax at the higher rate of 40 per cent, so that is the rate he pays on the gain.

So Ben must pay 40 per cent of £2,267 – a capital gains tax bill of £906.80.

Step 12: Add the net tapered gains together to get the total net tapered gain for the tax year. Deduct the tax-free capital gains tax allowance for the tax year from the total – this was £9,200 for 2007–8.

Step 13: Add the result to your taxable income for the year. If the total is less than £2,230, the gain is taxed at 10 per cent. If the total is less than £34,600 for the 2007–8 tax year, the rate of tax on the capital gain is 20 per cent (or a mix of 10 and 20 per cent). If the total is more than £34,600, tax on the amount over the limit is charged at 40 per cent.

Initial and final value

In most cases, the value of an asset when you acquire or sell it is what it cost you to acquire it or what you get on selling it. If you acquired something by inheritance, its initial value is its probate value.

With a gift, the value is its market value: what anyone selling it at the time of the gift would get for it on the open market. However, in certain circumstances, the initial value of a gift may be what the giver acquired it for if you agreed at the time of the gift to take over the giver's capital gain (see below).

The market value is also the final value if you dispose of an asset to a connected person, however much you sell it for. For capital gains tax, a connected person includes your husband or wife, your business partner and their spouse, a relative of yours or these others (brother, sister, parents, child, grandchild) and the spouse of one of these relatives.

When a person (the settlor) puts money or assets into trust, the trustees become connected with the settlor (and any people connected to the settlor).

There are special rules for valuing assets owned before April 1982 (see p. 129).

Gifts

With some things you are given, you may have agreed to take over the giver's capital gains tax bill by agreeing to a claim for hold-over relief (see p. 146). Since 14 March 1989, this can be done for only a limited range of gifts, but before that date it could be done with almost anything.

When you come to dispose of an asset on which hold-over relief has been claimed when you got it, its initial value is what the giver acquired it for, not its market value when you were given it.

Allowable expenses

Deducting the initial value of an asset from its final value gives you the gross capital gain or gross capital loss. However, you can then deduct certain allowable expenses in computing the gain on an asset for capital gains tax. These include:

■ acquisition costs, such as payments to a professional adviser (for example, surveyor, accountant, solicitor), conveyancing costs and stamp duty, and advertising to find a seller

■ what you spend improving the asset (though not your own time) provided the improvement is still reflected in the asset when you dispose of it

■ what you spend establishing or defending your rights or title to the asset

■ disposal costs, similar to acquisition costs, but including the cost of valuing it for capital gains tax.

Deducting these expenses gives you the net capital gain or net allowable loss. If the asset was a gift to you and the giver got hold-over relief (see above), you can also claim any allowable expenses incurred while the giver owned it.

Tax-saving idea 75

If you own a second home, investment property, antiques, collectables or other valuables, keep careful records of what they cost you to buy and maintain. You could face a capital gains tax bill when you dispose of them but allowable expenses can reduce the bill.

Part disposals

If you dispose of part of an asset, you will need to allocate expenses between the part you are getting rid of and the part you have kept.

Any expense connected only with the part being disposed of can be fully deducted from the proceeds in working out the gain. Anything connected only with the part you are keeping cannot be deducted. But some of the expenditure will be impossible to allocate in this way, and will thus have to be divided between the two parts, in proportion to their value. The proportion of such a cost that you can deduct from the gain is as follows:

$$\frac{\text{Disposal proceeds}}{\text{Disposal proceeds} + \text{Value of the part retained}}$$

Example

When Melanie Hill sold her holiday cottage in September 2007 for £138,000, she feared an enormous capital gains tax bill – she had bought it in August 1993 for £72,000. But she soon realised there were a lot of expenses she could claim to reduce the capital gain:

- acquisition costs of £1,935 – the £790 legal bill incurred in buying it, the £720 stamp duty and the £425 surveyor's fee for inspecting and valuing it
- improvement costs of £18,750 – the cost of installing modern plumbing and central heating, rewiring and building an extension which were all paid for in May 1994
- disposal costs of £4,140 – legal bills for the sale of £1,725 and £2,415 commission paid to the estate agent.

The net capital gain is worked out as follows:

Final value		£138,000
minus allowable expenses:		
original cost	£72,000	
acquisition costs	£1,935	
improvement costs	£18,750	
disposal costs	£4,140	
Total allowable expenses		£96,825
Net capital gain		**£41,175**

However, Melanie won't pay capital gains tax even on this net capital gain of £41,175 – she can claim indexation allowance (see below) and taper relief (p. 133).

There are special rules for allocating costs to shares and unit trusts where holdings are divided or added to (see p. 137).

Indexation allowance

If you end up with a net capital gain after deducting allowable expenses from the gross capital gain, you can claim indexation allowance to remove some or all of the gain created by inflation if you owned it between 1 April 1982 and 31 March 1998. But you can't use indexation allowance to create or increase a loss.

To calculate indexation allowance for assets held on 5 April 1998, the initial value and each allowable expense is multiplied by the indexation factor for the month in which the money was spent. The factors are in the table on p. 130 – for example, for money spent in June 1994, the factor is 0.124.

Example

Martin Thompson buys a house which he converts into a pair of flats. He spends £5,000 converting one into a weekend retreat for himself and £3,000 on doing up the other one to sell off.

Each of the flats is given identical valuations at the time of the sale. So any money spent on the whole house can be divided equally between the two flats. He can therefore claim the following expenses to reduce the gain on the flat he sells off:

■ the £3,000 spent improving the flat he sells off
■ the expenses of selling the flat
■ half the expenses of buying the house including the purchase price.

Assets owned on or before 31 March 1982

If you owned an asset on or before 31 March 1982, only the gain since that date is liable to capital gains tax. Any gain made before 1 April 1982 is effectively tax-free. With such assets, the initial value is normally its market value on 31 March 1982 and you do not deduct expenses incurred on or before that date. Indexation allowance runs from March 1982.

An alternative approach which does take into account earlier expenses can be adopted in some cases. But not if you have made a 'rebasing election' which means that you have chosen for all your gains and losses on assets owned on or before 31 March 1982 to be based on their market value at that date. The rebasing election had to be made within two years of the first disposal of such an asset and is irrevocable. For more details, see Help Sheet IR280 *Rebasing – assets held at 31 March 1982*.

Example

Ben Barber works out the indexation allowance he can claim on the paddock he disposed of in May 2007 (see p. 125). He can claim the allowance for the original cost of £7,000, the valuation fee of £100 and the cost of laying on the water supply of £500 – all of this £7,600 was spent in April 1987 when the indexation factor was 0.597.

The indexation allowance is as follows:

$$£7,600 \times 0.597$$
$$= £4,538$$

Ben's chargeable gain net of indexation allowance on the paddock is therefore £27,150 − £4,538 = £22,612.

Indexation factors

Year	Jan	Feb	Mar	Apr	May	Jun	Jul	Aug	Sep	Oct	Nov	Dec
						Month						
1982			1.047	1.006	0.992	0.987	0.986	0.985	0.987	0.977	0.967	0.971
1983	0.968	0.960	0.956	0.929	0.921	0.917	0.906	0.898	0.889	0.883	0.876	0.871
1984	0.872	0.865	0.859	0.834	0.828	0.823	0.825	0.808	0.804	0.793	0.788	0.789
1985	0.783	0.769	0.752	0.716	0.708	0.704	0.707	0.703	0.704	0.701	0.695	0.693
1986	0.689	0.683	0.681	0.665	0.662	0.663	0.667	0.662	0.654	0.652	0.638	0.632
1987	0.626	0.620	0.616	0.597	0.596	0.596	0.597	0.593	0.588	0.580	0.573	0.574
1988	0.574	0.568	0.562	0.537	0.531	0.525	0.524	0.507	0.500	0.485	0.478	0.474
1989	0.465	0.454	0.448	0.423	0.414	0.409	0.408	0.404	0.395	0.384	0.372	0.369
1990	0.361	0.353	0.339	0.300	0.288	0.283	0.282	0.269	0.258	0.248	0.251	0.252
1991	0.249	0.242	0.237	0.222	0.218	0.213	0.215	0.213	0.208	0.204	0.199	0.198
1992	0.199	0.193	0.189	0.171	0.167	0.167	0.171	0.171	0.166	0.162	0.164	0.168
1993	0.179	0.171	0.167	0.156	0.152	0.153	0.156	0.151	0.146	0.147	0.148	0.146
1994	0.151	0.144	0.141	0.128	0.124	0.124	0.129	0.124	0.121	0.120	0.119	0.114
1995	0.114	0.107	0.102	0.091	0.087	0.085	0.091	0.085	0.080	0.085	0.085	0.079
1996	0.083	0.078	0.073	0.066	0.063	0.063	0.067	0.062	0.057	0.057	0.057	0.053
1997	0.053	0.049	0.046	0.040	0.036	0.032	0.032	0.026	0.021	0.019	0.019	0.016
1998	0.019	0.014	0.011									

Special rules for personal belongings – chattels

Personal belongings with a useful life of less than 50 years count as wasting assets and any gains on their disposal are tax-free (see p. 120). When more enduring personal belongings – often referred to as chattels or tangible moveable property – are sold for less than £6,000, the gain is also tax-free. Chattels include, for example, furniture, silver, paintings and so on. A set (for example, a silver tea-set) counts as one chattel for this exemption.

Example

William Baxter bought a piece of furniture for £4,000 and sold it for £7,500 in 2007–8. This produces a gain of £7,500 − £4,000 = £3,500. The sale price is over the £6,000 chattels limit so the gain is not tax-free. But for capital gains tax purposes, the gain cannot be more than $\frac{5}{3}$ of £7,500 − £6,000. This is $\frac{5}{3}$ of £1,500 = £2,500, thus reducing William's taxable gain by £1,000.

If a chattel is sold for more than the tax-free limit, the taxable gain is restricted to $\frac{5}{3}$ of the amount of the disposal value over the limit. So the maximum gain on a chattel sold for £7,200 would be $\frac{5}{3}$ of £7,200 – £6,000 = $\frac{5}{3}$ of £1,200 = £2,000.

In most cases, disposing of an asset that would produce a tax-free gain means that you cannot claim any allowable loss made on such an asset. With a chattel, you can claim a loss even if it is sold for less than £6,000 – but the loss is calculated as if it had fetched £6,000.

Example

> William Baxter sold a painting for £4,500 which he had bought for £9,500. His gross loss is calculated as if he had sold it for £6,000: it is therefore £9,500 – £6,000 = £3,500 – rather than the £5,000 loss William actually made.

For more about chattels, ask for Help Sheet IR295 *Chattels and capital gains tax*.

Tax-saving idea 76

> The generous tax treatment of chattels means that collecting can be a very tax-efficient activity. This is especially true if the items in the collection can be sold individually and so taxed separately instead of being treated as a set. This might apply to, say, rare books or unrelated bits of silver.

Capital losses

If the initial cost of an asset and its expenses add up to more than its final value, you have made a net capital loss on that asset. Net capital losses are deducted from your chargeable gains to find the total chargeable gain on which your capital gains tax bill is based. If your net capital losses are bigger than your total chargeable gains, the difference – your net allowable loss – can be carried over to reduce your chargeable gains in later tax years.

Note that a loss made when you dispose of an asset to a connected person (p. 126) can be set off only against a gain made on a disposal to the same connected person. This is called a 'clogged loss' and applies even if the loss was made when you disposed of the asset for a genuine commercial value.

Warning

> For disposals made on or after 6 December 2006, you cannot claim as an allowable loss, any loss you make as a result of an arrangement if a main purpose of the arrangement was to save tax. The legislation is very widely drawn and could potentially catch any type of transaction. The Revenue has specifically said that it does not apply, for example, to timing your disposals so that losses can be set against gains for the same tax year, or giving an asset to your spouse or civil partner so they can sell it to realise a loss to set against other capital gains they have. At the time of writing, it was not clear whether other common arrangements, such as selling shares and repurchasing them within an individual savings account (see page 139) in order to realise a loss would be caught.

The tax-free allowance

The first slice of total chargeable gain in any tax year is free of capital gains tax. For 2006–7, the tax-free allowance was £8,800; for 2007–8, the allowance is £9,200.

Tax-saving ideas 77, 78 and 79

Try to use your tax-free allowance every year – you can't carry any unused part over to another year.

Spouses and civil partners each have a tax-free allowance, so in 2007–8 can have tax-free gains of £18,400 between them. Consider reorganising your possessions and investments (for example, holding them jointly) so that each of you uses up your full allowance before the other starts to pay tax.

You usually have to deduct losses made in the same tax year as a gain even if this takes your chargeable gains below the level of your tax-free allowance. This means some allowance is wasted. You may be able to avoid this if you can dispose of the item bearing the loss to a connected person. The loss is then clogged and can only be set against gains on disposals to the same person.

Example

Gus Henry made chargeable gains of £8,900 in 2007–8 and allowable losses of £3,250 in the same year. All the losses have to be set off against the gains for this tax year, even though this brings the net chargeable gain below the tax-free allowance of £9,200 for the tax year.

So his net chargeable gain is £8,900 – £3,250 = £5,650 – on which no tax is payable.

Losses from previous years

If your net chargeable gain for the tax year is bigger than the tax-free allowance, you must use any losses from previous tax years to reduce your tax bill. If you have enough such losses, you must reduce your total chargeable gain to the level of the tax-free allowance and pay no capital gains tax at all. Note that – unlike with losses from the same tax year – you don't have to deduct more than is necessary to get down to the tax-free amount.

If your losses from previous tax years are not sufficient to reduce your total chargeable gain below the level of the tax-free allowance, then they can be used to reduce your capital gains tax bill. The carried-forward losses are subtracted from the chargeable gains on individual assets in a way that ensures the biggest possible reduction in your tax bill by maximising the amount of taper relief you can claim – see opposite.

In general, losses can never be carried back to an earlier tax year. An exception is when you die. On death, your executors can carry back losses to set against gains you made in the three previous tax years – starting with the gains in the most recent year. There is further information in Help Sheet IR282 *Death, personal representatives and legatees*.

Claiming losses

You have to claim losses within five years and ten months of the end of the tax year in which they were made. So losses made in 2007–8 must be claimed by 31 January 2014.

You can claim the losses by giving details on the Capital gains pages of the tax return (see Chapter 22). If you haven't been sent these pages, write and tell your tax inspector about your losses.

Tax-saving idea 80

Do not forget to claim losses you make when you dispose of, say, shares or valuables. Make sure you claim them within the time limit and keep careful records so that you don't forget them later on.

Example

Elizabeth Ong has a total chargeable gain in 2007–8 of £10,000. The tax-free amount for that tax year is £9,200, which would mean paying capital gains tax on £10,000 – £9,200 = £800. But she has losses of £3,500 carried over from previous years and she can use £800 of this amount to reduce her total chargeable gain to nil – with no capital gains tax to pay.

This still leaves her with £3,500 – £800 = £2,700 of unused losses to be carried forward to 2008–9 and beyond.

Taper relief

Taper relief is designed to encourage you to invest for the longer term. It reduces the amount of the gain according to the number of complete years the asset has been owned after 5 April 1998. The reduction is bigger for business assets.

For a non-business asset owned for three full years, taper relief reduces the gain by 5 per cent – so 95 per cent of the gain on it is chargeable. After 10 years, taper relief rises to the maximum 40 per cent, leaving 60 per cent of the gain chargeable.

For business assets, the rate of taper relief is higher – a maximum of 75 per cent that leaves just 25 per cent of the gain chargeable. For disposals between 6 April 2000 and 5 April 2002, the maximum is reached after four years; and, for disposals from 6 April 2002 onwards, the maximum is reached after just two years.

If you owned a non-business asset before 17 March 1998, you will be given one bonus year of ownership if you sell it after 5 April 1998. So if you bought the asset on 1 January 1998 and sold it on 1 July 2007, you would be treated as having owned it for ten years after 5 April 1998 – the nine complete years after that date plus the one bonus year. Business assets disposed of on or after 6 April 2000 no longer qualify for a bonus year because taper relief was enhanced for such assets.

Number of complete years asset owned after 5 April 1998	Non-business assets		Business assets			
			Disposal on or after 6 April 2000 and before 6 April 2002		Disposal on or after 6 April 2002	
	Taper relief	% of gain chargeable	Taper relief	% of gain chargeable	Taper relief	% of gain chargeable
0	0	100	0	100	100	0
1	0	100	12.5	87.5	50	50
2	0	100	25	75	75	25
3	5	95	50	50	75	25
4	10	90	75	25	75	25
5	15	85	75	25	75	25
6	20	80	75	25	75	25
7	25	75	75	25	75	25
8	30	70	75	25	75	25
9	35	65	75	25	75	25
10	40	60	75	25	75	25

Taper relief is calculated on the chargeable gain after deducting any losses for the tax year and previous tax years. To maximise the amount of taper relief you can claim, losses are deducted first from the gains that qualify for least taper relief, then the next least and so on. So, for example, if you have a non-business asset that qualifies for 10 per cent taper relief and one that qualifies for 20 per cent, the losses are deducted from the first gain – if it is too small to use up all the losses, they are then deducted from the second gain. Note that a business asset owned for just a few years qualifies for a higher rate of taper relief than a non-business asset owned rather longer, so may come behind the non-business asset in the queue for losses.

Business assets

The definition of 'business asset' was changed from 6 April 2000 onwards and again from 6 April 2004 (see below).

If you have an asset that was a business asset for only part of the time you owned it (perhaps because of the changes to the definition), you must apportion any gain into two parts: a business part and a non-business part. Different rates of taper relief will apply to each part (see Example on p. 138).

What counts as a qualifying company for business asset taper relief

| Period to which definition applies | Definition of qualifying company | | |
	Your relationship with the company (apart from holding shares)	Type of company	Nature of your shareholding
6 April 1998 to 5 April 2000	None required	Trading company[1]	Shares giving you at least 25% of the voting rights
	Full-time working officer or employee	Trading company[1]	Shares giving you at least 5% of the voting rights
6 April 2000 onwards	None required	Unquoted trading company[1] [2]	Any
	None required	Quoted trading company[2]	Shares giving you at least 5% of the voting rights
	Officer or employee (full- or part-time)	Quoted trading company[2]	Any
	Officer or employee (full- or part-time)	Non-trading company	No more than 10% of any class of shares or 10% of the voting rights or rights to no more than 10% of distributable income or assets

(1) Or holding company of trading group.
(2) Quoted means listed on the London Stock Exchange or a recognised overseas exchange. Other companies are unquoted. 'Unquoted' includes shares listed on the Alternative Investment Market (AIM).

A business asset is:

- any item you use in your trade or profession

- from 6 April 2004 onwards, any item used in a trade or profession carried on by someone else

- until 5 April 2000, any item you held for the purpose of your employment (including as a director) by a trading company, provided you were required to devote at least 75 per cent of your working hours to that job

- from 6 April 2000 onwards, any item you hold for the purpose of your employment (including as a director) by a trading company

- shares or securities in a qualifying company – see table on p. 135 for what counts as a qualifying company.

Calculating your capital gains tax bill

If there is anything left after deducting expenses, indexation allowance, losses, taper relief and the tax-free allowance (£8,800 in 2006–7, £9,200 in 2007–8), there is capital gains tax to pay.

For 2007–8, your total net tapered gains minus the tax-free allowance of £9,200 is added to your taxable income for the year and taxed as if it was savings income. So if the combined total comes to less than £2,230, the tax rate on the gains is 10 per cent. Any amount over £34,600, the upper limit for the basic rate of income tax, is taxed at the top rate of 40 per cent. Between the upper and lower limit for the basic rate, gains are taxed at 20 per cent.

Similarly, for 2006–7, if adding your taxable gains to your taxable income comes to no more than £2,150, the gain is taxed at 10 per cent. If it comes to more than £33,300, the gain is taxed at 40 per cent. In between those limits, the gain is taxed at 20 per cent.

Tax-saving ideas 81 and 82

Since 6 April 2004, an asset used in a business can qualify for business asset taper relief even if it is not your own business. This can enhance the return you get from, say, investing in commercial property such as shops and offices.

Selling shares in the company you work for? From 6 April 2000, you can claim taper relief at the rate for business assets so you may be able to reduce the gain to just a quarter after two years. But bear in mind, if you get shares every year, that any sale will be matched first with the most recently acquired shares (see p. 138).

Shares and unit trusts

Shares and unit trusts are treated in the same way as other assets for capital gains tax purposes. But if you buy and sell identical shares in a particular company or units in a particular unit trust at different times, how do you decide which you have bought or sold when working out the gain? And there are further complications when companies merge, are taken over or otherwise reorganise their capital. This section explains the special rules for working out the gains and losses on share transactions. Help Sheet IR284 *Shares and capital gains tax* has more details.

Valuing shares

The market value of shares bought and sold on a stock exchange is normally the amount you paid for them or got for selling them.

But you should use the market value when valuing gifts or disposals to a connected person (see p. 126). If they are traded on the London Stock Exchange use the prices recorded in the Stock Exchange Daily Official List (which can be obtained from a stockbroker or bank or the Historic Price Service London Stock Exchange, 10 Paternoster Square, London EC4M 7LS or www.londonstockexchange.com). The market value is the lower of the following two figures, calculated using prices on the date of the gift or disposal:

■ the selling price, plus a quarter of the difference between the selling price and the (higher) buying price – the quarter-up rule

■ the half-way point between the highest and lowest prices of recorded bargains for the day.

With any disposal of unquoted shares, the market value must be agreed with Shares Valuation, part of the Revenue (Tel: 0115 974 2222). This cannot be negotiated in advance and reaching agreement can be a lengthy business.

Unit trusts and investment trusts

The gain on disposing of unit trusts and investment trusts is worked out in the same way as for shares. If you receive an equalisation payment with your first distribution from a unit trust, this is a return of part of your original investment and should be deducted from the acquisition price in working out your gain or loss.

Example

Reg Parsons and Jack Gill both hold 10 per cent of the shares of a company (which they do not work for). Reg got his shares in 1990 and Jack got his ten years later on 6 April 2000. They both sell their shares on 6 April 2007, realising a profit of £60,000.

Jack's shares have counted as a business asset throughout the seven years he has owned them and qualify for maximum taper relief of 75 per cent. This means only 25% × £60,000 = £15,000 of Jack's gain is taxable.

Reg has owned his shares for 17 years – ten years longer than Jack. However, taper relief was introduced from 6 April 1998 and this is the period which counts for taper relief purposes. The shares only became business assets when the rules changed from 6 April 2000. So for seven of the nine years, the shares count as business assets. Using the apportionment rules means that $\frac{7}{9}$ of the shares count as business assets, so $\frac{7}{9}$ × £60,000 = £46,667 of the gain qualifies for 75 per cent business taper relief, giving a taxable gain of 25% × £46,667 = £11,666. The remaining $\frac{2}{9}$ of the shares count as a non-business asset. As they have been held for nine years since 6 April 1998, non-business taper relief of 40% is due (nine years plus the bonus year). The gain of $\frac{2}{9}$ × £60,000 = £13,333 is tapered at 60% to £7,999. Reg's total taxable gain is £11,666 + £7,999 = £19,665.

Despite owning his shares for longer, Reg has a much higher taxable gain than Jack.

Which shares or unit trusts have you sold?

If you buy one batch of shares in a company and later sell it without any other dealings in the shares, it is quite simple to calculate the gain or loss. But if you buy shares in the same company on different occasions and then sell them – together or in parcels, disposals will be matched with acquisitions in the following order:

- first, shares acquired the same day
- second, shares acquired at any time in the next 30 days (see below)
- third, shares acquired before the day of sale and after 5 April 1998 – with the most recent acquisitions first (last in, first out, or LIFO)
- fourth, shares acquired between 6 April 1982 and 5 April 1998 – see the example on p. 141 for how their initial cost and indexation allowance are calculated
- fifth, shares acquired between 6 April 1965 and 5 April 1982
- finally, shares acquired on or before 5 April 1965.

Tax-saving idea 83

It could still pay you to sell some shares towards the end of the tax year to use up the tax-free allowance. In 2007–8, you can have chargeable gains of up to £9,200 tax-free – saving up to £3,680 in capital gains tax. You could buy the same shares back after the 30 days – taking the risk that the shares shoot up in price during the 30-day period. Or you could buy different shares – perhaps in a similar company. Another option is to sell shares you own directly and buy them back within a stocks and shares ISA or get your spouse or civil partner to buy the shares back – these are effective for tax purposes without waiting 30 days. Remember to take the costs of buying and selling shares into account. Be wary if you intend to sell shares and buy them back within an ISA in order to realise a capital loss to set against gains you have made on other assets – you could be caught by a new anti-avoidance rule (see p. 131).

Shares acquired at any time in the next 30 days

Shares bought in the 30 days after a sale are treated as those sold in the sale before those bought earlier – to stop a practice that was known as 'bed and breakfasting'. This involved selling some shares towards the end of the tax year and buying them back the next day to realise a gain which could help use up the tax-free allowance or realise a loss for offsetting gains made on other assets.

This can no longer be done. If you sell shares and buy them back within 30 days of the sale, the shares you sell are matched to those you buy back, not shares bought earlier. So if you sell some shares for £5 each which you originally bought for £3 and then buy them back for £5 the next day, the initial value of the shares you sold will be £5 each not £3 – and there would be no gain realised.

Shares acquired before 6 April 1998 and after 5 April 1982

Shares you acquired between these two dates qualify for indexation allowance, according to when the acquisition was made. If you acquired more than one batch of the same shares at different times between the two dates, they are pooled when working out the gain or loss – this means they are treated as a single asset. Each share is given the average initial value of all the shares in the pool, and each is entitled to the average indexation allowance. The example on p. 141 shows how pooling works.

Shares bought on or before 5 April 1982

Shares owned on or before 5 April 1982 and on or after 6 April 1965 are kept in a separate pool, and treated like other assets owned before 1 April 1982:

- the gain is based on their value on 31 March 1982, unless it is to your advantage to base it on their cost when you bought them (see p. 129)

- indexation allowance runs only from March 1982.

Shares bought before 6 April 1965

Shares acquired before 6 April 1965 are kept completely separate. They are the last to be sold if you have bought batches since that date – all shares bought after that date are sold first. When you come to sell pre-April 1965 quoted shares, it is assumed the last to be bought are the first to be sold.

However, you can elect for your shares acquired before 6 April 1965 to be added to your pre-April 1982 pool. This is usually to your advantage, as their value on 31 March 1982 is likely to be higher than what you paid for them more than 17 years before.

Employee share schemes

Employee share schemes allow employees to acquire shares in their companies free or cheaply – and if they are certain types approved by the Revenue, without an income tax bill. There could be a capital gains tax bill when the shares are disposed of, though from 6 April 2000 onwards the gain will qualify for the higher rates of taper relief for business assets (see p. 134).

The initial cost of the shares and when you are deemed to have received them depends on the type of scheme:

- approved savings-related share option schemes – you acquire the shares at the price you paid on the day that you opted to buy them

- approved profit-sharing schemes – you acquire the shares at the market value on the day they are allocated to you, even though you can't sell them for three years

- approved discretionary share option schemes – you acquire the shares at the price you pay for them on the day you exercise the option. If you paid anything for the option, this is an allowable expense

■ share incentive plan – when the shares are first awarded to you or, in the case of partnership shares, first acquired on your behalf, even though you have to hold them for a minimum period (see Chapter 16).

You can transfer shares from a savings-related share option scheme or share incentive plan direct to an ISA (see p. 92) or pension scheme (see p. 82). Shares transferred in this way are free of capital gains tax on transfer and when they are subsequently sold.

Example

Diana Nichols bought 2,000 ordinary shares in United Enterprises plc in June 1983 at a cost of £7,000. In December 1988, she added another 2,000 United Enterprises shares for £10,000. That gave her a pool of 4,000 United Enterprises shares bought before 6 April 1998 and after 5 April 1982. She works out the average cost and indexation allowance of the shares in the pool using the following figures for indexation factor:

■ June 1983 – 0.917
■ December 1988 – 0.474

First Diana calculates the average initial cost of the shares in the pool. The total cost is £7,000 + £10,000 = £17,000, which bought her 4,000 shares. So the average cost is:

$$\frac{£17,000}{4,000} = £4.25$$

Then she works out the indexation allowance on the 2,000 shares bought in June 1983:

$$£7,000 \times 0.917 = £6,419$$

The indexation allowance on the 2,000 shares bought in December 1988 is:

$$£10,000 \times 0.474 = £4,740$$

Total indexation allowance on the 4,000 shares is:

$$£6,419 + £4,740 = £11,159$$

Average indexation allowance for each share in the pool is:

$$\frac{£11,159}{4,000} = £2.79$$

So if she sells 1,000 shares in the pool, the initial cost is taken to be 1,000 × £4.25 = £4,250. The indexation allowance is 1,000 × £2.79 = £2,790.

Identical shares acquired on the same day are normally pooled together. But, if you acquire shares from two employee schemes on the same day (or from one employee scheme and buy a second batch on the open market on the same day), you can opt to match a disposal with the shares that have the higher initial value (i.e. produce the lowest gain).

Help Sheet IR287 *Employee share schemes and capital gains tax* has more details.

Rights issues

If you get extra shares through a rights issue or a bonus issue, they are allocated to the relevant shares or pool. So if half your shares were bought in May 1990 and half in July 1998, the rights issue is split 50:50 between the July 1998 shares and the pool of 1982–98 shares. Whatever you pay for the rights issue is added to the initial costs of the two lots of shares, with any indexation allowance running from the time the payment was made. Taper relief on the new shares is calculated from the time the shares they relate to were acquired, since rights and bonus issues are treated as share reorganisations.

Stock dividends and accumulation unit trusts

If you get extra shares instead of dividends, this is known as a stock dividend (or scrip dividend). The value of the new shares is the amount of dividend foregone excluding the value of the tax credit – the cash equivalent. Any indexation allowance or taper relief runs from the date of the dividend. Accumulation unit trusts work in a similar way, with extra units allocated to the appropriate pool.

Takeovers and mergers

If you own shares in a company which is taken over, you may get shares in the new parent company in exchange for your old shares. This exchange does not count as a disposal. The new shares are assumed to have been acquired at the cost of the old ones and on the same dates.

If part of the price for the old shares is cash, this is a disposal. For example, if you get half cash, half shares, you have disposed of half the old shares.

Sometimes you are offered loan notes as an alternative to taking cash. Usually, these are treated as the same asset as the shares you have given up, so no disposal takes place until you cash in the loan notes.

Tax-saving idea 84

If you accept cash for shares in a takeover, this counts as a disposal for capital gains tax. Sometimes you can opt for loan notes instead. If so, the disposal is deferred until you cash in the loan notes. This is useful if putting off the disposal would reduce the tax you pay (for example, by using a new tax year's allowance or increasing the taper relief you can claim).

When mutuals become PLCs

Some building societies and mutual insurance companies convert to public limited companies or are involved in other organisational changes that may produce benefits for members. If you receive shares or cash – or both – in such circumstances, there may be a bill for income tax or capital gains tax. Ask the building society or insurance company for guidance.

Payment by instalments

If you have bought newly issued shares, you may have paid for them in instalments. Indexation allowance and taper relief on the full purchase price runs from when the shares were acquired only if all the instalments were paid within 12 months of acquisition. If instalments are paid more than 12 months after the shares were acquired, indexation allowance and taper relief on those instalments runs from when the payments were made.

However, if you paid in instalments when buying newly issued shares in a privatised state enterprise, indexation allowance and taper relief run from the date you acquired the shares (even though you hand over some of the money months or even years later).

Monthly savings schemes

If you have invested in unit trusts or investment trusts through a monthly savings scheme since before 6 April 1998, working out your gains and losses could be very complicated. (But because of changes to the share identification rules the complications disappear for investments made on or after 6 April 1998.) For these pre-April 1998 savings, you would have to work out the gain, indexation allowance and taper relief for each instalment you invested when making a disposal. If you have been investing in a monthly savings scheme since before 6 April 1998, you can opt for a simplified method of working out the initial costs and indexation allowance for instalments invested up to the end of the accounting year of the fund after that date.

For each year the simplified method applies, it assumes that all 12 monthly instalments for a year were made in the seventh month. So if you invested £100 a month in a fund with an accounting year that runs from 1 January to 31 December, you could assume that you invested 12 × £100 = £1,200 in July, the seventh month.

You may have to add in or deduct extra amounts:

- any distribution or dividend reinvested during the year is added to your investment. So a £50 dividend added to your fund in the above example would take the amount you had invested in July to £1,200 + £50 = £1,250

- extra savings over and above the regular instalments are included, provided you don't add more than twice the monthly instalment in any month – a bigger payment is treated as a separate investment

- if you increase the monthly instalments, the extra is added to the year's investment so long as the increase is in or before the seventh month (if later, it is added to next year's fund)

- small withdrawals are deducted if they are less than a quarter of the amount invested in the year by regular instalments (if withdrawals exceed this amount, the simplified calculation cannot be used).

To opt for this simplified method, you must write to your tax inspector within two years of the end of the first tax year after 6 April 1998 in which you dispose of the units or shares and any of the following applies:

- you face a capital gains tax bill

- the disposal proceeds are more than twice the amount of the tax-free band for the year (more than £18,400 for the 2007–8 tax year, more than £17,600 for 2006–7)

- your other disposals in the year create net losses.

Details are contained in Revenue statement of practice SP2/99 available from tax offices and www.hmrc.gov.uk.

How to reduce or delay your capital gains tax bill

There are a number of ways to reduce or delay a CGT bill. For a start, it is important to claim all the allowable expenses you can (p. 127), indexation allowance (p. 128) and taper relief (p. 133). Also, take advantage of the special rules for disposing of assets owned before 31 March 1982 (p. 129). Then use the tax-free capital gains allowance you can make each year (see p. 136) and don't overlook losses which you can set off against gains (see p. 131).

These are all ways to minimise your tax bill once you have made a disposal. But there are several steps you can take before reaching a disposal to keep your tax bill down:

- ▩ take advantage of the allowances of your spouse or civil partner (below)

- ▩ make the best use of losses (see p. 146)

- ▩ pass the tax bill for gifts of business assets ànd certain other gifts on to the recipient if possible, or pay it in instalments if not (see p. 146)

- ▩ invest the gains from any disposals in growing businesses if you don't need the proceeds immediately – you may be able to defer the tax bill by claiming capital gains deferral relief on buying shares through the EIS (see pp. 96 and 148)

- ▩ claim the special reliefs which can reduce your tax bill if you are disposing of a business or farm (see p. 148).

It will help in minimising your capital gains tax bill if you keep a record of the assets you have acquired which may fall into the tax net, together with relevant receipts (for example, for allowable expenses).

Husbands, wives and civil partners

Spouses and civil partners are treated as separate individuals for capital gains tax. They pay tax on their own gains and can deduct their losses only from their own gains. They have their own tax-free allowances to deduct from their own net chargeable gains.

But if a married or registered couple living together dispose of assets to each other, this is ignored for the purposes of capital gains tax. For example, if a husband buys shares worth £10,000 in June 2002 and gives them to his wife at a later date, her gain or loss when she sells them will be calculated as if she had bought them for £10,000 in June 2002. Anything they pay each other on such transfers is ignored.

A married or registered couple is treated as living together unless legally separated or where the separation appears to be permanent. Gifts between spouses or civil partners in the year of separation are free of capital gains tax, but after this, tax may be payable. For more about marriage and capital gains tax, see Help Sheet IR281 *Husband and wife, divorce and separation*. The information in this Help Sheet also applies to civil partners.

Tax-saving ideas 85 and 86

Since there is no capital gains tax on gifts between spouses or civil partners, you can effectively double your tax-free band if you are married by giving assets to your spouse to dispose of. So in 2007–8 a married couple can effectively make £18,400 of disposals.

A gift of more recently acquired shares to your husband or wife can help you drill down through the share identification rules to match a sale with an earlier purchase.

Making the best use of losses

If your allowable losses in a tax year look likely to mean you will not be able to use the whole tax-free allowance for the year, there are two options:

■ make more disposals to increase your chargeable gains – by selling some shares that have done well, for example

■ hold back on loss-making disposals to a later year when there are no gains or they can be used to reduce future gains.

Gifts

If you give away certain assets or sell them for less than their market value, you can avoid paying capital gains tax by claiming hold-over relief. This means the recipient is treated as having acquired the assets when you did and having paid the costs you paid (less anything paid to you). The recipient's agreement is necessary, since he or she is taking over the tax bill for your period of ownership.

Hold-over relief is available only for the following gifts, however:

■ business assets

■ heritage property

■ gifts to political parties

■ gifts which result in an immediate inheritance tax bill. Since 22 March 2006, this includes lifetime gifts to most types of trust.

Hold-over relief cannot normally apply to a gift to a settlor-interested trust, in other words, a trust in which you have an interest (or later acquire an interest) by, for example, being one of a class of beneficiaries who can receive benefits from the trust. There are also restrictions if a trust (in which you do not have an interest) makes a gain on property which has been the subject of both a hold-over relief claim and a claim for private residence relief (see Chapter 6).

If the person you have made the gift to becomes non-resident without having sold or given it away, you might have to pay a capital gains tax bill.

There is no point in claiming hold-over relief if your net taxable gains for the year, including the gift, will be covered by the tax-free allowance (£9,200 in 2007–8 and £8,800 in 2006–7). There would be no capital gains tax for you to pay, but you might add to the tax the person you are making the gift to has to pay eventually.

Example

In August 2007, Suzy Richmond gave a second home to a discretionary trust under which the home could be used for the benefit of any of her grandchildren. (Suzy herself cannot benefit at all under the terms of the trust.) She had owned the home since April 1990 when she bought it for £60,000.

By August 2007, there was a chargeable gain of £100,000 on the property but, instead of paying tax on this, Suzy and the trust jointly claimed hold-over relief. This means when the trust eventually sells or gives away the property, the trust will be treated as if it had owned the home since April 1990 and the initial value will be £60,000.

However, under anti-avoidance rules introduced from 10 December 2003, the trust may not claim private residence relief if the grandchildren use the home as their main residence, having had hold-over relief. To be eligible for private residence relief, Suzy and the trust would have to forgo the claim for hold-over relief, in which case Suzy would have to pay tax on the £100,000 gain. The trust's initial value would then be the market value of the property at the time of the gift.

Business assets include land or buildings used by the business, goodwill, fixed plant and machinery, and shares or securities of a trading company, where the company is unlisted (but including those quoted on AIM – the Alternative Investment Market) or is the transferer's personal company.

If you make a gift of land or certain types of shareholdings which do not qualify for hold-over relief, you may be able to pay the capital gains tax in ten annual instalments. The shareholdings in question are a controlling shareholding in a company or minority holdings in unquoted companies. Interest is charged on the unpaid tax in the usual way. For more about hold-over relief, see Help Sheet IR295 *Relief for gifts and similar transactions*.

Tax-saving idea 87

If you give, say a second home to a discretionary trust and one of the beneficiaries uses the property as their main home, you have to choose between hold-over relief on the gift or private residence relief (see Example above). But provided the property counts as a business asset – say, a furnished holiday letting (see Chapter 19) – you can still claim both business asset hold-over relief and private residence relief.

Capital gains deferral relief

If you're facing a capital gains tax bill that you can't reduce by claiming losses or other reliefs, consider investing the gain in the shares of certain types of small companies through the Enterprise Investment Scheme (EIS) (see p. 96). You can claim deferral relief which allows you to put off the tax bill.

You must make the investment any time between one year before and three years after the disposal that produces the gain. The amount of the gain that you reinvest will generally be taxed only when you eventually sell the shares. If there is a gain when you dispose of EIS shares and you reinvest in shares in another EIS company, you can treat this as a single investment in calculating taper relief when you sell the second lot. This is designed to encourage 'serial entrepreneurs' by giving an incentive to reinvest gains on successful EIS companies in new ones.

Businesses and farms

If you are disposing of a business or farm, you could face an enormous tax bill on the gain. There are two reliefs to reduce the impact on entrepreneurs and others who create small businesses:

- claiming taper relief (see p. 133)
- roll-over relief if you replace business assets (see below). With large sums at stake, it would pay to seek professional advice on this relief to ensure you meet the complex requirements.

Roll-over relief

Roll-over relief allows you to defer the capital gains tax bill when you sell or otherwise dispose of assets from your business, providing you replace them in the three years after the sale or the one year before it. You can claim relief even if you do not buy an identical replacement as long as you use the proceeds to buy another qualifying business asset. Assets which qualify include land or buildings used by the business, goodwill, fixed plant and machinery.

You usually get the relief by deducting the gain for the old asset from the acquisition cost of the new one. So when you come to sell the new asset, the gain on it has been increased by the gain on the old asset. However, if you replace again, you can claim further roll-over relief, and currently capital gains tax will not have to be paid until you fail to replace the business asset.

You can make a claim for roll-over relief up to five years after 31 January following the end of the tax year in which you dispose of the asset or the year in which you replace it if this is later. You must reinvest all of the sale proceeds from the disposal of the first asset to get full relief.

For more information see Revenue Help Sheet IR290 *Business asset rollover relief.*

10

Gifts and passing your money on

There is no space on the 2007 tax return for inheritance tax. This is because it is largely a tax on what you leave when you die (including gifts made in the seven years before). The number of estates which are taxed has been rising in recent years and now stands at around one estate in 16.

The tax rate is a hefty 40 per cent of anything over £300,000 in 2007–8. There is plenty that can be done to reduce the amount paid – as long as you plan carefully.

This chapter tells you how inheritance tax works and how to reduce the amount that goes to the Revenue. It also explains the pre-owned assets tax which came into effect from 6 April 2005 and which does have to be reported on your tax return.

How inheritance tax works

When you die, everything you own – your home, possessions, investments and savings – goes into your estate. So does money paid out by life insurance policies unless they are written in trust (see p. 159), and the value of things you have given away but reserved the right to use for yourself (gifts with reservation – see p. 161). Debts such as outstanding mortgages and funeral expenses are deducted from the total to find the value of your estate.

Inheritance tax is worked out on a rolling total of gifts you have made over the last seven years. What you leave on death is in effect your final gift. So to the estate you leave are added any gifts you made in the seven years before death unless they were tax-free gifts (see p. 153).

Some or all of your estate may be free of inheritance tax: anything left to your spouse or civil partner, or to a UK charity, for example (for a full list of what is tax-free, see opposite). These tax-free bequests and legacies are deducted from the value of your estate before the tax bill is worked out.

If the resulting total exceeds a certain limit – see table below – inheritance tax is payable on the excess at 40 per cent. So in 2007–8 if the total is £350,000, tax is payable on £350,000 – £300,000 = £50,000 and the bill would be 40% × £50,000 = £20,000.

Inheritance tax-free limits

Tax year	2006–7	2007–8	2008–9	2009–10	2010–11
Tax-free limit	£285,000	£300,000	£312,000	£325,000	£350,000

Quite separately from tax on your estate, potentially exempt transfers (see p. 154) and taxable gifts you made in the last seven years are reassessed on death and tax (or extra tax) may be due on them. Initially the person you made the gift to will be asked to pay. If they can't or won't, tax is paid from your estate. But taper relief can be claimed to reduce the tax bill if the gift was made more than three years before death (see below). Note that taper relief does not reduce the tax bill on the estate, and will only be useful if the life-time gifts exceed the nil band of £300,000.

Years between gift and death	% of inheritance tax payable
Up to 3	100%
More than 3 and up to 4	80%
More than 4 and up to 5	60%
More than 5 and up to 6	40%
More than 6 and up to 7	20%

Example

Angela Framing died in May 2007, leaving an estate worth £304,000 (largely the value of her home). In December 1999, she had made a taxable gift of £10,000 to help a grandchild with the cost of studying. Subsequently, in August 2000, she gave another grandchild a taxable gift of £5,000 to start a business.

In calculating the tax due on Angela's estate, the £15,000 of taxable lifetime gifts is added to the £304,000 left on death to produce a total of £319,000. The first £300,000 of that is free of tax, leaving £319,000 – £300,000 = £19,000 on which tax is due.

Tax at 40 per cent on £19,000 is £7,600 – tax that will be entirely paid out of Angela's estate, since the life-time gifts are deemed to use up the £300,000 before the balance is used to calculate the tax on the estate.

Gifts free of inheritance tax

Gifts that are always tax-free:

■ gifts between husband and wife or civil partners – even if the two are legally separated. But only the first £55,000 is tax-free if the gifts are to someone who is not domiciled in the UK (domicile reflects the individual's natural home, see Chapter 23).

■ gifts to UK charities and community amateur sports clubs

■ gifts to certain national institutions such as the National Trust, National Gallery, British Museum (and their Scottish, Welsh and Northern Ireland equivalents)

■ gifts of certain types of heritage property such as paintings, archives, land or historic buildings to non-profit-making concerns like local museums

■ gifts of land in the UK to registered housing associations

■ gifts of shares in a company into a trust for the benefit of most or all of the employees which will control the company

■ gifts to established political parties.

Gifts that are tax-free on death only:

■ lump sums paid out on your death by a pension scheme provided the trustees of the scheme have discretion about who gets the money

■ refunds of personal pension contributions (and interest) paid directly to someone else or a trust – in other words, not paid into your estate

■ the estate of anyone killed on active military service in war or whose death was hastened by such service

■ £10,000 ex gratia payments received by survivors (and their spouses) held as Japanese prisoners of war during World War Two and amounts from other specified schemes that also provide compensation for wrongs suffered during the war.

Gifts that are tax-free in lifetime only:

■ anything given to an individual more than seven years before your death – unless there are strings attached (see p. 161)

■ small gifts worth up to £250 to any number of people in any tax year. But you can't give anyone more than this limit and claim exemption on the first £250 – if you give someone £500, the whole £500 will be taxable unless it is tax-free for one of the other reasons below

- regular gifts that are treated as normal expenditure out of income. The gifts must come out of your after-tax income and not from your capital. After paying for the gifts, you should have enough income to maintain your normal standard of living

- gifts on marriage to a bride or groom or on registration to civil partners: each parent of the bride, groom or partner can give £5,000, grandparents or remoter relatives and the bride, groom or partners themselves can give £2,500 and anyone else £1,000. The gifts must be made before the big day – and if the marriage or registration is called off, the gift becomes taxable

- gifts for the maintenance of your family – your current or a former husband, wife or civil partner, certain dependent relatives and children under 18 or still in full-time education. The children can be yours, stepchildren, adopted children or any other children in your care

- up to £3,000 in total a year of other gifts. If you don't use the whole £3,000 annual exemption in one year, you can carry forward the unused part to the next tax year only. You can't use the annual exemption to top up the small gifts exemption. If you give someone more than £250 in a year, all of it must come off the annual exemption if it is to be free of inheritance tax.

Planning for inheritance tax

If your estate is likely to be well below the threshold for paying inheritance tax, there is no need to worry about it. But if it looks as if you are above it, there is much you can do to reduce the tax bill. An important first step is to draw up a will which will make you think about what you own and how you want it to be disposed of after you die.

Many of the ways of minimising inheritance tax involve making gifts which are free of tax or making potentially taxable gifts more than seven years before your death. But remember your heirs will still gain from what you leave them even if tax is due on your estate. Don't give away so much that you or your spouse are left impoverished in old age, merely to cheat the Revenue of every last penny of tax.

Tax-free gifts and PETs

If you do have some resources to spare, make as full use as possible of the annual £3,000 exemption, regular gifts out of income and such like. And make sure your spouse has enough to make similar gifts tax-free.

Tax-saving ideas 88, 89 and 90

Draw up a will. There are simple steps you can take to minimise the tax payable on your estate when you die and to reduce the complications for those you leave behind.

Make as full use as possible of the lifetime gifts you can make which do not fall into the inheritance tax net, such as those which count as normal expenditure from income or fall within the £3,000 annual allowance.

Share your wealth with your spouse or civil partner so that you can each make tax-free lifetime gifts and efficient wills. There is no inheritance tax or capital gains tax (see Chapter 9) on gifts between spouses or civil partners.

If you want to make larger gifts, the earlier you make them the better – because inheritance tax may have to be paid on a gift if you die within seven years of making it. For this reason, most lifetime gifts are called potentially exempt transfers (PETs). They are potentially free of inheritance tax but you must survive for seven years after they are made for the tax to be avoided.

Even if you die within seven years of making the gift, there will be no inheritance tax if the gift is fully covered by your nil-rate band. If tax is payable, it will be reduced by taper relief (see p. 152) if the gift was made more than three years before your death. Tax is initially due from the person to whom you made the gift but, if they can't or won't pay, your estate has to pick up the bill.

Note that gifts in your lifetime, other than cash, may mean a capital gains tax bill – see Chapter 9.

Share your wealth

A married couple or civil partners can share their wealth – what they give to each other is free of inheritance tax. Each can then make tax-free gifts and leave a taxable estate of up to £300,000 without paying inheritance tax.

In practice, it may not be easy to split your worldly goods and give them away during your lifetime. It may make more sense to pass all or most of them on to the survivor so he or she has enough to live on. But this principle of estate-splitting is a basic strategy to be followed where possible.

Example

Veronica McGough wants to give away as much as possible free of inheritance tax before she dies.

First, she gives £1,000 a year to each of her three children – taking advantage of the £3,000 a year annual exemption. Then she makes £250 gifts every year to each of her ten grandchildren – a total of £2,500 a year free of inheritance tax as small gifts. She also gives the maximum £2,500 to any of her grandchildren who get married.

She can afford to pay the premiums on insurance policies on her own life out of her income. So she takes out policies written in trust (see p. 159) for each of her three children. The premiums come to £60 a month each and will be tax-free as normal expenditure out of income. (When she dies, the money from the insurance policies will be paid straight to the children without being taxable.)

Overall, Veronica manages to give away almost £7,660 every year free of inheritance tax. Even if she dies within seven years of making the gifts, there will be no inheritance tax to pay on them because they are all exempt gifts.

Your home

Your home is almost certainly your most valuable possession – and may be the main reason why your estate ends up over the threshold for paying inheritance tax. But it is one of the hardest assets to remove from the tax net – assuming you intend to go on living in it until you die.

For example, you can't make a lifetime gift of it to your children on condition you can continue to live in it. That would count as a gift with reservation (see p. 161), and the home would still be treated as yours. More complex planning might trigger a charge to the pre-owned asset tax (see p. 163).

If your home is jointly owned with someone as joint tenants, your share automatically goes to the survivor when one of you dies. But if you jointly own your home with someone else as tenants in common, you can bequeath your half-share to anyone you please. For example, if you had a tenancy in common with your spouse, you could bequeath half of your half-share to your spouse and the other half to a trust set up under your will (see opposite). This would reduce the size of your spouse's estate but leave them in control of at least part of the home.

Example

Alan and Meg Riordan realise there could be a hefty inheritance tax bill when they die, since most of their assets are in Alan's name. They decide to reduce the future bill by estate-splitting.

They divide their assets between them, and bequeath £300,000 each to their children in their wills, with the rest to each other. When the first dies, the £300,000 bequest to the children will be at or below the threshold for inheritance tax.

The second to die will thus leave £300,000 less to fall into the tax net, saving £120,000 in tax.

There is no inheritance tax to pay if you leave part or all of a home to your spouse or civil partner, since such gifts are always tax-free. But a gift to anyone who is not your spouse or civil partner is taxable, unless it falls within the £300,000 tax-free limit.

Consider will trusts

One way spouses and civil partners may be able to leave assets, including the family home, to each other and still use their £300,000 tax-free limit is by each setting up a discretionary trust in their will. The will should leave £300,000 to the trust – say, a £300,000 share in the family home – and appoint trustees who have the right to allow anyone in a specified class of beneficiaries to live in the home. The bequest to the trust, which is not tax-free, uses the £300,000 tax-free limit and is not part of the estate of the surviving spouse or partner. A variation on this scheme is that the surviving spouse or partner gets the whole home but issues an IOU to the discretionary trust for the £300,000 due under the terms of their late-spouse's or partner's will.

Due to changes in the way trusts are subject to inheritance tax from 22 March 2006 onwards (see box overleaf), another option would be to set up an interest-in-possession trust on your death provided that it did not comply with the rules for an immediate-post-death-interest (IPDI) trust. You could use this to give your spouse the right to remain in the home during their lifetime with the home passing to your children on your spouse's death.

Inheritance tax and trusts

A trust is a legal arrangement where one or more people (the trustees) hold assets (the trust property) to be used for the benefit of one or more people (the beneficiaries) in accordance with the rules of the trust. The person who gives the trust property is called the settlor. There are two main types of trust:

- **interest in possession trust.** The beneficiary/ies have the right to use the trust property or receive income from it during their lifetime or for some other specified period. They are said to have the life interest. Other beneficiaries, or sometimes the same people, have the right to become the outright owners of the trust property when the life interest ends – this is called the reversionary interest
- **discretionary trust.** The trustees decide who among the beneficiaries will receive payments of income and/or capital from the trust and when this will be, subject to whatever the trust rules say.

Under the discretionary trust regime, gifts to the trust are taxable, so there is inheritance tax to pay at the time of the gift unless it falls within the £300,000 limit. In addition, there is an inheritance tax charge every ten years on the value of the trust property and exit charges when assets leave the trust. Before 22 March 2006, interest in possession trusts and certain discretionary trusts, called accumulation and maintenance (A&M) trusts, were subject to a more lenient regime under which gifts to the trust counted as potentially exempt transfers, there were no ten-yearly or exit charges and, where someone had a life interest, they were treated as if they owned the trust assets for inheritance tax purposes.

From 22 March 2006 onwards, the discretionary trust regime applies to nearly all types of trust, including interest in possession trusts and A&M trusts. The few exceptions are:

- immediate-post-death-interest (IPDI) trusts set up in a will to give a life interest to a survivor
- bereaved minor trusts set up in a will to benefit a dependent child of the person who has died
- disabled person's trusts set up either in life or on death to benefit a person with a physical or mental disability.

Transitional rules apply to trusts already in existence at 22 March 2006.

The wording of the trust document must be absolutely correct and the trust properly run. Be aware, too, that stamp duty land tax might be payable on the transfer of all or part of the home to the trust. However, this can usually be avoided. It is essential to get the help of a solicitor.

Life insurance

If you want to make sure there is enough money to pay an inheritance tax bill on a home or business, you can take out a term life insurance policy which pays out if you die within seven years of giving it away. And if you plan to leave a large asset on death, whole life insurance policies pay out whenever you die, again providing cash to pay the inheritance tax.

Tax-saving ideas 91, 92 and 93

Holding assets as tenants in common rather than joint tenants gives you flexibility over how you leave your share of those assets and so can save tax. You can sever a joint tenancy by writing to the co-owner(s).

Using your will to set up a will trust may let you use your £300,000 tax-free limit (ultimately saving £120,000 – or more) and still ensure that your spouse or civil partner is financially secure or able to stay on in the family home.

Use life insurance to blunt the impact of inheritance tax. Policies written in trust go straight to the beneficiary and don't form part of your estate. Premiums you pay are tax-free gifts if they count as normal expenditure out of income or fall within the £3,000 a year exemption.

Make sure you have any such policies written in trust to the person you want to have the money. The proceeds will then be paid directly to that person on your death and be free of inheritance tax. The premiums for a policy written in trust count as gifts, but will be free of inheritance tax if the policy is for your spouse or civil partner. And if you pay the premiums as normal spending out of income or the £3,000 annual allowance applies, they will be tax-free whoever benefits.

Shares

The market value of any shares left on death must normally be included in your estate in working out the inheritance tax bill. But some sorts of shares qualify for business relief (also available on lifetime gifts). This reduces the value for inheritance tax purposes – or even removes them from the calculation altogether:

- shares in a listed company which form a controlling interest, the value of the shares is halved

- unquoted shares in most companies – including those listed on the Alternative Investment Market (AIM) – qualify for full relief

- unquoted securities which either alone or with other securities and unquoted shares give you a controlling interest qualify for full relief.

To prevent 'death-bed' purchases of business property, all these shares and securities must have been owned for at least two years.

Your own business or farm

If you own or have an interest in a small business or a farm, seek professional advice on inheritance tax, since there are substantial concessions which can reduce or eliminate the tax:

- business relief means there will be no inheritance tax to pay on business assets such as goodwill, land, buildings, plant, stock, patents and so on (reduced by debts incurred in the business)
- agricultural relief can mean no inheritance tax on the agricultural value of owner-occupied farmlands and farm tenancies (including cottages and farm buildings). There are also reliefs for landowners who let farmland.

Estate freezing

Estate freezing is a way of freezing some of the value of your wealth now so the increase in value in future years benefits someone else.

A simple way of doing this is by investing in an endowment or unit-linked life insurance policy written in trust for your children or grandchildren (see p. 159). Any growth in its value accumulates in the policy free of inheritance tax. Some unit trust managers can do something similar with investments in unit trusts.

Changing inheritances after a death

Whether or not there is a will, those who are entitled to a share of a dead person's estate can agree to vary the way the estate is divided up and this may save tax. For example, the variation could direct some of the estate towards tax-free bequests – from the children to the dead person's husband or wife, for example. The variation must be made within two years of the date of death. Get advice from a solicitor who can draw up a suitably worded deed.

Tax-saving ideas 94, 95 and 96

Consider estate freezing by, for example, paying premiums to an investment-type life insurance policy written in trust for the person to whom you wish to make the gift. They get any growth in the value of the investment instead of it counting as part of your estate.

A deed of variation can be used to alter the way an estate is shared out. This could save tax on a subsequent death where, say, part of a tax-free bequest to a spouse or civil partner was diverted instead to a child or grandchild and the new gift fell within the deceased's £300,000 tax-free limit.

If a subsequent death occurs within two years, it may be more tax-efficient to use a deed of variation rather than claim successive charges relief (see p. 163).

Inheritance tax planning pitfalls

You might think that there are some rather obvious wheezes that will help you avoid inheritance tax. It is unlikely that the Revenue will not have thought of them and blocked their use.

Gifts with strings attached

If you give something away but reserve the right to use it, it counts as a gift with reservation – and is treated as remaining your property. The gift would not be recognised for inheritance tax purposes and its value would be added to your estate when you died. This applies to any such gifts made on or after 18 March 1986.

For example, if you give your home to a child on condition that you can go on living in it until your death, this would count as a gift with reservation. This could apply even if there was no formal agreement that you go on living in the home.

Accountants, insurance companies and others have been fairly successful in devising schemes – often using trusts and generally complicated – that let you continue to enjoy the income or use of an asset that you have given away without falling foul of the gift with reservation rules. The Revenue has now pulled the plug on most of these schemes by introducing the pre-owned assets tax (see p. 163).

Associated operations

If you try to get round the inheritance tax rules by making a series of gifts, the Revenue is allowed to treat them as associated operations which form a single direct gift. For example, you might think you could give an extra £2,500 to an adult child by making ten tax-free gifts of £250 to friends which they pass on. The taxman will treat this as a single £2,500 gift, however – and potentially subject to tax.

Related property

In working out the value of a bequest or gift, the Revenue may treat as yours property which it reckons is related to yours – in particular, anything owned by your husband, wife or civil partner. This means you can't reduce its value by splitting it with your spouse or partner.

Suppose, for example, you own 30 per cent of the shares in a company and your spouse owns another 30 per cent. The Revenue will value your 30 per cent as worth half the value of a 60 per cent controlling interest, which is generally higher than the value of a 30 per cent minority interest.

Retroactive/retrospective legislation

The government has made clear that it is prepared to introduce further new tax charges (like the pre-owned assets tax – see p. 163) to ensure that successful tax-avoidance schemes do not after all save tax.

Payment of inheritance tax

Inheritance tax is due six months after the end of the month in which death occurred. If tax is due, you need to make a return to the Revenue on form IHT200. In other cases, you can normally use the much simpler form IHT210. In general, the property in the estate cannot be distributed until probate has been granted, but probate will not be granted until the tax has been paid. Therefore, the personal representatives may have to borrow to pay the tax bill. However, certain National Savings & Investments products can be used before probate solely for paying tax and, since 2003, the balances in the deceased's bank and building society accounts can usually also be used in this way.

Interest is charged if the tax is paid after the six-month deadline, running from the time the tax was due. Likewise, if you pay too much inheritance tax, you will get interest on the over-payment from the Revenue.

Example

Maurice Thornton inherits a half-share of his mother's estate, worth £160,000. Inheritance tax of £7,000 is due on this share.

However, Maurice's mother had inherited £80,000 from her father only two-and-a-half years earlier – an inheritance on which tax of £20,000 had been paid. Because Maurice's legacy is within five years of his mother's own legacy, he is entitled to reduce the inheritance tax on his legacy by a fraction of what was paid on hers.

The fraction of the tax bill on his mother's legacy which can be taken into account is worked out as follows:

$$\frac{£80,000}{£80,000 + £20,000}$$
$$= \frac{£80,000}{£100,000}$$
$$= \%$$

This means if the second death had occurred within one year of the first, the tax bill would be reduced to % × £20,000 = £16,000. However, the period between the two deaths is two-and-a-half years, so the fraction is reduced to just 60 per cent (100 per cent less 20 per cent for each complete year) of %. This means the tax bill can be reduced by 60% × £16,000 = £9,600.

If you take out a loan to pay inheritance tax before probate is granted, you can get tax relief on the interest on it for up to 12 months by setting it against taxable income accruing to the estate after death and before distribution.

You can spread inheritance tax on land, property and business assets over ten equal yearly instalments.

If you inherit investments or land and buildings which fall in value after the death of the person who bequeathed them, you might be able to reduce the inheritance tax bill.

Where you make a lifetime gift that is neither tax-free nor a PET, you must report the gift to the Revenue on form IHT100 if the total of such gifts during the tax year comes to more than £10,000 or your running total of such gifts over the past ten years comes to more than £40,000. Report the gift within 12 months of the end of the month in which you made it.

Facing a second inheritance tax bill within five years?

If you inherit something that has only recently been subject to inheritance tax, the tax due on this second change of ownership is reduced by what is known as successive charges relief (formerly quick succession relief). Provided the death which led to the first payment was within five years of the death that has led to a second tax bill, the second bill can be reduced by a fraction of the first bill.

If the first death was within one year of the second death, the second bill is reduced by the following fraction of the first bill:

$$\frac{\text{Value of inheritance at the time of first transfer}}{\text{Value of inheritance at transfer + tax paid on first transfer}}$$

If the first death was more than one year before the second death, the fraction is reduced by 20 per cent for each complete year – see example opposite.

Pre-owned assets tax

If you still use something you have given away or sold for less than its full value at any time since 18 March 1986 and the gift is not caught by the gift with reservation rules (see p. 161) it may from 6 April 2005 be caught instead by the pre-owned assets tax (POAT). The tax may also apply to something you use which belongs to someone to whom you made a cash gift in the last seven years.

POAT is an extra charge to income tax that aims to tax the yearly benefit you are deemed to get from your continued use of the gift. You can be liable for POAT even if you have no income with which to pay it. You will need to report any POAT liability on your tax return (see p. 206).

With land and property, the benefit you are deemed to get is the market rent you would otherwise pay. For chattels (for example, paintings and antiques) and other assets, the benefit is a percentage of the asset's market value. The percentage is the official rate of interest (see p. 116) which was 6.25 per cent in April 2007. The taxable value is reduced by anything you actually pay for using the asset under a legally binding agreement. Land, property and chattels need to be valued every five years.

There are some exceptions. For example, there will be no POAT charge if:

- the value of all the items otherwise subject to POAT is £5,000 or less (before deducting anything you pay)
- you sold the whole of the asset you still use for its full market value
- the gift was covered by the £3,000 yearly inheritance tax exemption or the £250 small gift exemption (see p. 153–4)
- you gave away your home to your children, say, but now have to live with them because of old age or illness
- you gave away a part-share of the asset – for example, your home – which you share with the co-owner(s) and you pay your full share of the expenses (or more) so you derive no benefit from the arrangement
- this is an equity release scheme with a commercial company. Non-commercial equity release schemes (for example, where a family member buys a share of your home) are exempt if the transaction was completed before 7 March 2005 or the payment is not in money or readily convertible assets (for example, in return for personal care when you have become infirm). But the transaction is not exempt if you have sold only part of your home to someone connected to you. 'Connected' is defined very widely to mean any ancestor (parent, grandparent and so on), any descendant (child, grandchild and so on), brother, sister, uncle, aunt, nephew, niece, your spouse or civil partner and any of their relatives, and any husbands and wives of any of your, your spouse's or civil partner's relatives.

Tax-saving ideas 97, 98 and 99

If a relative – say, a son or daughter – offers to buy part of your home as a way of giving you cash while you still live in the home, the arrangement will be caught by POAT and you may have to pay tax each year on the benefit you are deemed to receive. But POAT will not apply if you sell them the whole of your home at its full market value. And, even where you sell only part of the property, POAT does not apply if the buyer is not treated as connected to you – for example, an unmarried partner.

To provide you with financial help, instead of a relative buying a share of your home, they could lend you money to be repaid eventually out of your estate. This would not be caught by POAT.

You will be caught by POAT if assets you use that are owned by someone else can be matched to any cash you gave them within the previous seven years. But there are no forward matching rules. So you may escape POAT if, say, your children pay for your home by building a granny annexe onto their home and later on you are able to give them some financial help.

What to do about POAT

Make the most of the exemptions opposite. But if POAT seems likely to apply, you have three choices:

■ stay within the POAT regime. You can reduce or eliminate the bill if under a legally binding agreement you pay the owner of the asset for using it

■ unravel the arrangement so that it is instead caught by the gift with reservation rules

■ elect to be treated as if the gift with reservation rules apply. This means the asset will be treated as if it is part of your estate on your death so inheritance tax may become due. But there is no elimination of capital gains on your death (see p. 123) and the current owner's acquisition value for CGT is still the value at the time of the gift.

To elect to be treated as if gift with reservation applies, for assets you already used before 6 April 2005, you had to make the election by 31 January 2007 for it to apply from 6 April 2005 onwards. For assets you start to use after that date, you must make the election by 31 January following the end of the tax year in which you first become liable for POAT. For example, if you first start to use the asset in the 2007–8 tax year, you must make the election by 31 January 2009. However, following Budget 2007, all is not lost if you miss the deadline because the Revenue has been given new powers to accept a late election. The election is made by you alone but you might wish to discuss it with the owner of the asset who could become liable for inheritance tax on your death. Make the election on form IHT500 and send it to the Revenue Capital Taxes Office (see Appendix E).

Tax-saving ideas 100 and 101

If a transaction is caught by POAT but you want to make future gifts to the person to whom you sold or gave the asset, consider paying them a full market rent under a legally binding agreement. POAT is then reduced to zero and the rent stands in place of the gifts you want to make. But the recipient will be taxed on the rental income.

If you use an asset you gave away and are caught by POAT, consider electing for the gift with reservation rules to apply instead if the value of your estate will in any case be below the inheritance tax-free limit (£300,000 in 2007–8).

Filling in your tax return

11

Getting started

When you receive your tax return for the 2006–7 tax year, this is what you should have:

- a 12-page booklet entitled Tax Return. We show you how to complete these pages in Chapters 12 to 14

- supplementary pages for the tax return to cater for your individual circumstances – there are nine sets of supplementary pages (see below). If your tax office knows that a supplement is relevant to you it may be bound into your tax return. We explain how to complete these pages in Chapters 15 to 23. There is also a new one-page additional form on which to report less common situations relating to pension schemes (see page 179).

- a Tax Return Guide. This consists of 34 pages which explain how to complete the 12 pages of the tax return (see above) plus extra pages on how to fill in any supplements bound into your tax return

- a 17-page Tax Calculation Guide. But if your tax affairs are complex, you'll need to ask for the 34-page Comprehensive Tax Calculation Guide or use the Revenue's Internet Service (see Chapter 3).

Short tax returns

You may have received a short tax return (four pages and no supplements). See Appendix C on p. 372 for a guide to completing the short return.

What you should do next

Step 1

Make sure you have the correct supplementary pages.

Step 2

If one or more of the supplementary pages you need are missing, contact the Revenue. The Orderline is open every day from 8 am to 10 pm, except Christmas Day, Boxing Day and New Year's Day. The phone number is 0845 9000 404, fax number is 0845 9000 604 or you can write to PO Box 37, St Austell, PL25 5YN. Alternatively, you can download the pages you need from the Revenue website www.hmrc.gov.uk/sa/forms/content.htm.

Step 3

Gather together all your records and supporting documentation, which you need to fill in the tax return.

Step 4

Fill in your supplementary pages FIRST, using the advice in Chapters 15 to 23 of this Guide. If you need further help, contact your tax office (see your return or correspondence) or, if that is closed, the Revenue helpline on 0845 9000 444. The helpline is open 8 am to 8 pm every day except Christmas Day, Boxing Day and New Year's Day and can give general advice.

Step 5

After filling in the supplementary pages, complete the tax return.

Step 6

If you are not going to work out your tax bill yourself, send in your tax return and supplementary pages by 30 September 2007, or by 31 January 2008 if you file by internet (see Chapter 3).

Step 7

If you want to calculate your own tax – and we recommend that you don't – use your Tax Calculation Guide. But if any of the following apply, you will not be able to use the guide sent with your tax return:

■ you have filled in any of the supplementary pages other than the

Employment pages, Self-employment pages or Land and property pages

▪ you received any scrip dividends or non-qualifying distributions (boxes 10.21 to 10.26 on page 3 of the main tax return)

▪ you received any gains on UK life insurance policies or refund of additional voluntary contributions (question 12 on the main return)

▪ you received any taxable lump sums (box 1.29 in the Employment supplement)

▪ you received a lump sum as a result of deferring your state pension

▪ you can claim higher rate relief on annuity or covenant payments you make for commercial reasons connected to your business (box 15.9 on page 6 of the main tax return)

▪ you have made a compulsory payment to an employer's scheme to provide death benefits for your widow, widower or children and unusually you did not get relief through PAYE (box 15.11)

▪ you are claiming an allowance against higher rate tax on cash received from the redemption of bonus shares (box 15.12).

If any of these apply and you want to calculate your own tax, contact the Orderline (see p. 170) and ask for the Comprehensive Tax Calculation Guide or consider using software to file by internet (see Chapter 3).

Step 8

If you are an employee and the tax you owe is less than £2,000, choose to send in your tax return and supplementary pages by 30 September, or, if you use the internet, by 30 December. Then you can ask to pay your tax bill through the PAYE system on a monthly basis starting in April 2008.

Step 9

Otherwise send in your tax return, supplementary pages and tax calculation by 31 January 2008. Send your final tax payment for the 2006–7 tax year by the same date. If you pay tax by making payments on account (see Chapter 3), you must also make your first payment for 2007–8 at this time.

The supplementary pages

On page 2 of the basic tax return you are asked nine questions. If you answer yes to a question you will need to fill in the corresponding supplementary pages. If you have not been sent those pages automatically you will need to ask for them from the Orderline (see p. 170).

Employment

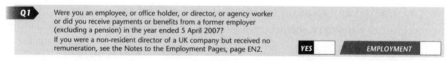

You are required to fill in the Employment supplementary pages if you answer YES to this question. If you have more than one job, you will need a set of Employment pages for each job. The Revenue will regard you as an employee even if you work on a part-time or casual basis. There are more guidelines on who counts as an employee in Chapter 15.

Share schemes

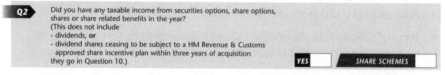

If you receive shares or options under one of the special approved schemes which are tax-free and you kept to the rules of scheme, you aren't required to complete this supplement. You will have to fill it in if in 2006–7 you have received securities options, share options, shares or share-related benefits in any other way or you have broken the rules of an approved scheme. Chapter 16 gives a lot of background information on share schemes and guides you through the completion of this supplement.

Self-employment

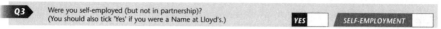

If you carried on a trade, profession or vocation as a self-employed person during 2006–7 you need to complete this supplementary section. Chapter 17 has guidelines on who counts as self-employed.

If you are in partnership you need to complete a different set of supplementary pages (see below).

Partnership

If you are in business with one or more partners, you should answer YES to this question and complete a set of supplementary pages. There is a short version and a long version. You will find guidance on which version you should complete in Chapter 18.

Land and Property

You need to complete these supplementary pages if you receive income from land and property, furnished holiday accommodation, or providing furnished accommodation in your home during 2006–7. However, if you provide additional services, such as meals, you will need to complete the Self-employment supplementary pages instead, as you are considered to be carrying on a trade. You can get more guidance by turning to Chapter 19.

If you have a property abroad that you rent out, you need the Foreign supplement (see below) not this one.

Foreign

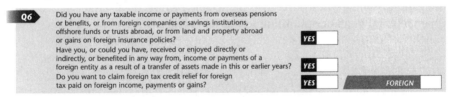

There are five supplementary pages which have space to give details about your foreign savings, pensions and benefits, income from offshore trusts, gains on foreign life policies, property income and other investment income from abroad. Ask for it if you received any such income or benefit in 2006–7 or if you answered yes to any of the three questions above. If you turn to Chapter 20 you will find more information on what is foreign income and how it is taxed.

Trusts etc.

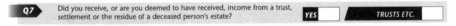

You need to complete this supplement if you were a beneficiary or settlor of a trust, or had income from the estate of someone who has died. You can find more information and guidance on filling in this supplementary page in Chapter 21. A beneficiary of a bare trust enters the income in the basic tax return, see p. 182.

Capital gains

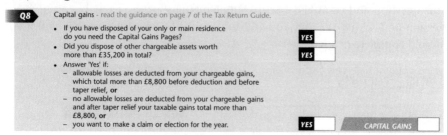

You must complete these supplementary pages if you have made a capital gain (with some exceptions – see below) or you wish to claim an allowable capital loss for 2006–7.

You normally won't need to return the supplementary pages if your gains for the year totalled £8,800 or less (the tax-free slice for the year) and the value of the assets you disposed of totalled no more than £35,200 (four times the tax-free slice). Do not include tax-free gains or assets in these calculations (such as the sale of your main home if the gain was tax-free).

For more information on which gains are tax-free and guidance on whether the gain on selling your home will be taxable or not, see Chapter 9. See Chapter 22 for guidance on filling in the supplement.

Non-residence etc.

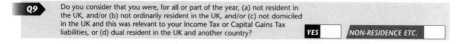

If at any time during 2006–7, you consider yourself to be non-resident, not ordinarily resident or not domiciled in the UK, or resident in the UK at the same time as being resident in a country with which the UK has a double taxation agreement, then you will need to complete this supplement. Chapter 23 will give you guidance.

Pensions – tax charges and taxable lump sums

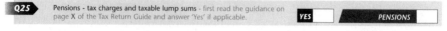

You will need this extra page if:

- you have drawn benefits from a pension scheme and, when added to previously drawn benefits, their value exceeds your lifetime allowance (£1.5 million in 2006–7 for most people)

■ the value of your pension savings has increased by more than the annual allowance (£215,000 in 2006–7)

■ you have received any unauthorised payments from a pension scheme on which tax is due

■ you have received certain lump sum payments from overseas pension schemes.

This is a complex area and your pension scheme should be able to help you decide whether you need to complete this page. You do not need this page if you are simply receiving a pension from a scheme – you report this on the main tax return.

Completing the tax return

You can fill in the first half of the tax return, using Chapters 12–14 of this guide. Chapter 12 completes the Income pages, Chapter 13 explains the Reliefs sections and Chapter 14 deals with the Allowances pages.

In the last half of the tax return, you are asked for information about student loan repayments, your tax bill, tax repayments and refunds. The main return continues onto the extra Pensions page if that is relevant to you.

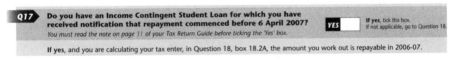

Q17 Do you have an Income Contingent Student Loan for which you have received notification that repayment commenced before 6 April 2007? **YES** If yes, tick this box. If not applicable, go to Question 18. *You must read the note on page 31 of your Tax Return Guide before ticking the 'Yes' box.*

If yes, and you are calculating your tax enter, in Question 18, box 18.2A, the amount you work out is repayable in 2006-07.

Student loans taken out from August 1998 onwards are 'income contingent'. This means under the current rules that you start to repay them once you're earning and your income exceeds a set threshold – £15,000 a year from 6 April 2005 (£10,000 in earlier years). If your income for 2006–7 exceeds £15,000, you are required to make a loan repayment equal to 9 per cent of the income in excess of £15,000. Some income is ignored, for example, unearned income (from savings, pensions, benefits, and so on) unless it comes to more than £2,000, and benefits in kind. In calculating your income, relief is given for pension contributions and some types of losses that qualify for tax relief. For more information, see Revenue Help Sheet IR235 *Calculation of student loan repayments on a income contingent student loan*.

If the Student Loan Company has notified you that repayment of your loan started before 6 April 2007 (and you had not fully repaid the loan before the start of the tax year on 6 April 2006), tick YES. Provided you send in your tax return by 30 September 2007, your tax office will work out the repayment due. If you are calculating the payment yourself, enter the amount later in Box 18.2A. Any amounts you've already paid back through PAYE (see p. 256) are deducted to arrive at the amount due. If you have paid back too much (which may happen in the year you finish repaying the loan if the PAYE deductions were not stopped in time), you will receive a refund.

Q18 Do you want to calculate your tax and, if appropriate, Class 4 National Insurance contributions and Student Loan Repayment? **YES** | Use your Tax Calculation Guide then fill in boxes 18.1 to 18.8 as appropriate.

Tick YES if you intend to work out your own tax bill, although we recommend that you send in your return by 30 September to let the Revenue work out the sum for you.

If you are not going to work out your own tax bill, move on to Q19.

Q19 Do you want to claim a repayment if you have paid too much tax? *(If you do not tick 'Yes' or the tax you have overpaid is below £10, we will use the amount you are owed to reduce your next tax bill.)* **YES** | If yes, tick this box. Then, if you want to give all or part of your repayment to a nominated charity, go to Question 19A; if you want to claim a repayment, go to Question 19B. If not applicable, go to Question 20.

Tick YES to claim a repayment. If you want any of the repayment paid out to you, fill in the boxes in Q19B as appropriate. The Revenue assumes you will accept repayment direct to your bank or building society account unless you don't have one. While direct payment is more secure, you can't be forced to accept payment this way. If you have an account but would prefer a cheque, tick box 19B.8.

Q19A Do you want to nominate a charity to receive all or part of your repayment? *See page 31 of your Tax Return Guide.* **YES** | If yes, tick this box and then read page 31 and 32 of your Tax Return Guide. Fill in boxes 19A.1 to 19A.5 as appropriate. If not applicable, go to Question 19B.

Alternatively you can use your tax return to instruct that part or all of a repayment be paid direct to a single charity, in which case tick YES at Q19A. You can choose only from participating charities and need to get a code for the charity from the Revenue (Tel: 0845 9000 444, www.hmrc.gov.uk or contact a local tax office). Tick box 19A.4 if you want this to be a Gift Aid donation (see p. 220 for details). You will be able to claim higher-rate tax relief on the donation if you are a higher rate taxpayer in 2007–8 by entering details at Q15A in next year's tax return (not this one).

Tax-saving idea 102

If you use your tax return to donate a tax rebate to charity, do not opt for Gift Aid (by ticking box 19A.4) if you are a non-taxpayer or you pay too little tax to cover the tax relief due on the donation. In that event, you will get a tax bill to cover the relief given. See p. 221 for more information.

If you are not sure how much your rebate will be, you can limit your donation to a maximum amount by writing a sum in box 19A.2 (instead of donating the whole rebate through box 19A.1). If your rebate comes to less than the amount in 19A.2, the whole rebate will go to charity. If the rebate comes to more, the excess will be paid back to you.

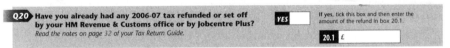

If this does not apply to you, go direct to Q21.

If YES enter the amount you were refunded, either directly from your tax office (including repayments of tax deducted from investments) or from Jobcentre Plus (such as refunds of tax deducted from jobseeker's allowance). You should also include similar amounts which, rather than being repaid directly to you, have been set against payments of tax you owe.

Enter the amount refunded for the 2006–7 tax year in box 20.1.

If your tax office sent you the return, check your details on the front page. If they are wrong, correct them, and also put a tick in the box on this page.

Q22 ▶ **Please give other personal details in boxes 22.1 to 22.7.** *This information helps us to be more efficient and effective.*

Complete the boxes with your phone number, first names, marital status and date of birth. Also give your national insurance number if you know it. If an agent (such as an accountant or tax adviser) deals with your tax return for you, include their contact details.

- If you owe tax for 2006-07 and have a PAYE tax code, we will try and collect the tax due (if it is less than £2,000) through your tax code for 2008-09. Tick box 23.1 if you do not want the tax collected through your PAYE tax code *read Key Dates on page 3 of your Tax Return Guide before completing this box.* [23.1]

If you are on PAYE and owe tax of less than £2,000, it will normally be collected through the PAYE system. You are asked to tick box 23.1 if you do not want this to happen, but do not do so without some thought. PAYE spreads out and delays the payment of your tax.

- Tick box 23.1A if you are likely to owe tax for 2007-08 on income other than employed earnings or pensions and you do not want us to use your 2007-08 PAYE tax code to collect that tax during the year [23.1A]

You may have non-PAYE income for 2006–7 which is expected to continue in 2007–8 and on which tax or extra tax is expected to be due. This might include, say, interest from savings, rents from property or earnings from freelance work. Where this income is £10,000 or less, the Revenue will usually adjust your PAYE code for 2007–8 to collect the estimated tax due. But, if you would prefer to wait and sort out the tax bill after the end of the tax year, tick box 23.1A.

- Tick box 23.2 if this Tax Return contains figures that are provisional because you do not yet have final figures. Page 31 of the Tax Return Guide explains the circumstances in which provisional figures may be used and asks for some additional information to be provided in box 23.9, on page 10

23.2

In box 23.2, you have to say whether any of the figures are provisional. If they are, don't delay sending in your tax return. In the Additional information space(s), explain which figures are provisional (including the box numbers), why they are provisional and when they will be finalised. If you know you are not going to be able to give reliable figures, because you have lost information or have had to estimate a valuation, for example, explain what they are and how you have arrived at the estimates.

If you negligently submit a provisional figure which is inaccurate or unnecessary, you may be liable to a penalty.

Do not tick box 23.2 if your tax return includes estimated figures (such as valuations) which you reckon to be final. Give details of how such figures have been estimated either in the appropriate supplements or in the additional information box 23.9 on page 10 of the main return.

- **Disclosure of tax avoidance schemes** - if you are a party to one or more disclosable tax avoidance schemes you must complete boxes 23.5 and 23.6. Give details of each scheme on a separate line. If you are party to more than 3 schemes give further details in the 'Additional information' box, box 23.9, on page 10

Scheme reference number

23.5								

Tax year in which the expected advantage arises - year ended 5 April

23.6			

Firms or employers that promote schemes designed to reduce or eliminate income tax, capital gains tax or certain other taxes are required to tell the Revenue about each scheme. Examples would be arrangements (often complicated involving, say, trusts, loans or derivatives) to reduce capital gains tax or to escape national insurance contributions on part of your pay. The Revenue allocates a number to each scheme which must be passed on to each individual using the scheme. If you have entered into such a scheme, you must declare it in boxes 23.5 and 23.6.

- **Business Premises Renovation Allowance (BPRA)** - Read page 33 of the Guide and enter the amounts of BPRA included in the capital allowances and balancing charges boxes on the Self-employment and Land and Property Pages

Capital allowance

23.7	£

Balancing charge

23.8	£

If you convert or renovate business premises in a deprived area that have been vacant for a year or more and bring them back into commercial use, you will eventually be able to claim tax relief for the full cost of your expenditure in the year you incur the expense. But the scheme did not get EU approval until 11 April 2007, so you won't need to fill in these boxes yet.

And finally

At Q24, tick any additional pages you are sending with the basic tax return. In the case of employment, self-employment and partnership, you might be including more than one set of supplementary pages (if you have changed job during the year or you have more than one job or business). So write in the relevant box the number of supplements you are sending back (even if only one). Don't forget to sign and date the declaration. If you are signing for someone else, state in what capacity you are doing this.

Tax-saving idea 103

Avoid simple mistakes that could cause your tax return to be rejected and possibly cause a £100 late-filing penalty. Common errors include: ticking yes to any of Qs 1 to 9 but failing to send the supplementary pages, sending information on a separate sheet instead of on the tax return itself, writing notes such as 'per accounts' or 'information to follow' instead of putting in figures (albeit provisional ones), and failing to sign and date the return.

Pensions

From the 2006–7 tax return onwards, there is an extra single page form on which to report the some common situations relating to pension schemes under the new pension regime which started on 6 April 2006.

Tax charges arising from UK or overseas pension savings

If you are subject to tax charges arising from UK or overseas pension savings fill in boxes 25.1 to 25.7.
Tax on pensions, retirement annuities, triviality lump sums and wind-up lump sums should not be returned here but in Question 11 of your Tax Return.

There is no limit on the pension savings you can have, but any excess over the lifetime allowance (£1.5 million for most people in 2006–7) is taxed when you draw benefits from the scheme (see Chapter 7). Give details of any excess drawn as a lump sum in box 25.1 and any excess drawn as income in box 25.2. Tax on the excess already paid by your pension scheme goes in box 25.3.

While your pension is building up, the value of your savings can increase by up to £215,000 in 2006–7. Any increase above this annual allowance is taxable and goes in box 25.4.

There are a variety of payments from pension schemes – called 'unautho-rised payments' – that attract an extra tax charge. They include, for example, a loan to you from the scheme and, in most cases, any benefit you derive from using the pension scheme's assets. Your scheme should warn you if a payment is unauthorised. Give details in boxes 25.5 to 25.7.

Taxable lump sum payments from overseas pension schemes

Fill in boxes 25.8 and 25.10 if you receive a refund of contributions (called a 'short service refund lump sum') from an overseas pension scheme. You are liable for tax at 20 per cent on the first £10,800 of the payments and 40 per cent on anything more. But you can get a credit for any foreign tax you have already paid on the refund. (Ignore box 25.9, which applies only to personal representatives filling in the tax return for someone who has died.)

12

Income

The first stage in working out your income tax bill for 2006–7 is to find your taxable income. Pages 3 and 4 of the basic tax return set out various different types of income, such as income from savings and investments, pensions and benefits, life insurance gains and other bits and pieces. You should complete this income section to tell your tax inspector what types of income and how much of each type you received. You may find it helpful to read Chapter 7.

This is not the only way in which your tax inspector will find out about your income. There are also supplementary pages, including Employment, Self-employment and Land and property, where you must give details of other sorts of income. And these should be filled in before you tackle the basic tax return.

You don't need to enter in the tax return any income which is tax-free. A comprehensive list is given in Appendix A (see p. 365).

INCOME for the year ended 5 April 2007

When entering your income in the tax return, you should enter the amount you received in 2006–7 (although in a few cases there are special rules for what counts as received). If you receive income of the same type from more than one source – for example, you have several savings accounts – enter the overall total for each type, but keep records for each separate account in case your tax office asks to see them.

When you enter amounts of income, round any odd pence down to the nearest £. When you enter amounts of tax credits or tax already deducted, round any odd pence up to the nearest £. If you are entering the total of income or tax from several sources (several savings accounts, say), add up each amount including the pence and round just the total.

Savings and investment income

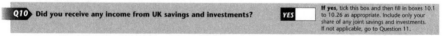

Q10 Did you receive any income from UK savings and investments?   YES   If yes, tick this box and then fill in boxes 10.1 to 10.26 as appropriate. Include only your share of any joint savings and investments. If not applicable, go to Question 11.

You can get an income from your investments or savings in the form of interest, dividends or distributions; for example, interest on a building society account, dividends from shares or distributions from unit trusts. Although the income from these sources can be paid out to you, this is not always the case. For example, interest can be added to your account rather than paid out, and with distributions from unit trusts it can be reinvested if you choose. It counts as income whether it is paid out to you or not. If you have any investment income (unless it is tax-free, see p. 184), you should tick the YES box at Q10 and fill in boxes 10.1 to 10.26.

Only enter details of investments you own. If you own an investment jointly, you need to enter only the amount in the tax return which is your share. If you are married or in a civil partnership, the income from a jointly owned investment normally will be split equally. But if you own an investment in a different proportion, the income can be split to reflect ownership (see p. 52).

Tax-saving idea 104

> Take advantage of the many ways you can save which are free of tax: pension schemes, some ISAs and many National Savings & Investment (NS&I) products. These are especially helpful if you are a higher rate taxpayer. If you are a basic rate taxpayer, check to see that any expenses, for example for managing an ISA, are not more than the tax saved.

There are many opportunities for tax saving and tax planning with investments. Chapter 7 should help you maximise your tax-efficient investing.

If you are the beneficiary of a bare trust, that is one in which you have an immediate absolute title to the capital and income, you should enter the amount of (or your share of) the income on this page of the return. Your trustee will be able to give you the details of your share. Which boxes you complete on this page depends on the type of income concerned. Income from other types of trust goes in the Trust supplement (see Chapter 21).

Your income from investments includes income from investments which you have given to your children aged 18 or less and unmarried. You need to enter details if the amount of income per child for the tax year is more than £100 before tax. This tax treatment applies even to a bare trust you have set up for your child, if the trust was set up on or after 9 March 1999. If you make additional gifts on or after that date to an existing trust, income from the extra gifts is also treated in the same way. This tax treatment also applies to money you have given your child to invest in a cash ISA, even though interest from the ISA would otherwise be tax-free. However, income produced by sums you pay into your son's or daughter's child trust fund and some other investments (see p. 94) will not be treated as your income.

Which investment income should not be included on page 3 of your tax return?

You shouldn't include in your tax return any investment income which counts as tax-free, such as income from ISAs (see box overleaf). If all your investment income is tax-free, you can skip Q10 and go straight to Q11.

These other types of income may be taxable but should go elsewhere in the tax return:

■ income from an annuity under a personal pension plan or retirement annuity contract or trust scheme. Enter on page 4 under Q11

■ gains on UK life insurance policies or life annuities or capital redemption policies. These should be included on page 4 under Q12

■ a share of any partnership investment income should be entered in the Partnership supplement

■ annual payments from UK unauthorised unit trusts. Enter under Q13.

Example

Sidney Barrow has the following investments and accounts: NS&I Certificates, a stocks and shares ISA, a cash ISA and a bank current account which pays interest on credit balances. If he didn't have the bank current account Q10 would not apply to him. But the interest payable on his bank current account means that he has to tick the YES box.

Tax-saving idea 105

Couples, where one person pays tax at the higher rate and the other does not, can adjust their investments between them, so that more investments are in the name of the lower taxpayer. Thus less of the return will be taxed at the higher rate. Couples, where one pays tax at the starting rate or pays no tax at all and the other pays at the basic rate, can save tax in the same way by shifting interest-earning investments (but not shares or unit trusts) to the lower taxpayer.

Tax-free investment income

Some investment income is free of income tax. This income does not have to be entered in the tax return. Income from the following investments count as tax-free:

- prizes from premium bonds, National Lottery and gambling
- an ISA (individual savings account). (Since 6 April 2004, dividends and similar income from investments within a stocks and shares ISA do have some tax deducted which you cannot reclaim. But these still count as tax-free investments)
- a PEP (personal equity plan), but not if you withdraw more than £180 in interest. Like ISAs (see above), dividends and similar income from investment within a PEP have some tax deducted but count as tax-free investments. From a date yet to be announced, PEPs will be reclassified as ISAs (see Chapter 7)
- SAYE schemes
- NS&I Certificates, including the index-linked ones
- NS&I Children's Bonus Bonds
- Ulster Savings Certificates, if you normally live in Northern Ireland and you bought the certificates or they were repaid while you were living there
- dividends on shares in venture capital trusts (up to £200,000 of shares) a year from 6 April 2004 (£100,000 in earlier years)
- Savings Gateway bonus (which is technically a capital gain – see Chapter 7).

There are other less obvious forms of investment income which are also tax-free and don't need to be entered in the tax return:

- interest awarded by a UK court as part of a claim for damages for personal injury or death. There is an extra-statutory concession which means that this can also apply to awards from a foreign court
- interest awarded as part of compensation for being mis-sold a personal pension or free-standing AVC scheme. However, interest that is part of a compensation award for being mis-sold an endowment policy (typically as part of a mortgage) is not tax-free and should be entered in boxes 10.12 to 10.14.
- lump sum compensation made in accordance with Financial Services Authority policies relating to being mis-sold a free-standing AVC scheme
- compensation (which would normally count as interest for tax purposes) paid by UK and foreign banks and building societies on dormant accounts opened by Holocaust victims and frozen during World War Two.

Tax-saving idea 106

Compensation paid by UK banks to Holocaust victims or their heirs has been tax-free since 8 May 2000. This exemption has now been extended to similar compensation paid by foreign banks. The extension is back-dated and such payments have become tax-free from 1996–7 onwards. If you have paid tax on such a payment in the past, you should now send an amended tax return to your tax office in order to claim the tax back – the normal time limit for amending returns does not apply.

The documents you need

Get together all your interest statements, tax deduction certificates, dividend and distribution tax vouchers and trust vouchers. Keep them safe; don't send them with your tax return.

Interest

Interest and alternative finance receipts

■ *Interest and alternative finance receipts*

● Interest and alternative finance receipts from UK banks or building societies including UK Internet accounts.
  If you have more than one bank or building society account enter **totals** *in the boxes.*

Most savings income (and equivalent income from Shariah-compliant products – see p. 77 – which in your tax return are called 'alternative finance receipts') is now paid with tax deducted and the rate of tax for 2006–7 is 20 per cent. Income from most accounts in UK banks, building societies, finance houses, organisations offering high-interest cheque accounts and other licensed deposit takers is paid after deduction of tax. There is no further tax bill to pay if you pay tax at the basic rate only on your income, which applies to most taxpayers. If you pay tax at the higher rate, there will be extra tax to pay, at the rate of 20 per cent (see Chapter 7). If your top rate of tax is the starting rate, tax due on your savings income is reduced to 10 per cent – you can claim back the excess tax already deducted. If you are a non-taxpayer, you can claim back all of any tax already deducted. See p. 41 for how to make your claim. If you expect to carry on being a non-taxpayer, you should register to receive your interest before any tax is deducted – see Chapter 7.

- enter any bank or building society interest and alternative finance receipts that **have not had tax taken off**. (Interest and alternative finance receipts are usually taxed before you receive them so make sure you should be filling in box 10.1, rather than boxes 10.2 to 10.4.) Enter other types of interest and alternative finance receipts in boxes 10.5 to 10.14, as appropriate.

Taxable amount

10.1 £

You may have received interest from your bank or building society paid gross, that is without tax deducted. The most common circumstance where this might apply is if you have registered to receive interest gross because you are a non-taxpayer (see p. 75). If you get gross interest from an offshore bank account, do not enter it here, it goes on the Foreign supplement.

Add up all the interest you have received without tax deducted from your bank, building society or deposit taker in 2006–7 and enter it in box 10.1.

If you are a beneficiary of a trust and you are entitled to income as it arises, you should include in box 10.1 any untaxed interest paid direct to you because the trustee has authorised the payer to do so.

Don't include NS&I interest here (it goes in box 10.8).

- enter details of **taxed** bank or building society interest and **taxed** alternative finance receipts. *The Working Sheet on page 11 of your Tax Return Guide will help you fill in boxes 10.2 to 10.4.*

Amount **after** tax taken off	Tax taken off	Gross amount **before** tax
10.2 £	**10.3** £	**10.4** £

You can get the information for these boxes from your statements or pass books or ask your bank, building society or deposit taker direct to give you a tax deduction certificate. Enter the totals for all three figures in the boxes.

If your statement only shows the after-tax figure, you will need to gross it up, see Appendix B on p. 369.

You may have received cash or shares when two or more building societies have merged or a building society has converted to a bank or been taken over by a bank. You may have to pay either income or capital gains tax and your building society should be able to tell you this. If you have received a cash payment on which you should pay income tax, put the details in boxes 10.2 to 10.4. If you don't know whether you have to pay income tax, put the details under Q13 on page 5, but also tick box 23.2 on page 9 and explain the situation in the Additional information box 23.9. Any capital gain should be entered in the Capital gains supplementary pages. If you have received shares, you may not need to supply details until you dispose of the shares.

If you are self-employed and have included interest on your business bank account in box 3.50 on the Self-employment supplement, to ensure the correct amount of tax is paid, deduct it again in box 3.71 and add it here to boxes 10.2 to 10.4.

Unit trusts

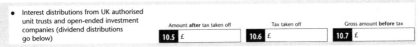

Some types of unit trusts and open-ended investment companies pay interest rather than dividends. These include unit trusts which invest in gilts and other fixed-interest investments. In these cases, 20 per cent tax has been deducted from the income before you get it in the same way as for bank or building society interest (see p. 73) and you will get a tax voucher telling you the amount paid. You may be able to claim some or all of it back, or you may have to pay more tax in the same way as for bank or building society interest.

The interest might not be paid out to you but automatically reinvested in accumulation or other units. However, you still have to enter the interest in your tax return.

Add up all the interest you receive after tax has been deducted and enter the total in box 10.5. Put the tax deducted in box 10.6. Then add together boxes 10.5 and 10.6 and enter the sum in box 10.7 (gross amount before tax). If you received interest without any tax deducted, enter nil in boxes 10.5 and 10.6 and enter the before-tax amount in box 10.7.

When you buy units in a unit trust, part of the purchase price includes an amount for income which the trust has received but not yet paid out. The first payment you receive will include an equalisation payment, which is not income, but a refund of part of the original purchase price you paid. It is not taxable, so do not enter it here. (Note that it is deducted for CGT purposes – see p. 137.)

Don't enter dividend distributions from unit trusts here, but in boxes 10.18 to 10.20.

National Savings & Investments

- National Savings & Investments (other than First Option Bonds and Fixed Rate Savings Bonds and the first £70 of interest from an Ordinary Account) — Taxable amount **10.8** £

You will receive or be credited with interest paid before deduction of tax from the following NS&I investments:

■ Easy Access Savings Account

■ Investment Account

- Deposit Bonds

- Income Bonds

- Capital Bonds

- Pensioners' Guaranteed Income Bonds.

Tot up the before-tax interest you received (or added to your account) in 2006–7. Do not include interest from FIRST option bonds or fixed rate savings bonds (see below).

The return from NS&I guaranteed equity bonds is usually taxable only at the end of the five-year term. But if the holder died in the 2006–7 year, any gain is paid without deduction of tax and should be entered in box 10.14 (see below), not here.

Enter the total amount you received in box 10.8.

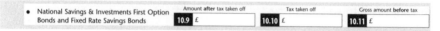

You receive interest after tax at the savings rate has already been deducted, if you invest in FIRST option bonds or fixed rate savings bonds. Enter in box 10.9 the amount you received, in box 10.10 the amount of tax deducted and in box 10.11 the amount of interest before tax.

Gilts and other interest-paying investments

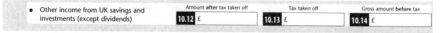

There is a hotch-potch of interest from other investments which should be entered here. Depending on the nature of the interest, it may be paid without tax being deducted or after tax is deducted. Tot up the relevant amounts and enter in boxes 10.12 to 10.14. If no tax has been deducted, put the interest in box 10.14 only and put nil in boxes 10.12 and 10.13. If tax has been deducted fill in all the boxes.

Here are examples of the investments to include:

- certificates of tax deposit when the certificate is applied to payment of a tax bill

- Gilts (British Government stock) – see opposite

- other loan stocks, such as corporate bonds and local authority loans and stocks

- permanent interest bearing shares (PIBS) of building societies

■ loans to an individual or organisation

■ income from credit unions and friendly societies

■ interest from Enterprise Zone trusts

■ discount on deeply discounted securities (enter in box 10.14)

■ discount from gilt strips (enter in box 10.14)

■ income from securities to which you have sold or transferred the right to the income, but not the security – even if you have not received the income (enter in box 10.14)

■ purchased life annuities (see below).

Corporate bonds

Since 1 April 2001, corporate bonds listed on a recognised stock exchange pay interest gross – in other words, without any tax deducted. Before that date, interest was usually paid with tax at the savings rate already deducted.

Gilts (British Government stock)

Tax at the rate of 20 per cent for 2006–7 may have been deducted from the interest on your gilts before you receive it. You can arrange to have future interest paid without tax deducted.

If tax has been deducted, your interest payment should be accompanied by a tax voucher which lets you know how much tax has been paid. If you are a non-taxpayer, you should be able to claim back the amount deducted. If you are a basic rate taxpayer, there is no more tax to pay. Enter the appropriate amounts in the three boxes 10.12, 10.13 and 10.14.

Accrued income scheme

If you own fixed-interest securities with a nominal value in excess of £5,000, and you buy or sell them, there are special tax rules designed to stop tax avoidance by turning income into capital gains. See the Revenue guidance at www.hmrc.gov.uk/guidance/ais.htm or, if you do not have internet access, ask your tax office to send you a copy of these web pages. The government has been reviewing the scheme for the past three years and changes are expected in due course.

Deeply discounted securities

Some corporate and other bonds do not pay interest. Instead you get a return by selling or redeeming the bond at a higher price than you paid –

the difference is called the 'discount'. (In the past, these investments were often called 'deep discount bonds'.) Usually, you are taxed on the proceeds only when you sell the bond or it is redeemed (but see below for different rules applying to gilt strips). In box 10.14, enter the sale or redemption proceeds less the price you originally paid. Note that NS&I guaranteed equity bonds count as deeply discounted securities.

You used to be able to claim tax relief for any loss provided you had other taxable income for the same tax year. But this now applies only where you started to own the securities before 27 March 2003 and the security was listed on a recognised stock exchange, in which case you enter a loss not here but in box 15.8 on page 6 of the return. There is no tax relief for losses made on securities acquired on or after 27 March 2003.

Gilt strips

A traditional gilt provides regular interest payments (usually twice a year) and possibly a capital sum at the end of its lifespan. Each of these payments can be stripped out and sold as a separate investment, called a gilt strip. A gilt strip entitles you to one payment on a specified future date. Strips can be bought and sold before the payment falls due at a market price which is at a discount to the payment. Strips are taxed in a special way. At the end of each tax year, you are treated as if you had sold each strip and bought it back the following day. You are then taxed on any increase in value over the tax year. So, in 2006–7, income tax is due on any increase in the market value of the strip between 6 April 2006 (or, if later, the date you bought the strip) and 5 April 2007. The relevant market values are available from your tax office. Enter the change in value in box 10.14. Enter any loss on actual disposal or redemption in box 15.8 on page 6 of the return. Since 15 January 2004, rules prevent claims for tax relief through the artificial creation of losses on strips.

For securities owned from 27 March 2003 onwards, the above rules also apply to strips of securities issued by non-UK governments.

Annuities

An annuity is an investment made with a life insurance company. You invest a lump sum and in return the insurance company will pay you an income. Sometimes this could be for a particular period, say ten years, or it could be until you die. The income which you receive is considered to be in two parts: some of it is your original investment being returned to you. There is tax to pay only on the interest.

The annuity payment is usually made to you with tax at the rate of 20 per cent of the interest part already deducted. The tax voucher which accompanies the payment will tell you how much tax has been deducted. If you are a starting-rate or non-taxpayer you can claim back some or all of the tax deducted. Non-taxpayers can arrange to receive the income without any tax deducted – see p. 75.

With an annuity which you buy as part of your pension, the tax treatment is different. Tax will be deducted from the whole payment through the PAYE system. Details of annuities bought under personal pension schemes or retirement annuity contracts should be entered on page 4 of the tax return under Q11.

Dividends

■ *Dividends*

You will receive share dividends from UK companies and distributions from authorised unit trusts with no more basic rate tax to pay because you also receive a tax credit. The payments are accompanied by a tax voucher which sets out the amount of the tax credit (10 per cent for 2006–7). You work out the gross amount of dividend by adding together the net dividend and the tax credit (see p. 78).

Since 6 April 1999, non-taxpayers cannot claim back the tax credit. Starting rate and basic rate taxpayers have no further tax to pay, but higher rate taxpayers pay extra bringing the rate they pay up to 32.5 per cent.

If you are a beneficiary of a trust and you are entitled to income as it arises, include in these boxes any dividends or distributions shown on your trust voucher.

Shares in UK companies

Your dividend voucher should show the amount of the dividend and the tax credit. Put these in boxes 10.15 and 10.16 and add them together to enter the sum in box 10.17. Note that scrip dividends are included below in boxes 10.21 to 10.23. If you have received dividends from a real estate investment rust (REIT), do not enter them here – they go in box 13.1 on page 5 of the return.

Include dividends you get from shares acquired through employee share schemes, unless the dividends were used to buy more shares through a share incentive plan (see Chapter 16). However, if during the year you've sold shares bought with dividends before holding the shares three years, include them here after all – enter the amount of the dividend originally reinvested.

A company can make other distributions as well as dividends – for example, if it sells you an asset at less than the open-market price. Some distributions are defined as non-qualifying and are entered in boxes 10.24 to 10.26 (see p. 194). All other distributions are qualifying and entered here in boxes 10.15 to 10.17. Explain how you got the distribution in the Additional information box on page 9.

In the past, you may have had a bonus issue of redeemable shares. If they are now redeemed, the amount you receive counts as a qualifying distribution and should be entered in boxes 10.15 to 10.17. If, when you originally got the shares, you paid higher rate tax on them, you can now claim some tax relief in box 15.12 on page 6 of the return (see p. 219).

IR35 companies

Do not include dividends you have received from your own personal service company if the company's tax office has agreed that the dividends are not taxable in your hands. This may be the case if, under the 'IR35 rules', you are treated as if you were an employee of your client(s) and your company has been deemed to pay you a salary (whether or not it actually did) on which income tax and national insurance contributions have been charged. If, in fact, you take money out of the company in the form of dividends rather than salary, you would be taxed twice on the same income if the dividends were taxed as well. Your company rather than you must claim relief for the dividends. Once the Revenue has agreed the claim, you do not include the dividends on your tax return at all.

Tax-saving idea 107

If you are an owner/manager of your own company and your spouse or civil partner owns shares in it but you do substantially all of the work, your tax office may have argued that any of the company's dividends paid to your spouse or partner were, in effect, gifts from you and should be taxed as your income. This treatment has been the subject of lengthy litigation (in a case known as *Jones* v *Garnett* or 'Arctic Systems') and, in December 2005, the Court of Appeal decided the Revenue view was wrong and that such dividends should correctly be treated as income of the spouse or partner. The Revenue has been given leave to appeal to the House of Lords for a final judgment but this appeal will not be heard until June 2007. If you send in your return before the judgment is published, you do not have to include your spouse's or partner's dividends on your tax return. (However, to be on the safe side, note in box 23.9 on page 10 and box 7.32 of the Trusts pages – see Chapter 21 – that you have completed your return on the basis of the *Jones* v *Garnett* Court of Appeal ruling.) If the House of Lords rules in the Revenue's favour, your tax position will then need to be corrected and interest will be charged on tax paid late. Returns sent in after the Lords' ruling should comply with whatever judgment they make. To check the latest news on *Jones* v *Garnett*, see www.pcg.org.uk.

Unit trusts and open-ended investment companies

Distributions from most authorised unit trusts and open-ended investment companies (oeics) are treated in the same way as dividends (see p. 78). If you have invested in an accumulation unit trust or oeic, you don't receive the income but the unit trust or oeic managers reinvest it for you in more units or oeic shares. However, for tax purposes this is treated in exactly the same way as if you received the cash. You will receive a tax voucher with a tax credit.

Your dividend vouchers show the amount of the dividend and the tax credit. If you own units in more than one unit trust, add up the distributions and tax credits and enter the totals for each in boxes 10.18 and 10.19. Add them together to get the entry for box 10.20. Don't enter any equalisation payments (see p. 137).

Scrip dividends

If you received new shares instead of cash as a dividend, this is known as a scrip dividend. The value of the scrip dividend is its cash equivalent and is the amount of cash dividend forgone. It should be shown on your dividend statement as 'the appropriate amount in cash'. This is what you enter in the dividend box. For 2006–7, you are treated as having received the cash equivalent grossed up at 10 per cent (see Appendix B on p. 369).

Do not confuse scrip dividends with shares you get through a dividend reinvestment plan (DRIP). Under a DRIP, your cash dividend is automatically used to buy additional shares in the company. But you still need to declare the cash dividend as usual in boxes 10.15 to 10.17.

Enter in box 10.21 the appropriate amount of cash. In box 10.22 enter the notional tax (11.11 per cent of the cash equivalent). Add together boxes 10.21 and box 10.22, and enter the sum in box 10.23.

Non-qualifying distributions

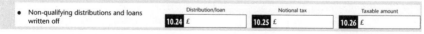

A non-qualifying distribution is broadly one which gives a future rather than a current claim on the company's assets, such as a bonus issue of redeemable shares. The amount of the distribution is the nominal value of the securities you received less any consideration (for example, cash) you paid.

Enter the amount of the distribution in box 10.26. Multiply box 10.26 by 10 per cent to get the amount of notional tax to enter in box 10.25. Leave box 10.24 blank. If you are a higher rate taxpayer, you'll have extra tax to pay on this distribution. When the shares are eventually redeemed, there could be further higher rate tax to pay (see p. 192) but you will then be able to claim relief to prevent your having been taxed twice on the same income (see p. 219).

For loans written off, contact your tax adviser or tax office.

Pensions and social security benefits

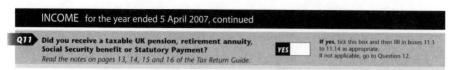

If you received none of these, go straight to Q12. But if you received one or more of these, you will need to find out whether what you received should be entered here in your tax return. Some pensions and benefits are not taxable.

Pensions and benefits that should not be included in your tax return

If you received any of the following, you do not need to give details here in the tax return because they are tax-free:

- attendance allowance, disability living allowance, severe disablement allowance, including age-related addition
- bereavement payment
- council tax benefit, housing benefit (rent rebates and allowances), home renovation and repair grants
- educational maintenance allowance
- Employment Zone payments
- guardian's allowance
- incapacity benefit for the first 28 weeks (and not taxable after that time if you were receiving invalidity benefit before 13 April 1995 unless there is a break in your claim; incapacity benefit replaced invalidity benefit)
- income support (if you're not required to be available for work)
- industrial injuries benefit (except death benefit)
- jobfinder's grant, employment training and employment rehabilitation allowances, back-to-work bonus and New Deal training allowances
- maternity allowance, child benefit, child tax credit, additions to benefits or state pensions because you have a dependent child, school uniform grants and fares to school
- pension credit, pensioners' Christmas bonus, over-70s payment to help pensioner households meet increases in council tax bills
- pensions and benefits for wounds or disability in military service or for other war injuries, war widow's pension and some similar pensions for dependants. See Helpsheet IR310 *War widow's and dependants' pensions* from the Orderline (see p. 170)
- social fund payments
- student grants, bursaries, scholarships and loans
- vaccine damage payments
- winter fuel payments and cold weather payments
- working tax credit
- similar benefits to those above paid by foreign governments.

Pensions and benefits that should be entered in your tax return

Details of the following should be entered here:

- additions to benefits or state pensions for an adult dependant
- carer's allowance
- income withdrawals from a personal pension plan where the purchase of an annuity has been deferred
- industrial death benefit pension (but not child allowance), pension for injuries at work or for work-related illnesses
- jobseeker's allowance (up to the taxable amount)
- pension from a former employer or a pension from your late husband or wife's employer, pension from a free-standing additional voluntary contribution, pension from service in the armed forces
- pension from a personal pension scheme or retirement annuity contract or trust scheme
- state retirement pension, including the basic pension, state additional pension and graduated pension and lump sum from deferring state pension
- statutory sick pay, statutory maternity pay, statutory paternity pay and statutory adoption pay paid by the Revenue, taxable incapacity benefit
- widowed mother's allowance and widowed parent's allowance, widow's pension and bereavement pension.

If you receive any of the above pensions or benefits, tick the YES box in answer to Q11.

Refunds of surplus additional voluntary contributions are not entered here. Details should be put in boxes 12.10 to 12.12. Overseas pensions and taxable benefits paid under the rules of another country should be entered in the Foreign supplementary pages (covered in Chapter 20).

The documents you need

Gather details of any state retirement pension and bereavement benefits – you can ask for form BR735 showing how much you have received during the tax year by phoning Pensions Direct on 0845 301 3011 or from your local Pensions Centre. The Department for Work and Pensions (DWP) should send you details of the taxable amount of other social security benefits that you have had, for example on form P60U or P45U for jobseeker's allowance. For non-state pensions, you need the P60 the pension payer gives you or any other certificate of pension paid and tax deducted.

State pensions and benefits

Enter the amount of pension or benefit you were entitled to for 2006–7, whether or not you actually received that amount in the year. You should enter the total of all the weekly amounts which you were entitled to in the year, even if you chose to receive your pension or benefit monthly or quarterly.

State retirement pension

The state retirement pension is taxable but paid without tax deducted. So if you have other income you will find that tax on your state retirement pension might be collected from your other income.

In box 11.1, you should enter the amount you were entitled to receive in 2006–7, but excluding any amount for a dependent child, the Christmas bonus, winter fuel payment and over-70s payment to help with council tax.

A married woman might receive a pension which is based on her husband's contributions and not her own. This pension (but not any dependency allowance which he receives for her before her 60th birthday) should be entered in her tax return, not her husband's.

If you have chosen to defer your state pension (to earn extra pension or a lump sum), while your pension is deferred you do not have any income to enter in box 11.1. Once your pension restarts, the amount in 11.1 should include any extra pension you have earned.

State pension lump sum

		Tax taken off	Gross amount **before** tax
● State Pension Lump Sum		**11.1A** £	**11.1B** £

If you have previously deferred your state pension and chosen to take a lump sum that was paid to you during 2006–7, enter the full amount of the lump sum in box 11.1B. The DWP deducts tax from this before making the payment. Enter the tax deducted in box 11.1A.

Tax-saving ideas 108 and 109

Taking a lump sum as a result of deferring your state pension will not push you into a higher tax bracket. The whole lump sum is taxed at the highest rate you were paying without the lump sum (ignoring the special rate that applies to savings income and dividends). For example, a starting rate taxpayer pays tax on the whole lump sum at 10 per cent. The lump sum does not affect age allowance (see Chapter 2).

You usually get the state pension lump sum when your state pension starts to be paid and the lump sum is taxed at your top rate for that year. But you can opt to delay receiving the lump sum until the following year. This will normally be worth doing if you expect your top rate of tax to be lower in the following year.

Widow's pension or bereavement allowance

From 6 April 2001, widow's pension was replaced by bereavement allowance for new claimants. If you first claimed before that date, you continue to receive widow's pension. Bereavement allowance is available to widowers as well as widows.

• Widow's Pension or Bereavement Allowance	11.2 £

Enter the full amount you were entitled to receive in 2006–7, including any earnings-related additional pension, in box 11.2. For more information on the benefits available to widows and widowers, ask for leaflet GL14 *Widowed?* from your local Jobcentre Plus or the DWP website.

Widowed mother's allowance or widowed parent's allowance

• Widowed Mother's Allowance or Widowed Parent's Allowance	11.3 £

From 6 April 2001, widowed mother's allowance was replaced by widowed parent's allowance for new claimants. If you first claimed before that date, you continue to receive widowed mother's allowance. Widowed parent's allowance is available to widowers as well as widows.

Include in box 11.3 the flat rate basic allowance and any earnings-related increase, but not any child dependency increase.

Industrial death benefit pension

• Industrial Death Benefit Pension	11.4 £

In box 11.4 you should enter the yearly pension you are entitled to receive under the industrial death benefit scheme. But do not include industrial death benefit child allowance which is tax-free.

Jobseeker's allowance

● Jobseeker's Allowance	**11.5** £

Jobseeker's allowance is taxable but paid without any tax deducted. There are two kinds of allowance, one based on your national insurance contribution record and one means-tested. There is a limit on the overall amount that is treated as taxable.

The DWP usually gives you a statement of the total jobseeker's allowance paid and the taxable portion (either Form P60U or Form P45U). Enter the taxable amount in box 11.5. If you haven't received a P60U, contact your social security office; if you haven't received a P45U, tell your tax office.

Carer's allowance

● Carer's Allowance	**11.6** £

Enter the amount you were entitled to receive in 2006–7. Include any addition for a dependent adult, but exclude any additional amount for a dependent child, because this is tax-free.

Statutory payments paid by the Revenue

● Statutory Sick, Maternity, Paternity and Adoption Pay paid by HM Revenue & Customs	**11.7** £

Generally, any statutory sick, maternity, paternity or adoption pay is paid by your employer and taxed under the PAYE system (see Chapter 3). Such payments will be included in your P60 or P45. Details should be entered in the Employment supplementary pages.

But if your employer didn't pay you, and the Revenue did so instead, enter the total received here in box 11.7.

Taxable incapacity benefit

	Tax taken off	Gross amount before tax
● Taxable Incapacity Benefit	**11.8** £	**11.9** £

Some incapacity benefit is tax-free. You will not pay tax on it when you receive it during your first 28 weeks of incapacity or you are receiving it for a period of incapacity which began before 13 April 1995, and for which invalidity benefit used to be payable.

The DWP will give you a form showing you whether your incapacity benefit is taxable or not. If it is taxable, enter the amount of the benefit in box 11.9 and any tax that has been deducted in box 11.8.

Other pensions

Apart from the state pension, you can get a pension from your employer, from what you have paid into a personal pension scheme or a retirement annuity contract.

■ *Other pensions and retirement annuities*

You should enter here details of pensions paid to you by someone in the UK unless they are paying you on behalf of someone outside the UK. Pensions received from abroad will be entered in the Foreign pages (see Chapter 20).

● Pensions (other than State Pensions), retirement annuities and triviality and wind-up lump sum pension payments - *If you have more than one pension or annuity, please add together and complete boxes 11.10 to 11.12. Provide the name of the pension payer, amount of pension and tax deducted of each one in box 11.14 or box 23.9 if there is insufficient space. Read the notes on page xx of the Tax Return Guide.*

	Amount after tax taken off	Tax taken off	Gross amount before tax
	11.10 £	**11.11** £	**11.12** £

You should total the amount you receive from all your pensions (excluding state pension) and put it in box 11.10. You should include in the total:

■ pension from a previous employer's occupational scheme (unless it is tax-free, see below)

■ annuity payments from a personal pension scheme

■ if you have taken advantage of the ability to defer buying the annuity, the income withdrawals which you receive during the deferred period

■ any annual payments from a retirement contract.

Put the amount of tax deducted in box 11.11. The information about an employer's pension or personal pension should be on your P60 and for other pensions from a certificate given to you by the pension payer. Adding up boxes 11.10 and 11.11 should give you the total for box 11.12, unless you have received some non-cash benefit. If you have, you'll need to ask your tax office what to do.

If the amounts you have entered include pensions or annuities from more than one source, give details in box 11.14. If there is not enough space here, use the Additional information box 23.9 on page 10 of the return.

Part of your pension may be tax-free if you receive it as a former employee who was awarded a pension on retirement because you were disabled by injury on duty or a work-related illness. If that pension is more than the amount you would receive if you had retired at the same time on the grounds of ordinary ill-health, the extra amount is free of tax. You should not enter any tax-free amounts in the tax return.

10 per cent deduction

- **Deduction** - *see the note for box 11.13 on page 15 of your Tax Return Guide.*   Amount of deduction **11.13** £   **11.14**

This applies to some UK pensions for service for certain overseas governments. Only 90 per cent of the basic amount of such pensions is taxed. Enter the 10 per cent deduction in box 11.13 and the reduced amount of pension in box 11.12.

Other income to be entered here

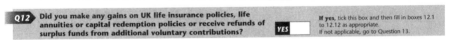

Q12 Did you make any gains on UK life insurance policies, life annuities or capital redemption policies or receive refunds of surplus funds from additional voluntary contributions?   **YES**   **If yes**, tick this box and then fill in boxes 12.1 to 12.12 as appropriate. If not applicable, go to Question 13.

Question 12 asks about payments from life insurance policies and certain other investments and pension schemes that are treated as income.

Life insurance policies

Gains on life insurance policies, contracts for life annuities and capital redemption policies are treated as investment income and may be taxable.

With most policies, the life insurance company will have paid tax on the income and gains which its life fund makes as they arise. This is deemed to be equivalent to income tax at the savings rate (20 per cent in 2006–7). So if you pay tax at the basic rate or less, there is no tax for you personally to pay. But you cannot reclaim any of the tax already paid even if you personally would not be liable for tax on income or gains or would be liable only at the starting rate.

The further tax treatment of a life insurance gain depends on whether the policy is qualifying or non-qualifying. Most policies where you pay regular premiums are qualifying. If you pay just a single premium, the policy will be non-qualifying and have less favourable tax treatment.

Taxation of qualifying policies

Tax at the savings rate is treated as already paid. There is usually no higher rate tax when the policy matures – that is, comes to the end of its term or the person insured by the policy dies. You do not enter details in your tax return.

The exception is if you cash in the policy or make it paid up before it has run for ten years, or three-quarters of its term if this is less. The policy is then treated as a non-qualifying policy (see below).

Taxation of non-qualifying policies

Higher rate income tax may be due when you receive proceeds from a non-qualifying policy. A gain from this type of policy can cause you to lose age allowance (see pp. 24 and 54) or tax credits (see p. 60).

A chargeable event may occur when a policy matures, the holder dies, the policy is assigned or surrendered, or a partial withdrawal is made. Each time there is an event, the gain (if any) is calculated. The gain is usually the total you have received from the policy since it started less any earlier gains that have already been taxed and less whatever you have paid into the policy. Where the person insured dies, the calculation uses the cash-in value just before death, which may be less than the death benefit actually paid out.

Where a life insurance policy is transferred from one spouse to another as part of a divorce settlement, this was often in the past treated as giving rise to a chargeable gain and a possible tax bill. The Revenue's view has now changed and such transfers, provided they are ordered or ratified by a court, do not now create a gain or tax bill.

Many non-qualifying policies let you draw an income by cashing in part of the policy. There is no tax to pay at the time you make such withdrawals provided they come to no more than 5 per cent a year of the amount you have paid into the policy. If you don't cash in the full 5 per cent each year, you can carry forward the unused amount, meaning you may be able to cash in more than 5 per cent in a later year. You can make 5 per cent withdrawals for up to 20 years. When the policy comes to an end, the amounts you have withdrawn are added to your final gain or loss to work out the tax due.

If in any year, you withdraw more than the cumulative 5 per cent a year limit, there may be an immediate tax bill on the excess. If, on maturity, you make a loss, you can claim deficiency relief in box 12.9 (see p. 204) up to the amount of the earlier withdrawals on which tax was paid.

Whenever there is a chargeable event producing a gain, the insurance company must send you a 'chargeable event certificate'. This tells you the amount of the gain, whether savings rate tax is treated as already paid and, if so, the amount. There will be higher rate tax to pay if your taxable income plus the gain come to more than the threshold at which higher rate tax starts to be paid. For 2006–7, this is usually £33,300 but will be higher if you have paid pension contributions or made Gift Aid donations.

Tax is due at the difference between the higher and savings rates: 40 – 20 = 20 per cent. But if it is to your advantage, you automatically get top-slicing relief: divide the gain by the number of full years you held the policy to find the average gain. Work out the tax due if the average gain was added to your income and multiply this by the number of years the policy was held.

Although most UK life insurance gains are treated as having had savings rate tax deducted, some are not. The chargeable event certificate should make clear where this is the case.

Taxation of personal portfolio bonds

A personal portfolio bond is an investment-type life insurance policy where the return is linked to a fund of investments usually chosen by or on behalf of a single policyholder. The return on the investments is taxed as that of the insurance company rather than the policyholder. If, as is typical, an off-shore insurer issues the policy, the investments roll up within the fund free of UK taxes. The government treats this as tax avoidance, and there is an extra tax charge for holders of these bonds (though some pre-1999 bonds are not affected). As well as the normal rules applying to non-qualifying policies (see above), there is an annual tax charge on a deemed gain equal to 15 per cent of the premiums paid up to the end of each policy year plus the total of deemed gains for earlier years.

If you have made a single gain and it is not treated as having had basic rate tax deducted, put the amount of the gain in box 12.2 and the number of complete years since the insurance was made in box 12.1. These figures are shown on the chargeable event certificate.

If you have made a single gain and it is treated as having had basic rate tax deducted, put the amount of the gain in box 12.5 and the notional tax in box 12.4 (20 per cent of the amount in box 12.5). Enter the number of complete years in box 12.3. Copy these figures from the chargeable event certificate.

Where you have made more than one sort of gain, or you hold a cluster of policies, things become complex. You will probably need to put additional information on page 10 of the tax return. Ask the Orderline (see p. 170) for a copy of Help Sheet IR320 *Gains on UK life insurance policies*. Consult your tax office or tax adviser for more guidance.

Normally, gains on life insurance policies held within an ISA are tax-free and you do not include them in your tax return. But there are strict rules on the types of policy which qualify to be held through an ISA. If it's found that the life policy you hold does not qualify or has ceased to qualify, the policy may come to an end and there may be tax to pay on any gain. Tax is worked out as for a non-qualifying policy – see p. 202. Your ISA manager will give you the information you need. Enter the amount of gain in box 12.8, the number of complete years the policy ran in box 12.6 and tax already paid by the ISA manager in box 12.7.

Deficiency relief

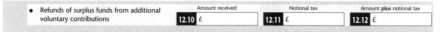

If you had a life insurance policy on which you made a loss on final surrender, you may be able to claim a relief to ensure that the amount treated as income is not more than the total gain made under the policy (see p. 202). Ask for Help Sheet IR320 *Gains on UK life insurance policies*.

Refunds of surplus funds from additional voluntary contributions

Additional voluntary contributions are extra payments you choose to make to boost your pension savings. It's possible you might pay in too much – though this is less likely since changes to the pension regime from 6 April 2006 onwards – in which case you may receive a refund. Usually you enter the refund here. But if it counts as an 'unauthorised payment', enter it instead at question 25 on the new pensions form (see p. 179). The pension scheme provider can tell you if the payment is unauthorised.

Your certificate from your pension scheme provider should show you the amount of surplus contributions and the tax refunded to you. Enter the total amount in box 12.12, the amount actually repaid to you in box 12.10 and the tax deducted in box 12.11. (But don't include any refund of contributions because you have left a scheme after less than two years.)

Any other income

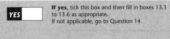

Q13 Did you receive any other taxable income or benefit which you have not already entered elsewhere in your Tax Return? **YES** ☐
*Fill in any supplementary Pages **before** answering Question 13.*
(Supplementary Pages follow page 10, or are available from the Orderline, or www.hmrc.gov.uk)

If yes, tick this box and then fill in boxes 13.1 to 13.6 as appropriate.
If not applicable, go to Question 14.

You should already have filled in the appropriate supplementary pages for income from employment, share schemes, trusts and abroad. Similarly, business income should already be entered in the supplement for self-employment, partnership or land and property, as appropriate. This section of the tax return is for odd bits of income you have not entered elsewhere. The income can be divided into two sorts:

A: Income against which you can set losses

- ▪ freelance or casual income
- ▪ profits from the odd literary or artistic activity
- ▪ income received after you close a business (post-cessation receipts). This could include money which you have recovered from a bad debt or royalties arising after the business ceased from contracts made before it ceased. You can claim to have this treated as income for the year in which the business ceased (tick box 23.4 on page 9 of the tax return). Or you can enter the total here
- ▪ any recovery of expenses or debts for which you claimed relief as post-cessation expenses
- ▪ sale of patent rights if you received a capital sum
- ▪ rental from leasing equipment you own
- ▪ income from guaranteeing loans, dealing in futures and some income from underwriting
- ▪ other miscellaneous sources.

B: Income you can't set losses against

- ▪ receipts from covenants entered into for genuine commercial reasons in connection with the payer's trade, profession or vocation
- ▪ annual payments received in the year, including those from UK unauthorised unit trusts and annual payments paid by a former employer that do not count as a pension
- ▪ benefits of certain insurance policies relating to sickness or disability

■ a taxable lump sum from an unapproved retirement benefits scheme

■ the taxable value of benefit you are deemed to receive from any pre-owned assets (see Chapter 10)

■ distributions from UK real estate investment trusts (REITs).

If you have more than one source of other income, you should ask for Help Sheet IR325 *Other taxable income*, which contains a Worksheet to help you keep track of your different income sources and the losses you can claim.

From any type of income in list A above (but not list B), you can deduct expenses that you had to incur wholly in order to earn the income. You can't deduct expenses incurred partly or wholly for private reasons. And, if you had to buy capital items, instead deduct capital allowances (see p. 283).

If your expenses come to more than the income from a particular source, you have made a loss. You can set the loss against any of the types of income in list A above, but not against any of the income in list B. If you can't use up all your losses in 2006–7, you can carry them forward to set against any of the list-A types of income in future years. Similarly, if you have made losses in previous years and elected to carry them forward, you can now set part or all of them against any list-A income you have in 2006–7.

● Other taxable income (including dividends from the tax-exempt profits of a UK Real Estate Investment Trust that are normally paid under deduction of tax and any benefit arising from a pre-owned asset.) *Read the notes on pages 19 and 20 of the Tax Return Guide. Also provide details in box 23.9.*		
Amount **after** tax taken off	Tax taken off	Amount before tax
13.1 £	**13.2** £	**13.3** £

● Tick box 13.1A if you have claimed enhanced capital allowances for designated environmentally beneficial plant and machinery to arrive at box 13.1		
	Losses brought forward	Earlier years' losses used in 2006-07
13.1A	**13.4** £	**13.5** £
	2006-07 losses carried forward	
	13.6 £	

In box 13.1, put the total of your other income from all the sources after any tax deducted and after subtracting any allowable expenses and capital allowances. If you have deducted any first-year capital allowances for environmentally friendly expenditure (see p. 285) tick box 13.1A. If overall you have made a loss, enter zero. In box 13.2, put the amount of tax deducted from any of the payments you received. Add together boxes 13.1 and 13.2 and, if applicable, deduct any losses made on list-A income in 2006–7 from other list-A income for the year. Enter the result in box 13.3.

If, in box 13.3, you cannot use up all your losses made in 2006–7, put the remainder in box 13.6 to carry them forward to a future tax year.

In box 13.4, enter the amount of losses you are bringing forward from earlier years. If you are setting any of these losses against list-A income for 2006–7, enter the amount in box 13.5.

The total losses you can carry forward to future years equal box 13.4 less box 13.5 plus box 13.6.

Tax-saving idea 110

Because a tax bill may now arise because of something you did many years ago, it is easy to overlook the pre-owned assets tax and think it does not apply to you. But, if you still use or benefit from: anything which you sold or gave away at any time as far back as 18 March 1986; or something owned by someone else and you gave them cash within the last seven years, you may be caught by the tax. There may be steps you can take now to reduce or remove yourself from the tax – see Chapter 10 for details. If tax is due, complete boxes 13.1 to 13.3 and give details in box 23.9 on page 10. Failure to report and pay any tax due will result in interest and possibly penalties (see Chapter 4).

Cashbacks and incentives

Enter as other income any cashbacks or other incentives you received to take out a mortgage or purchase something (such as a car) if there is tax to pay. Ask the person who gave you the incentive or check with your tax office to find out if it is taxable. Include it in box 13.3. If you're not sure whether there is tax to pay, enter the amount you received in box 13.3, but also tick box 23.2 on page 9 and give details in the Additional information box 23.9.

Insurance policies relating to sickness and disability

Some part of income received under an income protection (also called 'permanent health') insurance policy may be taxable and should be entered as other income. This does not include income from a policy which you paid for yourself, as that is tax-free. Income from your employer for sickness and disability should go on the Employment pages. But if you have left your employer and you are still receiving benefits because you are covered by your former employer's scheme, you should enter that amount here (part might be tax-free if you contributed to the cost of the scheme). Check with your tax office if you are not sure how much is taxable, and ask for leaflet IR153 *Tax exemption for sickness or unemployment insurance payments*.

Unapproved retirement benefit schemes

Most, but not all, pension schemes set up by employers are approved and so qualify for special tax treatment. If you belong to an unapproved scheme, any lump sum you receive from it is treated as taxable income unless you can show that the lump sum had built up from contributions you paid yourself or contributions paid by your employer but on which you paid tax, or the payment was made because of accidental death or disablement. If the lump sum is the only retirement benefit you get from that employment and you do not also belong to an approved pension scheme, the lump sum might be tax-free – contact your tax office. If you have filled in the Employment supplement, you should have entered this income in boxes 1.26 and 1.28 and do not need to give details again here.

13

Reliefs

You can pay less tax by spending more money on things the government wants to encourage – and thus gives tax relief on – such as pensions and gifts to charity. In some instances you can get tax relief at your highest rate of tax, which could be 40 per cent or in some cases effectively more – see box. Assuming that you want to spend the money, buying any of these things could be highly advantageous. You claim for them on pages 5 and 6 of the basic tax return.

You get your tax relief in different ways. Frequently you get basic rate tax relief by deducting it from what you spend. Any higher rate tax relief that is due you will claim here in the tax return and give yourself the relief when you are working out your tax bill. Or you could get higher rate relief through your PAYE code. Non-taxpayers will not have to repay the tax deducted, except in the case of Gift Aid.

If you don't get basic rate relief by deducting it from what you pay, you will claim the relief here in the tax return and get it through your tax bill or your PAYE code.

The documents you need

You must gather together all the supporting documents you need to be able to prove to your tax inspector that you are entitled to the relief you are claiming (but keep the documents safe, don't send them with your tax return). These could include:

- certificates of premiums paid from your pension provider
- certificates of interest paid on loans

- maintenance agreements, court order, Child Support Agency assessments

- share certificate in a venture capital trust

- Forms EIS3 or EIS5 for Enterprise Investment Scheme

- certificates from community development finance institutions

- details of donations to charity by Gift Aid

- certificates from charities accepting gifts of land or buildings.

Tax-saving idea 111

If you are a higher rate taxpayer you get higher rate relief on personal pension contributions and Gift Aid donations by adding the grossed-up amount paid to your basic rate band (see p. 21). This takes some or all of your income that would otherwise have been taxed at the higher rate tax out of the top tax band. If your top slice of income is earnings, the effect of making the contribution or donation is to save you tax at 40 per cent (22 per cent tax relief at source on the payment plus 18 per cent higher rate tax saved on your top slice of income). If your top slice of income is savings, you effectively save 42 per cent tax (22 per cent relief at source plus 20 per cent higher rate tax). If the top slice is dividends, you save 44.5 per cent (22 per cent at source plus 22.5 per cent at the higher rate). If the payment also increases the amount you can claim in tax credits, the saving is even greater – see pp. 63–4.

What deductions can you claim?

INCOME AND RELIEFS   for the year ended 5 April 2007

You can claim here for:

- pension contributions

- additional voluntary contributions to a pension scheme

- interest paid on qualifying loans

- maintenance payments

- investments in growing business (venture capital trusts or enterprise investment scheme)

- investments in certain community development schemes

- post-cessation expenses for a business and losses on relevant discounted securities

- payments under annuities made in connection with your business

- certain payments to a trade union or friendly society

- certain contributions to a compulsory employer's scheme to provide benefits for your husband, wife or children in the event of your death

■ relief for higher rate tax paid on the issue of bonus shares where they are subsequently redeemed

■ payments to charities (through Gift Aid)

■ gifts of shares, unit trusts or property to charities.

Tax-saving idea 112

You can go back nearly six years to claim deductions which you forgot to claim at the time or didn't know you were able to. You will get tax relief at the rate you should have got it if you had claimed the deduction at the right time. Provided you claim by 31 January 2008, you can go back as far as the 2001–2 tax year.

Example

Tony Jabot is saving for his retirement through a stakeholder pension scheme. He pays in £1,000 in 2006–7, but this costs him just £780 because he is a basic rate taxpayer and gets 22 per cent tax relief.

Pensions

For 2006–7, you can get tax relief at your highest rate of tax on contributions to a pension scheme. If you are an employee, your employer can also make contributions to an approved pension scheme for you, and these do not count as a taxable fringe benefit for you. See p. 81 for details.

Here is what you need to put on your tax return to make sure you get all the tax relief due.

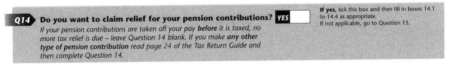

Q14 **Do you want to claim relief for your pension contributions?** **YES** ☐ **If yes**, tick this box and then fill in boxes 14.1 to 14.4 as appropriate. If not applicable, go to Question 15.

If your pension contributions are taken off your pay before it is taxed, no more tax relief is due – leave Question 14 blank. If you make any other type of pension contribution read page 24 of the Tax Return Guide and then complete Question 14.

With an occupational pension scheme, you are likely to get tax relief on your contributions deducted at source (they will be deducted from your salary before your employer works out your income tax through the PAYE system). If this is the only way you are saving for a pension, or if you are not saving at all for a pension, you can skip Q14 and go on to Q15.

Contributions you paid with basic rate deducted

- Enter the full amount of the contribution and add back the basic rate tax deducted. *Read the notes on page 24 of your Tax Return Guide.*   `14.1` £

Tax relief on contributions you pay to most types of pension scheme that you arrange for yourself – such as personal pensions, stakeholder schemes and free-standing additional voluntary contribution schemes – is given at source. This means the amount you pay in is treated as if tax relief at the basic rate (22 per cent in 2006–7) has been deducted. The scheme provider then claims this relief from the Revenue and adds it to your plan. For example, if you pay in £1,000, the provider claims £282 from the Revenue which is 22 per cent of the total £1,282 that goes into your plan.

You get the full amount of this basic rate relief even if you are a non-tax-payer or pay tax only at the starting rate. If you are a higher-rate taxpayer, you qualify for extra relief. (This extra relief is given by adding the gross value of the contributions to your basic rate band when working out your tax bill for the year.)

Add together the amount you actually paid in 2006–7 and the basic rate tax relief. The amounts should be shown on your certificate of premiums paid. Enter the total in box 14.1.

Contributions you paid in full

- Contributions under a retirement annuity contract paid in full without deducting basic rate tax   `14.2` £
- Contributions paid to your employer's occupational pension scheme which were not deducted from your pay before tax   `14.3` £
- Contributions paid to a non-UK registered overseas pension scheme which are eligible for tax relief, and were not deducted from your pay before tax   `14.4` £

Contributions to most retirement annuity contracts (an old type of personal pension started before July 1988) are paid without any tax relief deducted. You get tax relief on them up to your top rate by deducting the contributions from your income before working out your tax bill for the year. Enter the amount you paid in box 14.2.

Contributions to overseas pension schemes are usually also paid in this way. So too are contributions to a UK employer's scheme where unusually tax relief was not given through PAYE.

Retirement annuity contract providers can opt to accept contributions using the tax-relief-at-source system. If this applies to any contributions you paid during 2006–7, enter them in box 14.1, not here.

Tax-saving ideas 113 and 114

Nearly everyone can pay up to £3,600 a year into a pension scheme (see p. 82). This works out at £2,808 a year after deducting the basic rate tax relief. You get the relief even if you are a non-taxpayer or pay tax only at the starting rate.

You can no longer ask for pension contributions paid in one tax year to be treated as if they were paid in the previous year. As these carry back rules have been abolished, you may now need to plan more carefully to maximise tax relief on your pension contributions. Be prepared to vary them from year-to-year so that you pay more in years when your taxable income is higher. Varying the amount you contribute each year can also maximise the amount of tax credits you can claim (see p. 63–4).

Other reliefs you can claim

Q15 **Do you want to claim any of the following reliefs?**
*If you have made any annual payments, after basic rate tax, answer 'Yes'
to Question 15 and fill in box 15.9. If you have made any gifts to charity go to
Question 15A.*

YES

If yes, tick this box and then fill in boxes 15.1
to 15.12, as appropriate.
If not applicable, go to Question 15A.

Your tax return on pages 5 to 6 lists a variety of reliefs you might be able to claim. If you are not entitled to any of these deductions from your income, go to Q15A.

Loan interest

	Amount of payment
● Interest and alternative finance payments eligible for relief on qualifying loans and arrangements	**15.1** £

Claim here for tax relief on the interest for a variety of loans, including loans to buy:

- ■ a share in or putting capital into a co-operative or a partnership (but not if you are a limited partner)

- ■ plant or machinery (but not a car – see p. 255) for use in your job if you are an employee or partner (if you are self-employed you claim in the Self-employment supplementary pages)

- ■ shares in or putting capital into a close company (see below). To be eligible you should own more than 5 per cent of the company or be a shareholder and work for most of your time in the business. Broadly, a close company is one which is controlled by five or fewer 'participators', such as shareholders, or any number of shareholder directors.

Provided the loan is for one of the purposes above, if it is a low-interest loan from your employer (see p. 116), the loan is a tax-free benefit and you can claim relief for any interest you actually pay by including the amount paid in box 15.1.

Don't enter here to claim tax relief on the interest on a loan for a self-employed business (use box 3.60) or to buy a property you let (use box 5.26) or a mortgage that is part of a home income plan (see p. 65). Nor should you enter interest on a loan to purchase your home, an overdraft or credit cards – they do not qualify for tax relief.

You claim tax relief in the same way for payments you make for Shariah-compliant products (called 'alternative finance payments' in your tax return) for the purposes listed above.

Maintenance payments

• Maintenance or alimony payments you have made under a court order, Child Support Agency assessment or other legally binding order or agreement	Amount claimed, up to £2,350
	15.2 £

In general, from 6 April 2000 onwards, you can no longer get tax relief on maintenance payments you make to your former (or separated) wife, husband or civil partner. However, if either of you were born before 6 April 1935, you can still qualify for some relief. If you can claim because of your spouse's age, put their date of birth in box 15.2A.

Provided you or your former spouse or civil partner were aged 72 or over on 5 April 2007, you can claim relief for payments made under a legally binding agreement, such as a court order, a Child Support Agency assessment, or a written agreement.

No relief is available for voluntary payments. Although maintenance paid to your former spouse or civil partner to maintain your children under the age of 21 is allowed, payments made *to* your children do not qualify for relief.

Payments cease to qualify for relief from the date on which your former wife or husband remarries.

Only payments up to a set limit qualify for relief. The limit is £2,350 in 2006–7. The £2,350 limit applies even if you are making payments to more than one former spouse or partner. You do not get tax relief at the rate of tax you pay. Relief is given at a fixed rate of 10 per cent in 2006–7.

Example

Peter Smith, aged 69, pays maintenance to his ex-wife, Pat, who is three years older than him. Since Pat was born before 6 April 1935, Peter's maintenance payments qualify for tax relief. In 2006–7, Peter paid Pat £400 on the first day of each month (£4,800 over the whole year). However, Pat remarried on 20 October 2006, and although Peter carried on paying maintenance, the payments from that date onwards do not qualify for relief. Peter's qualifying payments (May to October) come to £2,400. This is more than the maximum relief of £2,350, so he puts £2,350 in box 15.2.

In box 15.2, enter the amount of qualifying maintenance you paid during 2006–7 or £2,350, whichever is lower. Give details of the relevant court order or agreement under Additional information on page 10.

Investing in growing businesses

There are some schemes which encourage investment into growing businesses which require risk capital. These types of investments can carry a high degree of risk and to compensate for this investors are offered tax incentives. For more details, see Chapter 7.

Venture capital trusts

● Subscriptions for Venture Capital Trust shares (up to £200,000)

Amount on which relief is claimed
15.3 £

If you invest in a venture capital trust (VCT), you are not investing directly in these companies but in a fund like an investment trust which is quoted on the Stock Exchange.

When you buy new ordinary shares in a venture capital trust, you can get income tax relief at 30 per cent on an investment up to £200,000 in 2006–7. If 30 per cent tax relief would come to more, relief is restricted to your tax bill for the year in which you make the investment. In working this out, the effect of most other reliefs – such as some allowances, enterprise investment scheme relief, Gift Aid relief, and so on – is ignored.

Any dividends paid out by the venture capital trust and gains you make on the shares in the trust are all free of tax.

In box 15.3, put the amount you have invested in venture capital trusts, up to a maximum of £200,000. Keep in a safe place any certificates you get from venture capital trusts as your tax office may ask to see them.

Enterprise Investment Scheme

● Subscriptions under the Enterprise Investment Scheme (up to £400,000) - *also provide details in the 'Additional information' box, box 23.9, on page 10 - see page 26 of your Tax Return Guide.*

Amount on which relief is claimed
15.4 £

You can get tax relief of 20 per cent on investments (not more than £400,000 in 2006–7) made in the shares of unquoted trading companies. If 20 per cent tax relief would come to more, relief is restricted to your tax bill for the year in which you make the investment. In working this out, the effect of most other reliefs – such as some allowances, Gift Aid relief, and so on – is ignored.

You can claim here in this tax return for an investment only if you have received form EIS3 from the company in which you invested (form EIS5 for an investment made through a fund). This form certifies that the company qualifies for the scheme.

If you have invested in shares eligible for the enterprise investment scheme after 5 April, but before 6 October 2007, you can ask for half the investment up to a maximum of £50,000 to be deducted from your income for 2006–7. Make this carry back claim on form EIS3.

Any gain you make on the shares may be free of capital gains tax. You can also claim capital gains tax deferral relief where the enterprise investment scheme investment was funded out of the proceeds of the disposal of another asset on which you made a capital gain – see p. 148. (Deferral relief is available regardless of whether you get any income tax relief.) There are a lot of detailed rules about which companies are eligible and whether you yourself are eligible (see p. 96).

Enter in box 15.4 the total investments (up to £200,000) for which you are claiming income tax relief in 2006–7, deducting any amount carried back to 2005–6. If you have made an investment for which you have not yet received form EIS3, or form EIS5, don't enter it here. Wait until you receive the EIS3 or EIS5 and then claim by sending the form that comes with it to your tax office.

Enter details of each investment for which you are claiming relief in the section headed Additional information on page 10 of the tax return.

Community investment tax relief

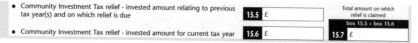

You can claim tax relief on loans you make to, or shares you buy in, a community development finance institution. These institutions have been set up to finance small businesses and social enterprise projects in disadvantaged communities. The institutions must be accredited by the Revenue and, to get tax relief, you must have a certificate from the institution.

You get income tax relief of up to 5 per cent a year of the amount you lend or invest for a maximum of five years. If the 5 per cent relief would come to more, relief is restricted to your tax bill for the year. In working this out, the effect of most other reliefs – such as some allowances, Gift Aid relief, and so on – is ignored. See Revenue Guidance Note *Community investment tax relief scheme. A brief guide for investors* at www.hmrc.gov.uk.

Enter the amount you lent or invested in 2006–7 in box 15.6 and the amount for earlier years in box 15.5. Put the total amount on which you are claiming relief in box 15.7.

Closing a business

Even after you have closed a business, you may find that there are certain obligations and expenses which you have to meet. For example, you may need to put right some defect in work which you carried out.

	Amount of payment/loss
● Post-cessation expenses, pre-incorporation losses brought forward and losses on deeply discounted securities, etc. - *see page 26 of your Tax Return Guide.*	**15.8** £

You can deduct some expenses from any other income and gains you have in the year in which the business expense arises, if you have no income from your closed business. The relief is available for expenses incurred within seven years after the business closure. You must claim for the relief by 31 January in the second year after the tax year in which you incurred the expense. So for an expense which you met in 2006–7, you must claim by 31 January 2009.

The expenses which qualify for this special relief are:

- costs of putting right defective work you did or faulty goods or services which you supplied and the cost of paying any damages as a result
- premiums for insurance against claims due to defective work or faulty goods and services
- legal and other professional expenses you incur in defending yourself against accusations of defective work or providing faulty goods or services
- debts owed to the business which you included in your accounts but which have subsequently turned out to be bad debts
- cost of collecting debts owed to the business and included in its accounts.

Expenses which don't qualify for post-cessation relief can only be set against future income which comes from the closed business. There are some special rules about unpaid expenses. Ask your tax adviser or tax office for help.

Enter in box 15.8 the amount of expenses which you want to deduct from your income in 2006–7 (and in box 8.5 of the Capital gains pages the amount you want to deduct from your capital gains). If you are later reimbursed for any expenses or bad debts entered in this section, remember to enter the amount recovered under Other taxable income (box 13.3 of the tax return – see p. 206).

If you used to run a business on a self-employed basis but have converted the business to a company, you may be able to claim relief for losses made while you were self-employed against your income from the company. You must previously have opted to carry forward the losses to set against future profits (see p. 304), you must have transferred the self-employed business solely or mainly in exchange for shares in the new company and you must meet certain other conditions. Enter the loss you are claiming in box 15.8.

You also claim in box 15.8 for losses on gilt strips, strips from other government securities, and the few other deeply discounted securities that still qualify for loss relief (see p. 190). A loss incurred in 2006–7 can be deducted only from the income in the same tax year.

Annuities

● Trade annuities and patent royalties   Payments made 15.9 £

Annuities and covenants entered into for full value, for genuine commercial reasons, that you pay in connection with your trade or profession and patent royalties are eligible for tax relief at your highest rate. (But covenants paid to individuals in other circumstances do not qualify for any relief.)

Your payments are treated as if basic rate tax relief has already been deducted. If you're a higher rate taxpayer, extra relief is given through your self-assessment tax bill.

In box 15.9, enter the total you actually paid during 2006–7.

Payments to a trade union or friendly society

● Payments to a trade union or friendly society for death benefits   Half amount of payment 15.10 £

Friendly societies supported their members before the arrival of the welfare state by paying sickness benefit, unemployment benefit and widow's pensions. Although rare, some continue in existence and you can get tax relief on premiums you pay on certain combined sickness and life insurance policies they offer. The tax relief is on one half of the premium; you can also get the same tax relief on part of your trade union subscription if it includes pension, funeral or life insurance benefits. With the friendly society policy, to be eligible for tax relief the premiums must be £25 or less a month and 40 per cent or less of the premium should be for the death benefit.

Ask your friendly society or trade union to tell you how much of the premium was for pension, life insurance, funeral or death benefit. Enter in box 15.10 half that amount.

Payment to employer's compulsory scheme for dependants' benefits

		Relief claimed
●	Payments to your employer's compulsory widow's, widower's, surviving civil partner's or orphan's benefit scheme - *available in some circumstances – first read the notes on page 27 of your Tax Return Guide.*	**15.11** £

Some employer's require you to join a scheme (separate from any occupational pension scheme) to provide a pension for your widow, widower or children in the event of your death. Contributions you make may qualify for tax relief that is normally given through PAYE, in which case you should leave box 15.11 blank.

Exceptionally (for example, where you have to make a lump sum contribution at retirement), you might not get all the relief you are entitled to through PAYE. You can claim relief at the basic rate on up to £100 of an otherwise unrelieved payment. In box 15.11 enter the amount of relief you are claiming (not the payment on which you are claiming relief). To work out the relief, take the lower of £100 or the payment on which you have not received relief through PAYE and multiply by 22 per cent. For example, if the payment was £50, enter 22% × £50 = £11 in box 15.11.

Relief on qualifying distributions on the redemption of bonus securities or shares

If you receive bonus shares or securities, when they are subsequently redeemed the amount you receive will count as a distribution for tax purposes. You will then receive a tax credit and, if you're a higher rate taxpayer, will have extra tax to pay.

	Relief claimed
● Relief claimed on a qualifying distribution on the **redemption** of bonus shares or securities	**15.12** £

This means that you could pay tax twice on the same income, because higher-rate taxpayers are also liable for extra tax when such shares are issued. To prevent this, you can claim an allowance equal to the extra tax paid on the issue of the shares. The allowance is given as a reduction in your tax bill.

If you are liable to higher rate tax on dividends during 2006–7 and have entered income from a redemption of the shares in box 10.17 (see p. 191), in box 15.12 enter the amount of relief you are claiming.

The amount of relief is the value of the shares when you first received them (box 10.26 on the relevant year's tax return) multiplied by the difference between the higher rate of tax charged on dividends and the rate treated as already paid. This is:

- for the period 6 April 1999 to 5 April 2007, 32.5% − 10% = 22.5%
- for the period 6 April 1993 to 5 April 1999, 40% − 20% = 20%
- for periods before 6 April 1993, 40% − basic rate tax.

Giving to charity

As well as making donations in the street, you can make more formal donations and use the tax system to reduce what it costs you to make the donation. You can get tax relief up to your highest rate on donations made using the Gift Aid scheme, which also includes any charitable donations you make by deed of covenant. You can also claim income tax relief on shares, similar investments and property that you give to charity or sell to a charity for less than their market value.

Gift Aid

In 2006–7, you get tax relief at your highest rate on any cash gifts made to charity under the Gift Aid scheme. There is no minimum or maximum on the amount of donations that can qualify. You can also use Gift Aid to make cash gifts to community amateur sports clubs registered with the Revenue. (Membership fees do not count as gifts.) For a list of registered clubs, see www.hmrc.gov.uk/casc/clubs.htm.

The amount you give is treated as a payment from which tax relief at the basic rate has already been deducted. The charity claims back the relief, so increasing the amount of your gift. If you are a higher rate taxpayer, you get extra relief deducted from your self-assessment tax bill or through PAYE.

Tax-saving ideas 115, 116 and 117

Provided you are a taxpayer, try to arrange gifts to charity through the Gift Aid scheme. The charity you support can receive more by reclaiming basic rate tax relief on what you give.

If you are a couple, make sure the donation is made by whichever one of you has the highest rate of tax.

If you're aged 65 or over and losing age allowance (see pp. 24 and 54), gifts to charity can be especially tax-efficient. This is because the grossed-up value of donations made under the Gift Aid scheme are deducted from your total income when working out how much age allowance you qualify for.

Example

An envelope is pushed through Julia West's door requesting a donation to the charity, Christian Aid. Julia gives £20 and completes the Gift Aid declaration on the back of the envelope. This is treated as if it is a gift from which basic rate tax relief of £5.64 has already been deducted. The charity claims £5.64 from the Revenue, bringing the total value of Julia's gift to £25.64. (£5.64 is 22 per cent of the grossed-up gift of £25.64). Because she is a higher rate taxpayer, Julia is entitled to more tax relief and claims it through her tax return. In box 15A.1, she enters the amount she actually gave, £20 (not the grossed-up amount of £25.64). She gets her higher rate tax relief as a deduction from her tax bill due on 31 January 2008.

If you don't pay enough income tax and/or capital gains tax to cover the relief you have deducted from your donation, you will have to hand money back to the Revenue. This may affect you if you pay tax at the starting rate in 2006–7 or you are a non-taxpayer. For example, if you made a donation of £78, the charity would claim back £22 bringing the gross amount of your donation to £100. If your tax bill for the year came to only £10, you would have to repay £22 − £10 = £12 to the Revenue (this is taken into account when working out your overall tax bill).

To qualify for tax relief, you must give the charity concerned a Gift Aid declaration, stating that you are a UK taxpayer and giving your name and address. If you do this over the phone, the charity no longer has to send you a written record of the declaration but you can request one. Keep a copy of any declarations.

You may be making regular donations to a charity using Gift Aid (for example, by direct debit). However, some or all of your gifts might be one-off payments that you will not necessarily repeat in another year. Enter the amount of such one-off payments in box 15A.2 so that your tax office knows not to include them as regular items when working out your PAYE code if you have one.

Tax-saving ideas 118 and 119

Gift Aid declarations are often indefinite covering any future donations you make to the charity concerned as well as your current gift. Be careful to stop any open-ended declarations if your circumstances change and you are no longer a taxpayer or if you want to make an unusually large gift (out of an inheritance say) which will not be matched by your tax bill. Otherwise you will find the Revenue billing you for tax relief that the charity claims.

It is worth carrying back a Gift Aid donation to the previous year if the tax you would save through higher rate tax relief on the donation or an increase in age allowance (see p. 24 and 54) in the earlier year would exceed the tax you could save in the year the donation was made.

• Gift Aid payments, including covenanted payments to charities, made between 6 April 2006 and 5 April 2007	**15A.1** £
• The total of any 'one-off' payments included in box 15A.1	**15A.2** £
• Gift Aid payments made after 5 April 2006 but treated as if made in the tax year 2005-06	**15A.3** £
• Gift Aid payments made after 5 April 2007 but to be treated as if made in the tax year 2006-07	**15A.4** £

You can elect for a Gift Aid donation made after 5 April 2007 to be carried back and treated as if you had paid it in 2006–7. You must have taxable income or gains in 2006–7 at least equal to the amount carried back plus the basic rate tax relief on it. The election must be in writing and must be made by the earlier of the date you file your tax return or 31 January 2008. Put the amount of any donation you want to carry back in this way in box 15A.4. In box 15A.3 put the amount of any Gift Aid donations made in the period 6 April 2006 to 31 January 2007 that last year you opted to carry back to 2005–6.

Gifts of shares, unit trusts and property to charities

• Gifts of qualifying investments to charities – shares and securities	**15A.6** £
• Gifts of qualifying investments to charities – real property	**15A.7** £

You can get income tax relief at your highest rate on gifts to charities of shares, units in unit trusts and shares in open-ended investment companies (oeics). Shares must be quoted on a recognised stock exchange either in the UK (including the Alternative Investment Market) or in another country. Unit trusts and oeics must be UK-authorised or equivalent foreign investment schemes.

Tax-saving idea 120

> If you're aged 65 or over and losing age allowance (see pp. 24 and 54), gifts of shares, unit trusts, oeics (open-ended investment companies) or property to charity can be especially tax-efficient. This is because the value of such gifts is deducted from your total income when working out how much age allowance you qualify for.

Similarly, since 6 April 2002, you can get income tax relief at your highest rate on a gift to a charity of a freehold or leasehold interest in UK land or buildings. You must have a certificate from the charity showing that it has accepted the gift.

If you own the property jointly, all the owners must agree to give the whole property to the charity and you get relief in proportion to your share.

If you or someone connected to you gets an interest or right in the property within five years of 31 January following the tax year in which you made the gift, the tax relief will be clawed back.

Tax-saving idea 121

> Gift Aid donations are especially tax-efficient if your income is above one of the tax-credit thresholds and a reduction in that income would increase your credits (see p. 60). For example, for every £10 you want the charity to receive, you give just £7.80 net of tax relief and your tax credits could increase by, say, £3.70 reducing the overall cost to you of each £10 donated to just £4.10. For tax credit purposes, donations count only in the year they are paid – there is no carry back arrangement.

Relief is given by deducting the value of your gift from your total income for 2006–7. (There is also no capital gains tax on gains made on shares or property given to charity – see Chapter 9.)

Enter the value of your gift in box 15A.6 or 15A.7 as appropriate. This is the market value of the shares, units or property at the time of the gift plus any disposal costs less any sum you receive (for example, if you are selling the shares or property to the charity at a knock-down price) and less the value of any benefits you receive from the charity as a result of the gift.

For more information, ask the Orderline (see p. 170) for Help Sheet IR342 *Charitable giving* and leaflet IR178 *Giving shares and securities to charity*.

Tax-saving idea 122

If you want to make a substantial gift to charity and you own shares or property which are standing at a substantial profit, it will usually be more tax-efficient to give the shares or property direct to the charity rather than selling them first and making a Gift Aid donation of the cash raised. But the tax relief you get can only be set against your income – not any capital gains.

14

Allowances

Another way of reducing the amount of income tax you have to pay is to claim any allowances to which you are entitled. These are deducted from your income, along with reliefs (deductions), to make your taxable income smaller – and so also your tax bill.

Personal allowances

Everyone gets a personal allowance. It comes automatically; you don't have to claim it in the tax return.

Tax-saving idea 123

You can go back nearly six years to claim an allowance which you forgot at the time or didn't know you were entitled to. You get tax relief at the rate of tax which would have applied if you claimed the deduction at the right time. Provided you claim by 31 January 2008, you can go back as far as the 2001–2 tax year.

Age-related personal allowances

However, people aged 65 or over during 2006–7, can claim a higher allowance. There is one level of age-related allowance if you were 65 or over during 2006–7 and a still higher rate if you were 75 or over. On the tax return it says if you were born before 6 April 1942, enter your date of birth in box 22.6 to claim the age-related allowance. Box 22.6 is in the middle of page 9 of the return.

ALLOWANCES AND OTHER INFORMATION   for the year ended 5 April 2007

Q16 **Do you want to claim blind person's allowance, or married couple's allowance?**
If you are resident in the UK you get your personal allowance of £5,035 automatically.
If you were born before 6 April 1942, enter your date of birth in box 22.6 *- you may get a higher age-related personal allowance.*

YES

If yes, tick this box and then read pages 28 to 31 of your Tax Return Guide. Fill in boxes 16.1 to 16.17 as appropriate.
If not applicable, go to Question 17.

Blind person's allowance

Anyone registered as blind with a local authority can claim blind person's allowance. The amount of the allowance for 2006–7 is £1,660.

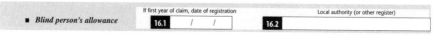

■ *Blind person's allowance*   If first year of claim, date of registration **16.1** / /   **16.2**   Local authority (or other register)

In box 16.1, enter the date you were registered blind if this is the first year you are claiming, and enter the name of the local authority in box 16.2.

If you are not registered until after 5 April 2007 but before 6 April 2008, you can still get the allowance for 2006–7 if you can show that you were blind at that date, for example, with an ophthalmologist's certificate.

The requirement for Scotland and Northern Ireland is different. You don't need to be registered. You can claim blind person's allowance if you are not able to perform any work for which eyesight was essential. To claim, write Scotland claim or Northern Ireland claim in box 16.2.

If your income is less than your allowances, including blind person's, and you are married and living with your husband or wife, or in a civil partnership and living with your partner, you can transfer the unused part of this allowance to your spouse or partner (see p. 229). If both of you are blind, you can claim two allowances.

Married couple's allowance

Where husband, wife or civil partner was born before 6 April 1935, a couple can claim the married couple's allowance. For other couples, the allowance was abolished from 6 April 2000 onwards. If you were both born on or after 6 April 1935, do not complete boxes 16.3 to 16.13.

The maximum allowance where either husband or wife reaches age 72 or more in 2006–7 is £6,065. Where either of you was aged 74 or over on 6 April 2006, the maximum allowance is £6,135. If the total income of the person to whom the allowance is initially awarded exceeds £20,100, the allowance is reduced but never to less than a basic amount of £2,350 (see

p. 54). The allowance gives tax relief at 10 per cent as a reduction in your tax bill.

A spouse or civil partner can claim married couple's allowance if they were married and living together for at least part of the tax year. A spouse or civil partner can also claim the allowance if they were living apart but neither intended the separation to be permanent.

Married couple's allowance is automatically given to the husband unless:

■ either of you has asked for half the basic amount to be given to the wife (in other words, £1,175 is transferred)

■ both of you have asked for the whole basic amount of £2,350 to be given to the wife, or

■ the first claim was made on or after 5 December 2005, in which case the award is made initially to whichever of the couple (in a marriage or civil partnership) has the highest income. In that case, half or all of the basic amount can be transferred to the other spouse or partner.

Any married couple's allowance in excess of £2,350 always stays with the person to whom the award was first made.

Normally, you must elect to transfer half or all of the basic allowance before the start of the tax year. But if you marry or register your partnership during the tax year, you have until the end of the year to elect for the transfer. This means it is too late to alter the way the allowance is given for 2006–7. It is also too late to alter the way the allowance is given for 2007–8, unless you marry or register on or after 6 April 2007. You have until 5 April 2008 to elect how the allowance is given for 2008–9. Make the election by writing to your tax office.

● Enter your date of birth (if born before 6 April 1935)	**16.3** / /
● Enter your spouse or civil partner's date of birth (**only** if born before 6 April 1935 **and** if they are older than you)	**16.4** / /

If you are claiming any of the allowance for 2006–7, put your date of birth in box 16.3. If your spouse or civil partner is older than you and was born before 6 April 1935, put their date of birth in box 16.4, otherwise leave 16.4 blank.

Then, if you are a married man, who married before 5 December 2005, or you married or formed a civil partnership on or after 5 December 2005 and you have the higher income, **fill in boxes 16.5 to 16.9.**

If you are a married woman, who married before 5 December 2005, or you married or formed a civil partnership on or after 5 December 2005 but you do not have the higher income, **fill in boxes 16.10 to 16.13** to claim half, or all, of the minimum amount of the married couple's allowance.

● Spouse or civil partner's full name **16.5**	● Date of marriage or formation of civil partnership (if after 5 April 2006) **16.6** / /

- Tick box 16.7 or box 16.8 where half, or all, of the minimum amount of the allowance has been allocated to your wife, husband or civil partner

Half | All
16.7 | 16.8

- Enter in box 16.9 the date of birth of any previous wife, husband or former civil partner, with whom you lived at any time during 2006-07. Read 'Special rules if you are married or formed a civil partnership in the year ended 5 April 2007' on page 30 of your Tax Return Guide before completing box 16.9.

16.9 | / | /

If you married or registered on or after 5 December 2005 and your income is lower than that of your spouse or partner, or if you are a woman who married before 5 December 2005, leave boxes 16.5 to 16.9 blank and go to box 16.10.

Otherwise, put your spouse's or partner's name in box 16.5. If your marriage took place before 6 April 2006 and you are receiving the whole married couple's allowance, leave boxes 16.6 to 16.9 blank.

If your marriage or registration took place on or after 6 April 2006, put its date in box 16.6. You can claim one-twelfth of the full allowance for each month of your marriage or partnership (see p. 56). If in the same tax year prior to your marriage or registration you were living with a previous spouse and either of you were born before 6 April 1935, you can instead claim the full married couple's allowance for 2006–7 and you should put your former spouse's date of birth in box 16.9.

- Tick box 16.10 or 16.11 where half, or all, of the minimum amount of the allowance has been allocated to you

Half | All
16.10 | 16.11

- Spouse or civil partner's full name

16.12

- Date of marriage or formation of civil partnership (if after 5 April 2006)

16.13 | / | /

If you are not the person to whom the allowance was initially allocated but you received all or part of the basic amount, tick either box 16.10 or 16.11 as appropriate. (But if your spouse or civil partner died during 2006–7 leave these boxes blank and tick box 16.28 – see below.)

Put your spouse's or civil partner's name in box 16.2. If the marriage or registration took place on or after 6 April 2006, give the date in box 16.13 unless you continue to qualify for all or part of the married couple's allowance for 2006–7 because of a previous marriage, in which case leave 16.13 blank.

Example

George, 71, was born on 7 June 1935 and would not qualify for married couple's allowance except that his wife, Hannah, who is older than him, was born on 23 February 1935. As a result George qualifies for an allowance of £6,065 in 2006–7. George and Hannah are both taxpayers. Before 6 April 2006, the couple wrote to their tax office electing to have the full basic allowance transferred to Hannah. This means Hannah gets £2,350 of the married couple's allowance, reducing her tax bill by 10% × £2,350 = £235. George keeps the other £3,715, reducing his tax bill by 10% × £3,715 = £371.50.

Transfer of surplus allowances

You can transfer any unused amount of married couple's or blind person's allowance to your spouse or civil partner if you did not have enough income in the year to use up the allowance and you lived with your spouse or partner for at least part of that year.

■ *Transfer of surplus allowances* - *read page 31 of your Tax Return Guide before you fill in boxes 16.14 to 16.17.*
● Tick box 16.14 if you want your spouse or civil partner to have your unused allowances   **16.14**
● Tick box 16.15 if you want to have your spouse's or civil partner's unused allowances   **16.15**
Please give details in the 'Additional information' box, box 23.9, on page 10
If you want to calculate your tax, enter the amount of the surplus allowances you can have
● Blind person's surplus allowance   **16.16** £
● Married couple's surplus allowance   **16.17** £

If you want your spouse or civil partner to have the surplus of married couple's or blind person's allowances, tick box 16.14. In the Additional information box on page 10 of your tax return, give your spouse's or partner's name, address, tax reference, national insurance number and tax office.

If you want to claim and use your spouse's or civil partner's unused allowances, tick box 16.15. Give your spouse's or partner's name, address, tax reference, national insurance number and tax office in the Additional information box on page 10.

If you are working out your own tax bill, enter in boxes 16.16 and 16.17 the amount of the surplus allowances you are claiming. You can ask your tax office for help if you are not sure of the amount.

15

Employment

It is usually easy to tell whether or not you are an employee. There are some grey areas, however, where the Revenue will seek to tax you as an employee even if you think of yourself as self-employed:

- if you are a company director (even if you own the company). Note that, from 6 April 2000, if you are a director of your own personal services company, special tax rules may apply and, from 10 April 2003, these were extended to domestic workers (such as nannies) operating through their own company (see p. 234). The Revenue considers that these special rules also apply to people working through managed services companies (in which workers have shares without usually being directors) but has had difficulty making these companies comply with the rules. Therefore the government plans to bring in new laws from 6 April 2007 onwards to ensure people working for managed service companies are taxed as employees

- if you work on a freelance or consultancy basis, but have to work closely under the control of your boss, working a set number of hours at an hourly rate, say, and at a particular location

- if you work on a casual, part-time basis

- if you work as a temp through an agency. This includes, for example, locum doctors; but it does not apply to entertainers or models working through an agency, or to people who work solely from home

■ you have more than one job: you may be classed as an employee for one job, even if you are clearly self-employed in another.

The key significance of being an employee is that in most cases your employer will have to operate PAYE (see Chapter 3) on your earnings from that job and deduct tax and national insurance before paying you. Exceptionally, the Revenue has agreed that most actors can count as employees for national insurance purposes but as self-employed for income tax (and is trying to backdate the same treatment to freelance musicians).

For many employees, the advantage of being paid under PAYE is that the right amount of tax on all their income should be deducted from their earnings and so they do not have to worry about paying a separate tax bill. If their income from their job is their only income many also do not need to fill in a tax return. But you may still have to fill one in if:

■ you are a higher rate taxpayer and get taxable perks such as a company car or receive investment income

■ you have other income which is paid out before tax is deducted, such as some types of investment income

■ your tax affairs are complex for any other reason.

If you are an employee and are sent a tax return, you need to tick the box at Q1 of the basic tax return and fill in a separate Employment page for each job you have. If you are not sure of your status, check with your tax office and try the Revenue's employment status indicator at www.hmrc.gv.uk/calc/esi.htm.

Your employer

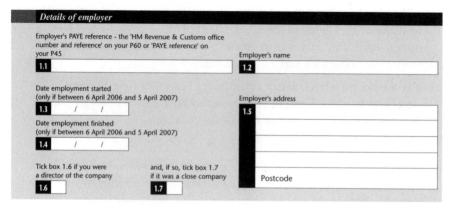

So that your tax office can tie up the information on your tax return with that provided by your employer, give your employer's name, address and PAYE reference (shown on the P60 or P45). If the employment started or ended during 2006–7, you also need to give the start or end dates of the job, the length of time you worked there, whether or not you are a director (box 1.6) and if it is a close company (box 1.7). This may affect how your perks and benefits are taxed.

Tax-saving idea 124

A disadvantage of being an employee is that you cannot deduct as many expenses from your taxable income as you could if you were self-employed. So if you are setting up on your own, check that you will meet the Revenue's conditions for self-employment.

What is taxed

Broadly speaking, the Revenue seeks to tax any benefit you get from being employed, even if you get it from someone other than your employer. The tax return organises your remuneration into the following categories:

■ money (including earnings from working abroad)

■ benefits (taxable perks given by your employer) and expenses payments (either flat-rate allowances or reimbursement for expenses you have incurred)

■ lump sums received on retirement, redundancy or death.

Not all of these will actually be taxable. But in general, you have to put it all down first, and the tax return then guides you to enter the various tax reliefs which you can deduct, for example, tax relief for expenses incurred in doing your job.

One thing you do not have to enter anywhere on your tax return is details of your national insurance contributions as an employee. These should all be sorted out for you by your employer.

The date income is taxable

As a general rule, you are counted as receiving income from employment from the earlier of:

■ the date you get it

■ the date you are entitled to it, even if you do not actually get it till later on.

So if, for example, you are entitled to payment on 15 March 2007, but do not actually receive it until 15 April, you must still include it in your tax return for 2006–7. If you receive payment early – on 15 March 2007, for work not completed until 15 April, for example – it is taxable from the date you received it, that is 15 March.

If you are a director, your earnings for a particular period may be decided on one date, credited to you in the company accounts on another date, but not paid out till much later. It is the earliest date that counts, unless the earnings for a particular period were decided before that period ended. In this case, you are treated as receiving them on the last day of the period to which the earnings relate.

IR35: special rules for personal service companies

Special rules may apply if you are a director of a company that hires out your services to clients and:

■ you or your family (including an unmarried partner) control more than 5 per cent of the ordinary share capital of the company, or

■ you or your family are entitled to more than 5 per cent of any dividends paid out by the company, or

■ the company can or does make payments to you other than salary but they are basically payment for the services you provide to clients.

Tax-saving idea 125

You must pay income tax and national insurance on any deemed payment for the tax year in which the money is earned by your personal service company. If that money is paid out to you as salary in a later year, tax and national insurance will again be due – in other words, the same income will be taxed twice. To avoid this, make sure any deemed payment retained within the company is eventually paid out as dividends, not salary. IR35 rules allow dividends up to the amount of any deemed payments to be paid without further tax being due (see p. 192) and dividends are not in any case subject to national insurance.

These so-called 'personal service companies' have been popular with people working as contractors or consultants, for example in the information technology and engineering industries. If you were employed direct by a client, you would pay tax and national insurance on your salary and the client would pay employer's national insurance. But if the client contracts with your personal service company to hire your services, the client pays a fee to your company on which there is no employer's national insurance. And if your company pays you dividends instead of salary, you also escape paying national insurance. The Revenue views this as tax avoidance.

For income earned by your company on or after 6 April 2000, the Revenue has closed this loophole. If in the absence of your company your work for a client would essentially be the same as that of an employee (rather than a self-employed person), you may be caught by the IR35 rules (named after the number of the press release which introduced them) and have to pay extra tax and national insurance. The Revenue uses the normal tests for deciding whether you count as an employee or self-employed (see p. 275).

Initially, the IR35 rules applied only where your company was contracted for business purposes. But from 10 April 2003, the rules were extended to apply to services performed for any person whether for business purposes or not. This brought domestic workers, such as nannies and butlers within the rules.

Example

Bill Brown is a software designer. He is owner-director of a company, BB-IT Ltd, which hires Bill out to clients. For the whole of 2006–7, Bill is contracted to Gigasoft plc, working full-time in their offices for a monthly fee of £6,000. The contract is caught by the IR35 rules. BB-IT Ltd paid Bill a salary of £24,000, £2,500 for an annual season ticket to cover travel to Gigasoft's offices and £4,000 to Bill's pension scheme. At the end of the year, BB-IT Ltd must work out whether there is any deemed payment under the IR35 rules on which income tax and National Insurance contributions are due:

Income caught by IR35 (12 × £6,000)	£72,000
Less	
Salary actually paid	£24,000
Employer's National Insurance already paid ([£24,000 − £5,035] × 12.8%)	£2,428
Employee-related expenses (i.e. season ticket) which would be allowed under normal rules	£2,500
Pension scheme contribution	£4,000
Expense allowance to cover costs of running personal service company (5% of £72,000)	£3,600
Deemed payment before deducting employer's national insurance	£35,472
Employer's national insurance on deemed payment (£31,447 × 12.8%)	£4,025
Deemed payment	£31,447

Bill is deemed to receive extra salary of £31,447 on 5 April 2007. The company is responsible via PAYE for paying Bill's income tax and employee's National Insurance on this amount as well as employer's national insurance of £4,025.

If the IR35 rules do apply, you will be treated for income tax and national insurance purposes as if you had received a salary (called a 'deemed payment') equal to:

■ the fees received by your company, less

■ any salary paid by the company on which you have paid tax and national insurance in the normal way, less

■ a 5 per cent expense allowance designed to cover the costs of running your personal service company.

The deemed payment is treated as paid on the last day of the tax year – in other words, 5 April 2007 in the case of the tax year covered by the current tax return. Tax and national insurance were due to be paid through the PAYE system by 19 April 2007.

The deemed payment, just like salaries that are actually paid out, is deducted from the company's profits when working out corporation tax.

Your company does not actually have to pay you the deemed payment – it could be retained within the company or paid to you as dividends. IR35 includes rules to allow special distributions (dividends) to be made during the tax year or later up to the amount of any deemed payment without further tax being due – see p. 192.

The IR35 rules affect only the income tax and national insurance position. They do not affect the legal status of your company's contract with the client.

The rules apply on a contract-by-contract basis. Some of the work you do through your personal service company may count as equivalent to self-employment and so fall outside the rules; other contracts may be deemed equivalent to employment and so fall within the rules. You can ask your tax office to advise on the status of existing contracts (but not draft contracts).

For more information, see www.hmrc.gov.uk/ir35/index.htm. If you do not have internet access, ask your tax office to send you a copy of these web pages.

Include any deemed payment in box 1.8. Income tax on the deemed payment paid through PAYE should be included in box 1.11.

The documents you need

Most of the information you need will be on Forms P60, P11D or P9D.

Your P60 is a form your employer must give you by 31 May after the end of the tax year (that is, by 31 May 2007 for the 2006–7 tax year). The P60 is a summary of how much you have been paid, and how much tax has been deducted. If you haven't got a P60, you should be able to find the information from your pay slips. If you left a job during a tax year, the information will be on your P45.

If you work through your own personal services company, your company must provide you with a P60 in the normal way. The P60 (and any P45) will show any deemed payment under the IR35 rules and tax on it in the same way as ordinary pay.

Your employer has to declare to the Revenue any taxable benefits or expenses you receive and the cash equivalent on form P11D or form P9D. Which form you get depends on how much you earn. You should get a copy from your employer by 6 July after the end of the tax year, that is by 6 July 2007 for the 2006–7 tax year.

Note that if you leave a job, you will not automatically be given a form P11D or P9D, but your ex-employer must give you one if you ask for it within three years after the end of the tax year in which you left. Your employer has 30 days from receiving your request in which to supply the form (if this is after the normal 6 July deadline).

Your P11D or P9D should be the starting point of all the expenses payments you have received. But you also need to keep receipts or documentation to back up your claim to deduct allowable expenses, particularly if they were not reimbursed by your employer and so did not appear on your P11D or P9D.

If you receive a lump sum from your employer, for example, when you left your job, it may be included on your P60, your P11D, or your P45, or you may just have a letter from your employer. Your employer should be able to help you decide which category a payment falls within. If there is any doubt, employers can get advance decisions from their tax office, so it is worth talking about the tax consequences with your employer before any payment is made.

Money from employment

Income from employment		
■ *Money* - see Notes, page EN3.		Before tax
● Payments from P60 (or P45)	**1.8** £	

You should enter as money:

■ salaries, deemed payments under IR35 rules, wages, fees, overtime, bonuses, commission and honoraria (after deducting money you have donated to a payroll giving scheme, or contributed to your employer's pension scheme, see below)

■ amounts voted to you as a director and credited to an account with the company, even if you cannot draw the money straight away

■ voluntary payments and gifts, whether from your employer or anyone else, such as tips and Christmas boxes (excluding some small gifts and personal gifts such as long-service awards, see Tax-free fringe benefits on p. 101)

■ incentive awards (but see below)

■ the taxable value of shares withdrawn early from an approved profit-sharing scheme

■ sick pay, including statutory sick pay and statutory maternity, paternity and adoption pay (see overleaf)

■ holiday pay

■ various payments to do with your employment which are not strictly pay. Examples are golden hellos paid to entice you to join the company; a loan written off because you satisfied or completed an employment condition; payments made to recognise changes in your conditions of service or employment; payments made if you leave a job and agree, in return for a lump sum, not to compete with your employer.

P60 forms vary slightly in design. The figure to look for is your pay 'for tax purposes' or 'this employment pay'. Enter the figure from Form P60 in box 1.8, but check that it does not include employer's contributions to a pension scheme or what you give under a payroll giving scheme (see below). If you were unemployed during the year, your P60 may give details of any jobseeker's allowance you received. Do not enter this in your Employment page – enter it instead in box 11.5 in the basic tax return.

Contributions to an occupational pension scheme

You can get tax relief on contributions you make to your employer's occupational pension scheme (see p. 81). This tax relief is given by deducting your contributions from your pay before tax is worked out on it, so giving you relief up to your top rate of tax. The figure you enter as taxable pay in box 1.8 should be the figure after deducting pension contributions.

Details of contributions to other types of pension plan or scheme do not go here, even if your employer arranges for them to be paid direct from your salary. Instead they go in boxes 14.1 to 14.4 in the basic tax return.

Payroll giving schemes

You can get tax relief on charitable donations of any amount through a payroll giving scheme offered by your employer. The biggest scheme run by the Charities Aid Foundation is called Give As You Earn, or GAYE. The money is deducted from your pay each week or month and passed straight to the charity by your employer. The donations are deducted from your pay before your tax is worked out on it, in the same way as contributions to an occupational pension scheme, so remember to check that what you enter in box 1.8. is your pay after deduction of payroll giving donations.

Incentive awards

Broadly speaking, these are taxable whether you receive them from your employer or from someone else in connection with your job; for example, a car sales representative may receive prizes from the car manufacturer. However, the person paying the award may pay the tax for you, through a taxed award scheme. In this case, the award still counts as part of your income, but the tax paid on your behalf will reduce your tax bill. Whoever makes the award should give you a Form P443 stating the value of the award and how much tax has been paid on it, unless the figures have been included on your P60. You should include the amount of the award in box 1.10 and the tax already paid in box 1.11.

Suggestion scheme awards are tax-free and need not be entered, provided that there is a formal scheme open to all employees, and the suggestion concerned is outside your normal job. If the suggestion is not taken up, the maximum award is £25; if it is implemented, the maximum award is 50 per cent of the first year's expected net benefit, or 10 per cent of the benefit over five years, with an overall maximum of £5,000.

Sick pay, maternity pay, paternity pay and adoption pay

If you are off work through illness or on maternity, paternity or adoption leave, any payment made to you by your employer, including statutory sick pay (SSP), statutory maternity pay (SMP), statutory paternity pay or statutory adoption pay, is taxable. It will be taxed before you get it and shown on your P60 or P45 in the same way as other income, and you enter it with your other taxable pay in box 1.8. There are two exceptions to this rule:

■ occasionally, these statutory payments may be paid directly to you by the Revenue. In this case, the benefit is still taxable, but tax is not deducted before it is paid to you and rather than enter it under Employment you should enter it in box 11.7 on page 4 of the basic tax return

■ if you pay part or all of the premiums for an insurance policy taken out by your employer to meet the cost of employees' sick pay. In this case, the proportion of the sick pay which arises from your contributions is tax-free and need not be entered on the tax return. Any sick pay arising from your employer's contributions is taxable. Put it in box 1.8.

Tips and other payments

Boxes 1.9 and 1.10 are there to catch any income which does not appear on your P60 (for example, because it is paid by people other than your employer or it comprises earnings from a foreign source earned in an earlier year but only remitted in 2006–7) and for which there is no other place on the Employment page.

Tax deducted

The tax your employer has deducted under PAYE is set against your tax bill. Enter it in box 1.11, together with any other tax deducted (for example, under a taxed incentive scheme). Occasionally, your employer may have given you more tax back as a refund than was actually deducted. If so, put the refund in box 1.11 but in brackets to show it is a negative sum.

If you left a job and later received a tax refund from the Revenue or the

Department for Work and Pensions, enter in box 1.11 the tax shown on your P45. Put the subsequent repayment in box 20.1 on the basic tax return (see p. 177).

Fringe benefits and expenses

■ *Benefits and expenses* - *see Notes, pages EN3 to EN6. If any benefits connected with termination of employment were received, or enjoyed, after that termination and were from a **former** employer you need Help Sheet IR204, available from the Orderline. Do not enter such benefits here.*

Many employers give their employees non-cash fringe benefits, such as a company car or free medical insurance (see Chapter 8). Generally, you are taxed on the cash equivalent of these benefits (and the same applies if the benefit or expense is paid to you by someone other than your employer). Benefits for your family or household are regarded as a payment to you. However, some types of benefits are tax-free for everyone, and others are tax-free if you count as low-paid.

Expense payments you receive are yoked together with benefits in this section and sometimes the dividing line between them can be a fine one; for example, a company car may be a way of covering your travelling costs for work, as well as a perk of the job.

Payments you do not need to enter

There are three sorts of payments which you can ignore when filling out the benefits and expenses section of the Employment supplementary page.

Dispensations

You do not need to enter in your tax return expense payments which are covered by a dispensation. A dispensation is a special permission from the Revenue which means that your employer does not have to include on your P11D or P9D expenses which would be tax-free anyway. Dispensations are usually given for things like travelling and subsistence expenses on an approved scale: they do not generally cover fringe benefits.

PAYE Settlement Agreements

The tax on some of your expenses and benefits may already have been paid by your employer under a PAYE Settlement Agreement (PSA). This is a voluntary agreement between an employer and the Revenue under which the employer undertakes to pay the tax otherwise due from you on some types of benefits and expenses. The advantage for your employer is the saving of paperwork; the advantage for you is that you do not need to enter the payments on your return and they are tax-free in your hands. Only some types of benefits and expenses can be covered by this sort of agreement, for example, minor expenses such as taxi fares and benefits such as parties shared by many employees.

Tax-saving idea 126

> Remember – you do not need to enter items covered by a dispensation or PAYE Settlement Agreement.

Tax-free fringe benefits

You do not need to enter the details of any fringe benefits which are tax-free (see Chapter 8 for a list). Note that there are conditions to be met before most of these benefits can be tax-free. Fuller information is given in Help Sheet IR207 *Non-taxable payments or benefits for employees*.

Payments you need to enter

There are some benefits which are always taxable and need to be entered on the tax return. They are assets which are transferred to you (including payments in kind), vouchers (except, since 6 April 2002, vouchers for minor benefits that are exempt from tax, such as a travel card for free travel on a works bus) and goods paid for by credit cards, living accommodation (with a few exceptions) and mileage allowance in excess of the Revenue authorised mileage allowance payments.

You may receive other benefits. But if you earn at a rate of less than £8,500 a year and are not a director they will be tax-free and you do not need to enter them on the tax return. Chapter 8 gives much more detail. It helps you work out whether you are paid at the rate of £8,500 a year or not and helps you work out the taxable value of benefits which you need to enter here.

Assets transferred to you and payments made for you

Payments in kind may be taxed in a number of ways, depending on how much you earn and whether you have the alternative of cash instead (see p. 107 to find out the taxable value). You should be able to get the amount to enter in box 1.12 from your P11D or P9D. If you earn less than £8,500, the taxable value is the second-hand value. But if you earn £8,500 or more, the taxable value is the larger of the second-hand value or the cost to the employer of providing the asset.

Payments your employer makes for you, like your phone bill, should also be entered in box 1.12. But don't put assets which remain the property of your employer and which you merely have the use of, or services supplied by your employer – these go in box 1.22, unless there is a more specific box.

Vouchers and credit cards

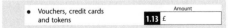

You may be given a voucher for a particular service (for example, a season ticket), a credit token or a company credit or charge card. If so, you are taxed on their cash equivalent unless they appear in the list of tax-free fringe benefits on pp. 101–6 (for example, luncheon vouchers, gift vouchers which count as a small gift, vouchers for minor benefits that are tax free). Cash vouchers worth a specified amount of cash should already have been taxed under PAYE, so you will not usually have to enter them here as a benefit. If you used vouchers or your company credit card to settle expenses of your job (such as train fares), include the full value of the vouchers or card bill here, but claim a deduction for 'Expenses you incurred in doing your job' on the back of the Employment page.

For vouchers and cards which count as a taxable fringe benefit, broadly speaking you pay tax on the expense incurred by the person who provided them, less any amount that you have paid yourself. You will not have to pay tax on any annual card fee or interest paid by your employer.

Company credit cards and charge cards are often provided as a convenient way of paying business expenses. If so, you still have to enter the value of any vouchers or goods or services obtained with a credit card or credit token in box 1.13. You can claim any allowable business expenses back in boxes 1.32 to 1.35. For more information see Help Sheet IR201 *Vouchers, credit cards and tokens*.

Living accommodation

The basic taxable charge for any living accommodation (unless it counts as a tax-free fringe benefit, see p. 104), and the extra charge if applicable, should be entered in box 1.14. However, if you have the alternative of getting cash instead of accommodation, and the cash alternative comes to more than the taxable value of the accommodation, you should enter the surplus cash (i.e. in excess of the taxable value) in box 1.12 and the taxable value in box 1.14. This applies even if you have decided to live in the accommodation.

Help Sheet IR202 *Living accommodation* explains how to work out the taxable value for various types of accommodation.

Mileage allowances

If you use your own car, motorbike or bicycle for work, you may be paid a mileage allowance for the business mileage you do. Since 6 April 2002, any allowance up to the Revenue approved mileage allowance payment (see pp. 101–2) is tax-free and you do not enter it on your tax return. But anything in excess of the approved payment is taxable and should be entered in box 1.15. This is the case even if your actual costs are higher than the authorised rate, so that you are not making any profit out of the excess allowance. The amount of any excess should be shown on the P11D.

Similarly, your employer can pay you a tax-free passenger allowance up to the approved payment if you carry a colleague in your vehicle on business trips (see p. 102). Any excess over the approved amount is taxable and must be entered in box 1.15.

If your employer does not pay you any mileage allowance or pays you less than the approved payment, you can claim a deduction up to the approved amount (regardless of your actual costs) in box 1.32 (see p. 251). This does not apply to passenger allowances.

For more information, see Revenue Help Sheet IR124 *Using your own vehicle for work*.

Company cars

A company car is taxable only if you earn at the rate of £8,500 a year or more (see p. 110). Put in box 1.16 the cash equivalent of cars made available to you (or to members of your family or household) for private use. Check the figure with your employer or on your form P11D. Chapter 8 and Help Sheet IR203 *Car benefits and car fuel benefits* will be useful.

Fuel for company cars

If you have a company car, you may get free fuel for private use as well. This is taxed in a similar way to company cars with the tax charge based on the car's carbon dioxide emissions (see p. 114). Enter the amount in box 1.17.

Tax-saving idea 127

> The taxable value of a company car is based on its carbon dioxide emissions. This makes larger company cars an expensive fringe benefit. Consider a low-emission car instead. You can find out about different cars' carbon dioxide emissions from www.vcacarfueldata.org.uk.

Vans

A van is taxable only if you earn at the rate of £8,500 a year or more (see p. 110). In 2006–7, the basic taxable value of a van is £500, but there may be reductions (see p. 115). Enter the adjusted taxable amount in box 1.18.

Vans are taxed much more heavily from 6 April 2007 onwards – see p. 115.

Interest-free and low-interest loans

Free or cheap loans are only taxable if you earn at the rate of £8,500 a year or more. The basic rule is that you have to pay tax on the difference between the interest you pay and the interest worked out at an official rate set by the Revenue. But there can be exceptions (see p. 116).

In box 1.19, you should put the cash equivalent (your employer should tell you what this is).

If the loan is for a qualifying purpose (for example, to buy an interest in a partnership) and you are paying interest on the loan, you should claim tax relief in box 15.1 of the basic tax return (see p. 213).

If the loan is eventually written off without your having to repay it, you pay tax on the amount written off. Include the amount with the taxable value of any other loans in box 1.19. There is no box 1.20.

Private medical or dental insurance

This is taxable only if you earn at the rate of £8,500 a year or more. Enter the taxable amount, which you should find on Form P11D, in box 1.21. For more explanation, see p. 117.

Other benefits

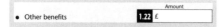

This is a box to sweep up any other taxable perks which you have not already entered elsewhere. Remember, though, that it applies only if you earn at a rate of £8,500 or more. The figures should be shown on your P11D. The main types of benefits you may have to enter here are listed on p. 117–8.

Tax-saving idea 128

The loan of a computer from your employer for your private use ceased to be a tax-free benefit for new loans from 6 April 2006 onwards. For new loans, the value of the benefit will be taxed as described on p. 118 and the taxable value should be entered in box 1.22. Where the computer was first lent to you before that date and qualified as tax-free, this exemption continues to apply and includes replacement of the computer under warranty (but not after the warranty period has expired), and upgrading software and ongoing maintenance contracts if part of the original pre-6-April-2006 agreement with your employer. But the exemption will be lost if, for example, your employer replaces the original computer with a new machine, so think carefully before accepting an upgrade.

Note: If your employer provides you with a computer solely for business use (whether at home or at work), this is not a taxable benefit provided any private use of the equipment is 'not significant'.

Expenses payments and balancing charges

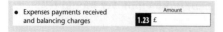

You should enter here the total expenses payments and expense allowances you received. You can deduct tax-free expense payments later on in boxes 1.32 to 1.35. The only expenses which you should not enter either here or later on are those for which your employer has a dispensation.

Your expenses payments should be shown in your P11D or P9D. In your P11D they will be broken down into the gross amount received, any contributions you made or amounts on which tax has already been deducted, and the taxable amount. Enter the taxable amount in box 1.23.

Balancing charges are not something you will see on your P11D or P9D. They apply only if you claimed capital allowances on something that you bought for your work and that you have now disposed of (see p. 287). You can find further information in Help Sheet IR206 *Capital allowances for employees and office holders*.

Lump sums and compensation

Income from employment continued

■ *Lump sums and compensation payments or benefits including such payments and benefits from a former employer*

You must read pages EN6 and EN7 of the Notes **before** filling in boxes 1.24 to 1.30.

You may have something to enter here if:

■ you received a lump sum when you left a job, such as redundancy pay

■ you retired and received a lump sum from a non-approved retirement scheme (that is, anything other than a Revenue approved, foreign government or other statutory pension scheme)

■ your employer (or ex-employer) paid you a lump sum which you have not already entered as pay (for example, in box 1.8 or box 1.10).

You will need Help Sheet IR204 *Lump sums and compensation payments* in order to work out what to enter in each of the boxes. It is important to enter the right bit in the right category because each is taxed under different parts of tax legislation. You can get various types of tax relief on some categories, but not on others. One payment might be made up of several different types. They may also affect your overall tax calculation.

- Tax taken off payments in boxes 1.27 to 1.29 - *leave blank if this tax is included in the box 1.11 figure but tick box 1.30A.*

Tax taken off

1.30 £

Your employer may deduct tax from any taxable sums you get before paying you. If so, make sure you enter it in box 1.30, so that it is taken into account when working out your tax bill. But do not put in this box any tax which you have already included in box 1.11 and, if that applies to you, tick box 1.30A.

Payment expected under the terms of your employment

Taxable lump sums

- From box B of *Help Sheet IR204*

1.27 £

Lump sums that you should enter here include:

■ any payment that you receive under the terms and conditions of your contract, or where the expectation that you would get it is firm enough for it to be regarded as part of your contract – for example, a payment based on length of service which it is your employer's established policy to make when a job ends

■ payments received in return for your undertaking not to carry out certain actions, sometimes called a restrictive covenant (if not already entered with other pay in box 1.8 or 1.10)

■ bonuses on leaving a job (for example, for doing extra work in the period leading up to redundancy). Do not enter redundancy payments themselves in this category – they go in box 1.29, after deducting various reliefs.

All these payments are taxable in full. For tax purposes, they are treated just like the rest of your pay.

Payments from non-approved retirement schemes

• Retirement and death lump sums	1.26 £
• From box K of *Help Sheet IR204*	1.28 £

Most pension schemes are registered by the Revenue or are statutory schemes, and the lump sums you receive from them are tax-free (within limits). Payments from a non-approved scheme are also tax-free if they:

■ arose because of an accident you suffered at work, or

■ were funded by a contribution from your employer on which you have already paid tax, or

■ arose from your own contributions, or

■ came from an overseas scheme, provided further conditions are met. (Ask your tax office about extra-statutory concession A10 *Lump sums paid under overseas pension schemes.*)

If you have any tax-free payments, the total should go in box 1.26. Any taxable payments you receive should be entered in box 1.28.

Other payments

Some payments are tax-free altogether if:

■ you get them as a result of accident or chronic illness which meant that you couldn't do your job

■ 75 per cent of your service in the job was foreign service, or if you worked abroad for at least ten out of the last 20 years (and 50 per cent of your time in the job, if longer than 20 years). If you can't meet these conditions, you may still get some relief – see Help Sheet IR204 *Lump sums and compensation payments.*

Enter these payments under reliefs in box 1.25.

● £30,000 exception	**1.24** £
● Foreign service and disability	**1.25** £

The first £30,000 of the following payments are also tax-free:

■ redundancy pay (either statutory or at the employer's discretion)

■ pay in lieu of notice which is not included in your terms and conditions of employment

■ any other payments on leaving a job which were not part of your terms and conditions, and not 'expected' or received as payment for work done.

Enter the first £30,000 (or total received) under reliefs in box 1.24. Anything over £30,000 is taxable and should be entered in box 1.29. Use Help Sheet IR204 to help you calculate the exact figure.

Foreign earnings

The broad principle of the UK tax system is that you are taxed on foreign earnings if you are resident or ordinarily resident in this country, even if your permanent home (your domicile) is elsewhere. A full explanation of all these terms is included in Chapter 23. If you think you may be able to claim non-residence you should read that chapter first.

You should include foreign earnings in boxes 1.8 to 1.10 (your employer may already have included foreign earnings in your P60). But if you are a UK resident, or a British citizen, a Crown employee or a citizen of some other countries you can claim personal allowances to set against your income. You may also be able to claim deductions in boxes 1.31, 1.37 and 1.38 which make the possibility of tax on foreign earnings a less fearsome prospect.

Foreign earnings not taxable in the UK

■ *Foreign earnings not taxable in the UK in the year ended 5 April 2007* - *see Notes, page EN7.*	**1.31** £

Depending on your residence status and the place where your duties of employment were carried out, you might not have to pay UK income tax on all your foreign earnings for 2006–7. For example, this might apply if you have included in the Employment Pages earnings which you are prevented from bringing back to the UK by law, because of government action or a shortage of foreign currency in the country concerned. The various situations in which your foreign earnings might be tax-free are complex and you should use the worksheet contained in Help Sheet IR211 *Employment – residence and domicile issues.*

Seafarers' earnings deduction

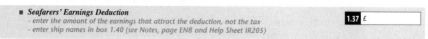

■ *Seafarers' Earnings Deduction*
   - *enter the amount of the earnings that attract the deduction, not the tax*
   - *enter ship names in box 1.40 (see Notes, page EN8 and Help Sheet IR205)*

1.37 £

This is a further deduction that can only be claimed by seafarers. You can get information on this from Help Sheet IR205 *Foreign Earnings Deduction: Seafarers.* Enter the names of the ships involved in box 1.40.

Foreign tax

■ *Foreign tax for which tax credit relief not claimed*   **1.38** £

If you work abroad, you may be liable to two lots of tax: tax charged by the country in which you earn the money and UK tax. You have two options for avoiding this double taxation:

■ claiming tax credit relief (if you are a UK resident)

■ deducting the foreign tax from your foreign earnings.

Because tax credit relief can wipe out all or part of the foreign tax, it is usually the best option, but it is not always available. There are various Revenue working sheets which may help you decide which is the best option for you (see Chapter 20 for more details). If you decide to claim tax credit relief, leave box 1.38 blank and complete the Foreign supplementary page. Otherwise, enter the amount of foreign tax in box 1.38.

Expenses incurred in doing your job

■ *Expenses you incurred in doing your job* - *see Notes, pages EN7 and EN8.*

You should already have entered all the expenses payments and allowances you received in box 1.23. However, not all these payments will be taxable, and there may be expenses for which you were not reimbursed and on which you can claim tax relief. So you should enter all your tax-allowable expenses, whether or not you were reimbursed, in boxes 1.32 to 1.36.

The only exception is expenses for which your employer has a dispensation (see p. 241). These should not be entered anywhere on your tax return, unless your allowable expenses came to more than the amount covered by the dispensation (in which case you should enter the extra). Your employer should be able to tell you what dispensations exist.

The overall rule is that only those expenses which are expended wholly, exclusively and necessarily in doing your job are allowable, except for travel and related meal and accommodation expenses, which must be necessarily incurred or incurred as a result of necessary business travel. In all cases, necessarily means that it would be necessary for anybody doing the job, not just necessary for you.

There is no neat list of definitions in tax law, and much depends on previous court judgments. In practice, a lot comes down to agreement with your tax officer and you should keep all the evidence you have (receipts, mileage details and so on) to back up your claims. However, the main tax-allowable expenses are listed below.

Travel and subsistence costs

● Travel and subsistence costs	1.32 £

You can claim tax relief for travel costs, for example fares, you incur making business journeys. If you use your own car, motorcycle or bicycle for work, any tax and tax relief are based on the Revenue approved payments (see p. 101) not your actual costs. Mileage allowance you receive up to the Revenue approved payment is tax-free and not entered on your tax return. Any excess is taxable and should already have been entered in box 1.15 (see p. 244), but you cannot claim any tax relief on the excess even if your actual costs exceeded the statutory payment. And you cannot claim capital allowances or interest on a loan to buy a vehicle. If you did not get any mileage allowance, or you received less than the approved payment, use box 1.32 to claim the shortfall up to the approved payment per mile (regardless of the actual expenses you incurred). You will need to have kept a record of your business mileage during 2006–7 and any allowance you had from your employer.

A business journey is either:

■ travel between one place of work and another required in the performance of your duties (travel 'on the job'), or

■ travel to and from a workplace, provided it does not count as ordinary commuting or private travel and attendance at the workplace is a requirement of your duties, not just a matter of personal convenience.

You can't claim for journeys that count as ordinary commuting, defined as travel between your home and your *permanent* workplace – even if the journeys take place at abnormal hours. However, the cost of travelling from home to work following an emergency call-out may be allowed in limited circumstances (for example, for NHS employees whose duties of employment commence before starting on the journey).

You can claim for journeys between home and a *temporary* workplace. A workplace counts as temporary if you go there for a limited duration or for a temporary purpose. But it loses its temporary status if you spend at least 40 per cent of your working time there over a period which lasts (or is likely to last) for more than 24 months.

If you have a permanent place of work, you might sometimes travel direct from home to another place where you are required to perform your duties, or travel from that place direct to home. In this situation, you can claim the actual travel expenses you incur unless the journey is not significantly different from the ordinary commuting journey.

If travelling is your job – for example, you are a travelling salesperson or a lorry driver – you might not have any permanent place of work. In that case, journeys from home to the places you visit on business may count as business travel. But if you work in a defined geographical area, any travel from home to the edge of that area, and back again, is ordinary commuting and you cannot claim the costs of that part of your journeys.

If a journey counts as business travel, you can also claim relief for:

■ meals and accommodation costs (subsistence) incurred in making the business journey

■ other business expenses arising because of the journey, for example telephone costs. You cannot deduct personal expenses, such as phone calls home, daily newspapers and personal laundry – but in practice, you may not have had to include these in box 1.23 in any case, since small amounts of personal expenses are tax-free (see pp. 102–3).

You should ask for and keep receipts for the subsistence and other business expenses you incur to back up your claim.

The rules can be interpreted in a number of different ways depending on the facts of the case. If you are unsure what you can claim, the Revenue guide 490: *Employee travel – a tax and NICs guide for employers* (to which your employer should have access and available from the Revenue website www.hmrc.gov.uk) gives the full rules and useful examples.

Add together all the allowable travel costs incurred, including accommodation and meal costs on business journeys and any other expenses of business journeys (such as business phone calls, but not personal items like phone calls home). Enter the total in box 1.32. If this box includes expenses of travelling between home and a permanent workplace, tick box 1.36.

Tax-saving idea 129

If your journey counts as business travel, don't forget to include the cost of any meals and accommodation which are attributable to the journey (other than the usual expenses you incur when at your normal place of work).

Fixed deductions for expenses

● Fixed deductions for expenses	1.33 £

The Revenue has agreed flat-rate expenses with various trade unions and other bodies to cover the costs of providing equipment and special clothing which is not provided by employers. For example, carpenters and joiners in the building trade can claim a flat-rate £105, uniformed bank employees can claim £45. Ask your union or other staff body if you are covered. You do not have to claim the flat-rate deduction – if you spend more, you can claim more, but if so, you should enter the amount in box 1.35, under other expenses, not here.

Professional fees and subscriptions

● Professional fees and subscriptions	1.34 £

You may pay for membership of a particular body or society which is relevant to your work. You can claim it in box 1.34 as an allowable expense provided that:

■ membership of the organisation, or registration with it, is a condition of your job, for example, as a dentist, optician or solicitor, or

■ the organisation is approved by the Revenue as being a non-profit body which exists for a worthy purpose such as to maintain professional standards, and membership is relevant to your work.

Any such organisation should be able to tell you whether it is on the Revenue's list of approved bodies. Or you can get the list from www.hmrc.gov.uk/list3/index.htm.

Other expenses and capital allowances

• Other expenses and capital allowances	**1.35** £

Other expenses must be wholly, exclusively and necessarily incurred in the performance of your duties. This means that you cannot claim expenses which merely put you in a position to do your job – for example, a journalist's expenditure on newspapers, employment agency fees, childcare. There are special rules for business entertaining – check with your employer whether these affect you. The expenses you should be allowed are:

■ the costs of providing and maintaining tools and special clothing which you have not already claimed a fixed deduction for in box 1.33. Special clothing does not cover clothes which you could wear outside work, even if you would never choose to do so

■ the cost of special security needed because of your job – you can claim this only if your employer paid for the security or reimbursed you, and you have already entered the appropriate amount as a benefit

■ costs and expenses if you are held liable for some wrongful act as an employee, or insurance premiums to cover you against such costs

■ training expenses for which you are not reimbursed, providing that your employer requires or encourages you to attend the course and gives you paid time off to do so, it is full-time (or virtually so) and lasts for at least four weeks. The expenses allowed are fees (unless you have already had tax relief on these), the cost of essential books and the full cost of daily travel to and from the course. You can claim any additional costs incurred if you have to stay away from home, provided you still have to meet the costs of maintaining or renting your own home

■ if you carry out some or all of the central duties of your job from home and the nature of the job itself requires that such work be done from home, a proportion of the heating and lighting costs, and, for a room used exclusively for work, council tax. You're not allowed to claim these expenses if you simply work from home from choice. Moreover, even if your contract of employment requires you to work from home, these expenses are not allowable if the work could in fact be done elsewhere. Do not include home-related expenses which your employer has reimbursed and which count as a tax-free benefit (see pp. 104)

■ cost of business calls you have to make on your home phone.

Tax-saving idea 130 and 131

Working from home could mean part being classified as business premises and so trigger a charge for business rates. But, in a case during 2003 (*Tully* v *Jorgensen*) – ironically involving a Revenue employee – a tribunal ruled that, where home-based working used furniture and equipment normally found in a home, there was no breach of residential use and business rates were not due. However, structural alterations, hiring staff, using specialist equipment and customers visiting your home-business could justify business rates.

The rules concerning working from home are less strict where your employer reimburses you for certain costs you incur. Since 6 April 2003, where you regularly work from home with your employer's agreement, you can receive up to £2 a week tax-free from your employer towards extra day-to-day costs of running part of your home as an office. Neither you nor your employer has to keep any records to back up these payments and there is no requirement to prove that working from home is a necessary feature of the job. Your employer can reimburse larger amounts tax-free but in that case you will need to produce records to back up the claim. The exemption does not apply where you work from home informally and not by arrangement with your employer. (The exemption applies only to expenses reimbursed by your employer or specifically covered by your salary. You cannot simply claim £2 a week as allowable expenses if your employer does not meet these expenses for you.)

You may also be able to claim capital allowances in this section if you buy equipment such as a computer which is necessary (as defined on p. 251) for your job. You cannot claim an allowance if your employer would have provided the equipment had you not chosen to do so. You used to be able to claim capital allowances on a car or other vehicle you bought to use in your job. But since 6 April 2002, capital allowances and interest on a loan to buy such a vehicle are already taken into account in the Revenue approved payments that can be either paid to you by your employer (see p. 244) or claimed by you as an allowable expense (see p. 251).

Tax-saving idea 132

For an employee to claim tax relief on expenses related to working from home, the work must be such that any employee doing the job would of necessity have to carry out some or all of the central duties from home. The Revenue has identified some types of employment where that condition is normally met. They are: insurance agent, university lecturer, councillor, examiner, midwife and minister of religion. If your tax office accepts your home as a workplace, you will also be able to claim the cost of travel to and from home on business.

When you finally dispose of an asset on which you claimed capital allowances there may be a balancing charge to add to your taxable income. (See Chapter 17 for how to work these out.)

Student loans

■ *Student Loans repaid by deduction by employer* - *see Notes, page EN8.* |1.39| £ _____

If your income for 2006–7 exceeds £15,000, you are required to start or continue repaying any income contingent student loans (see p. 175). The Revenue will have notified your employer to deduct repayments through PAYE. In some circumstances, the amount deducted might not be the full repayment due for the year. This will be the case where, for example:

■ you have more than one job. Each employer will ignore the first £15,000 of your earnings from the job concerned

■ you have unearned income of more than £2,000.

Any repayments due but not made through PAYE will now be collected through the self-assessment system. A person who has not received a tax return is not required to pay any more than has already been deducted through PAYE, but can voluntarily pay extra.

If you are a teacher, teaching a shortage subject, you may have been accepted into the Repayment of Teachers' Loan Scheme, in which case the government will gradually write off your loan over a period of up to ten years and your employer should not make deductions from your pay. If this applies to you, tick box 1.39A.

For each set of Employment pages you complete, in box 1.39 enter the amount of student loan repayments deducted by your employer as shown on your P60 or pay slips.

16

Share schemes

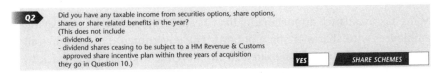

Q2 Did you have any taxable income from securities options, share options, shares or share related benefits in the year? (This does not include - dividends, **or** - dividend shares ceasing to be subject to a HM Revenue & Customs approved share incentive plan within three years of acquisition they go in Question 10.) **YES** **SHARE SCHEMES**

Part of your payment from a job may come in the form of shares (or share options – the right to buy shares at a set price at some point in the future) in your employer's company. Generally pay in the form of shares is taxable just as any other form of pay or benefit would be. However, there are special approved schemes under which you can get your shares or options tax-free. You only have to tick the YES box and complete these supplementary pages if your shares or share options are not received through an approved scheme, or if you are in a scheme but breach its rules in some respect. You have to complete pages 2 and 3 of the supplementary pages before page 1, and you need to fill in a separate page 2 and/or page 3 (or a photocopy) for each taxable event arising from a share scheme.

The benefit you get from share schemes may come in the following forms:

- a gift of the shares themselves, or a discount on the purchase price
- an option to buy a set number of shares, at a set price, at a particular time in the future
- dividends from the shares once they become your property
- a capital gain (or loss) arising from movements in the share price once the shares become your property.

The share dividends are taxed like the dividends from any share you own and you enter them at Q10 of the basic tax return (see Chapter 12) or the Foreign supplement (see Chapter 20) if they are paid by an overseas company. Similarly, the shares are generally subject to the normal capital gains tax rules (see Chapter 9). However, most employee shares benefit from a high level of capital gains tax taper relief even if you hold them for only a couple a years. This makes shares schemes a particularly attractive way of acquiring shares. You give details of capital gains on the Capital gains supplementary pages (Chapter 22). The Share scheme supplementary pages apply only on the gift (or discounted purchase) of the shares themselves, or an option to buy them, and to any associated advantages. Occasionally, with some unapproved schemes, they may also apply when you sell the shares themselves. The scope of the tax rules was widened to cover many more types of security from either 16 April 2003 onwards or 1 September 2003 onwards, depending on the type of security involved. For simplicity this chapter uses 'shares' to mean shares and other securities within the scope of the rules.

Many tax-avoidance arrangements have been developed involving paying employees with shares or share options. The government now requires all such arrangements to be declared to the Revenue and has been quick to change the law to close them down. It has also passed legislation enabling avoidance arrangements that emerge in future to be closed with their closure backdated as far as 2 December 2004.

Different types of share schemes

For tax purposes, share schemes fall within four broad categories:

- approved profit-sharing schemes
- share option schemes – either approved savings-related schemes or discretionary share option schemes (that is, company share option plans and their predecessor, executive share option schemes), enterprise management incentive options or unapproved schemes
- approved share incentive plan
- cheap or free gifts of shares through an unapproved scheme (sometimes called share incentive schemes).

Tax-saving idea 133

As an employee, you do not often have a choice of scheme, since employers are likely either to have just one scheme, or to have one scheme that is open to all employees and another which is open to a select few. But if you know that your employer is considering a scheme, try to make your voice heard so that the scheme which is chosen is one which suits you.

You may have come across Employee Share Ownership Trusts (ESOTs) – these are a special type of trust set up to acquire shares in the company and distribute them to employees. For the employee, the shares are taxable in the same way as shares received through an unapproved scheme (see p. 270).

If you received shares or share options which are taxable in 2006–7, you will need to declare them on the Share schemes supplementary pages, unless they have already been taxed under PAYE or have been included on Form P11D. If under PAYE, you should put the taxable value of the benefit in box 1.8 of the Employment page, and the tax in box 1.11. If on Form P11D, the taxable value goes in box 1.22.

The documents you need

You should have some correspondence from your employer concerning your scheme, including (where relevant) a share option certificate and a copy of the exercise note. You will also need to know the market price of the shares at various dates – if your employer cannot help, try a historic share price service, such as that run by the London Stock Exchange (www.londonstockexchange.com). If the company is not quoted on a recognised stock exchange, the market value has to be agreed with the Revenue.

Approved profit-sharing schemes

These are a way of transferring free shares in a company to its employees via a special trust. These schemes are being phased out. No new shares could be allocated after 31 December 2002.

The shares became taxable only if you sold them within three years of being allocated them so there should no longer be any tax charges associatd with these schemes and you will not need to enter them on the Share scheme pages.

Tax-saving idea 134

When you take your shares out of an approved profit-sharing scheme, savings-related share option scheme or approved share incentive plan, you can transfer them into an ISA (see p. 92), providing you do so within 90 days. Alternatively, shares from any of these schemes may be transferred within 90 days to a pension scheme (see p. 82). Both pension schemes and ISAs ensure that future growth in the value of your shares is free of capital gains tax.

Securities option schemes

For tax purposes, there are three key events in the life of an option:

- when you are first granted the option. If you receive the option through an approved scheme, there is never any tax to pay on the grant of the option. There could be a tax bill in the case of an unapproved scheme, but this has become less likely for options granted from 1 September 2003 onwards

- when you exercise your right to buy the shares. You have to pay tax on the exercise only if you fail to meet various conditions. You don't have to exercise the option and there is no tax if you just let it lapse

- if you receive some benefit for cancelling, transferring, releasing or otherwise not exercising your option. Tax is due on the value of the benefit (which may be adjusted if the value has been artificially reduced).

To work out the taxable amount (if any), you need to keep records of:

- the date on which each key event takes place

- the number of shares involved

- the share price – both the price you actually have to pay, and the market value at the time of each event

- any cash you contributed for the option, or any cash (or other benefit) you received for cancelling, transferring, releasing or otherwise not exercising it.

You have to give this information on page 2 of the Share schemes supplementary pages for each occasion on which your options are taxable (photocopy the form if necessary or ask the Orderline – see p. 170 – for extra copies).

Approved savings-related share options

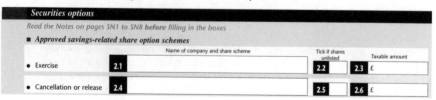

These schemes give you the right (or 'option') to buy a set number of ordinary shares in your employer's company at some point in the future, at a price fixed now, but you must do so using savings you build up in a Save-As-

You-Earn (SAYE) plan. If you meet the various conditions laid down by the Revenue, you will get your shares tax-free. For details, see the Revenue website at www.hmrc.gov.uk/shareschemes/saye_employees.htm. If you do not have Internet access, ask your tax office to send you a copy of these pages.

Among other conditions you must agree to:

■ save a set amount each month, with a minimum of £5 a month and a maximum of £250

■ save for a set period – three or five years. Five-year contracts may give you the option of leaving your money invested until the seventh anniversary.

The price of the shares (the subscription price) is fixed when you are granted the option, but cannot normally be less than 80 per cent of their market value at that time (or up to 30 days before). So if, for example, shares in Horridges' plc stand at 400 pence, the lowest subscription price is 320 pence. You have no tax to pay when the option is granted to you. You will not have tax to pay when the option is exercised unless:

■ you exercise your option when your company is taken over or sold, and you have not yet held it for three years. In this case, fill in the Options exercised column on page 2 of the Share schemes supplementary page (boxes 2.45 to 2.49 and 2.51) and carry the taxable amount to box 2.3 on page 1 (see overleaf for the calculation)

■ you benefit from the option in any way other than using it to buy shares – for example, if you receive compensation for not using or agreeing not to use your option. Fill in the Options assigned/released column on page 2 (boxes 2.45, 2.49 and 2.52) and then carry the taxable amount to box 2.6 on page 1.

Tax-saving idea 135

Whether or not you will benefit from a savings-related share option scheme depends on the option price and the share price when you exercise your option.

You do not have to exercise your option if you would make a loss and the return on SAYE schemes is tax-free. So if you are a higher rate taxpayer, or are optimistic that you will make some profit on the shares, joining the scheme is worthwhile.

Approved discretionary share options

Discretionary schemes may be restricted to groups of employees. Their original name was executive share option schemes, replaced in 1995 by company share option schemes. Broadly, options received under both these schemes are tax-free as long as you exercise them within strict time limits (see p. 263).

Unlike savings-related share option schemes, the price at which you can buy the shares under your option must not be less than the market value of the shares when the option is granted (or up to 30 days before). However, you may have been granted a discount of up to 15 per cent of the market value if you:

■ were granted options in an executive share option scheme after 1 January 1992 and before 17 July 1995, and

■ your company already had an approved savings-related share option scheme or approved profit-sharing scheme.

Tax on the exercise of an option

Step 1: take the market value of the share at the date the option was exercised (which you should have entered in box 2.51) and multiply by the number of shares you actually bought (entered at box 2.47). This gives you the market value of all the shares you have bought.

Step 2: take the price at which you exercised the option (in box 2.48) and multiply by the number of shares you bought (at box 2.47). This is the actual price.

Step 3: deduct the actual price (at Step 2) from the market value (at Step 1). If you paid anything for the option (box 2.49), you can deduct that too. The result is the taxable amount to enter on page 1 of the Share schemes supplementary page in box 2.3, 2.9, 2.15 or 2.24 as appropriate.

Rule changes from 1 September 2003

The meaning of 'exercise' was widened to include any acquisition of shares even if there is no actual exercise as such. For example, it includes automatically acquiring shares after a set time has passed. If someone else – say, a family member or someone you have a business connection with – benefits from your option (rather than you), you will still be taxed according to the rules here.

The grant of an option

With most unapproved share options there is no tax on the grant.

Cancellation etc. of an option

If you get any benefit in return for cancelling, transferring, releasing or otherwise not exercising your option, the taxable amount is what you received less anything you paid for the option. Fill in the 'cancellation or release' boxes on page S2 for the type of scheme concerned and transfer the amounts to page S1.

Tax-saving idea 136

> If you are granted options in an approved share option scheme, keep records of when you exercise them, and the dates by which you can next do so. For example, if you were granted options in 1997, you must exercise them by 2007 to avoid tax.

If you received a discounted option after those dates, it becomes an unapproved share option (see p. 266).

Under a company share option scheme, the maximum value of options you can be granted is £30,000.

You only have to pay tax on other options if:

■ you have received something for giving it up or not exercising it, or

■ the scheme had ceased to be approved by the time you exercised your options, or

■ you exercise the option within three years of being granted it (unless from 9 April 2003 onwards this happened because of injury, disability, redundancy or retirement as described on p. 269), or

■ you exercise the option more than ten years after being granted it.

If the first point applies, fill in the Options assigned/released column on page 2 of the Share schemes supplementary page (boxes 2.45, 2.49 and 2.52) and then fill in boxes 2.10 to 2.12 on page 1. If any of the other conditions apply, fill in the Options exercised column on page 2 (boxes 2.45 to 2.51) and then fill in boxes 2.7 to 2.9 on page 1.

Warning

> If there is a tax charge to pay when you exercise an option, it is based on the market value of the shares at that time. The tax charge will not be reduced if the value of the shares subsequently falls. Make sure you set aside enough money to pay the tax bill. This may mean selling some of the shares as soon as you get them. If you plan to sell shares later to meet the tax bill, you are gambling that the share price will not fall in the meantime.

Enterprise management incentive options

This scheme is designed to help small, high-risk firms recruit and retain key employees. Independent trading companies with assets of no more than £30 million that qualify for the scheme can offer share options to any number of employees. The maximum value of shares subject to unexercised options outstanding at any time is £3 million. The shares may be quoted or unquoted. The option must be capable of being exercised within ten years. Each employee can hold a maximum of £100,000 of unexercised options in total. (In the case of several different options, the value of each one is based on the share price on the date it was granted.)

To be an eligible employee, you must work for the company at least 25 hours a week or, if less, at least 75 per cent of your total work time, and you must control no more than 30 per cent of the company's ordinary share capital.

There is no income tax to pay when an option is granted. There is also no income tax to pay when you exercise an option unless:

■ it was a discounted option – in other words, the price you paid for the shares was less than the market value of the shares at the time the option was granted; or

■ a disqualifying event took place and you failed to exercise the option within the 40 days following the event.

If neither of these situations applies, you do not need to give any information on the Share scheme pages about your options under the scheme.

Tax-saving idea 137

If you acquire shares on or after 6 April 2002 on the same day from more than one share scheme and you later dispose of some of them, you can elect to have the shares from each scheme treated separately and the disposal matched to the shares that show the smallest capital gain (see p. 138).

For a discounted option, complete boxes 2.55, 2.57 to 2.60 and 2.62 in the Options exercised column on page 2 and also boxes 2.13 to 2.15 on page 1.

Example

In August 2006, under an enterprise management incentive scheme, Sam Wright is granted an option over 50,000 shares priced at £1 each at the time the option is granted. It gives him the right to buy the shares at 75p each when he exercises the option at any time up to July 2016. There is no tax to pay when the option is granted.

In December 2006, when the shares are priced at £1.50 each, the company ceases to qualify as a trading company, having moved into insurance business. Sam exercises his option in March 2007, when the share price has reached £2. Income tax is due when the option is exercised because it is a discounted option and because a 'disqualifying event' took place more than 40 days earlier. The taxable amount is worked out in two stages.

First, Sam must calculate the taxable amount resulting from the discount. The market value of the shares in August 2006 when the option was granted was 50,000 × £1 = £50,000. The price he paid for the shares in March 2007 was 50,000 × 75p = £37,500. Therefore gain from the discount is £50,000 − £37,500 = £12,500. But Sam has agreed to pay the employer's national insurance of 12.8% × £12,500 = £1,600 in respect of this gain, so the net amount on which income tax is due is £12,500 − £1,600 = £10,900.

Next, Sam must work out the taxable amount triggered by the disqualifying event. The market value of the shares in March 2007 when Sam exercised the option is 50,000 × £2 = £100,000. From this, Sam deducts the market value of the shares in December 2006 when the company changed its business (50,000 × £1.50 = £75,000). This gives a gain since the disqualifying event of £100,000 × £75,000 = £25,000. Sam can deduct the employer's national insurance he has paid in respect of this amount (12.8% × £25,000 = £3,200) leaving a net amount on which tax is due of £25,000 − £3,200 = £21,800.

The total taxable amount that Sam enters in box 2.15 is £10,900 + £21,800 = £32,700. Sam is a higher rate taxpayer, so pays income tax of 40% × £32,700 = £13,080 as a result of exercising his option. In addition he has paid £1,600 + £3,200 = £4,800 in employer's national insurance contributions and must pay employee's contributions of 1% × £32,700 = £327.

If a disqualifying event occurred more than 40 days before you exercised the option, complete boxes 2.55 to 2.59, 2.61 and 2.62 in the Options exercised column on page 2 as well as boxes 2.13 to 2.15 on page 1.

If the option was both discounted and affected by a disqualifying event more than 40 days before exercise, complete all the boxes 2.55 to 2.62 in the Options exercised column on page 2 as well as boxes 2.13 to 2.15 on page 1.

Your employer should be able to tell you if a disqualifying event has taken place. Disqualifying events are:

■ the company becomes a 51 per cent subsidiary of another company or, in some other way, comes under the control of another company. This is not a disqualifying event if, within six months of the takeover, your original option is replaced by an equivalent option over shares in the new company

- the company ceases to count as a trading company under the scheme rules. (Some 'low risk' trades are in any case excluded – for example, dealing in land or shares, banking, insurance, farming, market gardening, managing woodlands, running hotels, nursing homes or residential care homes, and so on.)

- the company had been preparing to become a trading company but this failed to materialise within two years of the option being granted

- you stop working for the company

- you no longer work 25 hours or more (or 75 per cent or more of your time) for the company

- the option is altered so that the market value of the option shares increases or the option ceases to meet the rules for the scheme

- the share capital of the company is altered without prior approval from the Revenue

- shares to which the option relates are converted to shares of a different class, unless all the shares of one class are converted to shares of one other class and certain other conditions are met

- relating to your employment with the same company, you are granted an option under an approved company share option plan (see p. 263) and together with your enterprise management incentive options this takes your holding of unexercised options above £100,000.

Unapproved securities options

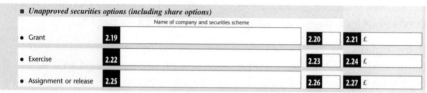

■ *Unapproved securities options (including share options)*

	Name of company and securities scheme		
• Grant	2.19	2.20	2.21 £
• Exercise	2.22	2.23	2.24 £
• Assignment or release	2.25	2.26	2.27 £

With unapproved schemes, since 1 September 2003, there is normally no tax on the grant of an option. Tax is generally payable only when the option is exercised, assigned, released or you receive any benefit in connection with the option (for example, for cancelling it). However, there is no income tax to pay if this occurs after your death.

Example

In 1997 Edward Brough was granted an option to buy 1,000 shares at £2 which can be exercised at any time between 1 January 2004 and 1 January 2009. This counts as a long option, so he had to pay tax when it was granted. At the time the market price of the shares was £3, so their market value was £3 × 1,000 = £3,000 against the option to buy at £2 × 1,000 = £2,000. The taxable amount was therefore £3,000 − £2,000 = £1,000 on which Edward paid tax of £400.

In October 2006 Edward exercised his option. This cost him £2,000. Since the market price had risen to £3.50, the market value of the shares was £3.50 × 1,000 = £3,500. The taxable amount is £3,500 − £2,000 = £1,500, less the £1,000 already taxed in 1997.

For options granted before 1 September 2003, income tax may be payable on grant if it is a 'long option'. A long option is one which can be exercised more than ten years after the date on which it was granted. Any amount already assessed for income tax can be set against income arising at a later date – for example, on exercising the option.

How to work out the taxable amount

In general, whatever type of share option scheme you have, and whether it is approved or unapproved, if the event (for example, the exercise or cancellation) is taxable, the amount is worked out as in the box on p. 262. You enter the amounts in the right-hand column of page 1 headed Taxable amount.

Slightly different rules apply if you have voluntarily agreed to pay any employer's national insurance contributions on the gain. When you exercise the option, your employer (and you) could be liable for national insurance contributions. The amount due will depend on the share price at the time of exercise which can't be predicted in advance. To save a company facing a large and unpredictable tax bill at some unknown future date, the company is allowed to make an agreement with you so that you pay the employer's national insurance contributions (as well as any employee's national insurance due) when you exercise the option. You can deduct any employer's (but not employee's) national insurance you pay in this way when working out the amount of income tax due.

Approved share incentive plans

Approved share incentive plans aim to give you a continuing stake in the company you work for. You can acquire shares in up to four different ways:

■ free shares – you can be awarded up to £3,000 of free shares each tax year. The award can be conditional on performance, length of service, and so on. You must normally keep the shares within the plan for a minimum holding period which can be no less than three years and no more than five years

■ partnership shares – you can ask your employer to deduct regular sums from your pay with which to buy shares in the company. The maximum deduction is £1,500 each year and total deductions must come to no more than 10 per cent of your pay (which could be your total pay or just part of it, e.g. excluding overtime). The plan can set a minimum deduction but this must be no more than £10. You can withdraw these shares from the plan at any time but this may trigger a tax charge (see opposite)

■ matching shares – your employer can decide to award you up to two matching shares for every partnership share you buy. You must normally keep the matching shares within the plan for a minimum holding period which can be no less than three years and no more than five years

■ dividend shares – you can opt to have cash dividends paid on any of the above shares reinvested to buy more shares. The maximum value of dividend shares you can buy in any year is £1,500. You must leave dividend shares within the plan for at least three years.

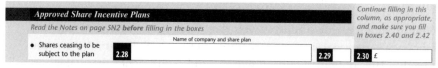

There is no tax to pay when any of these shares are acquired. You get tax relief through PAYE on any amount used to buy partnership shares. There is also no income tax due if you leave shares within the plan for at least five years (three years in the case of dividend shares).

Example

In December 2006, Lynne Harper was awarded 100 free shares in her employer's company, Treats plc, through its share incentive plan. Over the period September 2006 to February 2007, Lynne has also had £20 a month deducted from her pay to buy partnership shares in Treats plc. By February, 6 × £20 = £120 has been deducted and she has bought 24 partnership shares. As Lynne is a basic rate tax-payer, she gets tax relief of £4.40 on each £20 deduction, reducing the cost to her of £120-worth of shares to just £120 − (6 × £4.40) = £93.60.

In February 2007, Lynne takes a better job with another company. As she is leaving Treats plc, her shares cease to be subject to the share incentive plan and tax may now be due. Including the free shares, she has 124 shares in all. The share price stands at £5.50. The taxable value of the shares is 124 × £5.50 = £682. Basic rate tax on this comes to 22% × £682 = £150.04.

An income tax bill will only arise and you only need to give details on the Share scheme pages if any free shares, partnership shares or matching shares cease to be subject to the plan (for example, on your changing job) within five years of them being awarded to you or bought by you, and the reason they ceased was not due to your leaving employment because of:

∎ injury or disability

∎ redundancy

∎ a job transfer covered by the Transfer of Undertakings (Protection of Employment) Regulations 1981

∎ transfer or sale of the company out of a group running the plan

∎ retirement on or after an age specified in the plan (50 or above)

∎ death.

If the situation above has occurred and none of the exemptions listed applies, give details in boxes 2.64 to 2.68 on page 3 and boxes 2.28 to 2.30 on page 1.

There may also be income tax to pay if any dividend shares cease to be subject to the plan within three years of the date you bought them and none of the reasons listed above applies. In this case, you should enter the amount of cash dividend used to buy the shares in boxes 10.15 to 10.17 of the main tax return (see p. 191).

If you have already paid through PAYE any tax due on free shares, partnership shares, matching shares or dividend shares ceasing to be subject to the plan, enter the amount in box 2.41 on page 1 of the Share scheme supplement.

For more information, ask the Orderline (see p. 170) for Help Sheet IR2002 *Share incentive plans: a guide for employees*.

How to work out the taxable amount

Where free shares, partnership shares or matching shares cease to be subject to the plan within three years of being granted or bought, the taxable amount is the market value of the shares at the time they leave the plan.

Where free or matching shares cease to be subject to the plan after three years but within five years of being granted or bought, the taxable amount is the lower of the market value at the time they leave the plan and their market value at the time they were awarded to you.

Where partnership shares cease to be subject to the plan after three years but within five years of being granted or bought, the taxable amount is the lower of the market value at the time they leave the plan and the total deductions in pay used to buy them.

Tax-saving idea 138

Persuade your employer to set up a share incentive plan. Your employer can give you up to £6,000 of shares a year tax-free as long as you keep them in the scheme for five years.

Free or cheap shares through an unapproved scheme

Employers have many reasons for offering cheap or free shares. These count as part of your payment from the job. The exact tax treatment depends on whether the shares are counted as your earnings (and entered under Securities acquired from your employment in boxes 2.31 to 2.33), or treated as a fringe benefit (and entered under Securities as benefits in boxes 2.34 to 2.36), unless these have already been shown under Earnings from employment.

The distinction is fine, but significant: whereas with shares which count as earnings you are taxed on the difference between the market value of the shares and the price at which you acquired them, with shares which count as benefits you are taxed as if you received an interest-free loan from your employer (see p. 116). In some circumstances, this may mean no tax to pay.

You should enter under Securities as benefits:

- shares you are allowed to pay for in instalments (partly-paid shares)
- shares which you buy but where part of the purchase price is deferred, for example, when a particular profit target is met
- any other exceptional cases in which cheap or free shares do not count as earnings.

All other free or cheap shares should go under Securities acquired from your employment (see below). Even after you have acquired the shares, you may be considered to receive further taxable benefits from them, for example, an increase in their value when a restriction is lifted. You should enter these under Post-acquisition events in boxes 2.37 to 2.39.

Warning

A change in the law in 2005 means that, where you are an owner/manager of your own company and pay yourself mainly in the form of dividends, the Revenue might seek to tax the dividends as post-acquisition event benefits if it can show that the main purpose of your mode of payment is to avoid paying tax or national insurance.

Securities acquired from your employment

You may get some benefit tax-free if the company for which you work decides to sell shares (or other securities) to the public and offers shares on special terms to its employees. You have to distinguish between:

■ a discounted price offered to employees

■ a priority allocation of the shares.

The discounted price is taxable: you pay tax on the difference between the price you pay and that paid by the general public. Enter the taxable amount under Shares acquired from your employment.

The calculation is very straightforward. Take the market value of the shares at the time you acquired them. Deduct anything you paid for them. The result is the taxable amount. The benefit of the priority allocation itself is tax-free and need not be entered unless:

■ it is reserved for directors or higher-paid employees, or those who are entitled to it do not all get it on similar terms, and

■ the shares reserved for employees in their priority allocation are more than a certain percentage of the overall shares on offer – normally, more than 10 per cent of the total shares on offer.

Previously, the above rules applied only to shares and most other securities issued by companies. However, from either 16 April 2003 or 1 September 2005, depending on the type of securities involved, the scope of the rules was widened to include many other financial assets, such as government stocks, futures, units in a unit trust, and so on.

Other changes that took effect during 2003 include important elections to consider about when you might pay the income tax. This is a complicated area and you might want to seek advice from an accountant or tax specialist.

For more information, see Revenue Help Sheet IR219 *Securities acquired from your employment.*

Example

> Linden works for Good Holdings, which has just been offered for sale to the public. Using the priority allocation for employees, Linden bought 500 £1 shares, at the discounted staff price of 80p. Linden is not taxed on the benefit of the priority allocation. However, the discounted price is taxable. The market value of the 500 shares was £1 × 500 = £500, but Linden only paid 80p × 500 = £400. She is taxed on £500 − £400 = £100.

Securities as benefits

Anything entered under this category is treated as an interest-free loan. The loan is the difference between what you paid and the market value of the shares. The loan is taxable only if:

■ you count as earning at a rate of £8,500 or more or are a director (see p. 110 for how this is worked out)

■ the total amount of all the cheap or interest-free loans from your employer outstanding in the tax year comes to more than £5,000 (see p. 116).

If tax is payable, it will be spread out over the whole life of the deemed loan.

The taxable value of the loan is the theoretical interest you would have paid had you been charged interest at an official rate set down by the government.

Post-acquisition events

You are charged tax on any further benefit from securities (or an interest in them) which you acquire because of your employment. This applies even if you have since left the company. Events that may trigger a tax charge later on include:

- restrictions attached to the securities running out or being altered
- keeping securities in certain subsidiary companies for seven years
- receiving special benefits as a result of owning the securities
- the securities being converted into other securities under rights you have as a result of the employment
- the market value of the securities being artificially increased or reduced
- disposing of the securities in certain circumstances for more than their market value.

You need to enter information in boxes 2.37 to 2.39 on page 1 of the Share schemes supplementary page, giving the details on page 3.

Ask the Orderline (see p. 170) for Help Sheet IR217 *Shares acquired: post-acquisition charges*. Again this is a complicated area and you may want to seek advice from an accountant or tax specialist.

17

Self-employment

Q3 Were you self-employed (but not in partnership)?
(You should also tick 'Yes' if you were a Name at Lloyd's.)   **YES** [ ]   **SELF-EMPLOYMENT** [ ]

If any of your income for 2006–7 came from running your own business as a self-employed person, answer YES to Q3 on the basic tax return. You'll need to fill in a separate set of Self-employment supplementary pages for each business you have.

Self-employed people are able to claim more income tax reliefs than employed people and they usually pay less in national insurance, so you might need to prove to your tax office that you really are self-employed. Ask yourself the following questions:

- Do you control how your business is run? For example, do you decide what work you take on, where you do the work, what hours you keep?

- Is your own money at risk in the business? For example, have you had to pay for your own premises, do you have to finance the lag between incurring costs and receiving payments?

- Do you have to meet any losses as well as keeping any profits?

- Do you provide the major equipment necessary for your work – for example computer and photocopier for office-based work or machinery for an engineering business? It's not enough that you provide your own small tools – many employees do this too.

- Are you free to employ other people to help you fulfil the contracts you take on? Do you pay your employees yourself?

- If a job doesn't come up to scratch, do you have to redo it or correct it in your own time and at your expense?

The more of these question to which you can answer 'yes', the more likely it is that you are self-employed. And if you answer 'yes' to all of them, you generally will count as self-employed. But it is the whole picture and facts of your case that determine your work status. Sometimes the decision is not clear cut – for example, if you are newly in business doing work for just one client, perhaps working at a former employer's premises on a freelance basis. Beware if you work through an agency – for example as an agency carer or temporary secretary. Even if you choose whether or not to take on a particular job, you will almost certainly count as an employee rather than self-employed.

Tax-saving idea 139

As a self-employed person, you can claim more tax reliefs than an employee. Nonetheless, small businesses can still usually save income tax and national insurance by operating as a company provided they are judged to be genuinely in business on their own account (rather than as a device for disguising employee status). But the tax advantages will fall from 2008 onwards.

Bear in mind, too, that it is possible to be self-employed for some of your work but an employee for other jobs you do.

If you pay tax and national insurance as if you are self-employed, but later your tax office decides you are really an employee, you could face a large bill for back taxes, so it is important to get your status straight right from the start. If you're in any doubt, you can ask your tax office for a written decision about your employment status. If you don't agree with the decision, you can appeal. You can check your status and the verdict the Revenue is likely to give by using the Revenue's employment status indicator tool at www.hmrc.gov.uk/calc/esi.htm. Print off every page as you fill in the tool, so you have a record should you need it in discussions with the Revenue.

Business details

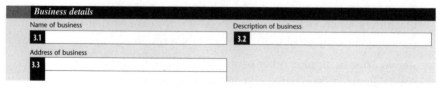

The first part of the supplement simply deals with basic details – the name and nature of your business and the address from which you trade.

Your accounting year

You also need to give the start and finish dates of the accounting period for which you are giving details. Normally, an accounting period is a year long, with the new accounting year starting immediately the previous year ends. But in the first and last year or two of your business, or if you change your accounting date, your accounting year might be longer or shorter (see below).

Tax-saving idea 140

If you take up fostering children, your receipts are tax-free up to a qualifying amount. In 2006–7, this amount is £10,000 a year per household plus £200 a week for each child under 11 and £250 a week for each child aged 11 or more. Private fostering arrangements are not eligible for this scheme.

Foster carers and adult carers are treated as if they run a business so need to complete the self-employment supplement. However, since 6 April 2003, receipts from foster caring are tax-free if they do not exceed a qualifying amount (see Tax-saving idea above). If fostering receipts exceed this amount, you can choose either to work out your profits in the normal way or use a simplified system. Adult carers also have a choice of ways to work out their profits. In both cases, you may not have to fill in all the boxes in this supplement, in which case tick box 3.9 so that the Revenue knows why some boxes have been left blank. For more information, get Help Sheet IR236 *Foster carers and adult placement carers*.

If you carry on your business completely overseas and think you should be taxed only on the remittance basis because of your residence status, fill in only boxes 3.1 to 3.13, 3.74, 3.75, 3.92, 3.93 and tick box 3.94. You also need to complete the Non-residence supplement (see Chapter 23). Tick box 3.9.

You may already have given information about your latest set of accounts in last year's return (for example, if your accounting periods overlap). If so, you do not need to give all the information again: you can leave boxes 3.14 to 3.73 and 3.99 to 3.115 blank, but tick box 3.10. Similarly, if your accounts do not run from the last accounting date, explain why in the Additional information box and tick box 3.11.

• Tick box 3.6 if details in boxes 3.1 or 3.3 have changed since your last Tax Return	**3.6**	

• Date of commencement if after 5 April 2004	**3.7**	/ /

• Date of cessation if before 6 April 2007	**3.8**	/ /

• Tick box 3.9 if the special arrangements for particular trades apply - read the Notes, page SEN11	**3.9**	

• Tick box 3.10 if you entered details for all relevant accounting periods on last year's Tax Return and boxes 3.14 to 3.73 and 3.99 to 3.115 will be blank (read Step 3 on page SEN2)	**3.10**

• Tick box 3.11 if your accounts do not cover the period from the last accounting date (explain why in the 'Additional information' box, box 3.116)	**3.11**

• Tick box 3.12 if your accounting date has changed (only if this is a permanent change and you want it to count for tax)	**3.12**

• Tick box 3.13 if this is the second or further change (explain in box 3.116 on Page SE4 why you have not used the same date as last year)	**3.13**

What profits are taxed

This first section of the Self-employment pages establishes which profits form the basis of your tax bill for 2006–7, and what information you need to give the Revenue about them. In most cases, your tax bill for 2006–7 will be based on the profits you make during the accounting period which ended during that tax year (the current year basis). However, there are special rules if you are in the opening or closing years of the business or, have changed your accounting date.

Starting or closing a business

If you become self-employed and liable to pay Class 2 national insurance contributions, you must register with the Revenue within three months of the end of the month you started in business. There is a £100 penalty for failing to do so. You can register by calling a helpline for the newly self-employed on 08459 154515 or by completing form CWF1 in the back of Revenue leaflet SE1: *Thinking of working for yourself?* Registration ensures that arrangements are made for you to pay the national insurance contri-butions (see p. 304) and that you will be sent a tax return at the appropriate time. You can also register for VAT (see p. 290).

The penalty is waived if you can show that your profits are less than £4,635 in 2007–8 or the pro-rata equivalent (£4,465 in 2006–7).

You must register – and incur the penalty if you don't – even if you are also an employee and pay enough class 1 contributions not to have to make any class 2 payments. Ask to defer the class 2 contributions (see p. 306).

If you do not register, under separate rules you must tell your tax office within six months of the end of the tax year (i.e. by the following 5 October) if you have any profits on which income tax is due.

When you start a business, special rules say how you will be taxed in the first two or three years.

First tax year during which you're in business

You are taxed on your profits from the date your business started to the end of the tax year (that is the following 5 April). This can be finalised only once your first set of accounts is drawn up and is then worked out by allocating a proportion of those profits to the period up to the end of the tax year. This is usually done on the basis of days, but weeks, months or other fractions of a year are also acceptable. For example, suppose you started in business on 1 January 2007 and your first accounting period runs to 31 January 2008. Out of that first 396-day accounting period, 95 days fall between 1 January to 5 April, so your profits for 2006–7 are deemed to be $^{95}/_{396}$ths of the profit for the whole accounting period.

Second tax year during which you're in business

In most cases, the end of an accounting period (not necessarily your first) will fall sometime during this second tax year. Provided you have been trading for at least 12 months, your tax bill will be based on profits for the 12 months up to that date. In the example above, there is an end accounting date falling within 2007–8. This is 31 January 2008 and, at that date, the business has been running for more than a year. Therefore, tax will be based on profits for the 12 months up to 31 January 2008 – that is $^{365}/_{396}$ths of the profits for the whole accounting period.

If there is an accounting date within the tax year, but you have been trading for less than 12 months, your tax is based on the first 12 months of trading, with a proportion of the profits from your next accounting period being used to make up the full 12 months. For example, suppose you started in business on 1 March 2006 and draw up your accounts to 30 June 2006 and then to each subsequent 30 June. Tax in your second year, the 2006–7 tax year, would be based on the whole of the profits for the period 1 March to 30 June 2006 (122 days) and $^{243}/_{365}$ths of the profits for the accounting year from 1 July 2006 to 30 June 2007.

If there is no accounting date at all during your second tax year, tax is based on the profits for the tax year itself – that is from 6 April to 5 April. For example, if you started in business on 1 March 2006 but did not draw up your first accounts until 30 June 2007, an accounting period of 487 days, you would be taxed on $^{487}/_{365}$ths of the profits for that whole period.

Third tax year during which you're in business

Normally, an accounting period at least 12 months after you started up finishes during your second tax year. From the third year onwards, you are simply taxed on the profits for the accounting year ending during the tax year – that is normal current year basis.

Example

Jim Newall started working as a freelance computer consultant on 1 July 2004 and drew up his first accounts on 30 April 2005. 30 April is his normal accounting year end. His profit and tax position for the first few years of business was as follows:

Accounting period	Profit for the period
1 July 2004–30 April 2005	£ 4,000
1 May 2005–30 April 2006	£ 8,500
1 May 2006–30 April 2007	£18,500

Tax year	Tax basis	Profits on which tax based
2004–5	Profits for tax year	$279 \div 304 \times £4,000 = £3,671$
2005–6	First 12 months of trading	$£4,000 + (61 \div 365 \times £8,500) = £5,420$
2006–7	Profits for 12 months to 30 April 2006	£8,500
2007–8	Profits for accounting year ending on 30 April 2007	£18,500

The profit for the period 1 July 2004 to 5 April 2005 is taxed twice, as is profit for the 61 days from 1 May to 30 June 2005. This gives Jim an overlap profit of $£3,671 + (61 \div 365 \times £8,500) = £3,671 + £1,420 = £5,091$.

Where unusually the first accounting period to end at least 12 months after start-up comes to a close in your third tax year of trading, you are taxed on profits for the 12 months to the end of that period. From the fourth year onwards, you are taxed on the normal current year basis.

Overlap profits

As you can see, the opening year rules described above mean that some profits may be taxed twice. For example, for the business which started on 1 January 2007, the profits for the first two years were as follows:

Tax year	Profits on which your tax bill is based
Year ending 5 April 2007	$^{95}\!/_{396}$ths × profit for accounting period from 1 January 2007 to 31 January 2008
Year ending 5 April 2008	$^{365}\!/_{396}$ths × profit for the period from 1 January 2007 to 31 January 2008

This means that (95 + 365) − 396 = 64 days' worth of profit have been taxed twice. This is called 'overlap profit' and the period over which it arose is called the 'overlap period'. One of the principles of the current year basis tax system is that, over the lifetime of your business, all your profits should be taxed, but only taxed once. Therefore, you are given overlap relief to compensate you for having paid tax on some profits twice in your opening year. But there is a snag: overlap relief is usually given only when you finally close the business down (see overleaf) and inflation in the meantime will reduce its value.

Businesses that started before 6 April 1994 also have overlap profit as a result of changes to the basis of taxing accounts from 6 April 1996 onwards. And a change of accounting date (see below) can create overlap profit.

Fiscal accounting

You can avoid all the problems of opening year rules and overlap relief, if you opt for fiscal accounting. This means using the tax year as your accounting year. By Revenue concession, this includes having an accounting date of 31 March, rather than exactly on the tax year end of 5 April.

For example, you might have started in business on 1 September 2006, drawing up your first accounts on 31 March 2007 and on each 31 March thereafter. Your tax for 2006–7 will be based on your profits from 1 September 2006 to 31 March 2007. Your tax for the next year will be based on profits for 1 April 2007 to 31 March 2008 and so on. For further information see Help Sheet IR222 *How to calculate your taxable profits*.

Tax-saving idea 141

Fiscal accounting makes accounting for tax very simple, especially in your opening years, but it has drawbacks too: you don't have long to make up your accounts and there's only a short delay between making your profits and paying tax on them (see p. 31).

If you don't choose fiscal accounting, try to keep your profits as low as possible during the first year or two, so that your overlap profit is small.

Changing your accounting date

For the Revenue to accept a change of accounting date for tax purposes, the following conditions must be met: the transitional accounting period running up to the new accounting date (called the 'relevant period') must not exceed 18 months; you must notify your tax office in your tax return by ticking box 3.12; and either there must have been no previous change of accounting date in the last five years or the Revenue must be satisfied that the current change is for bona fide commercial reasons. If you have changed the date within the last five years, tick box 3.13 and explain your reasons in box 3.116.

If you choose a new accounting date earlier in the tax year, the relevant period will be less than 12 months. Your tax bill will be based on your profits for the 12 months up to the new accounting date. This creates some overlap profit.

If you choose a new date which is later in the tax year, your tax bill will be based on the whole relevant period which will be longer than 12 months, but you are then allowed to use some of your overlap relief (see p. 281).

Closing your business

In the tax years up to the one before closure, you are taxed on the normal current year basis. For the tax year in which you close down, you're taxed on profits from your last accounting date up to the date on which you close down less any overlap profits which you have been carrying forward (see p. 280). (For how to claim relief on these overlap profits, see p. 301.) The position for a business closing down in 2006–7 is summarised below.

Tax year	Profits on which your tax bill is based
2005–6	Profits for accounting year ending in 2005–6
2006–7	Profits from day after end of accounting year ending 2005–6 up to date of closure less overlap profits

If your normal accounting date is early in the year, your final tax bill may be based on a long period – for example, if you closed in December 2006 and your normal accounting date was 30 April, your final tax bill will be based on the 20 months from May 2005 to December 2006. This can mean a large tax bill if the business is profitable even after using overlap relief.

Capital allowances

Your taxable profits are broadly your business income less your business expenses. But when you buy capital items for your business – that is things which will be in use for many years – you are not normally allowed to set the full cost against your business income in the year you buy the item. In your ordinary business accounts, you'll deduct depreciation each year which varies from business to business and is not allowed as an expense when working out your tax. Instead, for tax purposes, you deduct capital allowances calculated according to standard rules.

Tax-saving ideas 142 and 143

Do not claim more capital allowances than needed to reduce your taxable profits to the level of your personal allowances – unless you have other income or gains against which you want to set a loss (see p. 302).

Earmarking a capital item as a short-life asset means you can get full tax relief on the cost of the item in just five years.

To be eligible for capital allowances, the item you have bought must be wholly or partly for business use. You can claim a proportion of the allowance if the item is used partly for business and, in part, privately.

How much you can claim

The basic capital allowance is called a writing-down allowance and it is available for plant and machinery (which covers most of your ordinary business equipment), cars and vans, patents and know-how. In general, capital allowances are not given for what you spend on buying business premises (for example, a shop or office), but industrial and agricultural buildings and some hotels with ten or more bedrooms are exceptions. Expenditure which qualifies for allowances is lumped together in one or more pools (see p. 286) and you can claim a certain proportion of the pool at the end of each tax year as a writing-down allowance.

The maximum writing-down allowance you can claim is:

- 25 per cent a year (20 per cent from April 2008) for machinery, plant, vans, patents, know-how

- 25 per cent a year for cars, but for any car costing over £12,000, there is also a cash limit of £3,000 a year. (This system is under review)

- 4 per cent a year for industrial and agricultural buildings and qualifying hotels (or 25 per cent for industrial and commercial buildings in an Enterprise Zone if full first-year allowance – see below – is not claimed). These allowances are to be phased out.

With some types of expenditure, you can claim a higher capital allowance for the year in which you buy the item. (But from April 2008, these allowances are to be replaced – see Chapter 1.) Maximum first-year allowances are:

- 50 per cent in 2006–7 for spending on machinery, plant, vans and know-how – but excluding cars, items for leasing and long-life assets (with an expected life of at least 25 years) if you count as a small enterprise (see opposite). (The allowance was 40 per cent for spending between 6 April 2005 and 5 April 2006 and this still applies in 2006–7 to medium-sized enterprises)

- 100 per cent for industrial or commercial buildings in an Enterprise Zone

- 100 per cent for environmentally friendly spending (see table opposite)

- 100 per cent for spending on or after 11 May 2001 on renovating or converting residential space above shops or other commercial property into flats for rent, provided various conditions are met (see p. 323)

- from 6 April 2004 100 per cent for spending by residential landlords on up to £1,500 of loft and cavity wall insulation and solid wall insulation from 7 April 2005. Spending on draught-proofing and insulation of hot water systems has been added from 6 April 2006

- from 11 April 2007, 100 per cent first-year allowances for spending on renovating business premises vacant at least a year in designated deprived areas.

Tax-saving idea 144

An initial allowance of 50 per cent is generally available to small businesses buying machinery or plant (excluding cars).

What counts as environmentally friendly spending?*

Date spending incurred	Item	Description
31 March 2001 onwards	Energy-saving equipment	Items such as boilers, combined heat and power, refrigeration, and so on.
17 April 2002– 31 March 2008	Low-emission cars and refuelling	Low emission cars (emitting no more than 120 gm/km of carbon equipment dioxide or electrically propelled) used in your business or by employees. Equipment for refuelling with natural gas or hydrogen fuel
17 April 2002 onwards	Environmentally friendly spending on items for leasing, letting or hiring	Items as described above. (They are not eligible for the first-year allowance if bought before 17 April 2002 for leasing, letting or hiring)
1 April 2003 onwards	Technology to save water or improve water quality	Meters, efficient toilets and so on. For list, contact details as for energy-saving equipment above

* For further details, see www.eca.gov.uk or call the Environment and Energy Helpline on 0800 585 794.

What are SMEs?

Business must meet at least two of following three criteria:	Accounting periods ending before 30 January 2004		Accounting periods ending 30 January 2004 onwards	
	Small enterprise	Medium enterprise	Small enterprise	Medium enterprise
Turnover	£2.8m	£11.2m	£5.6m	£22.8m
Assets	£1.4m	£5.6m	£2.8	£11.4m
Employees	50	250	50	250

The definition of small and medium-sized enterprises (SMEs) changed in 2004.

You can claim less than the maximum first-year allowance or writing-down allowance. It would be worth restricting your claim if your taxable profits or income were so low that some of the maximum allowance would be wasted. The allowance is not lost. The effect is to carry forward a higher value of assets in your pool of expenditure. This increases the value of the maximum writing-down allowances you can claim in future years. For example, suppose your pool is valued at £10,000. If you claim the full 25 per cent, the writing-down allowance would be £2,500 and you would carry forward a £7,500 pool. Next year you could claim 25% × £7,500= £1,875. If you claim just 10 per cent in the first year (£1,000), next year you could claim 25% × £9,000 = £2,250.

Capital pools

Various categories of capital expenditure have to be allocated to their own separate pools. They include:

- any car costing more than £12,000 must usually be hived off to its own pool and the writing-down allowance is limited to the smaller of 25 per cent or £3,000 in each year. The exception is environmentally friendly cars as defined in the table on p. 285. Cars costing £12,000 or less are added to your main pool of expenditure. Vans, lorries and so on do not count as cars but motorbikes do

- industrial and agricultural buildings

- an asset used partly for private use must have its own pool and you can claim a proportion of the allowance reflecting the business use

- short-life assets. Capital equipment (other than cars) which you expect to have a useful life of no more than five years can be put in a separate pool. The advantage of doing this is that you get tax relief on the full cost of the item more rapidly than if it were in the general pool of expenditure (see Buying and selling capital items below).

Example

Joe Morris has been running a small dairy since 1979. He counts as a small enterprise and makes up his accounts to 31 December each year. For the year to 31 December 2006, he made the following purchases and sales of capital items:

Date	Capital item	Purchase/sale price
10 April 2006	New van bought	£17,000
5 May 2006	Old van sold (cost £12,000 when new)	£ 5,000
2 November 2006	Second-hand cream separator bought	£38,000

On 31 December 2005, after claiming writing-down allowances, Joe's general pool of capital expenditure stood at £158,000. Joe can claim an initial allowance for the cream separator of 50 per cent × £38,000 = £19,000. The van also qualifies for 50 per cent initial allowance, so he can claim 50 per cent × £17,000 = £8,500. Joe deducts the £5,000 from selling the old van to give a general pool expenditure at 31 December 2006 of £158,000 − £5,000 = £153,000. Joe can claim a maximum writing-down allowance of 25 per cent × £153,000 = £38,250. This gives allowances of £19,000 + £8,500 + £38,250 = £65,750 to set against his taxable income for the year. In fact, he has only enough profits and other income to use up £37,000 of the allowances. His capital pool at 1 January 2007 (including the balance of the expenditure on the van and the cream separator) becomes £158,000 − £5,000 (sale of van) + £17,000 (for van) + £38,000 (for cream separator) − £37,000 of allowances = £171,000.

You do not normally get capital allowances on items you lease rather than buy. Instead the leasing charge counts as an allowable expense (see p. 299). If you buy something on hire purchase, the capital element of the charges can qualify for capital allowances but the interest element is treated as an allowable expense (see p. 299).

If you close down your business, in the final accounting period you cannot claim writing-down allowances or first-year allowances. Instead, you may get a balancing allowance on the sale of the business assets (see below).

Buying and selling capital items

When you buy an item of capital, its cost (less any first-year allowance) is added to the appropriate pool of expenditure. This increases the year-end value of the pool in subsequent years on which the writing-down allowance is worked out.

When you first start in business, you might take into the business capital equipment you already own – for example, a desk, shelving, a computer. Although no money changes hands, you are treated as having sold the item to your business and you can claim capital allowances (but not first-year allowances) in the normal way. Value each item at its second-hand market value given its age, state of repair, and so on.

When you sell a capital item, the amount you get for it (up to its original cost) is deducted from the expenditure pool. Occasionally, this may be more than the total value of the pool, in which case, the excess (called a balancing charge) is added to your profits or (taxable income) for the year, increasing your tax bill. It is entered in box 3.15, 3.17, 3.19 or 3.21 as appropriate and added to your profits at box 3.68.

If you sell the item for less than its written-down value – at the extreme, you might scrap it for nothing – the shortfall remains in your pool of expenditure and continues to be written down. So you could be claiming allowances on an item for many years after you have sold it. Only when you finally close down the business can you claim a balancing allowance for any remaining value of the pool. This is where short-life assets come into their own.

If you scrap a short-life asset within five years, you can claim tax relief on the difference between what you get (if anything) for the asset and its written-down value. The relief is given in the tax year in which you scrap it – you don't have to wait until the business closes down. If, having declared an asset as short life, you actually go on using it beyond five years, it is transferred into your general pool of expenditure and treated like any other capital item.

If you are registered for VAT, the amount you put in your expenditure pools should not include VAT (unless you are unable to recover the VAT through your VAT returns or, in some cases, where you are using the VAT flat-rate scheme – see p. 291). If you are not registered for VAT, you claim capital allowances on the cost including VAT.

Claiming capital allowances

Capital allowances are given as a deduction in working out your taxable profits for the year. Enter the capital allowances you are claiming in boxes 3.14, 3.16, 3.18 and 3.20 and the total is deducted from your profits at box 3.70. If you are claiming first-year allowances for any environmentally friendly spending (see p. 285), tick box 3.22A.

Tax-saving idea 145

If your turnover is less than £64,000 in the year from 1 April 2007, you can choose whether or not to register for VAT. Being registered means you can reclaim VAT on things you buy for your business, but you must also charge your customers VAT on your whole turnover (not just the bit in excess of £64,000). Be wary of registering voluntarily if your customers cannot reclaim the VAT you charge them (because, for example, they are private individuals) – you probably won't be able to raise your prices in line with the VAT and unless you can claim back large amounts on things you buy, registration could cause your overall income to fall.

Being VAT-registered means you have the extra administration of keeping VAT accounts and dealing with payments and reclaims. But there are several schemes to reduce the administration for small businesses including the flat-rate scheme. However, you should check that the flat-rate scheme really does save on administration and that you do not end up paying more VAT as a result.

Income

If your turnover is less than £15,000 a year

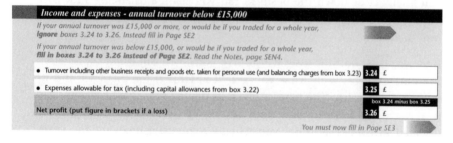

Complete boxes 3.24 to 3.26. You can get guidance on what expenses are allowable by reading pp. 292–300.

You do not need to give full details of your accounts. This does not mean that you can get away without preparing proper accounts – you must have these ready, in case your tax inspector asks to see them, together with all the background paperwork (see Chapter 3).

Note that £15,000 is the annual limit – if your accounts cover a period of under a year, it will be reduced proportionately, and increased if you have a longer accounting period.

Do not complete page 2 of the Self-employed supplement, but go straight to page 3. Turn to p. 300 for guidance on filling in boxes 3.74 and beyond.

If your turnover is £15,000 a year or more

You should complete the details asked for on page 2 of the Self-employed supplementary pages. You don't need to attach a copy of your accounts. If the headings do not tally with the headings you use in your own accounts, don't be tempted to leave any out. Instead, use your judgement to allocate them to boxes on page 2, but make sure that whatever method you adopt is the same as last year and next year's – in other words, be consistent.

If the period over which you are being taxed is covered by two sets of accounts, you need to complete two Self-employment supplements (unless you have already given all the information in last year's tax return).

If you produce a balance sheet, there is space for the entries on page 4 of the supplement. Enter the amounts in boxes 3.99 to 3.115. If you don't have a balance sheet, leave these boxes blank.

Warning

However small your business, the tax rules require you to prepare your business accounts in accordance with UK generally accepted accounting practice (GAAP). The GAAP rules are under constant review and change from time to time, making it hard for a lay person to keep abreast of the requirements. We recommend you use an accountant but, if you are a small business and want to prepare your own accounts, get a copy of *Financial Reporting Standards for Small Entities* (FRSSE) published by the Accounting Standards Board and downloadable free from www.frc.org.uk. FRSSE brings together most of the GAAP rules in one place, but you will still need to take account of recent changes not yet included in the latest version.

Value added tax (VAT)

You must fill in this Page if your annual turnover is £15,000 or more - read the Notes, pages SEN2, SEN4 to SEN7

If you were registered for VAT, will the
figures in boxes 3.29 to 3.64, include VAT? **3.27** □ or exclude VAT? **3.28** □

If your turnover is £61,000 a year or more from 1 April 2006 (£64,000 from 6 April 2007), you must register for VAT. Below that threshold, you can choose whether or not to register. Registration means that you must normally charge your customers VAT on the goods and services that you sell, but you can usually reclaim VAT on the things that you buy to sell, or use, in your business. You must regularly hand over to the Revenue the net amount of VAT you have collected (or claim a refund if what you are claiming comes to more than the VAT paid by your customers). Generally this VAT does not form part of your profits and needs to be stripped out before your tax bill is calculated. Your tax office needs to understand how you have stripped out the VAT.

Assuming you are not using the VAT flat-rate scheme (see below), you are likely to treat VAT in either of two ways. You can put in box 3.29 your turnover including VAT and also report in boxes 3.30 to 3.63 your costs and expenses including VAT. You then convert your profit to a VAT-exclusive amount by deducting the net amount of VAT you paid in box 3.63. In this case, your figures are shown including VAT and you should tick box 3.27. (Note that the VAT figure included in box 3.63 must be adjusted for any VAT on capital items and you should note the amount of the adjustment in the Additional information box on page 4.) Alternatively, you can record VAT-exclusive amounts throughout your accounts in which case, your figures in boxes 3.29 to 3.64 will already have had the VAT stripped out and you tick box 3.28.

From April 2003, businesses with a yearly taxable turnover before VAT up to £150,000 (and total turnover up to £187,500) can opt to join the VAT flat-rate scheme. Instead of basing your payments to the Revenue on full records of VAT on sales and purchases, under the flat-rate scheme they are a single percentage of your VAT-inclusive turnover. The percentage depends on the nature of your business. From 1 January 2004, they vary from 2 to 13.5 per cent with a 1 per cent reduction for newly VAT-registered businesses during their first year. For full details, see VAT Notice 733 from the Revenue website (www.hmrc.gov.uk) or Tel: 0845 010 9000.

When using the flat-rate scheme, in effect the actual VAT you pay on items for your business is not recoverable. Therefore it is usually easiest to fill in this supplement using your figures including VAT, in which case you tick box 3.27. In boxes 3.30 to 3.64, record your expenses including the VAT you paid on your purchases. In box 3.29, put your turnover including the actual VAT you charged your customers. You need to deduct the amount of flat-rate VAT you paid over to the Revenue. You can do this either as a reduction to turnover in box 3.29 or as an expense in box 3.63. You do not normally make any adjustment for VAT on capital items and, when working out capital allowances (see p. 283) you should normally use the cost of the item including VAT. The exception is where the capital item costs £2,000 or more including the VAT. In that case, by concession, you can reclaim the VAT you paid on that item. There is no adjustment to the amount in box 3.29 or 3.63 but your capital allowance for the item should be worked out using the VAT-exclusive amount.

Alternatively, when using the flat-rate scheme, you can record your figures excluding VAT (tick box 3.28). You will then need to work out the amount of flat-rate VAT you paid less the amount of VAT that would have been due had you not used the flat-rate scheme (which means you are no longer saving on administration and paperwork). If using the flat-rate scheme has saved you VAT, the amount saved must be included in box 3.50 as other income of your business. If you have paid more VAT through using the scheme, the extra paid can be deducted as an expense in box 3.63.

If you are not registered for VAT leave boxes 3.27 and 3.28 blank. You do not charge your customers VAT and the VAT you pay to your suppliers counts as a legitimate business expense. Your figures should include the VAT you have been charged. If you were registered for VAT for part of the year, but not for all, explain why, when the change occurred, and whether your figures are VAT-inclusive or not, in the Additional information box on page 4.

Gross profits

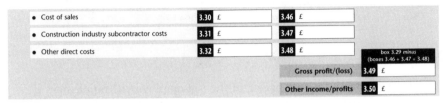

Your taxable profits are the income of your business less all the allowable expenses – that is the expenses you are allowed to deduct under the tax rules.

The starting point for working out your taxable profits is your gross profits. If you are in the business of selling something, this will be the income you get from sales less the cost of buying in the items you sell. If you sell your services, this will be the income you receive or have become entitled to receive. For more information on how to take stock and work in progress into account, see Help Sheet IR222 *How to calculate your taxable profits* and, if you sell your services, Help Sheet IR238 *Revenue recognition in service contracts – UITF40.*

In your accounts, direct costs (for example, marketing, sales discounts) might include a figure for depreciation of equipment or machinery used in producing your goods. This is not an allowable expense (see Capital allowances on p. 283) and should be entered in box 3.32.

Tax-saving ideas 146 and 147

Claim all the allowable expenses you can. If you're not sure whether an expense is allowable, deduct it from your taxable profits but ask your tax office to confirm whether this is correct.

Unless you can claim 100 per cent capital allowances (see p. 284), you will get tax relief more quickly if you can claim spending as an allowable expense (a revenue expense) rather than a capital outlay. If you need to spend on something to make it fit to use, this counts as capital spending. So make sure you do the minimum work needed and defer until later any extras that can count as revenue spending.

Other income or profits (box 3.50) includes things like income from renting out premises, interest on bank and building society accounts, discounts you get, and so on. If you receive any Business Start-up Allowance, put this in box 3.91, not here.

Tax-saving idea 148

Interest from your business bank account is taxable at the savings rate which is lower than the rate of tax charged on business profits. To ensure the correct amount of tax is paid, deduct any interest you include in box 3.50 by putting it in box 3.72 and instead include the interest in boxes 10.2 to 10.4 in the basic tax return (see p. 186).

Expenses

You don't need to complete page 2 of the Self-employment supplement if your annual turnover is less than £15,000. If it is £15,000 or more, you need to allocate your costs and expenses to boxes 3.30 to 3.63. In the boxes in the right-hand column you should enter total expenses under each heading. In the left-hand column you should enter the amount of any expenses not allowed but which have been included in the right-hand column.

Example

Hannah Brown has converted the garage at her home into an office which is used exclusively for her computer software business. She can claim part of her household expenses as allowable expenses for business purposes and, because she uses part of the home exclusively for business, she can also claim part of her mortgage interest. She makes the following calculation:

add up total household expenses	£1,800
add up the number of rooms in the house, ignoring separate toilets, halls and landings (unless large enough to be used as rooms)	8 rooms
divide the expenses by the number of rooms to give a cost per room figure	£1,800 ÷ 8 = £225 per room
multiply the cost per room by the number of rooms used for business (or by the relevant fraction of a room, if a room is used only partly for business)	1 × £225 = £225

She also claims one-eighth of her mortgage interest as a business expense. This comes to ⅛ × £3,600 = £450. However, Hannah may become liable for capital gains tax on the part of the proceeds, when she sells her home. If the garage is no longer suited to residential use, Hannah may also be liable for business rates (see below).

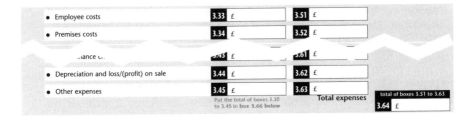

You total the amounts in boxes 3.30 to 3.45 and enter the total in box 3.66.

Tax-saving idea 149

Be wary of using part of your home exclusively for business – there may be capital gains tax on part of the proceeds when you come to sell your home. Ensuring some private use of your work space – for example, for private study, hobbies, civic duties or other voluntary work – reduces the proportion of home-related expenses you can claim as business expenses, but you should escape capital gains tax. A recent tribunal case clarified the circumstances in which you might have to pay business rates if you work from home – see p. 255. (The case is relevant to both employees and the self-employed.)

Deducting an expense from your business income has the effect of giving you tax relief at your top rate(s) of tax, so it is important to claim all the expenses you can. According to tax law, you get tax relief on an expense only if it is incurred wholly and exclusively for business. Strictly speaking, this means you can't get relief at all on expenditure which is partly for your private benefit. In practice, the Revenue does allow you to claim a proportion of some costs where something – for example, your car or home – is used partly for business. However, your tax office may baulk at some expenses which arise because of a joint business and private purpose – for example, combining a trip abroad to see a client with a holiday.

It is difficult to lay down hard and fast rules which apply to all businesses. Different types of businesses can claim different expenses and to a different extent. It is up to you to show that any claim is justified within the context of your own line of work.

You can claim expenses you incur before you open for business if they would have been allowable anyway. Treat them as expenditure incurred on the first day of business.

Tax-saving idea 150

> If you employ a family member in your business, there is no income tax or national insurance on their earnings if you pay them less than the 'primary threshold' (£5,225 in 2007–8). But consider paying them at least the 'lower earnings limit' (£4,524 in 2007–8), so they build up an entitlement to certain state benefits, such as state retirement pension.

Expenses that you incur after you close down can be set against any late income which comes into the closed business. However, if there is no income, tax relief on the expenditure is usually lost. With a few particular types of expense, you can get tax relief by setting the expenses against any other income or gains you have, provided the expense is incurred within seven years of the business ceasing (in box 15.8 of the basic tax return, see p. 217).

Employee costs

Normally allowed

Salaries, bonuses, overtime, commissions, etc. paid to your employees, together with the add-on costs, such as national insurance contributions, pension and insurance benefits. The costs of hiring locums to stand in for you or fees paid to people to whom you subcontract work. Training for employees. Council tax paid on behalf of employees if a genuine part of the pay package, taxed as normal through PAYE. Include the cost of employing your wife, husband or other family member in the business, provided their pay is reasonable for the work done (and bear in mind that the national minimum wage regulations may apply). Costs of entertaining staff – for example, a Christmas party.

Not allowed

Your own wages, national insurance, income tax, pension costs (though you can get personal tax relief for these), your drawings from the business. Wages to employees which remain unpaid nine months after the accounting date (although they can be deducted in the accounting period in which they are eventually paid). Payments to family members if excessive for the work done – be especially careful employing young children which might, in any case, be illegal. Cost of your own training might be allowed but claim in box 3.63 (see p. 299).

Premises costs

Normally allowed

If you work from dedicated business premises, include any rent, business rates, water rates, cost of lighting, heating, power, insurance, cleaning, security, and so on. If you work from home, you can claim a proportion of your home-related expenses – for example, heating, lighting, power, cleaning, maintenance, mortgage interest, rent, water rates and Council Tax. The proportion you claim must relate to your business use of the home – for example, based on the number of rooms used or floor area and the amount of time this space is devoted to business use. You should explain the basis used in the Additional information box on page 4 of the supplement.

Not allowed

Cost of buying premises (see Capital allowances on p. 283), costs relating to any part of the premises not used for business.

Repairs

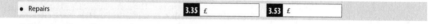

● Repairs   **3.35** £   **3.53** £

Normally allowed

General maintenance and repairs to your business premises and machinery, cost of replacing small tools.

Tax-saving idea 151

If you use your car on business, you must normally keep a record of your expenses and a log of both business and private mileage so you can claim the business proportion of your total motoring costs. However, if at the time you buy the car, your turnover is no more than the VAT registration threshold (£64,000 from 6 April 2007), you can opt instead to claim a fixed mileage allowance for use of the car on business. The fixed allowance must not exceed the approved mileage allowance payments that apply to employees (see p. 101). If you use the approved allowance, you cannot claim capital allowances, though you may (unlike employees) still claim relief for interest on a loan taken out to buy the car. The option to use the approved allowance is made when you buy the car and applies until you stop using that car in your business. Opting for the approved allowance could save you tax if your car is fairly cheap (perhaps second-hand) and small/fuel efficient. It also saves paperwork because the only record you need to keep is your business mileage.

Not allowed

Costs of alterations and improvements (see Capital allowances on p. 283 but also Tax-saving idea 130 on p. 255 which is also relevant to spending by businesses), costs relating to any part of the premises not used for business, general reserve for repairs.

General administrative expenses

● General administrative expenses   **3.36** £   **3.54** £

Normally allowed

Office expenses, such as postage, telephone, stationery, printing, subscriptions to trade journals, professional fees, accountancy and audit fees and regular expenses not included elsewhere. You can claim the cost of computer software where you pay a regular licence fee to use it or where the software has a limited lifetime (generally taken to be less than two years). In most other cases, software costs count as capital expenditure for which you can claim capital allowances (see p. 283). If you work from home and use your home phone for business, you can claim your business calls and a proportion of the line rental consistent with your business use of the phone. The same approach applies to internet connections.

Not allowed

Personal expenses, payments to political parties, most donations and fees to clubs, charities and churches. Any non-business part of a cost.

Motor expenses

Normally allowed

Costs of running a vehicle used in your business – for example, insurance, servicing, repairs, road tax, breakdown insurance, parking charges, fuel, hiring or leasing charges. A proportion of those costs if you also use the vehicle privately.

Not allowed

Travel between your home and business premises. Cost of buying a vehicle (see Capital allowances on p. 283). Parking fines, other fines.

Travel and subsistence

Normally allowed

Rail, air and taxi fares, hotel accommodation, cost of meals connected to an overnight stay whether included on your hotel bill or paid separately, modest additional expense of meals where your work is itinerant by nature (for example, commercial traveller) or during occasional journeys that are not part of your normal business pattern.

Not allowed

Cost of lunches and most other meals.

Advertising, promotion and entertainment

Normally allowed

Advertising, mail-shots, free samples, gifts up to £50 a year to any client provided they promote your firm or its products or services and are not food, drink or tobacco.

Not allowed

Entertaining clients, business associates, etc. (only entertaining staff is allowed), gifts except those specifically allowed (see above).

Legal and professional costs

Normally allowed

Fees charged by accountants (including extra costs due to a Revenue enquiry provided the enquiry does not reveal any negligent or fraudulent conduct), auditors, solicitors, surveyors, stocktakers, and so on, professional indemnity premiums.

Not allowed

Legal costs of buying premises, equipment, etc. (treated as part of their cost – see Capital allowances on p. 283), legal expenses on forming a company, cost of settling tax disputes, cost of fee protection insurance if it would cover cost of professional help in the event of tax fraud or negligence, fines, etc. as a result of acting illegally.

Bad debts

Normally allowed

Items you have sold or amounts you have invoiced but for which you no longer expect to be paid. A proportion of a bad debt given up under a voluntary arrangement. If in a later tax year you are paid, include the amount recovered in box 3.50 (other income/profits).

Not allowed

General reserve for bad debts.

Interest

● Interest and alternative finance payments 3.42 £ 3.60 £

Normally allowed

Interest and arrangement fees for a loan or overdraft used for business.

Not allowed

The part of loan payments which represents capital repayments.

Tax-saving idea 152

Whether interest on a loan counts as an allowable expense depends on how the money is used, not its source. Instead of overdrawing your business account or getting a business loan, a cheaper option might be extending the mortgage on your home. The part of the interest relating to business use is allowable and the Revenue assumes repayments pay off the personal debt before the business debt.

Other finance charges

● Other finance charges   3.43 £   3.61 £

Normally allowed

Charges on your business current account, credit card interest and fees, the interest element of hire purchase charges, leasing payments – but the amount you can claim is restricted in the case of a car whose retail price when new exceeded £12,000 unless it counts as environmentally friendly (see p. 285).

Not allowed

The part of any payment which represents capital repayment.

Depreciation and loss/(profit) on sale

● Depreciation and loss/(profit) on sale   3.44 £   3.62 £

Not allowed

None of these costs is allowable – instead you claim capital allowances (see p. 283). The figure you enter at 3.62 should exactly match the amount you put in box 3.44 – unless some of the costs relate to finance leases, in which case ask your tax office what you can deduct.

Other expenses

Normally allowed

Any expenses which you haven't found a place for in boxes 3.46 to 3.62. For example, any insurance premiums not included elsewhere, contributions to approved local enterprise agencies, training and enterprise councils, local enterprise councils and business link organisations, and part or all of subscriptions to trade or professional associations which secure some benefit for your business or to societies which have an arrangement with the Revenue. Cost of your own training provided it is wholly and exclusively for business and updates your existing knowledge and skills. This is also the place to strip out VAT if applicable (see p. 290).

Not allowed

The non-business element of any expenses included in box 3.63. This includes, for example, ordinary clothing even if you bought it specially for business and would not normally wear it otherwise, buying a patent (see Capital allowances on p. 283), cost of computer hardware and any software costs not claimed in box 3.54 (see Capital allowances on p. 283), cost of your own training if it provides you with new skills (including initial training for operating a franchise) – claim Capital allowances instead, see p. 283.

Tax adjustments to net profit or loss

All the expenses which are not allowable are added together and the total entered in box 3.66. In the next box, you must enter the selling price of any goods which you took for personal use. These are added to your profits. If you are a farmer, box 3.67 is also the place to enter any compensation from the compulsory slaughter of animals that you have opted to spread forward from an earlier year to 2006–7. Similarly, if you wish to spread forward any compensation received in 2006–7, put the deduction in box 3.71 and a note in the Additional information box 3.116. See Help Sheet IR224 *Farmers and market gardeners*.

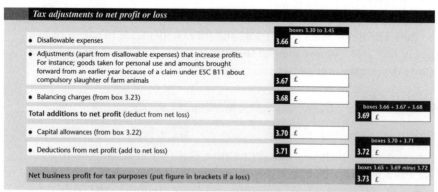

Adjustments

So far, in completing the Self-employment supplement, you have entered figures for one particular accounting period. As explained on p. 278 this may not be the same as the period over which you are actually taxed which is known to the Revenue as your basis period. After the first two or three years in business, your basis period (and the dates you enter in 3.74 and 3.75) will normally be the same as your accounting period. But in the early years of the business, or if you change your accounting date, you may have to enter different dates.

If your basis period does differ from your accounting period, you have to make an adjustment in box 3.77. Work this out by adding together and/or dividing the profits or losses for the relevant accounting periods. This is explained on p. 279 and in Help Sheet IR222 *How to calculate your taxable profits*. Remember to enter the adjustment in brackets if it is a deduction.

Overlap relief

In boxes 3.78 and 3.80, you should keep a record of the overlap profit (see p. 280) that you are carrying forward. You may be able to use part or all of it to reduce your profits or create a loss if you closed your business in 2006–7 (see p. 282) or you changed your accounting date (see p. 281). Enter the amount of overlap profit you want to use in this way in box 3.79. See IR222 *How to calculate your taxable profits*.

Example

Sam started his business as a self-employed landscape gardener on 6 July 2006. His basis period for the tax year ending 5 April 2007 is the period between 6 July 2006 and 5 April 2007. He draws up his first set of accounts on 5 June 2007. In all the boxes up to 3.76 he enters the figures for his first accounting period, running to 5 June 2006. His profit in this accounting period was £8,000. Because he was only in business for 274 of the 365 days in the year to 5 April 2007, his profits for the tax year were $^{274}/_{365} \times £8,000 = £6,005$. At box 3.77 he enters an adjustment (in brackets) of £8,000 − £6,005 = £1,995.

Adjustments to arrive at taxable profit or loss

Basis period begins	3.74 / / and ends	3.75 / /
Profit or loss of this account for tax purposes (box 3.26 or 3.73)		3.76 £
Adjustment to arrive at profit or loss for this basis period		3.77 £
● Overlap profit brought forward	3.78 £	● Deduct overlap relief used this year 3.79 £
● Overlap profit carried forward	3.80 £	
● Averaging for farmers and creators of literary or artistic works *(see Notes, page SEN7, if you made a loss for 2006-07)*		3.81 £
● Adjustment on change of basis		3.82 £

Farmers and creative workers (such as authors and artists) whose income varies substantially from year to year can make a claim to be taxed on the average of their earnings from consecutive years. In box 3.81 enter the increase or reduction in your income as a result of the claim. See Help Sheets IR224 *Farmers and market gardeners* or IR234 *Averaging for creators of literary or artistic works*.

Use box 3.82 to report any increase or decrease in your profits for 2006–7 as a result of a change in the basis on which you draw up your accounts. This may apply to you if you provide professional or other services (for example, as an accountant or solicitor) and you are affected by the new accounting guidance known as 'UITF40'. This guidance, which takes effect for accounting periods applied on or after 22 June 2005 (but could voluntarily be adopted earlier), requires you to account for the income notionally accrued on part-completion of contracts instead of including the full amount only on completion. Most people will have made the adjustment to the UITF40 basis in their 2005–6 tax return but, if your accounting year ends early in the tax year, you may be making the adjustment this year.

Tax-saving idea 153

If you are now adjusting your accounts to the UITF40 basis, you will need to restate your balance sheet at the start of your accounting period as if UITF40 had applied in the previous year. This is likely to result in an increase in your balance sheet total which counts as a 'prior period adjustment' and is taxable. But tax due on this adjustment will automatically be spread over a period of three to six tax years, unless you elect for the relief not to apply. When deciding whether or not to make an election, consider your whole tax position for the year and whether you might obtain tax relief instead by, say, making pension contributions.

Tax-saving idea 154

You do not have to make up your mind about how to get tax relief for your losses straightaway. You have a while to wait and see how your business affairs turn out. But the time limits for each option are strict, so don't delay so long that you miss them.

Losses

If you make a loss, there are several ways you can get tax relief on it.

Other income or gains for this year

Net profit for 2006–07 (if you made a loss, enter '0')		**3.83** £
Allowable loss for 2006–07 (if you made a profit, enter '0')	**3.84** £	
• Loss offset against other income for 2006–07	**3.85** £	
• Loss - relief to be calculated by reference to earlier years	**3.86** £	

Complete box 3.85 to set the loss against other income you have during 2006–7 – for example, from working for an employer or from your savings. If this does not use up all the loss, you can ask for the rest to be set against any taxable capital gains for 2006–7. If any loss still remains, you can ask for relief on it to be given in some other way. The time limit for making this choice with respect to losses made in the accounting period being declared for 2006–7 is 31 January 2009.

Tax-saving idea 155

Regardless of how you use a loss to claim tax relief, you may also be able to use it to make or increase a claim for tax credits (see p. 60).

Example

Sonja Frisk has been an antiques dealer for the last ten years. Normally, she makes a reasonable living but, in 2006, the sale of some expensive artifacts fell through and Sonja made a £7,000 loss for the tax year.

Sonja could set the remaining loss against other income which she had in the tax year ending 5 April 2007 from a part-time job lecturing in art history at the local university. Alternatively, she can carry back her loss to the tax year ending 5 April 2006, or carry it forward to set against future profits from her antiques business. She doesn't want to use her loss this year, because she will pay only 10 per cent tax on her lecturing income, compared with the 22 per cent top rate of tax she paid last year; nor is she keen to carry forward her loss because she does not expect to pay a higher rate of tax in future. She claims to carry back her loss to the year ending 5 April 2006, qualifying for tax relief of 22 per cent × £7,000 = £1,540.

Other income and gains for the previous year

• Loss - relief to be calculated by reference to earlier years	**3.86** £

Complete box 3.86 to carry back the loss to 2005–6 to set against your income from any source for that year. If this does not use up the full loss, you can ask for the rest to be set against any capital gains for 2005–6. If some loss still remains, you can ask for relief on it to be given in some other way. The time limit for making this choice is 31 January 2009.

Other income for earlier years

You can ask for a loss made in the first four years of the business to be carried back and set against income (but not gains) for the previous three tax years – that is, 2003–4, 2004–5 and 2005–6. The loss is set against the earliest year first. The time limit for this choice is also 31 January 2009.

Future profits

> • Loss to carry forward (that is allowable loss not claimed in any other way)   **3.87** £

Complete box 3.87 to carry the loss forward to set against your future profits from the same business. It will be set against the next profits you make with any remaining loss being rolled forward to set against the next profits and so on until the loss is completely used up. You have until 31 January 2013 to make this choice.

Closing down

If your business closed down during 2006–7, you have a further option. A loss you made during your last 12 months of trading can be set against your profits for the three previous tax years – that is you can go back to 2002–3. The time limit for this choice is also 31 January 2013. For more information see Help Sheet IR227 *Losses*.

National Insurance

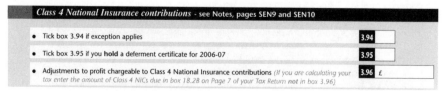

Running your own business, you will usually have to pay national insurance contributions (NICs) both for yourself and for any people you employ. You will have to pay: class 2 contributions at a flat-rate of £2.10 a week in 2006–7 (£2.20 in 2007–8). If your profits are less than £4,465 in 2006–7 (£4,635 in 2007–8), you can opt not to pay.

Class 2 NICs help you to qualify for certain state benefits, such as retirement pension and incapacity benefit, so it might be better to carry on paying even if your profits are low. Class 2 contributions are paid direct to the Revenue, usually by direct debit.

Tax-saving idea 156

At £2.20 a week, Class 2 national insurance contributions are a good value way of building up rights to state benefits such as state basic pension and incapacity benefit. If your profits are low, think twice before deciding not to pay these contributions.

You may also have to pay class 4 contributions. Unlike other types of national insurance, class 4 contributions do not entitle you to any state benefits – they are simply a tax on profits which is collected along with your income tax. In 2006–7, class 4 NICs were payable at a rate of 8 per cent on profits over £5,035 up to £33,540 and at a rate of 1 per cent on profits above £33,540. (In 2007–8, the rates are unchanged and the limits rise to £5,225 and £34,840.) If your profits are less than the lower limit, you do not pay any class 4 NICs at all.

Example

Jim Newall has profits for income tax purposes of £8,500 for 2006–7. These are also the profits on which his Class 4 NICs are based. They are calculated as follows:

Profit for Class 4 NICs purposes	=	£8,500
Less lower profit limit	=	£5,035
Amount chargeable (£8,500 − £5,035)	=	£3,465
Class 4 NICs at 8 per cent × £3,465	=	£277.20

Tax-saving ideas 157 and 158

Losses can be used to reduce your class 4 national insurance contributions as well as your income tax bill. And the treatment of losses is not necessarily identical: where, for income tax purposes, you elect for a loss to be set against income or gains other than profits from your business, that amount of loss is carried forward and set against future profits for class 4 purposes.

If you're paying both class 1 and class 4 national insurance on some of your income, ask to have the class 4 liability deferred until you know precisely how much is due. Otherwise, you could end up paying too much in contributions.

A few groups of people are excluded from having to pay class 4 NICs. They include people over state pension age (currently 60 for women and 65 for men), people under age 16 if they have been granted an exemption by the Revenue (ask for form CA2835U available from HM Revenue & Customs, NICO Deferment Services, Brenton Park View, Newcastle upon Tyne, NE98 1ZZ) and people who are not resident in the UK.

In some circumstances, you might have earnings which count as profits of your business but which have already had class 1 NICs deducted. In other cases, you might have earnings both as an employee (on which class 1 contributions are payable) and from self-employment. There is a cap on the overall amount you have to pay in national insurance, so it may be that class 4 NICs won't be payable after all. However, you usually don't know whether this is the case until after part of the class 4 NICs would have become payable, so you can ask to have payment deferred until the position is known by filling in form CA72B in the back of booklet CA72 *Deferring payment* from www.hmrc.gov.uk or tax offices.

If you are either excluded from paying class 4 NICs or your tax office has agreed that you can defer paying them, you should tick the box at 3.94 and put 0 in boxes 3.95 and 3.96. In all other cases, leave box 3.94 blank. If you have any losses from 2006–7 or previous years which have not yet been set against profits chargeable to class 4 contributions enter them in box 3.95 because they can reduce your profits used for working out class 4 NICs (as well as reducing your income tax liability). If you have paid interest for business purposes but it has not been deducted in working out your profits for income tax purposes, you might be able to deduct it for class 4 NICs purposes. If this applies enter the amount of interest also in box 3.95.

Box 3.96 invites you to write down the amount you owe in class 4 NICs. You don't have to do this sum yourself. Provided you send in your tax return by the 30 September deadline, you can leave the box blank and let your tax office do the sums. If you prefer to work out your class 4 NICs yourself, there is a calculator included in the notes accompanying your Self-employment supplement. (The calculator is not suitable if you run more than one business, see Help Sheet IR220 *More than one business*.)

Class 2 and class 4 contributions are not allowable expenses and can't be deducted when working out your profits for income tax purposes. If you have employees, you have to pay employer's class 1 NICs for them if they earn more than the primary threshold (£97 and £100 a week respectively for 2006–7 and 2007–8). In this case, the amount you pay counts as an allowable expense (see p. 294).

Tax-saving idea 159

If you employ someone, you must operate PAYE to deduct the correct tax and national insurance from their pay. In stages, all employers are being required to switch to filing PAYE returns electronically and by 6 April 2009 this will include small employers with fewer than 50 employees. If you voluntarily switch before then, you are eligible for incentive payments ranging from £250 to £75 a year. You can still pick up a total of £325 if you first file online by 19 May 2007. Ask your tax office for details.

18

Partnership

Q4 ▶ Were you in partnership?   **YES** ☐   *PARTNERSHIP* ☐

If you are in business with one or more partners, you should answer YES to Q4 in the basic tax return and fill in the Partnership supplement. There are two versions:

- short version. Use this if the partnership income is from trading profits or interest from bank or building society accounts which has already been taxed at the savings rate. This version will be adequate for most partners
- full version. If your partnership earnings are more complex because you have untaxed investment income, foreign income or income from land and property, for example, you'll need to complete this longer supplement.

The partnership should already have provided you with a Partnership Statement summarising your share of the profits, losses and other income. If you received the full statement, you need the full version of the supplementary pages; if you received a short statement, you need only the short supplement. If you haven't received a Partnership supplement or you need the full version, contact the Revenue Orderline (see p. 170).

You and your fellow partners are jointly responsible for the partnership tax return, although one partner may be nominated to deal with it. This is a separate document from the partnership supplement. Profits are calculated on the return as if the partnership were a single person using largely the same rules as for a self-employed person (see Chapter 17). How profits are shared between partners depends on your partnership agreement.

Once the partner dealing with the tax return has worked out the taxable profits for the partnership as a whole, he or she must show each partner's share of the profits, losses and tax suffered on the Partnership statement at the end of the Partnership return. The Partnership statement gives each individual partner the information needed to complete their own Partnership supplement. Each partner is then responsible for the tax on their own share of the profits.

Each partner is treated as if they were carrying on a business on their own, and the short version of the Partnership supplement is very similar to the Adjustments to arrive at taxable profit and loss and class 4 national insurance sections of the Self-employment supplement (see pp. 300 and 304). The other sections of the supplement simply summarise your share of any tax that the partnership has already suffered. For this reason, we have not gone through the Partnership supplement in detail.

Becoming a partner

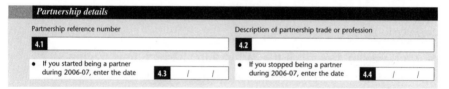

When you join a partnership, the normal opening rules described on pp. 279–80 apply. The period on which your tax is based is likely to be different from the accounting year for the partnership. The dates you put in boxes 4.5 and 4.6 should reflect how the opening year rules apply to you.

The opening year rules may result in overlap profits (see p. 280) on which you can eventually claim tax relief either when you leave the partnership or, possibly, if the partnership accounting date is changed.

Once the special opening year rules have worked through, you are taxed on the normal current year basis. The period on which your tax is based will then be the same as the accounting year of the partnership, so you put the start date of the partnership year in box 4.5 and the end date in box 4.6.

Ceasing to be a partner

If you leave a partnership you are treated as if you are closing down your own business. The normal closing rules apply (see p. 282), including the claiming of tax relief on any overlap profits carried forward from the opening years or a change of accounting date.

Partnerships providing personal services

If your partnership hires out your services to client companies and, in the absence of the partnership, your work would effectively amount to that of an employee, you may be caught by the 'IR35 rules' described on p. 234. Ask the Orderline (see p. 170) to send you Help Sheet IR222 *How to calculate your taxable profits*, which explains the adjustments you need to make.

Tax-saving idea 160

Partnerships providing services need to comply with the new UITF40 rule. This means the accounts must recognise revenue from projects which are only part-completed at the end of an accounting year. Switching to the UITF40 basis is likely to have resulted in a prior period adjustment (see p. 302). Tax on this will usually automatically be spread over three to six years. If a partner leaves, all the tax remaining to be collected is normally the responsibility of the remaining partners and any new partners who join, even though it relates to an earlier period. You might want to adjust your partnership agreement so you can charge leaving partners their share of the tax. Alternatively, consider electing not to use the spreading provisions so that all the tax is paid now.

Losses

Since 10 February 2004, if you are a partner but do not yourself spend a significant amount of time running the business, the amount of losses for which you can claim 'sideways loss relief' is limited to the amount you have contributed to the partnership. For example, if you paid £20,000 into the partnership, the loss relief is limited to a maximum of £20,000. 'Sideways loss relief' means the setting of losses against other income and gains (see p. 303), setting losses against profits for earlier years (see p. 304) and claiming relief for interest on a loan used to buy into the partnership (see p. 213). You can still claim relief without any restriction by carrying losses forward to set against future profits from the same business.

Warning

For investments you make from 2 March 2007 onwards, sideways loss relief for a non-active partner is restricted to the lower of the eligible amount as described above and £25,000. You will count as a non-active partner if you devote on average less than 10 hours a week to the business. There is an exception: the £25,000 limit will not apply where you are investing in a partnership carrying on a film-related trade.

19

Land and property

Q5 Did you receive any rent or other income from land and property in the UK?

YES   **LAND & PROPERTY**

If you ticked the YES box against Q5 on page 2 of the tax return, you will need the Land and property supplementary pages. Many people renting out the odd room in their home may have to do little more than tick one box on the first page. But there is also space for details of more substantial lettings businesses and for income from holiday homes.

If you take in lodgers in your home, providing meals and other services, this may amount to a form of business (but see the Rent a Room scheme below) and details should be entered on the Self-employment supplementary pages (see Chapter 17). Income from property abroad is entered on the Foreign pages (see Chapter 20).

Warning

> The Revenue is cracking down on people who fail to declare and pay tax on foreign sources of income. If you rent out a property abroad – say, a holiday home – you must in most cases declare this income even if you leave it in a bank account abroad and use it only for the upkeep and running of the property. Do not declare such income here – use the Foreign supplement (see Chapter 20).

The documents you need

You will need details of the rents you have received and any receipts or invoices for expenses. With furnished holiday lettings, you will also need records of the periods the properties were available for letting out.

If any of these properties is jointly owned, remember to enter only your share from these documents when filling in the tax return.

The Rent a Room scheme

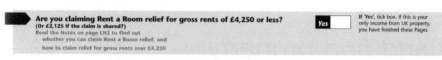

The Rent a Room scheme applies to rent from letting out furnished accommodation in your home and income from providing any related services, such as providing meals or doing your lodger's laundry. In the normal way you would pay tax on any profit you make – in other words, the income you get less allowable expenses you incur. If instead you opt for the Rent a Room scheme, the first slice of the income is tax-free, but you are not allowed to deduct any expenses.

Tax-saving idea 161

If you make a profit from taking in lodgers and your income from the lettings is £4,250 or less in 2006–7, there will be no tax to pay on this income if you opt for the Rent a Room scheme. If your gross income from the lettings is more than £4,250 but the expenses and allowances you can claim come to £4,250 or less, you will pay less tax if you opt for the Rent a Room scheme. Using the Rent a Room scheme can save you administration because, for tax purposes, you need only keep records of your income not any expenses.

The scheme can apply only to rooms you let in your only or main home (see Chapter 6). It doesn't matter whether you own the home or you yourself are a tenant (though bear in mind that you may need permission from a mortgage lender or landlord before taking in lodgers). The scheme is not intended to apply to rooms let as offices or for other business purposes. And you cannot claim Rent a Room relief if you yourself are not living in the property because, say, you have gone abroad or moved into job-related accommodation.

Under the scheme, in 2006–7, the first £4,250 of such income (without any expenses deducted) is tax-free. If anyone else living in the same home is letting out another room or you are jointly letting out room(s) with one or more other people, you each get £2,125 tax-free. The amount of Rent a Room relief has been unchanged since April 1997.

Example

Natalie Lean lets out three rooms in her house, bringing in a total of £150 a week in rent. This means her gross rental income for 2006–7 is £7,800, on which she could claim expenses and allowances of £2,350.

If the rental income is taxed as normal property income, she will pay tax on £7,800 − £2,350 = £5,450. But if she claims the Rent a Room relief, she will pay tax on the excess of the gross rental income of £7,800 over £4,250 – that is, on £3,550.

Rent a Room relief means Natalie will pay tax on £1,900 less income.

Unless you made a loss on the letting (in other words, your expenses came to more than the income), it will be worth claiming Rent a Room relief if your gross income from the letting(s) is £4,250 or less. All you need to do is tick the YES box if this is your only letting income. There is nothing more to enter – leave the rest of the Land and property pages blank.

In all other cases, which boxes you complete depends on how much profit or loss you made from the letting(s) in 2006–7:

- if you made a loss, follow the instructions for Other property income (see p. 325)
- if the expenses and allowances you can deduct from your letting income come to more than £4,250 (or £2,125 if you are sharing the relief), follow the instructions for Other property income (see p. 322)
- if the deductions you can make from your letting income come to £4,250 (£2,125) or less, opt for the Rent a Room scheme by putting your income in box 5.20 on page 2 and the Rent a Room relief you are claiming (either £4,250 or £2,125) in box 5.35. Don't enter any expenses in boxes 5.24 to 5.30 and don't claim any other deductions in boxes 5.36 (capital allowances) or 5.37 (wear and tear allowance).

Warning

It is commonly claimed that taking in lodgers through the Rent a Room scheme will not mean losing any of the private residence relief which prevents a capital gains tax bill when you sell your home (see Chapter 6). This is not correct. The Revenue's view is that if you have a single lodger (whether you use the Rent a Room scheme or not), you do not lose private residence relief. But if you have two or more lodgers (again, regardless of whether you have opted for the Rent a Room scheme), you are effectively running a business and so lose some of the capital gains tax relief on your home. However, you may instead claim lettings relief (see p. 71).

Furnished holiday lettings

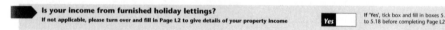

If you have no income from short-term furnished lettings, turn over to page L2 of the supplement and to p. 320 of this book.

Tax benefits of furnished holiday lettings

Income from furnished holiday lettings is treated differently from other forms of property income, to reflect the fact that it is a form of business for many owners. This offers several tax benefits:

- you can claim capital allowances on plant and equipment (see p. 283)

- losses can be set off against other income or gains for the same or previous tax year and losses in the first four years of the business can be deducted from other income from the previous three years (see p. 319)

- it counts as relevant earnings for tax relief on pension contributions (p. 82)

- you can claim the special business reliefs for capital gains tax (p. 148).

What income is taxed?

Income from land and property (other than that dealt with under the Rent a Room scheme) is all taxed in the same way – irrespective of its type. All income from land and property in the UK is added together. You pay tax on the income after deduction of allowable expenses, interest paid on loans to buy or improve the properties and losses from letting out property in the past. You can also claim allowances for some equipment you buy.

The tax you pay in a tax year is based on the property income and expenditure during that year. If you make up accounts for your property business for the year ending 5 April, the figures in your accounts will be the ones to use in filling in your tax return.

But if your accounting year runs to different dates, you will have to use two sets of accounts to work out what your property income and expenditure was for the tax year.

To count as furnished holiday lettings, the property must normally meet all the following conditions for 2006–7:

- be available for letting to the general public on a commercial basis (that is, with a view to a profit) for at least 140 days

■ actually let commercially for at least 70 of those days

■ periods when the property was occupied for more than 31 days in a row by the same person (called periods of longer-term occupation) do not count towards the 70 days. The total of any periods of longer-term occupation (which need not be consecutive) must not exceed 155 days.

If you first started letting the property during 2006–7, these conditions must be satisfied for the first 12 months of letting. If you finished letting the property during that tax year, the conditions must have been met for the 12 months ending with the last letting. If you own more than one furnished holiday letting, you can average out the letting for 70 days rule between all of them.

The property need not be a fixed building. It could, for example, be a caravan. But whatever its structure you will have to convince the Revenue that you are genuinely letting on a commercial basis not simply trying to offset some of the costs of your holiday home. For example, you should be able to produce a business plan and properly drawn-up accounts.

Tax-saving ideas 162 and 163

If you let out your second home, try to make sure you meet the conditions for the rent to be taxed as income from furnished holiday lettings. You can claim a wider variety of deductions against tax and you may be able to reduce or avoid capital gains tax when you sell the home (see pp. 148 and 316).

Furnished holiday lettings, as such, do not count as business property for the purpose of inheritance tax. But, if they are serviced lettings (for example, providing meals and laundry), they may qualify. You can employ someone else to provide these services. Provided certain conditions are met, gifts of business property qualify for 100 per cent business property relief which means they can be passed on or given away free of inheritance tax.

Income

Furnished holiday lettings in the UK

● Income from furnished holiday lettings	5.1 £

Enter the total income from all your furnished holiday lettings in the UK for 2006–7 – before any deductions such as agents' commission. Include any income for services provided to tenants, such as cleaning, linen hire and use of additional facilities. Also include any money received from insurance policies for loss of rent.

Expenses

■ *Expenses* (furnished holiday lettings only)

If your total property income, including that from furnished holiday lettings, is less than £15,000, enter your total expenses in box 5.7, as Other expenses – you don't need to give details of individual expenses. If your total property income is over this limit, you need to list expenses separately:

Rent, rates, insurance, ground rents, etc.

• Rent, rates, insurance, ground rents etc.　　**5.2** £

Enter the amount of rent, business rates, council tax, water rates, ground rent and insurance premiums on the furnished holiday lettings (including for insurance against loss of rents) in box 5.2.

Repairs, maintenance and renewals

• Repairs, maintenance and renewals　　**5.3** £

Claim in box 5.3. Any work that prevents the property deteriorating is a repair – such as painting and damp treatment. You can't claim here the cost of improvements, additions or extensive alterations even if such work makes repairs unnecessary.

If you aren't claiming capital allowances for the furniture, fixtures and fittings, you can claim a renewals deduction for the cost of replacing them. If the new items are better, you cannot claim the full cost. And if any of the old items are sold, the proceeds should be deducted from the amount you claim.

Tax-saving idea 164

The Revenue accepts that work which once counted as an improvement to a property may over time and due to technological advances now be accepted as a repair and so count as an allowable expense. The example it gives is replacing old windows with double glazing. If you are replacing an old feature with a modern equivalent, try claiming and ask your tax office to confirm that the expense is allowable.

Finance charges

• Finance charges, including interest　　**5.4** £

Enter in box 5.4 the cost of any loan you took out to buy the property – including interest paid and charges for setting up the loan.

Legal and professional costs

• Legal and professional costs	**5.5** £

You can claim legal and professional expenses for a letting of less than a year, including fees for agents, surveyors and accountants and commission. You can also claim such costs when renewing the lease for a longer letting provided it is for less than 50 years. But you cannot claim expenses incurred in the first letting of a property for more than a year. Nor can you claim costs of registering title to land, getting planning permission or in connection with the payment of a premium on renewal of a lease. Enter the total in box 5.5.

Cost of services provided

• Costs of services provided, including wages	**5.6** £

You can claim as an expense the cost of services such as gardening, cleaning and porterage. You can't claim the cost of your own time, but you can claim the cost of paying other people such as a member of your family.

Enter the total in box 5.6. If you are paid for any services you provide, this should be included as part of the income in box 5.1.

Tax-saving idea 165

Where you own a rental property with your spouse or civil partner, you must split the taxable income between you in the same shares as you own the property (usually equal shares unless you have made a declaration specifying some other split). But if you own property jointly with anyone else, you can agree to divide the income in different shares from those in which you own the property provided the actual shares you receive are the same as those agreed. For example, an unmarried couple who pay tax at different rates can agree to have more of the rent paid to the lower taxpayer.

Other expenses

		total of boxes 5.2 to 5.7
• Other expenses	**5.7** £	**5.8** £

Other expenses include advertising costs, stationery, telephone calls, rent collection and travel to the property when solely for the letting.

Add together the figures in boxes 5.2 to 5.7 and enter the total in box 5.8.

Net profit

	box 5.1 *minus* box 5.8
Net profit (put figures in brackets if a loss)	**5.9** £

Net profit is income minus expenses. Deduct the figure in box 5.8 from that in box 5.1 and put the amount in box 5.9, in brackets if it is a loss.

Tax adjustments

Private use

If a furnished holiday letting is partly used for your own enjoyment or that of friends staying cheaply or rent-free, this counts as private use. Part of the costs must be apportioned to this private use, and cannot be claimed as an expense. For example, if it was available for letting for nine months of the year and used by you for the rest of the time, you can claim only three-quarters of the costs of owning it. (You can still claim the full costs of letting it out as expenses.)

There are two ways to make an adjustment to reflect private use. You can enter the appropriate share of the costs in boxes 5.2 to 5.7, but let your tax inspector know what you've done. Or, better, you enter the costs in full in these boxes and enter in box 5.10 a figure for private use which is deducted from the total.

Capital allowances and balancing charges

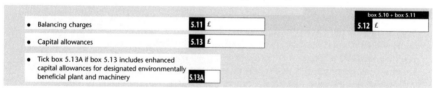

You can claim capital allowances for the cost of buying furniture, machinery such as a lawnmower or equipment such as a water pump. If you get rid of an item on which you have claimed capital allowances, a balancing charge may be added to your profits, reflecting the sale proceeds or the second-hand value. There's more on p. 283 about capital allowances and balancing charges. You might also find it useful to get Help Sheet IR250 *Capital allowances and balancing charges in a rental business* from the Orderline (see p. 170).

Enter the amount of any capital allowances you are claiming for the tax year ending 5 April 2006 in box 5.13 and the amount of any balancing charge in box 5.11. Add the figures in boxes 5.10 and 5.11 together and enter the total in box 5.12.

If you are claiming first-year capital allowances on something which counts as environmentally friendly spending (see table on p. 285), tick box 5.13A.

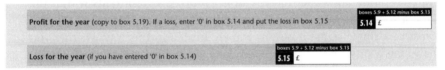

Total boxes 5.9 and 5.12 and subtract the amount in box 5.13. If the answer is a negative number, you have made a tax loss on your furnished holiday lettings. Enter 0 in box 5.14 and put the amount of the loss in box 5.15. If you have made a profit, enter it in box 5.14.

Losses for the year

Any loss in box 5.15 can be used to reduce the amount of tax you pay on other income or capital gains in 2006–7 or earlier tax years:

■ other income for 2006–7 (enter the amount you wish to claim in box 5.16)

■ capital gains for the same tax year – include the amount you wish to claim in the total you enter in box F4 or column K2 of the Capital gains supplementary pages (see p. 346)

■ income and gains for earlier tax years – enter the amount you wish to claim in box 5.17. If you have already claimed to offset this loss, still include it here but make a note of the amount in the Additional information box on page 10 of the basic tax return.

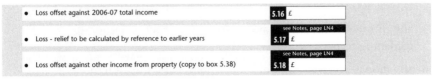

If you haven't used all the loss in box 5.15, you can set off what remains against other property income for 2006–7. Enter what is left in box 5.18 and copy it into box 5.38 on page L2 of the Land and property supplementary pages.

Tax-saving idea 166

Keep careful and detailed records so that you can claim for all your expenses. Don't forget to claim the interest on any mortgage used to finance the purchase of the property as an expense against letting income. The mortgage does not have to be secured against the let property in order to be allowable – it could be secured, for example, against your own home.

Other property income

All your rental and other income from property (except rents within the Rent a Room scheme – see p. 312) is added together and treated as the proceeds of a single rental business. You are treated in this way whether you have, say, a single buy-to-let property or a whole string of flats and houses.

Income

Other property income (not including dividends from a UK Real Estate Investment Trust - go to box 13.1 - 13.3 on page 5 of the Tax Return)

■ *Income*
    copy from box 5.14
● Furnished holiday lettings profits   5.19 £

Copy the figure for profits on furnished holiday lettings from box 5.14 to box 5.19.

Rents and other income from land and property

    Tax taken off
● Rents and other income from land and property 5.20 £   5.21 £

Enter in box 5.20 the total income from all your lettings in the UK except furnished holiday lettings for 2006–7 – before any deductions such as agents' commission. Include the following:

■ rent you will receive after 5 April 2007 which is payment in arrears for 2006–7 (equally, leave out any rent received in arrears this year that was included in last year's return, and any rent received on or before 5 April 2007 which is payment in advance for rent for periods after 5 April 2007)

■ any income for services provided to tenants, such as cleaning, gardening or porterage

■ any money received from insurance policies for loss of rent

■ ground rent and feu duties

■ grants from local authorities for repairs (you can claim the cost of repairs as an expense)

■ payments for using your land – for example, to shoot or graze.

If any tax has been deducted from the income before you get it, enter the total in box 5.21. The figure you enter in box 5.20 should be the before-tax amounts – so should include the amount in box 5.21.

If you own and let the property jointly with someone else, enter only your share of the income in box 5.20, and your share of the expenses lower down. If you only know your share of the profit after expenses, enter this in box 5.20 or any loss in box 5.29. Tick box 5.46 and give the name and address of the person who keeps the records for the shared property in the Additional information box on page 10 of the main tax return.

Chargeable premiums, reverse premiums

● Chargeable premiums	**5.22** £	
● Reverse premiums	**5.22A** £	boxes 5.19 + 5.20 + 5.22 + 5.22A **5.23** £

If you receive a premium from a tenant in return for granting a lease, you will have to pay income tax on part of it if the lease lasts 50 years or less (and capital gains tax on the rest). Any work the tenant agrees to do for you on being granted a lease counts as a premium.

Example

Miriam Patel has divided most of her house into furnished rooms which she lets out, providing cleaning. The total yearly income is £9,640 but she can deduct these expenses:

■ a proportion of the outgoings on the house (council tax, water rates, gas, electricity and insurance) which add up to £3,400 a year. Miriam is letting out three-quarters of the house and claims this proportion
■ the cost of cleaning (cleaner's wages plus materials) – £1,300 a year
■ an allowance for wear and tear of the furniture and furnishings – Miriam claims the actual cost of replacement (£500 for this year).

Thus Miriam's tax bill would be calculated as follows:

Total rent received		£9,640
Less expenses		
Three-quarters of the outgoings of £3,400 a year	£2,550	
Cost of cleaning	£1,300	
Cost of replacing furniture and furnishings	£500	
Total allowable expenses		£4,350
Taxable rental income		£5,290

If Miriam does the cleaning, no allowance can be made for her time. But if she pays someone else to do the work (her mum, say), she can claim this cost as an allowable expense.

If you are paid the premium in instalments, the total premium is still taxable in the year the lease is granted. But if paying in one go would cause you hardship, you can ask your tax inspector to allow you to pay by yearly instalments. The maximum number of instalments is eight (or the number of years you are getting the premium over, if less).

The proportion on which you will have to pay income tax is calculated as follows:

$$\frac{51 - \text{number of years of the lease}}{50}$$

So if the lease is a 20-year one, the proportion of the premium which is taxable as income is:

$$\frac{51 - 20}{50} = \frac{31}{50}$$

Enter the taxable amount in box 5.22.

A lease for more than 50 years is treated as capital rather than business income. There is no income tax to pay, but capital gains tax may be due (see Chapter 9).

If the property you let out is one you are yourself letting and you received a payment or other benefit, such as a contribution towards fitting out the property, to persuade you to take it on, this is a reverse premium. If actual money has been laid out by the landlord, it is taxed as income. Give the amount in box 5.22A – if you are not sure whether you have received a reverse premium, ask your tax inspector or your business adviser.

Add the figures in boxes 5.19, 5.20, 5.22 and 5.22A together and enter the total in box 5.23.

Expenses

■ *Expenses* (do not include figures you have already put in boxes 5.2 to 5.7 on Page L1)

• Rent, rates, insurance, ground rents etc.	**5.24** £	
• Repairs, maintenance and renewals	**5.25** £	
• Finance charges, including interest	**5.26** £	
• Legal and professional costs	**5.27** £	
• Costs of services provided, including wages	**5.28** £	total of boxes 5.24 to 5.29
• Other expenses	**5.29** £	**5.30** £

If your total property income, including income from furnished holiday lettings, for 2006–7 is less than £15,000, go to box 5.29 and enter your total expenses in it (but excluding any expenses relating to furnished holiday letting which you should have put in box 5.7 on page 1). If your total property income is over this limit, you need to list the expenses incurred in 2006–7 separately.

The details of what expenses you can claim in boxes 5.24 to 5.29 are given under Furnished holiday lettings on pp. 316–17. Note that with furnished property, you can claim a renewals deduction in box 5.25 for the cost of replacing furniture, fixtures and fittings, but not if you are already claiming a wear and tear allowance on the property (see opposite).

Don't include any expenses you have already claimed in boxes 5.2 to 5.7.

Add together the figures in boxes 5.24 to 5.29 and enter the total in box 5.30.

	box 5.23 *minus* box 5.30
Net profit (put figures in brackets if a loss)	**5.31** £

Subtract the figure in box 5.30 from that in box 5.23 to find the net profit or loss on the letting. Enter the figure in box 5.31, in brackets if it is a loss.

Tax adjustments

■ *Tax adjustments*		
● Private use	**5.32** £	
● Balancing charges - including those arising under Business Premises Renovation Allowance which should also be included in box 23.8	**5.33** £	box 5.32 + box 5.33 **5.34** £

Box 5.32 is where you enter a figure for any private use of the property, in the same way as for furnished holiday lettings (see p. 318).

Any balancing charges (see p. 318) should be put in box 5.33. Add together the amounts in boxes 5.32 and 5.33 and put the total in box 5.34.

Enter in box 5.35 any tax-free amount you are claiming under the Rent a Room scheme (see p. 312). Otherwise leave it empty.

If you want to claim capital allowances (see p. 318), enter the amount in box 5.36. You can't claim capital allowances on items used in a property let as a furnished home (unless it is a furnished holiday letting). You can instead claim a renewals deduction for the cost of replacing such items (in box 5.25 above). Or you can claim a wear and tear allowance in box 5.37 of 10 per cent of the rent less service charges and local taxes. Once you have chosen a method, you can't switch. And if you have been using a different method of allowing for wear and tear agreed with your tax inspector before 6 April 1976, you can carry on using it.

Usually, capital allowances let you claim only part of your costs in the year you incurred them. But you can claim a 100 per cent capital allowance to cover in full any amount you have spent in 2006–7 renovating or converting the space over a shop or other commercial property into flats for rent, provided certain conditions are met. The property must have been built before 1980, all or most of the ground floor must be for business use, it must have no more than five floors and the upstairs part must originally have been constructed primarily for residential use. The flats must pass a value test with the rents not exceeding given limits. The limits are set at £350 a week for a two-room flat in Greater London and £150 a week elsewhere rising to £480 a week for a four-room flat in Greater London and £300 a week elsewhere. Flats with five or more rooms do not qualify. 'Room' does not include kitchens, bathrooms and small hallways. If the figure you put in box 5.36 includes a claim for 100 per cent capital allowances for this purpose, tick box 5.36A. If you don't claim the full 100 per cent first-year allowance, you can claim writing-down allowance of 25 per cent in subsequent years.

• Rent a Room exempt amount	**5.35** £	
• Capital allowances - including Business Premises Renovation Allowance which should also be included in box 23.7	**5.36** £	
• Tick box 5.36A if box 5.36 includes a claim for 100% capital allowances for flats over shops	**5.36A**	
• Tick box 5.36B if box 5.36 includes enhanced capital allowances for designated environmentally beneficial plant and machinery	**5.36B**	
• Landlord's Energy Saving Allowance	**5.36C** £	
• 10% wear and tear	**5.37** £	
• Furnished holiday lettings losses	copy from box 5.18 **5.38** £	total of boxes 5.35 to box 5.38 **5.39** £

You may also be able to claim 100 per cent capital allowances on the cost of bringing property in a deprived area which has been vacant for over a year back into commercial use. (Though at the time of writing the scheme was still awaiting EU approval before being introduced.) Include the allowance in box 5.36 and also enter in box 23.7 on the main tax return (see p. 178).

If you are claiming first-year capital allowances on something which counts as environmentally friendly spending (see table on p. 285), tick box 5.36B.

You should already have filled in box 5.38 if you wish to set off a loss on furnished holiday lettings against other property income (see box 5.18).

In box 5.39 enter the total of boxes 5.35, 5.36, 5.37 and 5.38.

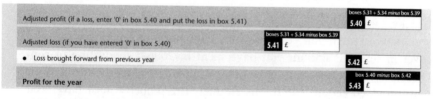

Add the figures in boxes 5.31 and 5.34 together and subtract the figure in box 5.39. If the answer is a negative number, you have made a tax loss on your property interests. Enter 0 in box 5.40 and put the amount of the loss in box 5.41. There are several ways that a tax loss on property income can be used to reduce your tax bill (see boxes 5.44 to 5.46, opposite).

If you have made a profit, enter it in box 5.40. You can reduce this – and the amount of tax you pay on your property income – if you made a loss on property income from 2005–6. Enter the total loss from that year in box 5.42, and subtract it from the figure in box 5.40.

If the answer is a negative number, enter 0 in box 5.43 and put the balance in box 5.45. If the answer is more than 0, you have made a taxable profit on your property income for 2006–7.

Losses

■	*Losses etc*		
●	Loss offset against total income read the note on page LN8	5.44 £	
●	Loss to carry forward to following year	5.45 £	

You can deduct a property income loss from other forms of income for 2006–7 but only in certain circumstances:

■ if you have claimed capital allowances in box 5.36. Even then, the maximum loss you can set off in this way is restricted. See the notes accompanying the Land and property supplement for details

■ if you have land used for agriculture and the loss is due to certain agricultural expenses. If this applies, see Help Sheet IR251 *Agricultural land*.

Enter the amount of loss you wish to deduct in this way in box 5.44. Alternatively, a loss which reflects an excess of capital allowances over balancing charges can be carried over to next year and set against your income for 2007–8. If this is what you would like to do, make a note of the figure to enter in the 2008 tax return.

Finally, any other unused losses can be carried over to deduct from future profits from property – enter these in box 5.45. If the figure in box 5.43 is 0 you will have already entered the right figure in box 5.45. If the figure in box 5.40 is 0, you find the figure to enter in box 5.45 by adding together the figures in boxes 5.41 and 5.42 and subtracting the figure in box 5.44.

●	Tick box 5.46 if these Pages include details of property let jointly	5.46
●	Tick box 5.47 if **all** property income ceased in the year to 5 April 2007 **and** you do not expect to receive such income again, in the year to 5 April 2008	5.47

Tick box 5.46 if you own and let property jointly with someone else – and give the name and address of the person who keeps the records in the Additional information box on page 10 of the basic tax return.

Tick box 5.47 if, during 2006–7, you stopped getting any income from property and you do not expect to have any property income in 2007–8.

20

Foreign income

Q6 Did you have any taxable income or payments from overseas pensions or benefits, or from foreign companies or savings institutions, offshore funds or trusts abroad, or from land and property abroad or gains on foreign insurance policies? **YES** ☐

Have you, or could you have, received or enjoyed directly or indirectly, or benefited in any way from, income or payments of a foreign entity as a result of a transfer of assets made in this or earlier years? **YES** ☐

Do you want to claim foreign tax credit relief for foreign tax paid on foreign income, payments or gains? **YES** ☐ **FOREIGN** ☐

If you ticked any of the three YES boxes at Q6 on page 2 of the basic tax return, you will need the supplementary pages called Foreign. These have space to give details about your foreign savings, pensions and benefits, property income and other investment income from abroad. Earnings from work abroad should be entered in the Employment, Self-Employment or Partnership pages of the tax return as appropriate, though you will need to use page 3 of the Foreign pages to claim any tax credit relief (see overleaf). Similarly, details of capital gains on overseas transactions should be entered in the capital gains supplement, though you will need to use page 3 of the Foreign pages to claim any tax credit relief (see overleaf).

Note that anywhere other than England, Scotland, Wales and Northern Ireland counts as 'foreign', so you should include, for example, interest from accounts held in the Channel Islands, Isle of Man or Republic of Ireland on the Foreign pages.

This chapter tells you how to fill in the Foreign pages, and about the expenses and allowances you can claim. But the tax treatment of people who live abroad is beyond the scope of this guide. If this applies to you, seek professional advice from your bank, accountant or tax adviser.

Warning

> The Revenue is conducting a sustained campaign to track down people who fail to declare and pay tax on foreign income. It has been given permission to require banks and building societies to hand over details of customers with foreign accounts or credit cards linked to foreign accounts. The data goes back six years, so will also cover people who have had foreign accounts in the past even though they might not have them now. If you are domiciled and resident in the UK, you are liable for UK tax on your income from anywhere in the world. This includes, for example, interest from a foreign bank account that you have simply to help you run a holiday home abroad as well as income from any offshore investments you might make. If you have failed to declare such income in the past, telling the Revenue now may reduce or avert penalties that will be due if you are 'found out' later.

How foreign income is taxed

Income from abroad is taxable in the UK, even if you have already paid foreign tax on it. You can deduct any foreign tax paid from the income before working out your UK tax bill – so you pay UK tax only on what you get after paying foreign tax.

But in most cases, you can instead claim a deduction from your UK tax bill to reflect the foreign tax paid, known as foreign tax credit relief. This is likely to mean paying less in UK tax than if you simply deduct the foreign tax from the gross income before working out the tax bill.

Example

> Bill Livingstone made £2,500 after expenses last year letting out his villa in Freedonia. He paid the equivalent of £400 tax on this to the Freedonian tax authorities.
>
> In calculating his UK tax, he could have simply deducted the £400 of Freedonian tax from the £2,500 and paid tax on £2,100. Since he paid tax on the income at the basic rate of 22 per cent, the tax bill would have been 22% × £2,100 = £462.
>
> But he claimed tax credit relief, so the full £2,500 was taxable at 22 per cent – £550 in tax. He could then deduct the £400 of Freedonian tax, making his UK tax bill just £150.

However, working out the amount of tax credit relief can be complicated and this guide assumes you are leaving the calculations to your tax officer. If you feel up to the calculations, you can use the guidance notes sent out by the Revenue to calculate your tax credit relief and thus your UK tax bill on such income.

Note that if the amount of foreign tax is adjusted, you must notify your tax inspector if it means any deduction for that tax was bigger than it should have been.

What income is taxed

The instructions below are for people who are domiciled in the UK and resident or ordinarily resident here. Their foreign income is taxed on an arising basis – when they get it or it is credited to them, regardless of whether or when it is brought back to the UK. You should enter the amounts you got in sterling, using the exchange rate on the date the income arose.

There are different rules for people who are not domiciled or not ordinarily resident in the UK – see Chapter 23 for how this is determined. If either applies, you will need to fill in the Non-residence supplementary pages (see Chapter 23). And your foreign income will be taxed on a remittance basis (i.e. only when income is brought into the UK rather than when it arose) – on the Foreign pages, enter the amounts of income received in the UK and the equivalent share of any foreign tax deducted from it.

Tax-free foreign income

The following types of foreign income are tax-free in the UK:

- pensions paid by Germany or Austria to the victims of Nazi persecution and to pensioners who have fled from persecution
- the extra foreign pension paid to you if you have been retired because you were disabled by injury on duty or by a work-related illness
- any part of a pension from overseas that reduces the amount of tax-free UK war widows' and dependants' pensions
- social security benefits which are similar to UK benefits that are tax-free – child benefit, maternity allowance, guardian's allowance, child's special allowance, bereavement payments, incapacity benefit (only for the first six months if it began on or after 13 April 1996), attendance allowance, disability living allowance and severe disablement allowance.

A tenth of overseas pensions funded by an overseas employer or pension fund is tax-free in the UK unless it is taxed on a remittance basis (see above).

Income stuck in a foreign country

In some cases, you will be unable to remit foreign income to the UK because it arises in a country which has exchange controls or is short of foreign exchange. If so, you can claim that the income should not after all be taxed in 2006–7. If income is unremittable, you will not be able to give all the information asked for on the pages of this supplement. In column A, enter the country and tick the box to show the income is unremittable. In column B, enter the amount of the income in foreign currency (delete the £ sign). In column D, enter the amount of any foreign tax paid on the income, again in the foreign currency concerned. Leave columns C and E blank.

The documents you need

You will need to gather together dividend vouchers for overseas shares, bank statements for overseas bank accounts, pension advice notes, foreign property bills – as well as details of any foreign tax paid.

Foreign savings

On page F1 give details of foreign interest and other savings income for 2006–7 unless you are taxed on a remittance basis (see p. 329). Savings taxed on a remittance basis go on page F2.

Enter each source of income on a separate line. If any of these types of income is from joint holdings, enter your share only. In column A, give the name of the country where the income arose. In column B, give the amount of income before deducting any foreign tax or UK tax but after subtracting any income which is unremittable. In column C, enter the amount of any foreign tax paid. If the income is unremittable, see 'Income stuck in a foreign country' above.

Foreign savings					
Fill in columns A to E, and tick the box in column E to claim foreign tax credit relief.					
Country tick box if income is unremittable ▼ **A**	**B** Amount before tax	**C** Foreign tax	**D** Special Withholding Tax	**E** Amount chargeable tick box to claim foreign tax credit relief ▼	
■ *Interest, and other income from overseas savings* - *see Notes, pages FN4 and FN5*	£	£	£	£	
	£	£	£	£	
	£	£	£	£	
	£	£	£	£	

Under double taxation agreements signed between the UK and more than 100 countries, tax should be deducted from investment income by the foreign country at a reduced rate which is then taken into account in calculating your UK tax bill. If the figure in column C is more than you should have paid under such an agreement, ask the foreign tax authority for a refund of the excess.

The amount you enter in column E depends on whether you wish to claim foreign tax credit relief (see p. 334):

■ if you intend to claim it, enter the amount from column B and tick the box

■ if you are not claiming tax credit relief, enter the figure from column B less any foreign tax from column C.

Add the figures in column E and enter the total in box 6.1.

Enter the same information for dividends received in 2006–7 unless you are taxed on a remittance basis (see p. 329). The following should not be included:

■ distributions by a foreign company in the form of shares (but enter any cash alternative you took instead)

■ stock dividends from foreign companies

■ bonus shares from a scrip issue by a foreign company

■ capital distributions – for example, the return of your capital or distributions in the course of a liquidation.

Tax-saving idea 167

Some countries, such as Jersey, Guernsey and the Isle of Man, pay gross interest on savings (in other words, without deducting any tax). If you are a UK taxpayer, you must declare this interest and pay UK tax on it. But there can be a delay between earning the interest and paying the tax. For example, if interest was paid or credited on 30 April 2007 and you pay tax through self-assessment, the tax is not due until 31 January 2009. In the meantime, you can earn extra interest on the uncollected tax.

Add the figures for dividends in column E and enter the total in box 6.2.

Foreign savings income taxable on the remittance basis and all other foreign income from overseas pensions or social security benefits, from land and property abroad, chargeable premiums or income/benefits received by/from overseas trusts, companies and other entities.

On page F2, give the same information for foreign pensions, social security benefits and property income. And if you are taxed on your foreign income on a remittance basis (see p. 329), this is where you give details of foreign interest, dividends and other savings income. In addition to columns A, B, D and E, you need to enter in column D any UK tax deducted from certain types of income.

Pensions and social security benefits

Exclude pensions and benefits which are free of UK tax – see p. 329. If only part of a payment is free of UK tax, give the amount which is not exempt in column E.

Income from foreign land and property

Income from overseas property is taxed in much the same way as that from UK property (see Chapter 19). You can deduct expenses including the cost of managing the property and collecting the income (for example, paying an agent). If you buy equipment, you may be able to claim a capital allowance or some other form of deduction (see p. 283). And you can deduct loan interest on the property.

As for UK property, there are certain expenses you cannot claim. These include personal expenses – such as the costs incurred while the property is not let. Nor can you claim any loss you make when you sell the property.

There is space on page F2 of the Foreign supplement for details of the income and tax paid on overseas property and land. But before you fill this in, you must turn to page F4 and complete a copy of it for each property, giving details of the income, expenses and other deductions for 2006–7. Then complete page F5. If your foreign income is taxed on a remittance basis (see p. 329), you do not need to complete pages F4 and F5.

Other overseas income

This is where you give details of miscellaneous other types of overseas income. If you have these complex investments, you should take specialised tax advice.

| • Disposals of holdings in offshore funds, income from non-resident trusts and benefits received from overseas trusts, companies and other entities - *see Notes, pages FN11 and FN12.* | 6.5 | £ |

Offshore funds

The income from an offshore fund should be entered as savings income on page F1 of the foreign pages. Here you must give details of any gain made on cashing in part or all of your investment unless the fund qualifies as a distributor fund – one which distributes most of its income as dividends. This is to stop investors rolling up income in offshore funds to create capital gains and so reduce their tax bills.

If the fund does not count as a distributor fund, enter the gain in box 6.5. If you have received an equalisation payment from a distributor fund, you should enter the part of the gain taxable as income in box 6.5. The taxable amount will be shown on the voucher given to you by the fund manager.

Following a review of the taxation of offshore trusts, the government has eased some of the conditions which must be met for a fund to qualify as a distributor fund.

Income from non-resident trusts

If you are entitled to the income from a trust that is not resident in the UK, enter the amount from foreign sources in box 6.5. Any of the trust's income from UK sources should have been entered in the appropriate boxes of the Income part of the tax return as if it had been paid direct to you.

Any income paid to you from a non-resident trust at the discretion of the trustees should be entered in box 6.5.

Income received by trusts or companies abroad

You may have transferred assets with the result that income becomes payable to a company, trust or other entity based abroad. If you or your husband or wife may at any time enjoy that income (say, because you are shareholders of the company or beneficiaries of the trust), or you receive or are entitled to receive a capital sum (including a loan) in connection with the transfer, the income or capital sum is taxable as income and should be entered on page F2 and included in boxes 6.3 and 6.3A or 6.4 and 6.4A unless you are ticking box 6.5A (see below).

If someone else makes a transfer to the company, trust or other entity described above, you are taxed on the income or other benefit to the extent that the company has 'unexpended income'. This means income that has not already passed to someone else or been spent by the company, trust or other entity. In this case, put the amount in box 6.5 unless you are ticking box 6.5A (see below).

In either case, give details of the assets transferred and the name and address of the company, trust or other entity concerned in box 6.39 on page F5.

If you have these complex types of investments, you should take special-ised tax advice.

If you can show that the purpose of the transfer of assets was not to avoid tax, you won't need to give details here. Tick box 6.5A.

Foreign life insurance policies

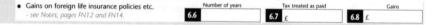

- Gains on foreign life insurance policies etc.
  - see Notes, pages FN12 and FN14.

Number of years	Tax treated as paid	Gains
6.6	6.7 £	6.8 £

Give details here of any gains you have made on foreign life insurance policies – whether because the policy has come to an end or because you have drawn some benefit from it. Enter the number of years you have held the policy in box 6.6 and the gain in box 6.8.

Most such gains are simply added to your taxable income because no foreign tax has been paid on them. If foreign tax has been deducted, you may be able to get a 'credit for notional savings rate tax' which means the gain will be taxed only at the difference between the savings and higher rates in the same way as a UK life insurance policy gain (see p. 202). Enter the amount of any notional income tax credit in box 6.7.

Foreign tax credit relief

With all types of foreign income, you can simply deduct any foreign tax already paid from the income before working out the UK tax bill. But you are likely to pay less UK tax if you claim foreign tax credit relief which reduces the UK tax bill to reflect the foreign tax already paid.

This section is for calculating tax credit relief on all your foreign income, including that from investments, pensions, benefits and property already entered above. But you can also claim the relief on foreign income from employment, self-employment and partnerships which you will have entered elsewhere on the tax return.

Foreign tax credit relief for foreign tax paid on employment, self-employment and other income

See Notes, pages FN14 and FN15

Enter in this column the Page number in your Tax Return from which information is taken. Do this for each item for which you are claiming foreign tax credit relief ▼	Country A	Foreign tax D	Amount chargeable E tick box to claim foreign tax credit relief ▼
		£	£
		£	£
		£	£

First you must enter details of these other forms of foreign income. Give the country the income arose in, the amount of foreign tax paid on it and the gross amount of the income before deduction of foreign tax. In the first column, give the page number of the tax return where the income is fully reported.

Box 6.9 gives you room to enter the amount of foreign tax credit relief you wish to claim on all of your foreign income. This is only for people who want to do the sums themselves – if you don't want to get involved in the calculations, go on to the next section.

If you want to work out your tax credit relief, you need to use the *Foreign Tax Credit Relief Working Sheet* on pages FN18 to FN23 of the *Notes on Foreign*. There are full instructions on pages FN15 to FN16, and all the data you need to complete it on the following pages. You won't be able to complete the working sheet until you have completed most of the rest of the tax return. Some of the figures you have to enter on it are drawn from the *Tax Calculation Guide* which you use to work out your overall tax bill.

● If you are calculating your tax, enter the total foreign tax credit relief on your income in box 6.9 - see Notes, pages FN15 and FN16.	**6.9** £

Fill in a separate working sheet for each item of foreign income you wish to claim relief for. Enter the total amount you wish to claim in box 6.9.

The bottom half of the page is for details of capital gains you wish to claim foreign tax credit relief on. Help Sheet IR261 *Foreign tax credit relief: capital gains* tells you what to enter and how to do the sums if you wish to calculate the tax credit relief on your foreign gains.

Foreign tax credit relief for foreign tax paid and Special Withholding Tax deducted on chargeable gains reported on your Capital Gains Pages

See Notes, page FN16

Amount of gain under UK rules	Period over which UK gain accrued	Amount of gain under foreign tax rules	Period over which foreign gain accrued	Foreign tax paid tick box to claim foreign tax credit relief **D**
£	days	£	days	£
£	days	£	days	£
£	days	£	days	£

● If you are calculating your tax, enter the total foreign tax credit relief on your gains in box 6.10 - see Notes, page FN15.	**6.10** £

If you have calculated the tax credit relief on your capital gains, enter the total in box 6.10.

21

Trusts

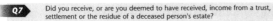

Q7 Did you receive, or are you deemed to have received, income from a trust, settlement or the residue of a deceased person's estate? **YES** **TRUSTS ETC.**

If you ticked the YES box at Q7 on page 2 of the basic tax return, you will need the supplementary page called Trusts etc. You should give details about taxable income from trusts and other forms of settlement such as a transfer of assets, and from the estates of people who have died. In some cases, you may have to give details of income from trusts you have set up. Even though the money has been paid to someone else, it may be treated as yours.

Do not enter any details in this supplement about income from a 'bare trust' – a trust to which you have an absolute right to both the income and assets. You are treated as the owner of the assets and any income or gains from them. You should enter income from a bare trust in the sections of the basic tax return and other supplements that deal with the particular type of income concerned.

The documents you need

With a payment from a trust or an estate, the trustees or personal representatives should have given you a form R185 setting out the details. There are different versions of the forms for interest in possession trusts, for other trusts and for estates.

If you have directly or indirectly provided funds for a settlement and are not sure whether the income will be treated as yours, Help Sheet IR270 *Trusts and settlements – income treated as the settlor's* should help. Ask the Orderline (p. 170).

Income from trusts and settlements

Income paid out by trusts and other forms of settlement in 2006–7 comes with a tax credit which reflects the amount of tax already deducted from it or deemed to have been paid on it. What you receive is the net (after-tax) amount of income. To find the gross (before-tax) amount, you need to add back the tax credit. You can find out the amount of the tax credit from certificate R185 or similar statement the trustees should give you.

How trust income is taxed

The amount of the tax credit depends on the type of trust:

- trust with an interest in possession where you have the 'absolute right' to the income from the trust. The tax credit will be at the rate of 20 per cent of the grossed-up amount of interest; 10 per cent of the grossed-up amount of share dividends and unit trust distributions; and for other sorts of income, such as rents or royalties, it will be at the basic rate of tax – 22 per cent for 2006–7

- a discretionary trust where the trustees have discretion about paying out the income. The tax credit will be at the 'rate applicable to trusts', which in 2006–7 is 40 per cent of the grossed-up income or 32.5 per cent for share dividends and distributions

- accumulation and maintenance trusts – the income also comes with a tax credit of 40 per cent or 32.5 per cent

- trust for a disabled person or minor child following death of a parent – the income may be taxed on the basis of the beneficiary's personal circumstances taking into account their allowances and tax bands.

Review of trust taxation

The government is considering, in future, taxing income from a discretionary trust at 10, 20 or 22 per cent as appropriate rather than 40 per cent where the income is paid out to beneficiaries by 31 December following the year in which the income arose. Major changes to the inheritance tax treatment of trusts were made from 22 March 2006 onwards – see Chapter 10 for details.

If the tax credit, other than the 10 per cent credit on share dividends and similar income, is more than the amount of tax you would have paid if the grossed-up income had come direct to you, you can claim a rebate. For example, if you get interest from a trust and your income – including the grossed-up trust income – is too low to pay tax, you could reclaim all the tax credit which comes with it. With a discretionary trust, anyone not liable to higher rate tax can reclaim part of the tax credits.

Tax-saving idea 168

Reclaim some or all of the tax credit that comes with income from trusts if it is more than you would have paid if the income had come straight to you. Unless you pay tax at the higher rate, you will always be entitled to a rebate on income from a discretionary trust.

Trust income that might be treated as yours

If you have directly or indirectly provided funds for a settlement, the income from those funds may be treated as yours – even though you haven't received it.

Example

Jimmy Hall received £250 from a discretionary trust in 2006–7, which comes with a tax credit of £166.67. He pays tax at no more than the basic rate (even when the grossed-up trust payment of £416.67 is added to his income). So he should have paid tax on the payment at the basic rate of 22 per cent only – a tax bill of 22 per cent of £416.67, or £91.67. He is thus entitled to a rebate of: £166.67 – £91.67 = £75.

The sorts of arrangement which might produce an income that would be treated as yours include:

- a trust from which you, your spouse, civil partner or children can benefit
- a trust that has lent or repaid money to you or your spouse or civil partner
- a trust where the capital would come back to you if the beneficiaries died before becoming entitled to it.

When your child's income might be treated as yours

This treatment might also apply if you make some investments on behalf of your children unless they have reached 18 or they are married – for example, opening a savings account in their names. Any income from such investments is treated as yours unless it is £100 a year or less before tax. This exception applies to gifts from each parent, so a child can have up to £200 a year before tax in income from gifts from both parents without a problem. This treatment does not apply to money you put into child trust funds.

Tax-saving idea 169

> If you want to give a child more capital and their income is approaching the limit at which it will be treated as yours, think about gifts in investments such as National Savings & Investments (NS&I) Children's Bonus Bonds, NS&I Certificates which produce a tax-free return or paying into a stakeholder pension scheme for your child. Income produced by sums you pay into your son's or daughter's child trust fund (see p. 93) will not be treated as your income.

You can't get round this by giving the funds to someone else who passes them on to your child. You would still have indirectly provided the funds and the income would be yours. The same would be true if you settled some money on a friend's child in return for him doing the same for you.

This income should be included as your own in Q10 in the basic tax return and not entered on the Trusts etc. pages unless you create a proper trust.

What to enter

Enter the income from trusts in 2006–7 in boxes 7.1 to 7.12. Also include here any income from trusts or settlements which is treated as yours even though you haven't received it. For discretionary trusts, put the actual amount received in box 7.1, the tax credit in box 7.2 and the gross income in box 7.3 (this should be the sum of boxes 7.1 and 7.2). For income from a trust with an interest in possession on which the tax credit is at the 22 per cent basic rate, give the same details in boxes 7.4 to 7.6. For savings income on which the tax credit is 20 per cent, enter the details in boxes 7.7 to 7.9. For dividends and distributions where the tax credit is 10 per cent, enter the details in boxes 7.10 to 7.12.

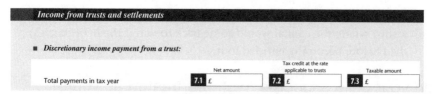

You don't need to enter the following here:

- scrip dividends or foreign income dividends received from a trust with an interest in possession and paid by UK companies, authorised unit trusts or open-ended investment companies – give details of these on page 3 of the basic tax return (see pp. 191–4)
- income from foreign sources paid to you by a trust with an interest in possession – give details on the Foreign supplementary pages (see p. 333)

■ income from a discretionary trust where the trustees are not resident in the UK – this should also go on the Foreign pages.

Income from estates

Income from the estates of deceased persons			

■ *Income taxed at:*

	Income receivable	UK tax or tax credit	Taxable amount
basic rate	7.13 £	7.14 £	7.15 £
lower rate	7.16 £	7.17 £	7.18 £
dividend rate	7.19 £	7.20 £	7.21 £
non-repayable basic rate	7.22 £	7.23 £	7.24 £
non-repayable lower rate	7.25 £	7.26 £	7.27 £
non-payable dividend rate	7.28 £	7.29 £	7.30 £

You do not pay income tax on anything you inherit from a dead person. And if you have inherited something which then produces an income, such as money in a bank savings account or properties that produce rent, you should enter the interest or other income in the appropriate part of the main tax return. You might receive interest along with a legacy because, say, there has been a delay between your inheriting the item and it being handed over. Do not include the interest on these pages – it should be entered under Q10 on the basic tax return.

However, you should give details in this section of the tax return of any income you receive from the estate that has been accrued while the estate is being wound up by the personal representatives – the executors or administrators. You would be entitled to this income if you were a residuary beneficiary – the person or one of the people who gets what is left after all the specific bequests and legacies have been made.

Such income will come with a tax credit in the same way as a trust with an interest in possession. For most types of income, this tax will be repayable if it is more than you would have paid; but the tax is not repayable for some types of income such as gains on life insurance policies and UK dividends.

The statement supplied by the personal representatives – tax certificate R185 (Estate income) – will show you the rate the income has been taxed at and whether it is repayable. Enter the details for 2006–7 in boxes 7.13 to 7.30. Give the name of the estate and the total amount paid to you in the Additional information box on page 2.

In some cases, income accrued during the life of the dead person and paid into the estate after their death will come to you after being taken into account in calculating the inheritance tax bill on the estate. There is a special tax relief that stops you having to pay higher rate tax on such income – ask your tax inspector for details.

Income from foreign estates

If you get income from a foreign estate, it will not have borne full UK tax – either because the personal representatives are outside the UK tax net or because the estate is that of someone who died while domiciled outside the UK and has income from non-UK sources. In this case, enter the full amount of such income in both boxes 7.13 and 7.15. Don't enter anything in box 7.14, even if some foreign tax has been deducted.

If the foreign estate has some income from UK sources, it will have paid some UK tax. In this case, you can reduce the amount entered in boxes 7.13 and 7.15 by the following amount:

$$\frac{\text{net amount of income subject to UK tax}}{\text{total estate income less UK tax}} \times \text{total estate income before UK tax}$$

Foreign tax paid

Total foreign tax for which foreign tax credit relief not claimed — **7.31** £

If you have been paid income from an estate which has already been taxed in a foreign country, you may end up paying two lots of tax on it: tax in the foreign country and tax in the UK. You may be able to reduce the amount of UK tax you pay on the income to reflect the foreign tax paid – this is known as tax credit relief.

To claim tax credit relief – which will usually be worthwhile – leave box 7.31 blank and make your claim on the Foreign supplementary pages (see p. 334).

If you don't want to claim tax credit relief – which can be quite complicated – you can instead deduct the foreign tax you have paid from the income. Enter the amount in box 7.31.

22

Capital gains

Q8 Capital gains - read the guidance on page 7 of the Tax Return Guide.

- If you have disposed of your only or main residence do you need the Capital Gains Pages? **YES**
- Did you dispose of other chargeable assets worth more than £35,200 in total? **YES**
- Answer 'Yes' if:
  - allowable losses are deducted from your chargeable gains, which total more than £8,800 before deduction and before taper relief, **or**
  - no allowable losses are deducted from your chargeable gains and after taper relief your taxable gains total more than £8,800, **or**
  - you want to make a claim or election for the year. **YES**   **CAPITAL GAINS**

If you have ticked any of the three YES boxes in Q8 on page 2 of the basic tax return, you will need the supplementary pages called Capital gains. These ask for details of taxable gains you have made on buying and selling assets such as shares, unit trusts and property. You may also have to report a taxable gain even though you haven't sold something – if you give it away, for example. And if you have made a loss on such assets, you should give details here also, since it might reduce your overall tax bill now or in the future.

This chapter tells you how to fill in the Capital gains supplementary pages. Chapter 9 explains how the tax works in detail with examples of the sometimes complicated calculations needed to fill in these pages. It also explains how to claim all the reliefs and allowances to minimise your capital gains tax bill.

The documents you need

You will need details of anything you have spent on buying or selling or maintaining the value of assets. With shares and unit trusts, you need any paperwork relating to share issues while you owned them or company reorganisations.

For assets owned on 31 March 1982, you may also need details of their value on that date (see p. 129). Use catalogues, press advertisements or stock market share price records to value them.

With assets that are jointly owned, you need enter only your share of any gains. With a husband and wife or civil partners, the gain or loss is split 50:50 between them unless they have told their tax officers that the asset is not owned equally (see p. 122).

Chargeable gains and allowable losses

The first page of the Capital gains pages has space at the top for you to write your name and the tax reference you will find on the front of your basic tax return. What you do next depends on what transactions you carried out in 2006–7.

If you have only made relatively straightforward transactions in quoted shares or securities, including unit trusts, you can use the simple grid on page CG1 (see opposite). But you cannot use this page if any of the shares were held at 31 March 1982, or you are able to claim taper relief on any of the gains made, or you want to claim any other tax relief that would reduce your gains other than indexation allowance.

If your transactions are more than just quoted shares, or you can claim taper relief, or you want to claim reliefs such as reinvestment relief, you must fill in pages CG2 to CG6 instead (see p. 347).

In some circumstances, you may need to give details of capital gains or losses even though you haven't disposed of the assets they relate to in 2006–7 For example, if you have been given something and agreed to take over the gain from its previous owner (hold-over relief), you have to pay tax on that gain if you become non-resident within six years of the end of the tax year in which the gift was made (see p. 146). Include any gains made by a trust that are treated as your gains because you are the settlor and, for example, you or your husband or wife can benefit from the trust.

Include anything you have been given as a result of the reconstruction or takeover of a company, building society or mutual insurance company (see p. 142–3). But you don't need to enter any details of disposals of assets on which gains are tax-free. Thus you should normally leave out possessions which are worth £6,000 or less when you disposed of them – these are known as chattels (see p. 130). However, if you made a loss on the disposal of such a chattel, you should give details since it could be used to reduce your tax bill.

Page CG1: quoted shares and securities only

A Enter details of quoted shares or other securities disposed of	B Tick box if estimate or valuation used	C Enter the date of disposal	D Disposal proceeds	E Gain or loss after indexation allowance, if due (enter loss in brackets)	F Further information, including any elections made
1		/ /	£	£	
2		/ /	£	£	

This page is for giving details of each taxable disposal of quoted shares and other securities made during 2006–7. 'Quoted shares and other securities' means:

■ shares or securities of a company which are quoted on the London Stock Exchange (including its subsidiary techMARK) throughout the period you held them. This does not include UK shares quoted on the Alternative Investment Market, Ofex or Tradepoint

■ shares or securities of a company listed on an overseas recognised stock exchange throughout the period you held them. This includes NASDAQ. It used also to include shares quoted on European junior markets, such as the Nouveau Marché and Neue Markt Frankfurt. But since 28 November 2001, these no longer count as recognised exchanges. Do not enter here any shares listed on these exchanges that you bought before 28 November 2001 – use pages CG2 and CG3 instead

■ units in a unit trust which was UK authorised throughout the period you held them

■ shares in a company which was an open-ended investment company (oeic) throughout the period you held them.

If you are likely to run out of space on page CG1, make photocopies before filling it in. Put your name and tax reference on each sheet.

Column A: Give details to identify the shares or unit trusts – the name of the company or unit trust fund manager, types of shares or units and the number disposed of.

Column B: Tick this box if your figures include any estimates or valuations. This would be the case if the shares or securities were acquired from or disposed of to a connected person (see p. 126). Give details of why you have used an estimate or how the valuation was arrived at in column F, or on page CG7 if there is not enough space.

Column C: Enter the date you disposed of the shares or securities, in numerical form (so 24 August 2006 would be 24/08/06).

Column D: Enter the total disposal proceeds, including any cash or other asset to be received in the future. But if the disposal was a gift or a sale to a connected person you should enter the market value of the asset (see p. 126).

Column E: Enter the net gain or loss after any indexation allowance you are claiming. Put losses in brackets. See Chapter 9 for how to work out the gain or loss and indexation allowance.

Column F: Give any other relevant details on the disposal, including if it is a disposal of part of a larger holding of shares (p. 127) or if you have exchanged shares in a company takeover or reconstruction.

You don't have to submit the calculations done to reach any of these figures – but you can if you want to. There's space on page CG7 to give details.

Total gains	**F1** £		*Total your gains in column E and enter the amount in box F1*
Total losses	**F2** £		*Total your losses in column E and enter the amount in box F2*

Add all your gains in column F and enter the total in box F1. Add all your losses and enter the total in box F2.

	box F1 *minus* box F2	*If you have a net loss go to Page CG8. If you have net gains*
Net gain/(loss)	**F3** £	*of £8,800 or less copy the figure in box F3 to box F7, then fill in Page CG8. Otherwise carry on to box F4*

Subtract your total losses in box F2 from your total gains in box F1 and enter the answer in box F3. If the amount in box F3 is more than £8,800, continue to box F4.

If the amount in box F3 is £8,800 or less, there is no capital gains tax to pay – enter the amount in box F7 and box 8.7 on page CG8. Leave box 8.8 on page CG8 blank. If the amount in box F3 is a net loss, go to p. 355 and fill in the Capital losses summary on page CG8.

minus income losses set against gains   **F4** £

There are losses on several types of income you can deduct from a net chargeable gain if you haven't enough income to set them off against:

- any trading losses from self-employment (p. 303) or a partnership

- losses from furnished holiday lettings (p. 319)

- certain expenses incurred in the seven years after you have closed a business which would have been allowable against business income (post-cessation expenditure) – for example bad debts, costs of rectifying faulty work (p. 217)

■ certain expenses incurred by employees up to six years after they have left their jobs (post-employment deductions) – for example, insurance premiums for policies that pay out against claims of faulty work.

If you have such losses, you can enter them in box F4 up to the amount in box F3.

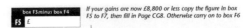

box F3 *minus* box F4

F5 £

If your gains are now £8,800 or less copy the figure in box F5 to F7, then fill in Page CG8. Otherwise carry on to box F6

Subtract the amount in box F4 from the amount in box F3 and enter the result in box F5. If the amount in box F5 is more than £8,800, continue to box F6.

If the amount in box F5 is £8,800 or less, there is no capital gains tax to pay – enter the amount in box F7 and box 8.7 on page CG8. Leave box 8.8 on page CG8 blank.

minus losses brought forward set against this year's gains   **F6** £

*Enter losses brought forward up to the **lower** of either the total losses brought forward, or the figure in box F5 **minus** £8,800. The figure you enter here should not be more than F5 minus £8,800*

You deduct any allowable losses left over from previous tax years from the amount in box F5 (see p. 132). If you have enough losses held over, you must reduce your total taxable gains to £8,800, the amount that is tax-free for 2006–7.

If your losses from previous years are not big enough to reduce the amount in box F5 to £8,800, enter the full amount carried over in box F6. If your losses from previous years are more than enough to reduce the amount in box F5 to £8,800 enter in Box F6 the amount that subtracted from the amount in box F5 will leave exactly £8,800.

Total taxable gains (do not enter losses here)   **F7** £

box F5 *minus* box F6

This box is for total taxable gains. Copy this figure to box 8.7 on Page CG8 and fill in Page CG8 as applicable

Subtract the amount in box F6 from the amount in box F5 and enter the result in box F7. This is your total taxable gains for 2006–7. Copy this figure to box 8.7 on page CG8 and fill in the rest of that page. If there is any additional information you need to give, there is space on page CG7.

Pages CG2 and CG3: disposals of more than quoted shares

Complete these pages if you have made disposals which include land, homes or unquoted shares either on their own or in addition to quoted shares and securities. Also fill in these pages if you are disposing of shares or securities held at 31 March 1982, or on which you are claiming taper relief or any other tax relief other than indexation allowance.

Your 2006-07 Capital Gains Tax liability

A	AA*	B	C	D	E	F	G
Brief description of asset	Type of disposal. Enter Q, U, L, T or O	Tick box if estimate or valuation used	Tick box if asset held at 31 March 1982	Enter the later of date of acquisition and 16 March 1998	Enter the date of disposal	Disposal proceeds	Enter details of any elections made, reliefs claimed or due and state amount (£)

Gains on assets which are either wholly business or wholly non-business

Losses

Brief description of asset	Type of * disposal. Enter Q, U, L or O	Tick box if estimate or valuation used	Tick box if asset held at 31 March 1982	Enter the later of date of acquisition and 16 March 1998	Enter the date of disposal	Disposal proceeds	Enter details of any elections made, reliefs claimed or due and state amount (£)

You will see there is space to give details of ten disposals that resulted in gains (two where the asset was used for both business and non-business purposes) and four that produced allowable losses. If you are likely to run out of space, make photocopies of pages CG2 and CG3 before filling them in. Put your name and tax reference on each extra sheet you submit.

Column A: Give details to identify the asset – the address of the property, for example, or the name of the company with shares, the type of share and the number disposed of.

Column AA: Enter one of the following letters in this column:

- Q for quoted shares or securities (for what these are, see p. 345)
- U for unquoted shares or securities
- L for land or property
- T for a trust gain treated as yours because you are the settlor if you have opted to set personal losses against these gains. Fill in all the columns except B to F. If you are not claiming personal losses against these gains, do not enter them here. Instead enter them at lines 11 and 12 with the total in box 8.4 (see p. 352)
- O for other assets (for example, chattels or goodwill).

Tax-saving idea 170

Normally a capital loss must be set against gains made in the same tax year even if that means some or all of your tax-free allowance (£8,800 in 2006–7) is wasted. However, a loss made on a disposal to a 'connected person' (see p. 126) must be carried forward until it can be set against gains on disposals to the same connected person. Therefore, you can avoid wasting your tax-free allowance by selling or giving the loss-making asset to a connected person (which could include a trust of which you are the settlor).

Column B: Tick this box if your figures include any estimates or valuations. This would be the case if you owned the asset on 31 March 1982 when you need to estimate its value on that date (p. 129). Transactions with connected people also involve market valuations (see p. 126). Give details of why you have used an estimate and the basis of any valuations in column G, or on page CG7 if there is not enough space.

Column C: Tick if you owned the asset on 31 March 1982 – there are special rules for calculating the gains and losses on such assets (see p. 129). Also tick if you are treated as having owned it then – for example, if your spouse did and has since given it to you.

Column D: Enter the date you acquired the asset if it was after 16 March 1998. If it was on or before then, enter 16 March 1998. Give the date in numerical form (so 24 August 2006 would be 24/08/06).

Column E: Enter the date you disposed of the asset, in numerical form.

Column F: Enter the total disposal proceeds, including any cash or other asset to be received in the future. But if the disposal was a gift or a sale to a connected person you should enter the market value of the asset (see p. 126).

If you have been given the right to something in the future in return for the disposal, this should also be included unless it would be taxed as income (for example, dividends or royalties). If it is not clear what you will get in the future – as with a share of any profits – include an estimate in the disposal proceeds. When that uncertain part is finally paid, this will count as another disposal – the right to the share of the profits will have been exchanged for real cash. There will then be another capital gain or loss to report at that time.

Column G: If you wish to claim any tax relief on the gain other than indexation allowance, give details here plus the amount claimed. These include private residence relief on your only or main home (Chapter 6) and rebasing relief (p. 129). Also say here if you are making any claim that defers the tax such as hold-over relief (p. 146), capital gains deferral relief (p. 148) or roll-over relief (p. 148). Special claim forms may be needed in addition to the tax return.

Column H: Enter in the Gains section the net gain after any indexation allowance or other relief, but before losses and taper relief. Enter any losses in the Losses section lower down the page. If the assets are for mixed business and non-business use, split the gains and losses appropriately.

H Chargeable Gains after reliefs but before losses and taper	I Enter 'Bus' if business asset	J Taper rate	K Losses deducted			L Gains after losses	M Tapered gains (gains from column L x % in column J)
			K1 Allowable losses of the year	K2 Income losses of 2006-07 set against gains	K3 Unused losses b/f from earlier years		
£		%	£	£	£	£	£
£		%	£	£	£	£	£
£		%	£	£	£	£	£

Add all your gains in column H and enter the total in box 8.1. Add all your losses and enter the total in box 8.2. Subtract the amount in box 8.2 from the amount in box 8.1. Provided you have no trust gains attributed to you not already dealt with by setting off of personal losses, continue with page CG3 unless any of the following applies:

■ If the answer is £8,800 or less, you have no capital gains tax to pay in 2006–7. Enter the answer in box 8.3 and in box 8.7 on page CG8. Enter 0 in box 8.4. Give any information needed on pages CG4 to CG6 and turn to page CG8.

■ If the answer is more than £8,800 and you have enough losses brought forward from a previous year to reduce your gains to £8,800, you have no capital gains tax to pay. Enter in box 8.6 the amount of losses from previous years needed to achieve this and enter £8,800 in box 8.3 and in box 8.7 on page CG8. Enter 0 in box 8.4. Give any information needed on pages CG4 to CG6 and turn to page CG8.

■ If the answer is a minus amount, your allowable losses are greater than your chargeable gains. You have no capital gains tax to pay – enter 0 in boxes 8.3, 8.4 and 8.7 on page CG8. Give any information needed on pages CG4 to CG6 and turn to page CG8.

From 6 April 2003 onwards, where gains made by a trust are attributed to you as settlor, any capital losses you personally have made which cannot be used against personal gains must be set against the trust gains.

The losses are set against the trust gains after deducting any trust losses but before deducting taper relief. Then the taper relief that the trustees would otherwise have applied is set against the net trust gains attributed to you. See Revenue Help Sheet IR277 *Trusts with settlor interest: taper and losses* for more information. For guidance on when trust gains are attributable to the settlor, see Revenue Help Sheets IR294 *Trusts and capital gains tax* and IR299 *Non-resident trusts and capital gains tax.*

Warning

From 6 April 2006, the definition of settlor-interested trusts for capital gains tax purposes has been aligned with the definition used in the income tax rules. This means that a trust you have set up that can benefit your minor child (under age 18 and unmarried) now also counts as a settlor-interested trust and so gains from it will be treated as yours.

Column I: Enter 'Bus' in this colum in the appropriate row if the asset was a business asset or used partly for business after 5 April 1998.

Column J: This column is for the taper rate on the disposal – the percentage of the net gain that is taxable after deducting taper relief. So if the rate of taper relief is 30 per cent, the taper rate is 70 per cent. Taper relief came into effect only from 1998 onwards (see p. 133). To find the taper rate you should use, see the table on p. 134.

Column K: This column is for entering any losses to be deducted from net gains – with three possible sources.

Column K1: Enter allowable losses from 2006–7. Allocate these against the gains on assets with the highest taper rates first. If you still have some losses unused after doing that, allocate the rest against the gains on the assets with the next highest taper rates.

Suppose, for example, you have a net gain of £10,000 with a taper rate of 100 per cent and another of £10,000 with a taper rate of 75 per cent. You have an allowable loss of £15,000. You allocate £10,000 of the loss to the gain with a taper rate of 100 per cent, the highest taper rate. The remaining £5,000 of the loss is allocated to the gain with the taper rate of 75 per cent. That leaves a net gain of £5,000 with a taper rate of 75 per cent. If losses were allocated the other way – £10,000 to the gain with a taper rate of 75 per cent – you would be left with a net gain of £5,000 with a taper rate of 100 per cent, and a higher tax bill.

Note that you must deduct the losses so long as there are gains to deduct them from – you can't hold losses from the same tax year back even if your total gains are going to end up below the tax-free allowance of £8,800 for 2006–7.

Column K2 is for entering losses on several types of income you can deduct from a net chargeable gain if you haven't enough income to set them off against. The income losses that can be used in this way are the same as those listed for box F4 on p. 346.

If you have such losses, you don't have to deduct them here – and you should not if deducting them means you would lose the benefit of your £8,800 tax-free allowance for 2006–7.

Column K3 is for losses carried forward from earlier tax years. Again you shouldn't deduct more than you need to reduce your total gains to the tax-free allowance of £8,800 for 2006–7.

Add the losses claimed in column K2 and enter the total in box 8.5. Add the losses claimed in column K3 and enter the total in box 8.6.

Column L: For each asset, subtract the losses in Columns K1, K2 and K3 from the net gain in Column J and enter the result in Column L. This is the gain after losses.

Column M: For each asset, multiply the amount in Column L by the taper rate in Column J and enter the result in Column M. This is the tapered gain on the disposal.

So if the gain after losses is £10,000 and the taper rate is 60 per cent, the tapered gain on disposal would be:

$$£10,000 \times 60\% = £6,000$$

Add the gains in column M and enter the total in box 8.3.

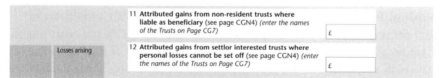

Enter any trust gains attributable to you as settlor where personal losses cannot be set off against them (see p. 348). Give the name of the trust on page CG7 and details of how the gains have been attributed to you. For more information, get Help Sheet IR277 *Trust with settlor interest: taper and losses.*

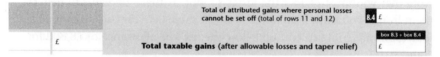

Add the amounts of attributed gains and enter the total in box 8.4.

Add the amount in box 8.3 to the amount in box 8.4 to find your total taxable gains. Enter the answer in the box and copy it to box 8.7 on page CG8. Complete pages CG4, CG5 and CG6 for all disposals not involving quoted shares or securities.

You don't have to submit the calculations done to reach these figures – but you can if you want to. There's space on page CG7 to give details.

Pages CG4 to CG6: further information

These pages are for giving extra details needed for any transactions in unquoted shares or securities, land and property or other assets. Each page has room for two such transactions – if you need more space, make copies.

Page CG7: additional information

This page is for any extra details you need to give.

Page CG8: chargeable gains and allowable losses

Start by completing the first few boxes which summarise what you have already filled in.

If you have used an estimate or valuation in listing any of your gains or losses, there will be a tick in column B on page CG1 or CG2. Tick YES in the first line if there are any ticks in column B.

Tax-saving idea 171

If you include estimates or valuations in your tax return, try to get a proper valuation from an independent, professional valuer. Give full details in the Additional information box explaining who carried out the valuation, their qualifications and the basis on which the valuation was made. This should be sufficient to stave off a discovery enquiry following the rules established in the *Langham* v *Veltema* case (see p. 44). This will give you the certainty that your tax affairs for 2006–7 are finalised by 31 January 2009 (or later date if you filed your tax return after 31 January 2008).

Chargeable gains and allowable losses	
Once you have completed Page CG1, or Pages CG2 to CG6, fill in this Page.	
Have you 'ticked' any row in Column B, 'Tick box if estimate or valuation used' on Pages CG1 or CG2 or in Column C on Page CG2 'Tick box if asset held at 31 March 1982'?	**YES**
Have you given details in Column G on Pages CG2 and CG3 of any Capital Gains reliefs claimed or due?	**YES**
Are you claiming, and/or using, any clogged losses (see Notes, page CGN11)?	**YES**

If you have filled in pages CG2 and CG3 and have claimed any tax relief on a gain other than indexation allowance in column G, tick YES in the second line.

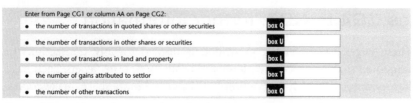

Enter the number of transactions in the five main categories:

- Box Q – quoted shares and securities (for what these are, see p. 345)
- Box U – unquoted shares or securities
- Box L – land or property
- Box T – gains from trusts attributed to you as settlor
- Box O – any other assets.

If you have filled in page CG1, all the transactions should be 'Q' – quoted shares or securities. If you have filled in pages CG2 and CG3, each transaction is categorised in column AA.

Enter the total taxable gains from Box F7 on page CG1 or from the total taxable gains box on page CG3, bottom right.

Subtract £8,800 from the amount in box 8.7 and enter the result in box 8.8. This is the net amount of chargeable capital gains you have to pay tax on in 2006–7.

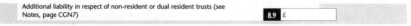

This is where you give details if you have benefited directly or indirectly from non-resident or dual resident trusts. You may be liable to capital gains tax on anything you receive from the trust – whether it be cash, a loan or an asset. You need to give details in box 8.9 of the amount of tax due on what you have received in 2006–7. To work this out, use the calculator on Help Sheet IR301 *Calculation of the increase in tax charge on capital gains from non-resident, dual resident and immigrant trusts*. Enter the name of the trust (and its tax reference if you know it) on page CG7.

Capital losses

This part of the Capital gains supplementary pages helps you keep track of your allowable losses. It summarises the losses you have made in 2006–7 and how you have used them. And it lists losses from previous years and whether these have been used. The information will be useful when you come to fill in next year's tax return.

There are some losses that can only be set against gains of certain types – called 'clogged losses'. These are losses on:

- disposals to connected persons (see p. 126). These losses can only be set against gains on disposals to the same connected person

- assets transferred to you after 15 June 1999 by trustees when you become absolutely entitled to settled property. These losses can only be set against gains on the same asset or an asset derived from that asset and have to be used before any other losses.

If you have clogged losses, make a copy of page CG8 for each one and keep separate records for each one. This will help you use them at the right time. Keep each copy until the clogged losses have been fully used up.

This year's losses

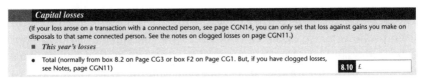

The first few boxes are for losses for 2006–7. Enter in box 8.10 the total allowable losses for the year – the figure from box F2 on page CG1 or box 8.2 on page CG3.

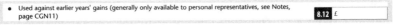

Enter in box 8.11 the amount of the allowable losses for 2006–7 used to reduce your chargeable gains in that year. This is the total of the amounts entered in column K1 on Page CG3, or the smaller of boxes F1 and F2 on Page CG1.

- Used against earlier years' gains (generally only available to personal representatives, see Notes, page CGN11)   **8.12** £

Personal representatives clearing up the estate of someone who has died and completing the tax return for the part of the tax year up to the date of that person's death can carry unused losses back to earlier tax years and effectively claim a tax rebate for the estate (see p. 133). Enter any amount this applies to in box 8.12.

If you have made losses on shares in unquoted trading companies, you can set them off against income from the same tax year or the previous tax year. For more information, see Help Sheets IR286 *Negligible value claims and income tax losses for shares you have subscribed for in qualifying trading companies* and IR297 *Enterprise Investment Scheme and Capital Gains Tax.*

If you make such a claim, enter the amount claimed against income for 2006–7 in box 8.13A, and the amount against the previous tax year in box 8.13B. Add boxes 8.13A and 8.13B and enter the total in box 8.13.

Add the amounts in boxes 8.11, 8.12 and 8.13 and subtract the total from the amount in box 8.10. Enter the result in box 8.14 – this is the total unused losses for 2006–7 which can be carried forward to future tax years.

Earlier years' losses

> • Unused losses of 1996-97 and later years   **8.15** £

The next few boxes record what has happened to losses carried forward from previous tax years. Enter in box 8.15 the amount carried over from 1996–7 and later tax years. You can find the figures you need on last year's tax return – the one for the 2005–6 tax year. Add the figures in boxes 8.14 and 8.15 of that tax return to fill in box 8.15 on this year's tax return.

> • Used this year (losses from box 8.15 are used in priority to losses from box 8.18)
> (column K3 on Page CG3 or box F6 on Page CG1)   **8.16** £

Enter in box 8.16 the amount of the losses from box 8.15 used this year – these losses must be used before losses from earlier years. The figure is the amount in box F6 on page CG1 or the total in column K3 on page CG3 – if none of these losses has been used, put 0 in box 8.16.

> box 8.15 *minus* box 8.16
> • Remaining unused losses of 1996-97 and later years   **8.17** £

Subtract the amount in box 8.16 from the amount in box 8.15 and enter the result in box 8.17. This is the remaining unused losses from 1996–7 and later years.

> • Unused losses of 1995-96 and earlier years   **8.18** £

Enter in box 8.18 the total of any unused losses from 1995–6 and earlier tax years. You can find this figure in box 8.12 of last year's tax return – the one for the 2005–6 tax year.

Box 8.19 records the amount of losses from 1995–6 and earlier tax years used in 2006–7. It can be found by subtracting the amount in box 8.16 or box F6 from the amount in box 8.6. If box 8.6 and box F6 are blank, put 0 in this box.

Total of unused losses to carry forward

Finally, the tax return has space to note down the totals of losses you can carry forward to future tax years.

Add the amounts in boxes 8.14 and 8.17 and enter the total in box 8.20. This is the amount of losses for 1996–7 and later tax years you can carry forward.

Subtract the amount in box 8.19 from the amount in box 8.18 and enter the result in box 8.21. This is the amount of losses for 1995–6 and earlier tax years you can carry forward.

23

Non-residence

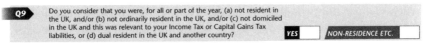

Q9 Do you consider that you were, for all or part of the year, (a) not resident in the UK, and/or (b) not ordinarily resident in the UK, and/or (c) not domiciled in the UK and this was relevant to your Income Tax or Capital Gains Tax liabilities, or (d) dual resident in the UK and another country? **YES** **NON-RESIDENCE ETC.**

If you are a resident of the UK, you are liable for UK tax on all your income whether it comes from within the UK or abroad. But, if you count as a non-resident, there is no UK tax on your income from abroad, only on any income which originates in the UK.

If you want to claim non-residence (or non-domicile) for 2006–7, you need to fill in the Non-residence Supplement which you can get through the Orderline (see p. 170). You are likely to need this if:

■ you are normally a UK resident but you are working abroad for an extended period

■ you have been a UK resident but you are going to live abroad permanently or indefinitely – for example because you are retiring abroad

■ you have been resident elsewhere but you are based in the UK for now or you have returned for permanent residence.

This guide cannot give you all the detail you may need so you should consult a professional adviser. See also Revenue booklet IR20 *Residents and non-residents etc*. At the time of writing, the government was still consulting on possible changes to the rules regarding domicile and residence, having announced a review in the 2002 Budget. So far, no substantial changes have been made and the rules described here continue to apply for 2006–7.

Residency is not defined in the tax legislation, but it has been the subject of much case law. Broadly, it means the place where you usually live.

Because different countries use different criteria to decide who is resident, it is possible to count as a resident of more than one country at the same time, in which case you could pay two lots of tax on the same income. However, the UK has double taxation agreements with many countries to avoid this situation.

In general, payment of UK taxes depends on whether or not you were resident during the particular tax year in question. Occasionally, it may hinge on where you are ordinarily resident. Again, there is no hard and fast definition, but basically your ordinary residence is the country you are resident in year after year, which you use as your base, returning to it for extended periods, and probably where you have an established home.

Your domicile can be the key to whether or not there is tax on foreign income and gains you receive and any inheritance tax to pay on your estate when you die. Your country of domicile is the place which you consider to be your permanent home and where you would intend to end your days. You can have only one country of domicile and it is not necessarily the country in which you are resident or ordinarily resident. Claims for foreign domicile should be made as soon as possible on form DOM1.

Note that even if you are non-resident for tax purposes, you might still be able to claim the UK personal tax allowances to set against your income from UK sources, for example, if you are a citizen of a Commonwealth country or a European country within the European Economic Area (this includes the UK), a Crown employee (or a widow or widower of someone who was a Crown employee) or employed by a UK missionary service.

Warning

There are Revenue concessions which might apply to you. You can claim the concessions, providing you don't use them simply as a means of avoiding tax. If the Revenue suspects that tax avoidance is your main motive, it will refuse you the concession.

How do you count as being non-resident?

If you have generally been considered as a UK resident, to count as non-resident for tax purposes, you need to pass all four of the following tests:

- the motive test
- the absent for a whole tax year test
- the 183 days test
- the 91 days test.

The notes which accompany the Non-residence supplement include a calculator which will help you to work out whether you pass all these tests.

The motive test

You will pass this test if you leave the UK to work full-time, providing the other tests are also met. Whether or not your job is full-time is judged, first, by comparing your hours with the norm in the UK, but if your job is less structured it will be assessed on its own merits and in the light of what is normal for your type of work and the country you are going to. You could also count as working full-time if you have two or more part-time jobs.

By concession, if you count as non-resident because of your work abroad, your wife or husband, if they go with you, will also count as non-resident, providing they pass the other tests.

Another way to pass the test is if you go abroad to live permanently or at least indefinitely. The Revenue will want evidence that this is your intention – for example, that you have bought a home abroad or you are going to marry someone in another country. If you still have a UK home, it wants to know how that fits with your plans to live overseas. Once you've lived abroad for three years, it will be accepted that you are non-resident.

If you can't pass this test at the time you go away, the situation can be reviewed later on, if new evidence of your motive becomes available or once you have been abroad for three years.

The absent for a whole tax year test

To count as non-resident for a tax year, if you work abroad, your job must last for at least a whole tax year and you must be out of the country for the whole tax year or longer, except for visits within the other rules (see below). Similarly, if you go to live abroad permanently or indefinitely, you must be out of the country for at least a whole tax year.

By concession, in the year you leave and the year you return, you can count as non-resident for just part of the year, provided that year is part of a longer period of non-residency. If you want to claim this split year treatment, you must give details of your date of arrival in or departure from the UK in box 9.25 or box 9.26 of the supplementary pages.

The 183 days test

You will always count as resident for the tax year if you spend 183 days or more in the UK. There are no exceptions to this rule. For example, if you make visits back home during a period working abroad, the total of your visits during any tax year must come to less than 183 days if you are not to lose your status as a non-resident. For the purposes of this rule and the next, the days on which you travel do not count as days spent in the UK.

The 91 days test

In addition to the 183 days test, the average time you spend in the UK must come to less than 91 days in a tax year. This is worked out over the period since you left until you have been away for four tax years. After that it is worked out over the most recent four tax years. You are allowed to ignore periods you had to spend in the UK for reasons beyond your control – for example, because someone in your family was ill.

Warning

> Bear in mind that you have to pass all four of the above tests. For example, the 91-day and 183-day rules apply only to temporary visits back to the UK where the Revenue is satisfied that the motive test has been met and you have permanently left the UK. In a recent case (*Gaines-Cooper* v *Revenue & Customs* [2006]), the Special Commissioners decided that a businessman who had a permanent home in the Seychelles was still UK resident as well because, for example, he maintained a home and club memberships in the UK, his son had attended school in the UK, and he made regular trips to the UK to socialise and take part in sporting activities. Taking all the evidence as a whole, the Revenue successfully argued that Mr Gaines-Cooper had not left the UK and therefore the 91-day test was not relevant.

Mobile workers

You might have the sort of job that takes you on frequent trips abroad, possibly working abroad all week and just returning home to the UK for weekends. Even if you pass the 183 and 91 days tests, the Revenue takes the view that you are unlikely to count as non-resident, if your home and domestic life continue to be UK-based. It argues that, in these circumstances, you have not genuinely left the UK. In the past, the Revenue may have granted non-resident status to people in these circumstances and it has indicated that it might review these cases if there is reason to believe that the earlier decision was not based on a full disclosure of all the relevant facts.

How do you count as being non-domiciled in the UK?

Your domicile is relevant only if it will affect the tax you must pay, so unless you fall into one of the following categories, you do not need to fill in boxes 9.27 to 9.31, and you should also leave box 9.5 blank. The tax areas which might be affected are where:

- you have income or gains from foreign investments which you will not be bringing in full into the UK

- you are claiming UK tax relief on contributions to a foreign pension scheme made out of earnings from a non-UK resident employer

- the costs of travelling between the UK and your normal home have been paid by your employer

- you worked abroad for a non-UK employer and have not brought all the earnings into the UK.

Tax-saving ideas 172, 173 and 174

If you go to work or live abroad, make sure your trips back home average less than 91 days a year and come to less than 183 days in any single tax year to avoid paying UK taxes on your overseas income.

Taking a long lease of three years on a home abroad would help to show that you intended to live abroad permanently.

If you are returning permanently to the UK after a period of non-residence abroad and you have been saving through an offshore roll-up fund, make sure you sell your investment before you become a UK resident again. If you don't, you will become liable for tax on the rolled-up income.

You can have only one domicile at a time and there are three ways in which it can be established: by birth, by dependency or by choice. From birth, you normally have the domicile of your father – that is not necessarily the same as the country in which you were born. If the domicile of the person on whom you are dependent changes, so will yours. Similarly, if you become dependent on someone else of a different domicile, your own domicile will fall into line with that. Women no longer acquire their husbands' domicile on marriage. Once you reach the age of 16, you have the right to choose a new domicile but the change is not easily made. You would need to show that you had settled in the new country of domicile with a view to staying there permanently. Your home, business interests, social and family ties, and the form of any will would all be relevant, but other factors could also be just as important.

If you are a woman who married before 1 January 1974, you automatically acquired the domicile of your husband. This is unaffected by subsequent divorce or bereavement.

Appendix A

Tax-free income

Income from a job

Check with your employer if you are uncertain about whether any of these forms of income is taxable

- work-related expenses reimbursed to you by your employer and covered by an agreement with the Revenue that they do not need to be declared (see p. 241)

- some fringe benefits, such as canteen meals, mileage allowance up to the authorised rates if you use your own transport for business and certain help with childcare costs (see pp. 101–6)

- foreign service allowances paid to diplomats and other servants of the Crown

- goods and services your employer lets you have cheaply (see p. 101)

- miners' free coal or cash allowances in lieu of coal

- long-service awards so long as they are not in cash and are within set limits (see p. 105)

- awards from approved suggestions schemes (see p. 239)

- payments for moving because of your job, within set limits (see p. 104)

- genuine personal gifts – for example, wedding presents

- compensation due to medical reasons linked to service in the armed forces, whether or not you continue in service

- armed forces operational allowance paid to members of the armed forces serving in some areas, such as Iraq and Afghanistan.

Income on leaving a job

Check with your ex-employer

- gratuities from the armed forces
- payments relating to certain foreign service
- lump-sum compensation for an injury or disability that means you can no longer do the job
- tax-free lump sum instead of part of a pension and certain other *ex gratia* payments on retirement or death
- up to £30,000 of other compensation on leaving a job, including statutory redundancy payments, pay in lieu of notice (provided receiving it was not part of your contract of employment or customary) and counselling and outplacement services (see p. 247).

Pensions and benefits

Check with the organisation paying the pension or benefit

- pension credit, Christmas bonus with state pension, winter fuel payment, payment to help pensioner households with council tax bills
- war widows' and orphans' pensions and equivalent overseas pensions
- bereavement payment
- certain compensation payments and pensions paid to victims of Nazi persecution
- war disablement pensions
- additional pensions paid to holders of some bravery awards, such as the Victoria Cross
- the part of a pension paid to a former employee who retires because of a disability caused by injury at work or a work-related illness which is in excess of the pension paid to an employee who retires on normal ill-health grounds
- income support paid to single parents with a child under 16 and those staying at home to look after a severely disabled person. Part of income support paid to unemployed people may be tax-free – see your statement of taxable benefits (p. 196)
- jobfinder's grant, most youth training scheme allowances, employment rehabilitation and training allowances, back to work bonus

- housing benefit and council tax benefit
- improvement and renovation grants for your home
- payments from the social fund
- maternity allowance (but statutory maternity pay is taxable)
- child benefit, one-parent benefit, school uniform grants
- additions for dependent children paid with a state pension or social security benefit
- guardian's allowance
- student grants and educational maintenance allowance
- incapacity benefit for first 28 weeks (and if paid to replace invalidity benefit)
- industrial disablement benefits
- disability living allowance
- attendance allowance
- working tax credit and child tax credit although the amount you get is reduced if your before-tax income exceeds certain thresholds (see p. 60).

Investment income

If in doubt, check with the organisation paying the income

- interest on National Savings & Investment (NS&I) Certificates (and Ulster Savings Certificates, if you normally live in Northern Ireland), NS&I Children's Bonus Bonds
- interest and terminal bonuses on bank and building society Save As You Earn (SAYE) schemes
- income from savings accounts and bond-based investments held in an individual savings account (ISA) or child trust fund (CTF)
- income from share-based ISAs, CTFs, personal equity plans (PEPs) and certain friendly society plans counts as tax-free and does not have to be included on your tax return but, since 6 April 2004, the income has in effect been taxed at 10 per cent
- dividends on ordinary shares in a venture capital trust
- part of the income paid by an annuity (other than a pension annuity)
- savings gateway bonus (technically a capital gain)

■ loan interest paid to members of a credit union.

Other tax-free income

If in doubt, check with the organisation paying out the money

■ what you receive in maintenance payments from a former spouse

■ up to £4,250 a year of income from letting out a furnished room in your only or main home – the Rent a Room scheme (p. 312)

■ gambling winnings (as long as you are not a bookmaker or similar)

■ lottery winnings

■ premium bond prizes

■ income from qualifying life insurance policies that pay out on death – for example, mortgage protection policies, family income benefit policies

■ income from insurance policies to cover mortgage payments if you are sick or unemployed

■ income from income protection policies you yourself pay for, creditor insurance and some long-term care policies

■ pay-outs under some accident insurance policies (usually group ones)

■ interest on a delayed settlement for damages for personal injury or death

■ compensation for being wrongly sold a personal pension (but not any interest element of compensation for endowment mis-selling)

■ compensation from UK and foreign banks to Holocaust victims and their heirs for assets frozen during World War Two.

■ interest on a tax rebate

■ foster carer's receipts up to £10,000 a year per household plus £200 a week per child under 11 and £250 a week for older children.

■ provided you are not carrying on a trade, income you make from putting into the national grid surplus power from domestic solar panels, wind turbines and other microgeneration methods.

Appendix B

Converting net income to gross

Some forms of income are paid net – after some tax has been deducted from them. For example, 20 per cent tax is normally deducted from the interest on savings accounts in banks and building societies before it is paid out to you or added to your account (unless it is a tax-exempt special savings account or individual savings account). In working out your tax bill, you may need to know how much the income was before the tax was deducted – the gross income.

You can find the gross income by grossing-up the net income using the ready reckoners overleaf. The first is for grossing-up income which comes with a tax credit of 10 per cent – share dividends and most unit trust distributions. With most forms of savings income, tax will have been deducted at 20 per cent, so that is the rate in the second ready reckoner. The third is for grossing-up income where tax has been deducted at the basic rate of 22 per cent (or payments where tax relief has been deducted at 22 per cent).

If the tax rates change the tables here will not apply, but you can use the following formula to work out the grossed-up income:

$$\text{Amount paid to you net} \times \left(\frac{100}{100\% - \text{rate of tax}}\right)$$

So, looking back to the tax year ending 5 April 2000, the basic rate was 23 per cent. If you had received £50 after tax, you could have found the grossed-up amount as follows:

$$£50 \times \left(\frac{100}{100 - 23} \right)$$

$$= £50 \times \frac{100}{77}$$

$$= £64.94$$

Grossing-up at 10 per cent

Net amount £	Gross amount £	Net amount £	Gross amount £	Net amount £	Gross amount £
1	1.11	10	11.11	100	111.11
2	2.22	20	22.22	200	222.22
3	3.33	30	33.33	300	333.33
4	4.44	40	44.44	400	444.44
5	5.56	50	55.56	500	555.56
6	6.67	60	66.67	600	666.67
7	7.78	70	77.78	700	777.78
8	8.89	80	88.89	800	888.89
9	10.00	90	100.00	900	1,000.00
				1,000	1,111.11

Grossing-up at 20 per cent

Net amount £	Gross amount £	Net amount £	Gross amount £	Net amount £	Gross amount £
1	1.25	10	12.50	100	125.00
2	2.50	20	25.00	200	250.00
3	3.75	30	37.50	300	375.00
4	5.00	40	50.00	400	500.00
5	6.25	50	62.50	500	625.00
6	7.50	60	75.00	600	750.00
7	8.75	70	87.50	700	875.00
8	10.00	80	100.00	800	1,000.00
9	11.25	90	112.50	900	1,125.00
				1,000	1,250.00

Grossing-up at 22 per cent

Net amount £	Gross amount £	Net amount £	Gross amount £	Net amount £	Gross amount £
1	1.28	10	12.82	100	128.21
2	2.56	20	25.64	200	256.41
3	3.85	30	38.46	300	384.61
4	5.13	40	51.28	400	512.82
5	6.41	50	64.10	500	641.03
6	7.69	60	76.92	600	769.23
7	8.97	70	89.74	700	897.44
8	10.26	80	102.56	800	1,025.64
9	11.54	90	115.38	900	1,153.85
				1,000	1,282.05

Appendix C

The short tax return

You may be one of the 1.5 million people invited to complete a short four-page tax return for 2006–7 instead of the normal full return.

Check you have the right form

The short return is designed for people with relatively straightforward tax affairs. The Revenue will have selected you on the basis of your previous tax returns, but the onus is on you to check that this is correct. If your tax affairs have become more complicated since last year, you may need a full return instead which you can get from the Revenue Orderline (see p. 170).

For example, you cannot use the short return if in 2006–7 you:

- were repaying a student loan (see p. 175) or want to send in your own tax calculation
- received a state pension lump sum (see p. 197)
- received a lump sum from your employer or on leaving a job unless it counts as a tax-free payment under £30,000 (see p. 247)
- were a company director
- received shares from an employee share scheme or exercised share options
- were self-employed and your turnover was more than £15,000, you had more than one business, you changed your accounting date or you want to claim businesses losses against non-business income or income for an earlier year (see Chapter 17)
- were in partnership

- had income from property of more than £15,000, from more than one property or from furnished holiday lettings (see Chapter 19)
- received life insurance gains (see p. 201), had income from abroad, from a trust, from the estate of someone who has died
- you are not both resident and domiciled in the UK.

Filing the short tax return

You will need to complete the full return if you prefer to file by internet since there is no internet version of the short return. Submit the short return either by post or by using a phone (telefiling) service.

You are encouraged to send in your short return by 30 September 2007 so that the Revenue can work out your tax bill for you in good time to settle any outstanding bill by the 31 January 2008 deadline. (You are not expected to work out your tax yourself.) However, the actual deadline for filing the short return is 31 January 2008. If you miss the filing and tax payment deadlines, the normal penalties apply (see Chapter 4).

From the 2008 tax return onwards, the deadline is changing. You will need to file the short tax return for the 2007–8 year by 31 October 2008 to avoid a penalty. The deadline for paying your tax bill will still be the following 31 January.

Completing the short tax return

Take care completing the return. It will be read by an electronic scanner so it is important that you keep to the boxes, leave blank boxes that do not apply to you, follow the instructions for mistakes and do not fold the form. If you need a replacement, call the helpline number given in the guidance notes.

Although Part II of this book deals with the full tax return, the information and guidance is just as relevant if you are filling in the short return. The table overleaf shows which sections of this guide to read for each set of questions on the short return.

Where to find help in this book when filling in the short return

Section of short tax return (questions)	Sections of this book which you may find helpful
Employment income (2.1 to 2.6)	Chapter 15 (income, benefits and allowable expenses), Chapter 8 (fringe benefits)
Self-employment income (3.1 to 3.13)	Chapter 17 (turnover, capital allowances, allowable expenses, losses, class 4 national insurance)
UK pensions and state benefits received (4.1 to 4.5)	Chapter 2 (p. 19), Chapter 12 (pensions – see p. 194)
UK interest and dividends (5.1 to 5.5)	Chapter 12 (p. 182), Chapter 7 (savings, investments)
UK land and property (6.1 to 6.5)	Chapter 19 (income, expenses, losses)
Other UK income for 2006–7 (7.1 to 7.3)	Chapter 12 (p. 201)
Gift Aid (8.1 to 8.2)	Chapter 13 (p. 220)
Paying into registered pension schemes (9.1 to 9.2)	Chapter 13 (p. 211), Chapter 7 (p. 81)
Blind person's allowance (10.1 to 10.2)	Chapter 14 (p. 226)
Married couple's allowance (11.1 to 11.4)	Chapter 14 (p. 226), Chapter 5 (p. 53)
If you have paid too much or too little tax? (12.1 to 12.12)	Chapter 11 (p. 176)

Appendix D

Tax deadlines

Within 60 days

■ Tell your tax office if you disagree with the statement of taxable social security benefits you receive from Jobcentre Plus or The Pension Service

On or before 31 May 2007

■ Form P60 should have been given to all employees by employer

On or before 4 June 2007

■ Choose to pay tax in instalments on exercise of option in 2006–7 to acquire shares through an approved scheme

On or before 5 July 2007

■ Send in your first tax credit claim form to get credits for the full year ending 5 April 2008

On or before 6 July 2007

■ Form P9D (or Form P11D) should have been given to employees receiving fringe benefits, plus details of other benefits provided by someone else

On or before 31 July 2007

■ Second interim payment of tax due for 2006–7

31 August 2007

■ Send in renewal form for tax credits to finalise award to 5 April 2007 and renew claim for 2007–8

On or before 30 September 2007

■ Send in tax return if you want the Revenue to work out tax due

■ Employees who owe less than £2,000 tax should send in their tax return so that tax will be collected through the PAYE system (unless they file by internet)

On or before 5 October 2007

■ Tell your tax inspector about any new source of income or capital gain for the 2006–7 tax year

On or before 30 December 2007

■ Employees who owe less than £2,000 should file their tax return by internet, so that the tax will be collected through the PAYE system

On or before 31 January 2008

■ Claim to reduce payments on account for 2007–8

■ Send in your tax return, along with calculation of any tax due, plus payment for any unpaid tax for 2006–7

■ Make first interim payment on account of tax due for 2007–8 (statement received from Revenue based on previous year's tax bill or your own self assessment calculation)

■ Choose to carry back Gift Aid donations made in 2007–8 to previous year (unless you have already sent in your tax return)

■ Last chance to claim for allowances and deductions for 2001–2

■ Send in actual income details for 2006–7 if, for tax credits, you could provide only estimates by 31 August 2007

On or before 31 January 2009

■ Set losses made in a new business for 2006–7 against other income for the previous three tax years

■ Set business losses made in 2006–7 against other income

On or before 5 April 2009

■ Register for primary or enhanced protection if your pension savings exceed the lifetime allowance or are likely to do so.

On or before 31 January 2013

■ Claim for allowances and deductions left out of tax return by mistake for 2006–7

■ Set business losses made in 2006–7 against future profits of the same business

Appendix E

Useful leaflets, forms and contacts

You can get these leaflets from any tax office (look in the phone book under HM Revenue & Customs or the former name, Inland Revenue). Most are also available from www.hmrc.gov.uk or by calling 08459 000 404.

Increasingly, the Revenue is ceasing to publish printed leaflets and instead putting information on its website where it can easily be kept up to date. If you do not have access to the internet, you can phone the helplines listed in this Appendix and asked to be sent a print-out of the information on the website.

Introductions to self assessment

SA/BK4	Self assessment. A general guide to keeping records
SA/BK8	Self assessment. Your guide

General guides to the Revenue

	Tax appeals
IR160	Enquiries under self assessment
AO1	The Adjudicator's Office for complaints
COP1	Putting things right. How to complain
COP10	Information and advice
COP11	Enquiries into tax returns by local tax offices

Income tax for particular groups

IR115	Income tax, National Insurance contributions and childcare
IR121	Approaching retirement – a guide to tax and National Insurance contributions

Tax credits

WTC1   Child tax credit and working tax credit. An introduction
WTC5   Help with the cost of childcare
WTC/AP   Child tax credit and working tax credit: how to appeal against a
          tax credit decision or award
COP26   What happens if we have paid you too much tax credit
WTC/FS1   Tax credits enquiries

Income tax and international issues

IR20   Residents and non-residents – liability to tax in the UK

Income tax – general

IR10   Paying the right tax on your earnings or pension
IR46   Clubs, societies and voluntary associations

Savings and investments

IR111   Bank and building society interest – are you paying tax when
          you don't need to?
          ISA factsheet

Employees

480   Expenses and benefits. A tax guide
IR115   Childcare provided by employers
IR177   Share incentive plans and your entitlement to benefits
P3   Understanding your tax code

Self-employed

SE1   Thinking of working for yourself
IR56   Employed or self-employed? A guide to employment status for
          tax and National Insurance
CA72B   Deferring self-employed National Insurance contributions

Employers (also see *Employees* above)

490   Employee travel. A tax and NICs guide for employers
P11DX   How to cut down on your paperwork: dispensations
IR109   Employer compliance reviews and negotiations

COP3   Reviews of employers' and contractors' records

Capital gains tax

CGT1   Capital gains tax – an introduction

Inheritance tax

HM Revenue & Customs no longer publishes any leaflets about inheritance tax. Instead see its customer's guide to inheritance tax at http://www.hmrc.gov.uk/cto/cutomerguide/page1.htm.

Inheritance tax is not dealt with by your usual tax office. Instead contact HMRC Inheritance Tax at:
England and Wales: Ferrers House, PO Box 38, Castle Meadow Road, Nottingham, NG2 1BB
Scotland: Meldrum House, 15 Drumsheugh Gardens, Edinburgh EH3 7UG
Northern Ireland: Dorchester House, 52–58 Great Victoria Street, Belfast BT2 7QL

Revenue background notes on businesses

The Revenue prepares Tactical and Information Packages (TIPs) which give tax officers background information, such as average profit margins, about particular businesses. This information may help the officer decide whether to open an enquiry into your return and what areas to investigate. TIPs replace the earlier Business Economic Notes (BENs). The Revenue has recently started to publish its TIPs on its website at http://www.hmrc.gov.uk/tips/index.htm. At the date of writing, only the TIPs below were so far available but more are expected to be added to the website in future. If you are the subject of an enquiry and there is no TIP relating to your business on the website, ask the officer dealing with your case whether they are drawing on information from a TIP and, if so, try asking for a copy.

TIPs available at March 2007:

- Estate agents
- Mortgage brokers
- Franchises
- Confectioners, tobacconists and newsagents
- Waste disposal and landfill sites

Useful Revenue forms

You can get these forms from tax offices, the Revenue website www.hmrc.gov.uk or by calling 08459 000 404.

CWF1	To register if you are newly self-employed
DOM1	To claim you are not domiciled in the UK
IHT100	To report a taxable lifetime gift for inheritance tax*
IHT200	Return of estate on which inheritance tax due*
IHT210	Simplified return of estate where no inheritance tax due*
P11D	Summary of your taxable fringe benefits (from your employer)
P2	Notice of coding
P38S	For students working in holidays who want to be paid gross
P50	To claim back tax deducted from earnings
P60	End of year certificate of PAYE deductions (from your employer)
P810	Tax review form if you pay tax through PAYE
R40	To claim a tax repayment
R85	To register to receive savings interest gross
SA100	The full tax return (main form). You may need supplements as well
SA200	Short tax return (not available from website)
SA300	Self assessment statement if you pay tax under self assessment
SA303	To claim to reduce payments on account
VAT1	To register for VAT

* From website or IHT Inheritance Tax and Probate Helpline 0845 30 20 900.

Revenue helplines

Here are a few examples. For a full list visit www.hmrc.gov.uk

Helpline for newly Self-Employed: 0845 9154515
Individual Savings Accounts Helpline: 0845 604 1701
Inheritance Tax and Probate Helpline: 0845 302 0900
New Employer Helpline (NESI): 0845 60 70 143
Self Assessment Helpline: 0845 9000444
Self-Employed Contact Centre: 0845 9154655
Tax Credits: 0845 300 3900 (Northern Ireland: 0845 603 2000)
Ten Percent Helpline (if your highest tax rate is 10 per cent): 0845 307 5555
VAT National Advice Service: 0845 010 9000

Advice about tax

Chartered Institute of Taxation
12 Upper Belgrave Street, London SW1X 8BB
Tel: 020 7235 9381
www.tax.org.uk
For list of members who give professional tax advice for a fee

Tax Aid
Room 304, Linton House, 164–180 Union Street, London SE1 0LH
Tel: 0845 120 3779
www.taxaid.org.uk
Free tax help for people on a low income

Tax Help for Older People (TOP)
Pineapple Business Park, Salway Ash, Bridport, Dorset DT6 5DB
Tel: 0845 601 3321
www.taxvol.org.uk
Free tax help for older people on a low income

Tax-saving idea 175

Whenever you contact HM Revenue & Customs, make sure you make a note of the conversation for your records in case of dispute later on.

Index